THE ARCHAEOLOGY
OF BOATS & SHIPS

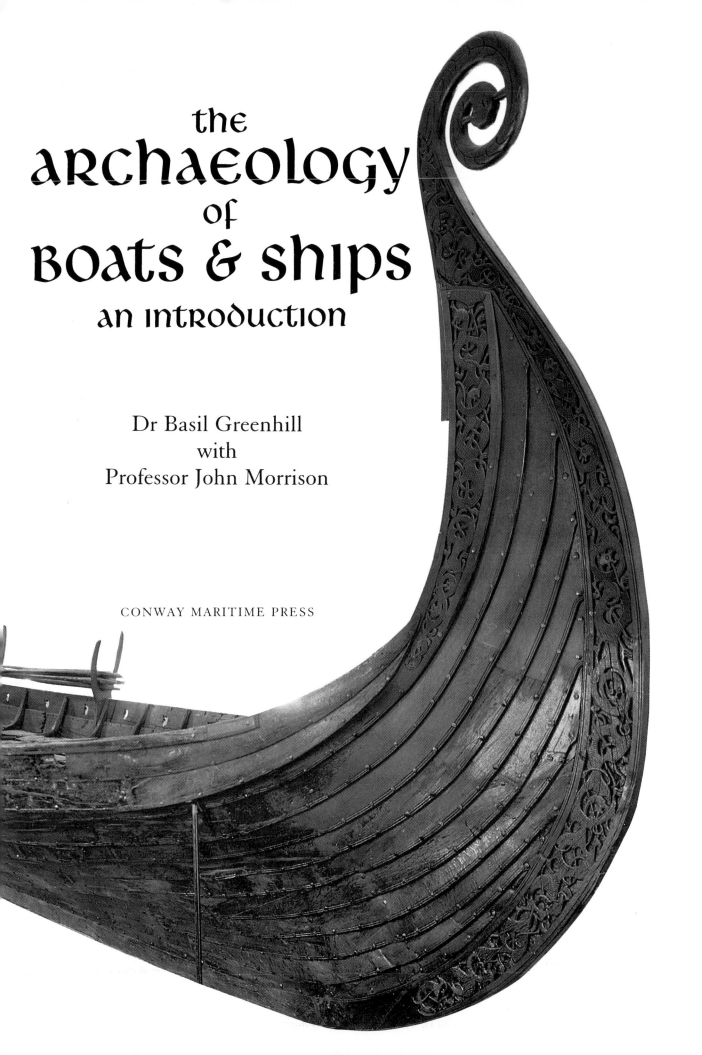

the
ARCHAEOLOGY
of
BOATS & SHIPS
an introduction

Dr Basil Greenhill
with
Professor John Morrison

CONWAY MARITIME PRESS

Frontispiece: The impressive Oseberg ship was built around AD 820 and intended for service in the relatively sheltered inshore waters of southern Norway. She was discovered in 1905 and stands today, as she was reconstructed, in the Viking Ship Museum outside Oslo. [Courtesy University Museum of National Antiquities, Oslo

© Basil Greenhill 1976 and 1995

Published by Conway Maritime Press 1995,
an imprint of Brassey's (UK) Ltd,
33 John Street,
London WC1N 2AT

This edition is based upon the author's earlier work *The Archaeology of the Boat*, published by A & C Black in 1976

British Library Cataloguing in Publication Data
Greenhill, Basil
    Archaeology of Boats and Ships:
    Introduction
    I. Title II. Morrison, J.S.

ISBN 0 85177 652 3

Designed by John Leath, MSTD

Typeset by Dorwyn Ltd, Rowlands Castle

Printed and bound in Great Britain by Page Bros Ltd, Norwich

Contents

Author's Note		7
Introduction – by Professor Séan McGrail		11

Part One   The General Theory

1	A New Study	14
2	Six Boats and Their Builders	26
3	Shells, Skeletons, and Things-in-Between	47

Part Two   The Roots of Boatbuilding

4	The Roots of Boatbuilding	74
5	The First Root, the Raft	78
6	The Second Root, the Skin Boat	91
7	The Third Root, the Bark Boat	97
8	The Fourth Root, the Logboat	101

**Part Three   Aspects of the Evolution of Boats and Vessels
in Europe, North America and Asia**

9	The Sewn Plank Boat	118
10	Ships and Boats of the Mediterranean from 3000 to 500 BC: by John Morrison	131
11	The Warships of the Mediterranean 500 to 31 BC: by John Morrison	151
12	The European Clinker-Built Boat Before the Viking Era	173
13	The Round-Hulled Boat Before the Viking Era: A Different Tradition	183
14	The Flat-Bottomed Boat Before the Viking Era	186
15	The Viking Age	191
16	The Viking Ships and the Graveney Boat	194
17	The Clinker-Built Boat after the Viking Period	216
18	The Cog and the Flat-Bottomed Boat after the Vikings	225
19	The Mysterious Hulk	250
20	Skeletons Everywhere	256

Selected Bibliography		274
Glossary		283
Index		285

Author's Note

Maritime Archaeology is a broad subject, covering ports and harbours, cargoes, navigation, maritime communities, trade and trade routes and the development of boats and ships. This book is about this last sub-division of the subject only and is intended as a simple guide to introduce and outline aspects of the present state of the study of boats and boatbuilding development, written by a layman for laymen.

In the twenty years since an earlier version of this book was published in 1976 the study of the archaeology and ethnography of boats and vessels has advanced very greatly. Perhaps more has been done to increase our knowledge than in the whole history of the study of the subject before.

Much remains to be done but, as the selective bibliographies in this new book show, there are now many publications in several languages giving professional accounts of the study of many finds of the remains of vessels on land and under water. There has also been substantial published ethnographic work. Of very great value in both fields have been the published reports of a number of international conferences held in the last twenty years, especially those of the gatherings of the International Symposium of Boat and Ship Archaeology which was founded in London in 1980.

Moreover very scholarly general studies, such as Professor McGrail's *Ancient Boats of North-West Europe* and *Ancient Boats of the World*, and the late Eric McKee's *Working Boats of Britain* have been published. The volumes entitled *The Earliest Ships, The Age of the Galley* and *Cogs, Caravels and Galleons* in the multi-volume *Conway's History of the Ship*, to which some of the world's leading specialists in their fields have contributed chapters, have become available in the 1990s. In North America the published descriptive work of John Gardner, Maynard Bray, Thomas Gilmer, David Taylor and many others, together with the continued archaeological publications of Professors Lionel Casson, George Bass, J Richard Steffy, and many others have carried forward the study very substantially. Very great progress has been made in the field of experimental archaeology in Denmark at Roskilde. A number of reconstructions of Viking vessels have been built and subjected to prolonged trials on long sea voyages. From the island of Gotland in Sweden Dr Nylén has taken his *Krampmarken* through Poland to the Russian border, along one of the routes taken by the Swedish Vikings in their penetration of what is now Russia and the Ukraine to the Black Sea. The largest and most fully documented experiment of all has been the Anglo-Greek reconstruction of a hypothetical trireme, headed up by a contributor to this volume, John Morrison, and the naval architect John Coates, which emerged from a conference held at the former Archaeological Research Centre at Greenwich.

All these developments underline the hazards implicit in venturing again, as a layman, to provide fellow laymen with a general guide to the state of the study of the archaeology and ethnography of boats and ships at the end of the twentieth century. This book is in no sense an academic treatise. Like its predecessor it is a book for the general reader seeking an introduction to the subject. John Morrison adopts a somewhat more academic approach, but in most of the chapters there are no footnotes and few specific references in the text. The very full bibliographies at the end of each chapter, which cover the publications actually consulted in writing each chapter, and at the end of the book will, it is hoped, function as a guide to the reader who wishes to pursue further particular themes and subjects. Look at the chapter bibliographies first and then follow up with the main bibliography.

Such has been the profusion of archaeological work internationally in the last twenty years that one must be very selective in the examples described. Inevitably there is some concentration on sites which have been published. There is also some bias towards sites on which I have worked and on the boats of regions with which I am personally familiar. There is emphasis on northwest Europe. The distribution of the subject matter over time is inevitably uneven. More attention is given to the last thousand years than to the preceding three thousand. But the central themes of this book remain. They are, first, that the study of the archaeology of boats and ships and the study of boats and ships in use in recent times usually by pre-industrial societies, the 'ethnography' of boats, are complimentary and neither should be pursued in isolation from the other. Thus a number of chapters in this book deal with archaeological matters, others largely with ethnographic, and some are a mixture of both.

As Professor McGrail has said on page 3 of his *Ancient Boats of North West Europe*,

> Ethnographic descriptions of material culture in recent, non-industrial, generally illiterate, small-scale societies are of great use in the technological interpretation of excavated material as they enable the archaeologist to escape the bounds of his own culture and become aware of other technologies. There are problems in using analogies cross-culturally but the more alike in environmental, technological and economic terms two cultures (one ancient, one modern) can be shown to be, the greater the likelihood that ethnographic studies will be of relevance to the understanding of ancient cultures. Descriptions of recent methods of building and handling simple forms of water transport thus form a significant element in this book;

This view is endorsed by Ole Crumlin-Pedersen who on page 70 of *Aspects of Maritime Scandinavia* writes,

> Thus, the ethnographic study of recent vessels can sometimes contribute valuable understanding of archaeological finds, in a way already well known to archaeologists studying house construction.

The second theme is that the broadest classification of boat structures in history is into boats of which the planks comprising the outer skin are joined to one another at the edges and boats the planks of which are not joined edge to edge. I formulated this theory as a result of my own field observations in Bangladesh in the 1950s and I subsequently tested the idea by looking at boats all over the world. I first published it in 1972 and it has become widely accepted. I have of course devoted much the greater part of the relevant text of this book to the examination of the long and complex history of edge-joined, shell constructed boats and devoted relatively little space to the post-medieval development of non edge-joined, skeleton structures. Both these terms and what lies behind them are examined at length in this book.

One of the major changes which have taken place in the last twenty years has been in the thinking about the development of skeleton, that is non edge-joined construction. A generation ago it was less clear than it has become now, as a result of a number of discoveries of remains of medieval vessels, that the development of full skeleton construction was a very slow process. It now appears that there was a period, lasting, perhaps, far into the 1600s, when forms of construction which might be considered to be in varying degrees intermediate between shell and skeleton, differing from one another in many details, were in use in European shipbuilding.

The third theme is that of the basic nature of the problems the boatbuilder meets – those of shaping the strakes; what to do with the plank ends; joining the strakes; or building a simple boat with the minimum of skilled work. The same problems have occurred whenever and wherever men have built boats of wood – hence the importance of the ethnographic approach. On the whole, similar solutions tend to recur, especially in the western world. The broad characteristics of the boats which are built are governed by the solutions adopted to these basic problems. Thus the builders of the medieval hulk and of the river cargo boats of Bangladesh in the 1970s may have adopted similar solutions to problems of strake shape and plank ends.

Inevitably the question will be asked by laymen, 'when does a boat become a ship?'. This is a very difficult matter, although not, perhaps, as important as all that, since it depends so much on what people thought at the place and time. For instance, it can be argued that ships are structures which constituted significant elements in the economies of the societies which built and operated them. To such economically and socially significant floating mobile nautical structures may be given the name of ship, although the word, in its different forms in Germanic languages, has had different significances over the years and in different societies.

By this definition of economic and social significance the large vessels of the classical world, like the big Scandinavian-built vessels of the Migration and Viking periods, which carried people and goods, were ships, as were, later, the cogs of north Germany and the hulks of Britain, and, in due course, the early two- and three-masted vessels of western Europe in the late 1300s and early 1400s. All these vessels represented significant capital investment, large use of scarce resources of materials and labour, on structures which were very important in the activities of the societies which produced them. Such structures we may call ships and, for purposes of convenience perhaps, describe all less significant contemporary mobile floating structures as boats, whatever their construction and lineage.

If we go further back in time this definition will not stand up. In a technically primitive and poor society a logboat may represent a significant element in the local economy. But in such societies the distinction will not have been made anyway, since the logboat will represent the whole of the transport – there will be no 'boats' and 'ships'. There is more difficulty where we simply do not know how societies looked at their vessels, whether, for instance, the Nydam Oak 'boat' was looked on as a special investment by those who built and operated her. She may well have been, in which case a number of the vessels which have been listed for years as 'boats' should properly be 'ships' – including 'vessels of the Ferriby type' (one wonders whether the language spoken by the builders of Ferriby allowed of the distinction), Hjortspring find and Graveney – all described in this book. In the reverse direction the 'farm boat' Skuldelev Wreck 3, probably not representing a significant element in the local economy but the equivalent of an early twentieth-century *storbåt* (in Swedish) should be described as a boat while the small 'freighter', Skuldelev Wreck 1, qualifies as the equivalent of a twentieth-century *jagt* and is thus a ship.

Perhaps the real answer to this not very important question is very simple. A ship is what in a particular group at a particular time people called a ship. A boat is what they called a boat.

In 1976 I referred to the archaeological work going forward at the National Maritime Museum, Greenwich. This work blossomed, and the major contributions made to the study, expressed in a comprehensive series of publications reporting on much archaeological and ethnographic work, rapidly gained international respect. The trustees must have thought long and deep before they closed down the operation in the mid 1980s. Their reasoning has never been explained but their decision had international implications. This was the saddest blow to the progress of nautical archaeology in Britain in the last twenty years and it destroyed the developing focus of the study in this country.

Although post graduate schools of nautical archaeology in the mid-1990s exist at the Universities of St Andrews, Bristol and Southampton, European leadership passed some time ago to Denmark, where the vigorous initiatives of the Danish National Museum led by Ole Crumlin-Pedersen have furthered the study most significantly. To him especially, and to Detlev Ellmers of the German National Maritime Museum at Bremerhaven, to Carl Olof Cederlund of the National Maritime Museum in Stockholm, to Jerzy Litwin of the Polish National Maritime Museum at Gdańsk and to Arne Emile Christensen Junior of the University Museum of National Antiquities in Oslo, I owe great debts in the preparation of this book, as I do to the late Eric McKee. I am also most grateful to Dr Margaret Rule for her help. I also happily acknowledge the inspiration and help in the United States of John Gardner of Mystic Seaport, of Maynard Bray and of the late Howard I Chapelle. I wish to thank especially my very old friend Captain W J Lewis Parker of the United States coastguard, retired, and in Canada Niels Jannasch, seaman, formerly Director of the Maritime Museum of the Atlantic at Halifax and Lunenburg, Nova Scotia, and Robert Grenier who enabled me to participate briefly in the work at Red Bay in Labrador. Ann Giffard has provided rigorous criticism and correction of drafts for which I am most grateful as I am doubly grateful for her compilation of the main bibliography.

I also want to thank two gentlemen, both now long deceased, who patiently endured hours of interrogation in the mid-1940s. They were Sawyer Waldron of Bideford, who had worked for Robert Cock and Sons at Appledore at the building of the *Katie* and other schooners for the Atlantic trade with Canada at the turn of the nineteenth to the twentieth centuries, and Sawyer William Drew of Falmouth who as a boy worked at the building of the ketch *Hobah* at Trelew Creek in south Cornwall in the late 1870s. Between them these vastly experienced men laid the foundations of my understanding of the processes used in skeleton building as it was practised in south west Britain more than one hundred years before this book was written, and they kindled an interest which has never died. Equally important in the development of my interest was the help of Lutfur Rahman of Dhaka who, over several years in the 1950s indoctrinated me into the mysteries of shell construction in its living forms in Bangladesh.

But my greatest acknowledgement is to the leader of the study of the archaeology of boats and ships in Britain, Professor Seán McGrail, late of the University of Oxford. His rigorous and creative thought encapsulated in a most formidable list of publications has been an inspiration to us all who are involved with the archaeology of water transport and he has done a great deal to further this new study in Britain and Europe.

BASIL GREENHILL
Boetheric.

1995.

Introduction

In the twenty years that have passed since the first edition of this book, 'boat archaeology' has broadened its scope and become 'maritime archaeology', the study of Man's age-old interaction with the waters of the world – lakes, rivers, seas and oceans. Moreover, the subject is no longer the preserve of nautical specialists for it now attracts the attention of mainstream archaeologists and others who clearly see that the evidence for cultural, technological and environmental history is not restricted to land sites but can be found beyond lake margins, river banks and high water marks. Nevertheless, boat archaeology, the subject of this very useful and readable book, remains a major element of the maritime sub-discipline of archaeology; indeed, it is one of its two focal points, the other being the study of ancient harbours, waterfronts and related structures.

The boat, or perhaps its cousin the raft, enabled Man to colonise Greater Australia from Southeast Asia, well before 40,000 BC. The ship, the boat's younger but larger brother, was the means by which aspects of European culture – ideas as well as people and artifacts – were dispersed across the oceans in the late fifteenth and early sixteenth centuries, to a large part of the world: to the Americas, southern Africa, India, Southeast Asia and Oceania. And water transport, especially the boat, continues today to be a mainstay of economic and social life for millions of people, as it has been throughout the world since Man first went afloat. The importance of the boat can thus scarcely be over emphasised; and how the boat in its various forms has been developed, worldwide, over millennia is one of the most intriguing and challenging archaeological problems.

Since 1976, there have been some striking advances in our knowledge of early boats due, not just to the excavation of important vessels, but also to a marked improvement in the techniques used in the field, at the desk and in the laboratory to extract information from these recent finds, and, indeed from earlier ones. There has also been an increasingly rigorous approach to the formulation of hypotheses about the structure and performance of the original boats represented by the incomplete, fragmented and distorted remains that are excavated. This approach can also be seen in the way experimental boat archaeology is now tackled. The building and testing of reconstructions of ancient boats is done in a more scientific manner than it was twenty years ago, with the result that the best of these experiments can throw light on the operational capabilities of certain ancient boats: their speed, cargo capacity, weatherliness, and so on. For all these reasons, a revised edition of this book is to be warmly welcomed, not least because these significant advances in our knowledge of the boat can now be brought to the attention of a wider audience.

A notable feature of the 1976 edition – and one that is extensively used in the present work – was the inclusion of descriptions of how rafts and boats are built today, in simple, pre-industrial societies. For a principal way of gaining some understanding of the problems faced by ancient boatbuilders, and of appreciating their solutions to these problems, is to study the methods used in these twentieth-century boat 'fossils' and to learn, whenever possible, the reasoning behind them. By the juxtaposition, in this book, of the present day Polish *galar* and the Brigg 'raft' of about 800 BC, Basil Greenhill encourages us to begin to visualise those parts missing from the excavated remains, and to fill the gaps in our knowledge about the building and use of river craft in Bronze Age Britain.

In the year that this book was first published, Dr Greenhill established an Archaeological Research Centre at the National Maritime Museum. By the time he retired from Greenwich that Centre was playing a prominent role in Maritime Archaeology within Britain, indeed generally in northwestern Europe, especially in the field of ancient boats. Within a year, however, the National Maritime Museum had decided to discontinue archaeological research; the subsequent, adverse effect on ancient boat studies can be felt today, when there is still no focal point in Britain for such research. There was, however, one beneficial – although unforeseen – outcome of the dispersal of Greenwich's archaeological staff: Maritime Archaeology began to be studied seriously in British universities. This is where the future of ancient boat studies now lies: in a small group of universities – or possibly within a Maritime Institute – where maritime archaeologists and historians will be trained, and maritime-orientated research will be pursued. The aims of such institutions must not be to create yet another specialisation, uninfluencing and uninfluenced by mainstream studies, but to help to build up a holistic view of the past to replace the present emphasis (in some cases the exclusive concentration) on the landsman and on land-based activities.

In his Author's Note, Basil Greenhill tells us that this book was 'written by a layman for laymen'. I venture to suggest that this is wrong on two counts. First, as far as the subject matter of this book is concerned, Dr Greenhill is not a layman. Although he may have no formal qualifications in archaeology or in naval architecture, he is certainly an experienced seafarer and boatman, familiar with sail and oar from an early age. Furthermore, he is an astute observer and recorder of boatbuilding techniques, as his many other publications demonstrate. Second, this book, which is about a technical subject, is not just for laymen. Though it is written in terms which the technically-challenged can readily understand, that understanding is further deepened by the many explanatory illustrations. These are qualities that everyone welcomes, the professional archaeologist and historian as well as the layman. I commend this book to all who are interested in the boats and boatmen of today and in their predecessors of yesterday, back in time to the Bronze Age and beyond.

SEÁN MCGRAIL

Department of Archaeology
University of Southampton

ONE

The General Theory

A New Study

Why is it especially useful now to compile an up-to-date short, simple, popular, introductory handbook on the history of boats and boatbuilding?

There are several good reasons for doing so. One is that the study of the development of boats in history and prehistory has in the last generation been the subject of much intensive if somewhat uneven study. Other artefacts of man – pottery, houses, temples and churches, fortifications, tools, jewellery, metal work – all developed their own disciplines, but it took a long time for the boat to do so. This was partly because wooden boats do not survive the centuries as well as pottery and stone. There were until the last quarter of the twentieth century few scientific excavations and a poor record of publication of discoveries. There had been no specialists in the field, partly perhaps because of the classic alienation of the seafarer from the rest of society, and to a lesser extent, by association, the alienation of those who followed trades closely allied to seafaring.

As Campbell MacMurray's investigations of social and working conditions in merchant ships and naval vessels in the early years of this century demonstrate, the two separate worlds of the seamen and the landsman must have developed very early in the course of mankind's encounter with the sea, and they persist as separate entities to the present day. The seaman's world is alien to the landsman unless he makes a lifetime study of part or all of it, and the more so since the seaman's very alienation makes him difficult to communicate with, makes his world not only other, but also closed. Consequently, scholars whose lives have been involved with the history of the landsman have rightly been inclined to avoid the otherness of the world of seamen and boatmen. When they have ventured into it they have frequently gone rapidly adrift and lost their bearings for lack of intense study of sufficient examples and of knowledge of the background of the artefacts. Their conclusions have in consequence sometimes been superficial, occasionally even inaccurate.

Worse still, this alienation has led archaeologists in general into the error of extending 'otherness' to the maritime world. The archaeologist who specialises in maritime affairs is still likely, even now, to be looked upon as something of an eccentric, whose work cannot easily be assessed. The future of the archaeology of boats and ships, and all that goes with it in the study of past societies and their ways of life, depends on its absorption into the mainstream of archaeological work. But,

1

Appledore Quay, c1875. The polacca brigantine Newton *built in 1788 is listing towards the quay.* [Postcard

even at the end of the century, this has not yet happened. So in this book we deal with a subject still too often regarded as marginal to proper archaeological studies.

Boats were developed when there was a need for them, and were almost invariably built for basic utilitarian requirements: they were either necessary, beneficial, essential or important to help people live. Time, work and scarce raw materials were not put into boats for reasons of romance or, normally, of aesthetics. Men and women did not take to the water unless the benefits were considerable. They exploited their environment and if the land alone could not support them, they took to the sea, river or estuary to fish for food, to travel to new hunting grounds, to earn money by carrying other people's goods or by stealing in acts of piracy, or for any combination of these reasons.

People usually take to the sea when the land alone is not enough. Thus at Appledore in north Devon in England, a community with little land to farm grew up around a creek and on the rocks of the foreshore. By the mid-nineteenth century 75 per cent of all its inhabitants, the census of 1851 shows, were dependent for a living on the sea and shipping (Figure 1). Or they seek to exploit in varying degrees a mixed environment. Thus the German settlers, brought into Lunenburg County in Nova Scotia to replace the French who had been driven out by the British in the eighteenth century, were principally farmers, settled in good farming country. However, by the end of the nineteenth century (Figure 2) Lunenburgers had exploited the rich and accessible fishing grounds to the extent that Lunenburg was one of the world's great fishing ports and in 1913 as many as 135 big salt banker fishing schooners and a number of merchant schooners were owned there.

The ownership or occupation of land has been so important that it is still very widely regarded as a status symbol. In the village where this book was written, on the border between Devon and Cornwall, there is still an invisible gulf between those who work land owned or leased from the National Trust and those who work other men's land as employees, hired men. For this reason, among others, inside a society those who have been forced completely off the edge (full-time fishermen, seamen – boat people) have for many years often been lowly rated by their contemporaries, and their settlements, if such they have, regarded as poor, outlandish, even lawless places.

Thus even in the early twentieth century both Appledore and Lunenburg were to a degree socially isolated from the neighbouring communities. This social categorising may, indeed, unconsciously have become one of the factors in the fashionable archaeologists' attitudes to things maritime. The inhabitants of such settlements tend to become people apart. From the nature of their occupations, if they are full-time specialists, and the fact that their manfolk are cut off from ordinary human social intercourse for much of their working lives, the communities become more and more separate. Extreme cases of this situation occurred with the outports of Newfoundland in the early years of the twentieth century. But materially these communities developed their own status symbols, and the boat, like the horse among landsmen, probably very early became an important status symbol itself.

It is only since the early 1960s that intensive professional study of the development of boat structures has begun to evolve as a subject in its own right. Almost a new profession was needed to make this development possible. The men and women who follow it must have a deep feeling for boats and knowledge of boatmanship, a practical commitment over and above the requirements of normal academic study. As Arne Emil Christensen of the University Museum of National Antiquities in Oslo, one of the pioneers of the new study, said in the mid-century days when wooden boatbuilding was still a thriving business, 'the archaeologist may theorise as much as he wants, but boatbuilders will be able to give him definite answers, if he takes the trouble to ask them, and watch them at work'. The archaeologist must have the practical approach which enables him to appreciate the problems faced by boatbuilders working in wood and the way they solved them, for here lies the solution to many problems presented by other evidence from the past. This is no deskbound study, but one requiring extensive field work. He must acquire professional knowledge of boat structures and considerable archaeological experience and ethnographic knowledge. The process of generating such skills and interests is lengthy and experimental.

The present students of the development of boats have had their great forebears. For generations people have been examining occasional boat finds more or less rigorously and a few people have been studying the structures of boats around the world. In Britain the most significant pioneer contributor in ethnographic field studies was James Hornell, Director of Fisheries in the service of the Provincial Government of Madras in the old Imperial India. Hornell was of a type of professional expert now virtually extinct: without degrees or formal training he successfully filled a professional role. After his retirement he published in 1946 *Water Transport*, a book which remains unique, the only attempt in the author's own words 'to marshal in due order the major part of the knowledge . . . concerning the origins of the many devices upon which men . . . launched themselves upon river, lake and sea'. Because of its structure (it is mostly an assembly of previously published academic papers) it is not an easy book to follow and in some fundamental aspects Hornell's general conceptions have been overtaken by new studies, but nevertheless the book remains perhaps the most comprehensive single source of descriptions of boats all over the world. It was followed, in 1950, by the very valuable posthumous *Fishing in Many Waters*.

At the end of the century Hornell's work has been complemented, and to some extent overtaken, by Professor Seán McGrail's *Ancient Boats of the World*, a rigorous academic study of the world's vehicles of water transport. This book is a necessary work of reference for everyone who is interested in the subject.

The birth of the new full-time study of the development of the boat as a specialism in its own right can perhaps be considered really to have taken place with the discovery and examination of the series of five boats or ships of the Viking Age, the

2
Lunenburg, c1890. [Knickles Studio, Lunenburg

Skuldelev finds, in Roskilde fjord in Denmark in the late 1950s and their excavation, recovery and continuing study by Olaf Olsen, Ole Crumlin-Pedersen and others of the Danish National Museum. In Britain it really began with the excavation and recovery of the Graveney boat of *circa* AD 950 by the National Maritime Museum and the British Museum late in 1970, and the subsequent establishment of the Archaeological Research Centre at Greenwich, which during its short life gave a tremendous push to the development of maritime archaeology internationally.

This is not archaeology in a narrow sense, for the study of the development of boat structures involves not only the study of ancient boats but also of boats today. This is for the very good reason that in the other world of the seafarer the ancient and the modern co-exist side by side to a degree perhaps unusual with the artefacts of man. Not only does the log canoe still greet the steel diesel container ship in some Asian and African ports, but the same logboat still occasionally lies on the river bank alongside highly sophisticated wooden boats that have developed from logboat origins and less sophisticated boats representing intermediate stages in the development, as well as alongside plastic boats which predominate in number. There is a great deal to be learned about the development of boats from the detailed study of relatively modern survivors (as I shall show in succeeding chapters), providing that we do not assume that things were necessarily the same in the past as they are now, but use the study as a source of ideas and an indication of what is possible. So the new discipline involves ethnography as well as archaeology, and since each boat was made for a utilitarian purpose and the nature of the environment in which they worked has not changed appreciably in the last five thousand years, the naval architect can play a large part in any team working within it.

It has become indisputably clear, though, that for all the work that has been done, we are still, even now, in the early stages of the study of the history of boat structures. For example, the detailed study of the Graveney boat and the Ferriby/Brigg finds not only derived the maximum possible knowledge from these particular finds, but generated new methods and techniques for the future. Work in Denmark and Norway in the last twenty-five years has revealed a great deal about Viking Age shipbuilding within 250 miles of the Skaw, and there are a number of other fields that are proving very profitable to study. The intensive study in Germany of the cog and her world since the discovery of the Bremen cog has not only given us detailed knowledge of a vessel type previously known only from iconographic and literary evidence, but has added a new dimension to our understanding of the world of medieval North Europe (see Chapter 18). It is profoundly to be hoped that the discovery of the remains of an indisputable hulk (see Chapter 19) will soon cast more light on this mysterious vessel and her world.

The presentation of some of this work in recent years has perhaps begun to show traces of nationalistic sentiment reminiscent, in a very small way, of nineteenth-century fervour. In a Europe in the early stages of the general political and cultural absorption of its constituent parts, national identity may be strengthened by the widespread awareness of cultural history – particularly in its more spectacular and romantic forms. The rediscovery through maritime archaeology of earlier periods of international political and economic influence can be politically helpful to the government of a country which may have to struggle to assert itself in the new Europe. The building of reconstructions of spectacular vessels of the 'romantic' past may have widespread popular appeal and help in the strengthening of a feeling of historical and cultural identity.

There has been a good deal of maritime 'experimental archaeology' in the form of the full-sized reconstruction of vessels of which extensive remains have been excavated or, in the case of one of the very best of these experiments, the Greek trireme, for which extensive iconographic and literary evidence exists. Such experiments can be very fruitful, but strict rules must be observed.

The subject must be very carefully chosen. The boat must be sufficiently documented or have sufficient remains so that there is a reasonable probability of being able to deduce both the methods of building and the probable shape of missing parts, and indeed the probable shape of the boat as a whole. The boat must be sufficiently representative to make the information and experience gained a significant advance in general knowledge of boat archaeology. The builder or builders of a replica must be chosen very carefully because they must be able to make themselves think in terms of the boatbuilding techniques of the time and place of the original boat and must not impose their own professional solutions from their own experience and training. They must not seek to improve on the original, but must limit themselves to the form and structure of the original, and the materials and methods of the original builders.

Experience has already shown that boatbuilders trained in the modern west European traditions have great difficulty in adapting themselves to the use of solutions to which they themselves were not brought up, but unless they do so the experiment is rendered at least in part invalid. The environment in which the experiment is carried out is very important. The modern boatbuilders must work in circumstances in which they can appreciate some of the problems faced by their predecessors long ago. It is unlikely, for instance, that a successful experiment could be carried out in a modern boatyard and in a modern industrial environment. In a rural environment, that at least approximates to the surroundings in which the original boat was built, the various aspects of the experiment would in time interact naturally and authentically. The building techniques to be used should be determined only after exhaustive study of all available evidence. Where there are conscious deviations from what are known to be original methods, the decision to make them and the reasoning behind the decision must be fully recorded. The experimenters must be very clear in their minds as to how far they are seeking an exact replica, how far a boat with the general characteristics of an original, and how the decision as to what to build is likely to affect the value of the whole experiment. Lastly, the trials programme should be carried out rigorously and should be designed preferably on lines that enable the results to be matched with those of other experiments to answer specific questions asked in advance. Finally, the description of the building process, the arguments behind each stage and the process of the trials in detail must be recorded and published. Not all reconstructions in recent years have met these standards and their value has been reduced accordingly.

One particular series of experiments in the last twenty years has proved invaluable. A generation ago very little indeed was known about the structure of the sails and the techniques of shiphandling under sail in pre-medieval and medieval northern Europe. The chequered squaresails depicted so clearly on the picture stones of Gotland, with their complex pattern of ropes hanging from the foot, were still a mystery. The ability to windward of a vessel, whose sole aid was a single squaresail, was much in dispute. After all, in the western world the sailing of boats and ships rigged with only one squaresail on a mast stepped more or less amidships had not been regularly practised for seventy-five years or more, and then only in remote parts of northern Norway. Now as a result of the work of Bent and Erik Andersen and others in Denmark, of Erik Nylén and others in Gotland, Sweden, and of Owain Roberts in north Wales, we are beginning to understand something of the sails and sailing of the north a thousand years ago. This knowledge has been enhanced by the experience gained by the sailing of several Viking ship 'replicas' on ocean voyages. Further reference will be made to what has been learned and how in a later chapter. But when all this is added up these are still only fragments and every find, every new idea and every hypothesis enlarges the study of this new branch of the history of man's activities. In this regard the study of boats parallels a process going on in other areas of archaeology, where the development of scientific method and the use of the computer are leading to much re-assessment.

Any book such as this, which seeks to present a brief account of aspects of our present knowledge of boat development history, inevitably oversimplifies. The development of the boat has a vastly complex history. I have already pointed out that in the modern world very primitive boats that have changed little if at all in thousands of years co-exist with sophisticated structures that have developed much later. Boats that represent both the most basic and the most complex type of floating structure of the age continue to stand side by side on the same beach in China or Bangladesh, or indeed on the fashionable foreshore at Rio de Janeiro. This was probably as true of twelfth-century Britain as it was of the mid-twentieth century before the plastic age began. There has been a constant interplay throughout the history of man's encounter with the sea between different types of boat and between boats in different stages of development, and almost endless local variations have developed wherever boats have been built in any numbers. This will undoubtedly become more apparent as the number of finds of ancient boats increases. The various types of boat historically in use on one river in Britain provide enough material for a small book, the boats in use until recently on a major river in a heavily populated part of Asia enough for several volumes. A book such as this can do no more than indicate the general nature of a few trends and the general shape of developments in a few areas.

For a long time archaeologists will be at the information-gathering stage. Too much time has perhaps been spent in the past in building hypotheses on too slight a basis of evidence and on imposing on the study a premature rigidity when it has scarcely been born. My next chapter describes a few examples of boats of the old building traditions in Britain, western Europe and North America which still exist, or did so until very recently.

For the development of a new study to be possible, especially one which is by definition international, an agreed terminology is needed, and such terms should necessarily be comprehensible for ease of reporting and discussion. Terminology presents far greater difficulties than might at first appear because in the English language there never has been any standard nomenclature for the parts of traditional boats or the processes of boatbuilding. Just as boats and building methods varied greatly from area to area, even between adjoining counties or the opposite banks of the River Thames, so did the terms used to describe the constituent parts of the boats. Some degree of standardisation is essential to allow of consistency in archaeological reports. In Britain the problem has been highlighted by the necessity of an agreed terminology for use in the National Monuments Record.

The time is right, therefore, for a new review of parts of the field of knowledge as it now is. This review shows unevenness of emphasis and inadequacies because it is a book about a subject on which our knowledge is still uneven and inadequate, and because it draws for illustrations on arbitrarily assembled collections. Its emphasis and structure are derived from existing knowledge, and it is concerned essentially to present in simple terms some of what we know at present. It is mainly about the development of the boat in northern Europe, Britain and North America where the great majority of boat types probably evolved from logboats in different and devious ways, perhaps with influence in some areas from boats made by covering skeletons of wood with skins, and maybe with a little influence from those developed from rafts with sides built on to them. But there is, I hope, enough about the development of boats generally to help to set that of the boat in Britain and northern Europe into its world context.

Boats have developed all over the world in different ways and at different speeds. Their development has been conditioned by the geography of the local waters, climate, purposes for which the boat was needed, availability of materials for their construction, tradition of craftsmanship which grew up among the boatbuilders and the general state and nature of the culture of the people building them. Different types of boat developed in different environments. To give a few simple examples: if a lot of timber grew close to the water in the territory of a people and there were enough of them to provide labour, then if the timber was small, the climate benefi-cent and particularly if the waters to be navigated were sheltered, rafts would proba-bly be developed; if the timber was big and the climate colder we might expect to find single and double logs shaped into boats – logboats. If the timber was very small and there were skin-bearing animals which could be hunted, then skin boats made by stitching skins over frameworks of light branches would probably be built. In the few parts of the world where some of the trees have bark of the right properties, bark canoes developed. Indeed when a people has a need to build boats, that need is often so great that they will build them even though the choice of material available contains nothing that other and better endowed peoples would ever think of using for the purpose. It is only in sophisticated societies, which are rich enough to have a considerable degree of choice, that ideal boatbuilding timbers, and even ideal timber for particular types of boat, begin to be regarded. Thus, builders of Bridgwater river flatners in Somerset in the last century made the sides of the flatners of elm, because it was cheap and readily available in the sizes needed for the work. But boatbuilders in areas with a wide choice and where people were ready to put more money into their boats would never have used elm in this way.

From time to time in many parts of the world sophisticated techniques of boat-building have evolved and the end products have become highly efficient vessels for their area and purpose, often beautiful to look at and frequently the products of very skilled craftsmanship. For example the very developed and very different edge-joined overlapping plank building techniques of northern Europe and of Bangladesh have resulted in the construction of many boats that are so well designed for their purpose and so pleasing in form that they are almost works of art in their own right. The complex structures of the Viking ships found in Norway and Denmark, the high degree of technical sophistication which marks the design of the Graveney Boat and the beauty of form of these and many other boat finds of the ninth and tenth centuries justify the description of the clinker boatbuilding of that period as one of the greatest technical achievements of north European society before the building of the early cathedrals. It has been compared at its best to an act of sculpture.

These are perhaps extreme examples, but until a few years ago the world was full of beautiful boats built by men who constructed them within the disciplines of a strong local building tradition conveyed from generation to generation only by example and therefore strongly protected against hasty innovation. The raft boats of the southwest coast of Africa, the logboat fishing boats of the coasts of Brazil around Rio, the smooth-skinned fishing boats of Clovelly in southwest England and the dory from northeastern North America, France and Portugal were all products of different environments, societies, technologies and requirements, yet all highly developed, efficient and beautiful, each in its different way.

But a boat should be judged only, and I repeat only, in the light of the requirements for which she was built and the resources of the society that built her. She should never be judged by comparison with other boats built for different purposes of different materials in different circumstances. The basic question is one of the fitness of purpose in relation to broad local circumstance. To appreciate a boat one must be aware of the factors that gave rise to her building, the timber available, the general environment, the building traditions of the society which produced her and, above all, the purpose for which she was built.

Most boats since men began building them have been the products, not of an organised industry with full-time craftsmen specialised in their trades, but of the part-time work of men who also had other trades and who had learned local boatbuilding traditions as part of their preparation for life. It was in such circumstances that the oldest elements in local traditions lasted longest, so that boats built in recent years even showed evidence of their origins in the gouging and hollowing techniques of logboat building, or the techniques of the extension with planks of an expanded logboat's sides to make a boat.

Now, quite suddenly, all these traditions and skills are in grave danger of being lost within a very short time. The reason, of course, is simple. It is one of the many cumulative effects of the development of the world we live in, seen most obviously in the introduction of glass-reinforced plastic, plywood, and resin glues for boatbuilding. Less directly it is seen in the development of highly commercialised, centralised production of boats in factories, in the introduction by such bodies as the Food and Agriculture Organisation of the United Nations of standard designs, using standard materials and parts and to be built with the minimum of labour, and in the widespread adoption of power in the form of small outboard motors even in the most remote areas of the world, with consequent changes to the boats' shapes and structures. All these developments mean the early end of the widespread use of boatbuilding traditions which, in some local areas in some countries, go back more than one thousand years.

This great change, from the traditional disciplines of the local boatbuilder using simple readily and locally available materials to the techniques of the factory using exotic and largely artificial materials, is a further reason why it is especially necessary now to produce an up-to-date basic book on the history of boats and boatbuilding. Soon popular awareness of one of the oldest technologies is going to be lost altogether.

Or very largely lost. The demise of the commercial wooden boat gave rise in the United States and Fenno Scandia and much more recently in Britain to a recrudescence of interest in wooden boats and boatbuilding. This perhaps began with the work of Howard Chapelle and was greatly enhanced by the writings and example of John Gardner, whose chief vehicle of publication was at first *The Maine Coast Fisherman*, which became *The National Fisherman*. The highly successful magazine

Wooden Boat, published in Maine, spread the gospel of the aesthetic value of many traditional working boats while keeping its feet firmly on the ground. Some manifestations of the revived interest in wooden boats in North America became almost religious in their fervour for the subject.

As a result on both sides of the Atlantic there has been some revival of old skills for a specialist market. The danger, as the annual wooden boat show at Greenwich in England has clearly shown, is that those very expensive reconstructions became glossier and glossier, nearer to the gig of an 1890s steam yacht than to a working boat which was the vehicle by which hard men scraped a living by labour inconceivable a century later.

A working boat showed the scars and bruises of a hard life in a community which would now be considered as economically and socially deprived. She smelt of Stockholm tar, or fish, or linseed oil. Unless the economy in which her people worked was a rapidly expanding one, as happened at times in North America, the life of the working boatman was usually a life without hope. Prosperity for him was often unattainable. In the history of getting a living on the water this has been the situation of most boatmen. For an accurate account of the reality of one form of earning a living in boats, see the transcripts of interviews with former dorymen in Barss, *Images of Lunenburg County*. For another, see Jan Godel's paper on 'Traditions of Square-Sail Rigged Norwegian Boats' in *Sailing Into The Past*. For a third, see Stephen Reynold's description of the life of beach fishermen in south Devon, England, before the First World War in his book *A Poor Man's House*. It is a very long way from yacht varnish, synthetic fibre sails and patent winches. There is an unbridgeable gulf between working on the water for a living and for recreation. He who sails for a living ceases often only to die.

Of course, the new materials, glass-reinforced plastic and glued plywood, and sometimes the two used together in the form called wood-reinforced plastic, have many and great advantages. In a world where labour is everywhere becoming the largest component in costs they save labour time spent in boatbuilding. They are relatively cheap and readily obtainable in standard sizes and qualities. Above all, once the boat is built, they are strong, stable materials which will not change in shape and size with variations in humidity and temperature. The boat, therefore, does not have to be nursed like the relatively delicate, flexible structure of even the most massively built traditional wooden vessel. The materials will not dry out and leave gaping seams to 'take up' when she is put in the water, so that in the end the boat is destroyed if she is allowed to dry out too completely too often. They will not be destroyed by marine borers, commonly known as 'worm'. A working boat leads a very hard life and the plastic, or partly plastic, boat can lead it with less trouble and much less maintenance than a traditionally built wooden boat of any form. The factor of time in building is also very important in the modern world. Traditional boatbuilding was a slow business and the maintenance of the tools alone occupied a good deal of the boatbuilder's time. But the plastic boat will not have as long a life as a well maintained wooden one, though this becomes less and less important.

The skills of traditional boatbuilders all over the world were often fascinating examples of mankind's resource in adapting locally available materials in relation to environment and purpose. The boat has been an extremely important tool in the ascent of man. The boats of a society have occasionally, as with the Vikings in Europe and the Polynesians in the Pacific, represented not only the supreme technical achievement of the society, but more than that, perhaps its principal aesthetic and social achievement as well.

We have unfortunately no detailed contemporary professional description of the building of a Viking or Saxon ship, but Sir Joseph Banks (as he later became) was in

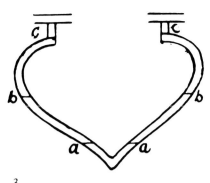

3
Joseph Banks' diagram of a section of a canoe from the island of Raiatea. [*National Maritime Museum*

modern terms the chief of scientific staff on the first of Captain James Cook's three great voyages of Pacific exploration 200 years ago, and this is how he described the building of a boat on the island of Raiatea in the Society Islands in a society in which there had been no recent technical innovations from outside (Figure 3).

. . . the inhabitants were at work makeing and repairing the large Canoes called by them Pahee, at which business they worked with incredible cleverness tho their tools were certainly as bad as possible. I will first give the dimensions and description of one of their boats and then their method of building. Its extreme length from stem to stern not reckoning the bending up of both those parts 51 feet; breadth in the clear at the top forward 14 inches, midships 18, aft 15; in the bilge forward 32 inches, midships 35, aft 33; depth midships 3 ft 4; hight from the ground she stood on 3 ft 6; her head raisd without the figure 4 ft 4 from the ground, the figure 11 inches; her stern 8 ft 9, the figure 2 feet. Alongside of her was lashd another like her in all parts but less in proportion being only 33 feet in her extreme length. The form of these Canoes is better to be expressed by a drawing than by any description. This annexd may serve to give some idea of a section: aa is the first seam, bb the second, cc the third. The first stage or keel under aa is made of trees hollowd out like a trough for which purpose they chuse the longest trees they can get, so that 2 or three make the bottom of their largest boats (some of which are much larger than that described here as I make a rule to describe everything of this kind from the common size); the next stage under bb is formd of stregtht plank about 4 feet long and 15 inches broad and 2 inches thick; the next stage under cc is made like the bottom of trunks of trees hollowd into its bilging form; the last or that above cc is formd also out of trunks of trees so that the moulding is of one peice with the plank. This work difficult as it would be to an European with his Iron tools they perform without Iron and with amazing dexterity; they hollow with their stone axes as fast at least as our Carpenters could do and dubb tho slowly with prodigious nicety; I have seen them take off a skin of an angular plank without missing a stroke, the skin itself scarce 1/16 part of an inch in thickness. Boring the holes throug which their sewing is to pass seems to be their greatest difficulty. Their tools are made of the bones of men, generaly the thin bone of the upper arm; these they grind very sharp and fix to a handle of wood, making the instrument serve the purpose of a gouge by striking it with a mallet made of a hard black wood, and with them would do as much work as with Iron tools was it not that the brittle Edge of the tool is very liable to be broke.

The boat as man's tool and toy has had very special significance in many societies; not only has it been essential to mankind's encounter with water, especially with the sea and to the development of the world as we know it, but it is also so fundamental that despite the low status in most societies of its professional users and their alienation from the majority of their fellow men, it has acquired aesthetic, religious and sexual significance beyond its great utilitarian importance. To take a very immediate and relevant modern example, the cult of the small yacht could not have been pushed, for commercial ends, to the degree that has been achieved in Europe and North America in the late twentieth century if the boat herself, and the simple fact of ownership of her, had not had a significance even beyond the return in leisure and pleasure her use gives.

On what materials can the professional boat archaeologist draw for his work? As I have said already, the account of the development of the boat available to us at present is still essentially fragmentary and we have as yet little real knowledge of the history of that development. At the end of the twentiety century the subject has been studied and recorded only here and there, as chance has brought informed observers into circumstances in which they could record in some degree the details of the structures of boats. Sometimes chance has brought about the survival of actual remains of ancient boats and their discovery and, sometimes, proper excavation; even more rarely, adequate recording and publication. There are illustrations or representations in one form or another of some ancient boats and there are a very few written accounts of them. It is from these sources, sometimes much more rigorously examined than they have been in the past, that the study is being developed.

There have been descriptions of ancient boats in literature from time to time since Homer. Some of them are relatively clear, like the famous passage in *De Bello Gallico*, Book III, in which Julius Caesar describes the boats of the Veneti. This is so detailed it might be a contemporary description of the building of a nineteenth-century vessel. Of course, a lot is still missing, and there has been a great deal of discussion of the description, but we can scarcely hope for anything better. Most descriptions are oblique and brief, but nevertheless much can be learned from them, as for instance from the references to boats in the Icelandic sagas. And the written descriptions are virtually all we have to go on for a number of nineteenth- and twentieth-century boat finds which are not adequately recorded in drawings or photographs and are not conserved.

Works of art provide some evidence about the history of boats, and can be of several kinds. There are actual models of boats, like the model of a Viking cargo ship found while excavating a Scandinavian settlement in Greenland; these are models made at the time the boats depicted were actually in use and which were therefore subject to contemporary criticism. There are carvings on rock, engravings on coins, images on seals and in later years, of course, there are actual paintings. There is a great deal of evidence about the development of boats and ships in and after the fifteenth century locked away in the art galleries of the world and in carvings, frescoes and decorations, which has never yet been adequately examined.

Of course this evidence can be very controversial and difficult to interpret. Right down to the present day when considering any painting or drawing representing a ship or a boat it has to be asked: 'Was the artist trying to make an authentic representation of a boat or vessel, or was he giving an impression?' In other words, was the result primarily a work of art or primarily an illustration and if the latter, how valuable is the illustration? Was the artist limited by materials with which he had to work or the tools he had to use? Was he strongly influenced by contemporary conventions in drawing, carving or engraving, so that he was not able for reasons practical or psychological to make an accurate picture of a boat? If his picture is not accurate are there still things which can be learned from it? Almost always there is something to be learned, some elements which convey accurate information.

Neither written evidence nor the evidence provided by works of art of different kinds provides information of the degree of detail and reliability to be gained from the actual remains of ancient boats. The remains of a boat are a first class primary source, since no longer are there author and artist between the archaeologist and the reality. But although this sounds very splendid, in fact the problems posed are still enormous because boat finds are never complete. Almost always the upper parts have been destroyed, quite often the boat is in a shattered state and has to be rebuilt and the wood from which it must be reassembled is often distorted, possibly even broken into fragments besides being water-logged and probably badly decayed, so that there are many problems in determining the original shape. Indeed, as part of the new approach to the study of the history of boats a new technical discipline has grown up in this country and in Denmark and Norway and in the USA in Texas, a system of methods for hypothesising the form and structure of an entire boat from remains which may resemble those of a crashed aeroplane and which may be a thousand years old or more, even, as in the case of the Brigg boat, 2,500 years old. In this kind of study, of course, the computer is becoming an ever more valuable tool.

The most important source of information other than major finds of ancient boats is that provided by the boats of the ancient building traditions which still exist today. These are to be found all over the world and they vary from the simplest logboats and skin boats to the most sophisticated plank-built constructions. They require detailed study by people knowledgeable in the history of boat structures and the mechanics and methods of boatbuilding. Every opportunity should be taken to record in detail not only the structures of old boats, but as far as possible the methods, processes and order by which they are still built and the materials used, and the way they were rowed, sailed, poled or paddled.

Bibliography

BALCOM, R A, *History of the Lunenburg Fishing Industry*, 1977

BARSS, P, *Images of Lunenburg County*, 1970

BASCH, L, 'Ancient Wrecks and the Archaeology of Ships', 1972

BASS, G F, 'Cape Gelydonia, a Bronze Age Shipwreck', 1967
    Archaeology Under Water, 1970
    (ed), *A History of Seafaring based on Underwater Archaeology*, 1972

BEAGLEHOLE, J C (ed), *The Endeavour Journal of Joseph Banks, 1760–1771*, 1962

BRUCE-MITFORD, R L S, *Sutton Hoo Ship Burial*, 1968

BUTLER, V, *The Little Nord Easter: Reminiscences of a Placentia Bayman*, 1975

CARPENTER, A C *et al*, *The Cattewater Wreck*, 1974

CASSON, L, *Ships and Seamanship in the Ancient World*, 1971

CHAPELLE, H I, *American Sailing Craft*, 1951

CHRISTENSEN, A E, 'Boatbuilding Tools and the Process of Learning', 1972
    'Lucien Basch: Ancient Wrecks and the Archaeology of Ships. A comment', 1973

CRUMLIN-PEDERSEN, O, 'Skin or Wood', 1972

CRUMLIN-PEDERSON, O, and VINNER, M (eds), *Sailing into the Past*, 1986

DUFFY, FISHER, GREENHILL and STARKEY (eds), *The New Maritime History of Devon*, Vol 2, 1994

ELLMERS, D, *Frühmittelalterliche Handelsschiffahrt in Mittel- und Nordeuropa*, 1972

EVANS, A C, 'The Sutton Hoo Ship', 1972

FENWICK, V H (ed), *The Graveney Boat*, 1978

FROST, H, 'The Third Campaign of Excavation of the Punic Ship, Marsala, Sicily', 1974

GREENHILL, B, *Boats and Boatmen of Pakistan*, 1971

GREENHILL, B and GIFFARD, A, *Westcountrymen in Prince Edward's Isle*, 1974

HAASUM, S, *Vikingatidens segling och navigation*, 1974

HASSLOF, O, 'Main Principles in the Technology of Shipbuilding', 1972

HEIDE, G D VAN DER, 'Ship Archaeological Investigations in the Netherlands', 1970

HORNELL, J, *Water Transport* 1946 and 1970
    Fishing in Many Waters, 1950

LANDSTRÖM, B, *The Ship*, 1961

MCGRAIL, S, 'Models, Replicas and Experiments in Nautical Archaeology', 1975A
    'The Brigg Raft Re-excavated', 1975B
    Ancient Boats of North West Europe, 1987
    Ancient Boats of the World, forthcoming

MCGRAIL, S and GREGSON, C, 'Archaeology of Wooden Boats', 1975

MCGRAIL, S and MCKEE, J E G, *Building and Trials of the Replica of an Ancient Boat: The Gokstad Faering*, 1974

MCKEE, J E G, *Clenched Lap or Clinker*, 1972
    'Flatners', 1970

MACMURRAY, Campbell, unpublished transcripts of interviews with former merchant and naval seamen, archives of the Royal Naval Museum, Portsmouth

MARSDEN, P R V, *Ships of the Port of London*, 1994

MARTIN, C J M, 'The Spanish Armada Expedition 1968–70', 1973

NICOLAYSEN, N, *Viking Ship discovered at Gokstad in Norway*, 1882

OLSEN, O and CRUMLIN-PEDERSEN, O, 'Skuldelev Ships', 1967

REYNOLDS, S, *A Poor Man's House*, 1908

SJOVOLD, T, *Oseberg Find*, 1969

SLADE, W J, *Out of Appledore*, 1970

TAYLOR, D A, *Boat Building in Winterton, Trinity Bay, Newfoundland*, 1982

WRIGHT, E V, 'The Ferriby Boats', 1990

ZINER, F, *Bluenose*, 1970

Six Boats and Their Builders

Carolina skiff

George Adams lives, let us imagine, near the little old town of Bath, North Carolina, on a tributary of the Pamlico River which flows into Pamlico Sound, inside the Outer Banks. He works at a filling station for several hours a day. He has a patch of ground where he can grow vegetables. He helps with odd building and carpentry jobs and he fishes, mostly for the family pot. Besides these occupations he builds the simplest kind of boats, flat-bottomed boats, or skiffs as they are locally known, and George's skiffs were the sweetest little rowing skiffs built for miles around. Nowadays there is no demand for rowing skiffs and he has to build them for outboard motors, which means the sterns are broader and they have a trunk to take the outboard (Figure 4).

The whole tradition of George's skiffs lies in the shaping of the lower edges of the sides. He always builds the same skiff, with some variation of the size, because he always begins with the same side shape. This side shape is the secret of his skill as a boatbuilder, which was transmitted to him by his father and grandfather. In his youth, George could use a single piece of fine white cedar for the side of a 14ft skiff; that is, the side was 14ft (4.27m) and the finished skiff was about 12ft 6in (3.81m). For a long time, however, such pieces of timber have not been obtainable at the price George's customers can possibly pay, so he now has to use plywood.

He begins building his skiff by cutting out the sides, two identical pieces, straight on top where the curves of the sloping sides will give a natural sheer, subtly shaped in a very elongated and flattened S on the lower edge, so that the bottom of the boat will be slightly raised forward; the heel of the stem just touching the water, the line of the bottom running straight and sloping downwards to just forward of amidships. Here the bottom is gently curved and then rises in a long straight line to the transom. This fore and aft rocker to the bottom gives a boat which will row well and perform well with a low-powered outboard. There is no rocker athwartships; the bottom is flat at its lowest point, just forward of amidships.

The whole secret of George's boats lies in the bottom curve of the sides, for there is no other cut curve to speak of; this bottom curve and the maximum beam between them absolutely determine the whole form of the finished boat. Occasionally, although there is more work involved, George builds a skiff with two or three planks, instead of a single sheet of plywood, on each side. It is cheaper in timber, but not in

4

An outboard skiff from the Pamlico river area of North Carolina. Note the kitchen chair used by the driver. [Basil Greenhill

labour, to do this. When he does so he has to shape only two planks, the lowest on each side, and these only on the bottom edges. He fastens cleats across the planks to hold them together and thus act as the skiff's only frames.

A completely flat-bottomed boat with no fore and aft rocker is even simpler to build. The outboard-powered skiffs built for the oyster fishery in the creeks in the New Bideford area at the west end of Richmond Bay, Prince Edward Island, eastern Canada, are an interesting example of a boat which has been developed locally in recent years by part-time builders, for a specific commercial purpose. Here the bottom edge of the plywood sides has only to be slightly arched to produce a boat otherwise comprised of straight lines except for the shape of the bottom in plan. This is the simplest of all boats to build (Figure 5).

When he has made up the sides, whichever method he uses, George makes up a solitary mould by tacking together some laths. This mould gives him the beam of the boat and the flare of the sides and, of course, this flare must exactly match the sides he has made to give the right rocker to the bottom. Then he fastens the front ends of the sides to the sides of the stem piece of the skiff, and places the mould in such a position that when the sides are wrapped round it the curve of the bottom will give the skiff shape; that is, long and sharp in front in plan, the maximum beam aft of amidships. With her flat bottom shaped in this way the skiff is less likely to pound

5

Oyster skiffs at New Bideford, Prince Edward Island, Canada. [Basil Greenhill

when being rowed or driven in a lop of water, and skiffs do pound if they are not properly shaped.

George draws the ends of his sides together with a Spanish windlass made of rope and a stick twisted in the rope. The straight upper edges of the sides then assume a curve in profile, which gives the boat a graceful sheer. He cuts the transom and fits it to the ends of the sides. When he has done this he turns the half-built skiff over, nails a chine beam along inside each side at the bottom, and cuts off the projecting corners of the chine beams and the sides to form a bed for the boat's bottom. Then he planks the bottom by laying on planks athwartships, taking great care to set the open ends of the annual rings' curves down on the chine, and that each plank is wedged in close against its neighbour before it is fastened to the chine beam and the sides. When planking is finished, he saws off the ends of the planks. Thus the bottom of the boat never exists at all as a separate unit. Its shape emerges from the bottom curve of the sides and the beam measurement. A few thwarts and some red paint, and the skiff is finished, and George goes off to lend a hand in building a frame house or barn. Probably the skiff's owner will give her a name, certainly she will be required by North Carolina State legislation to carry a number on her bows.

George, with his two secrets of side shape and cross-section amidships, is a very long way from the world of full-time professional boatbuilders of the last years of wooden boatbuilding, and from the working world of urban boatyards using building techniques and terminology which, though they vary greatly locally, are comprehensible throughout the trade.

Somerset turf boat

Like the housebuilder with his use of stock timber (straight cut planks from a lumber yard), George is still essentially of the industrial world in which such material is commercially available. His British near equivalent in the first half of the twentieth century built double-ended, flat-bottomed boats for carrying cut turf or peat down the canals or over the floods from the peat beds of the Somerset Levels around Shapwick and Mere to the roadsides where it was collected for sale. They were used for general farm transport purposes, like carts or pick-up trucks (Figure 6).

This man was a small farmer or a village carpenter who might also be the undertaker and coffin-maker. He scarcely thought in terms of plank-built boats at all, and the boats he built were probably the oldest in design and structure of any in use in twentieth-century Britain (Figure 7). He used simple natural shapes, grown curved timbers and forked branches as they came to hand. He built clinker, clenched lap, because it was easier to build in this way, rather than a boat with a smooth skin; he clearly revealed one of the factors in the origin of clinker construction in that he did not bother to smooth off the upper edges of his lower strakes, since this is not necessary, but left them rough and with the bark still on them. Technically, of course he need not have smoothed off the lower edges either, except for the bottom strake, but he did, for appearance's sake.

The massive stem and sternpost of his boat were evidence of its probably remote past as a logboat, as was the bottom, made from a single piece of wood from a very large tree. He was not concerned with stock timber bought from a merchant but with what could be made out of a suitable tree. The smooth lines in his boat were cut in the rough boards only when and where necessary and he never worked with a straight-sided plank at all. In reverse of George Adam's building process, he began with the bottom, added the 'noses' or stem and sternpost, then the first strake. The knees were then cut from grown crooks and fitted (Figure 8) and the second strake added. This strake was cut down at either end, so as to keep the sheer as low as

6
Turf boats loading peat near Shapwick, Somerset, c1890. [Somerset Year Book

possible to minimise the effect of wind on the boat and make it easy to pole. His tarred boat might be used for any farm purpose when the floods came, as they used to before the big drainage ditches were dug, the last of them in the 1960s, but they came again in early 1995 when perhaps peat boats – if any survived – may have been pressed into use again. His boat had no name, but the parts of it were named in strictly local terminology, quite unrecognisable in other regions – *hrung* for a floor timber, *drashels* for the side frames.

8
This turf boat was built in 1970 by Stanley Baker of West Hay, Somerset. He has at this stage roughly finished off the upper edges of the lower strakes. The piece he has cut off to give the arch of the lower edge is resting on the trestles. [Eric McKee

7
A Somerset turf boat. [Eric McKee

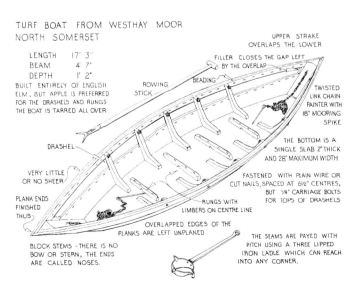

TURF BOAT FROM WESTHAY MOOR
NORTH SOMERSET

LENGTH   17' 3"
BEAM   4' 7"
DEPTH   1' 2"
BUILT ENTIRELY OF ENGLISH
ELM, BUT APPLE IS PREFERRED
FOR THE DRASHELS AND RUNGS
THE BOAT IS TARRED ALL OVER

UPPER STRAKE
OVERLAPS THE LOWER

FILLER CLOSES THE GAP LEFT
BY THE OVERLAP

ROWING
STICK

BEADING

TWISTED
LINK CHAIN
PAINTER WITH
18" MOORING
SPIKE

DRASHEL

THE BOTTOM IS A
SINGLE SLAB 2" THICK
AND 28" MAXIMUM WIDTH

VERY LITTLE
OR NO SHEER

FASTENED WITH PLAIN WIRE OR
CUT NAILS, SPACED AT 6½" CENTRES,
BUT ¼" CARRIAGE BOLTS
FOR TOPS OF DRASHELS

PLANK ENDS
FINISHED
THUS

RUNGS WITH
LIMBERS ON CENTRE LINE

OVERLAPPED EDGES OF THE
PLANKS ARE LEFT UNPLANED

BLOCK STEMS - THERE IS NO
BOW OR STERN, THE ENDS
ARE CALLED NOSES.

THE SEAMS ARE PAYED WITH
PITCH USING A THREE LIPPED
IRON LADLE WHICH CAN REACH
INTO ANY CORNER.

Cornish clinker-built working boat

These two men, George Adams and the undertaker/turf boatbuilder of the Somerset levels of the 1920s, both built boats very old in form but of simple construction, boats which served their purposes well but which were not amenable to much development. There are structural parallels between a turf boat and a medieval cog, between a Carolina skiff and some boats of the Netherlands in the first millennium AD, and flat-bottomed boats are used today and have been used widely across the world for many centuries. But an ordinary clinker-built working boat of the nineteenth century, is much more part of the mainstream of North European boatbuilding traditions.

10
Nugget. [*Basil Greenhill*

A boat of this kind spends the winters in a barn – by a farmhouse in southern England. The farmhouse was built in the early 1880s when trade on the tidal river, which runs half a mile away down across the fields in clear view of the front windows, was booming. The local copper mines were still prosperous, as were the brickworks, quarries and blacksmiths, the arsenic works and the riverside dealers in coal and fertilisers. In a local shipyard, some years before the farmhouse was built, a trading smack was launched. This smack's principal employment was to bring the groceries from the town on the sea coast up the river on the flood tide and land them at the quay on the river bank down below the farmhouse. Pack donkeys and carts pulled by horses took the groceries to the shops in the villages up the valley which ran down to the river at the quay. The coal for the villages came to the quay from south Wales in schooners, whose crews were among the best customers of the little beer shop in the cottage by the limekilns at the back of the quay. For manure on the farm they often used a load of horse dung, fermenting and stinking from the streets of the town on the sea coast, brought up on the flood tide in sailing barges, whose crews never seemed to notice the stench, though they sometimes slept in the little hutch-like cuddies while the barges lay in the creek by the quay, and with an easterly wind the stench was very apparent up at the farmhouse.

When the house was built the estate specified that the dairy and the kitchen should have floors of blue stone slate from the Delabole Quarries in north Cornwall. The slates, each about 3ft square and 1½in thick, were brought down from the quarries in wagons drawn by oxen to Porth Gaverne on the coast, and loaded into smacks which lay aground on the beach. They were loaded by women who wore long aprons of white leather and broad-brimmed hats. The cargoes were collected by a builder's merchant in a village on the river bank a mile above the quay below the farmhouse. Often a smack from Porth Gaverne would take on board a boat built at a yard in the village to take back home for the local fishery, for the village had a great name for its boats, which were exported in visiting vessels all around the west coast of Britain.

It is not too much to say that the whole life of the valley depended upon the tidal river, and had done so for a thousand years or more. Scandinavian raiders came up on the tide in great clinker-built boats and landed in a creek which still bears their name. Everything for the big house of the estate, all the furniture and tapestries, the kitchen and dairy equipment, the gardener's tools and all the foods that were not available locally, came up the river in smacks and barges. The river was alive with boats, ferries, salmon-fishing boats, boats used to collect seaweed from the beaches at the mouth of the river for use as fertilisers, farm boats used for family and working transport up and down.

The farmhouse was built in the yard in front of a much older building, a cottage which was demoted to become the dairy. The old barns which were around the old farm cottage still stand, and in one of them every winter lies the 13ft (3.96m) clinker-built wooden pulling and sailing boat. She was built on the quay with larch from a local wood lot, with local oak for the ribs and knees, elm for the transom and

9

Lines of the 13ft (3.96m) salmon netting boat Nugget *drawn by Eric McKee from measurements taken from the boat.* [*Basil Greenhill*

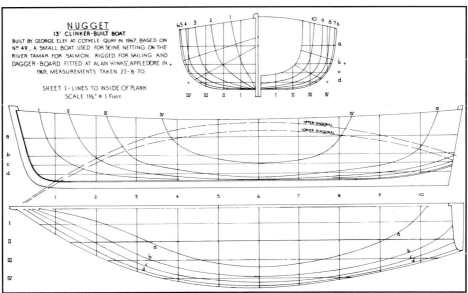

NUGGET
13' CLINKER-BUILT BOAT
BUILT BY GEORGE ELEY AT COTHELE QUAY IN 1967, BASED ON
No 49, A SMALL BOAT USED FOR SEINE NETTING ON THE
RIVER TAMAR FOR SALMON. RIGGED FOR SAILING AND
DAGGER-BOARD FITTED AT ALAN HINKS', APPLEDORE IN
1969. MEASUREMENTS TAKEN 22·8·70.

SHEET 1 - LINES TO INSIDE OF PLANK
SCALE 1½" ≡ 1 FOOT.

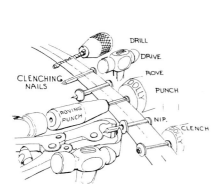

11

Fastening strakes in clinker building — a common method — and the tools used. [*Eric McKee*

imported pine for the thwarts and gunwales. She was built as a copy of an old boat, which worked off the quay in the net-fishing for salmon on the bend just below, by a skilled craftsman in wood, who built boats from time to time. The original boat had been built seventy years before on the river bank half a mile upstream, by a house-builder who turned out a few boats. Her shape, and the shape of her copy which lies in the barn each winter, was the one traditional in the late nineteenth century in this part of Britain for the salmon fishery: very full in the stern so that she could carry weights like a water-soaked natural fibre net and its warp without sinking herself to an unreasonable depth or becoming unstable; sharp and narrow forward so that she could be pulled easily (Figures 9 and 10).

The men who built her worked in a tradition as old, or older, originally than that of George Adams and the Somerset turf boatbuilders, but which developed into something infinitely more complex to become the main tradition of northern European boatbuilding. A clenched lap or clinker-built wooden boat at its best, which is by no means its most expensive or sophisticated, is a work of craftsmanship so developed as to verge upon art. Bob May, who built the original salmon net boat, did not think in terms of setting out to build an ideal boat, but of something of roughly the right shape he could put together from available timber, a gale-felled larch tree, some oak posts, some deals. Apart from the keel every line in the boat is shaped and curved. The planks, scarfed together to make the strakes, are all curved and recurved, high in the centre, dipping towards the ends and turning up again as may be necessary to take their place in the shell which they comprise when joined together. The strakes were fastened together with copper rivets, driven through from the outside and mushroomed out over round copper washers called roves, on the inside (Figure 11). The curves were developed as the boat was made, strake added to strake, by a process called spiling. This shell, formed with a few moulds, became the boat when the stiffening ribs and the gunwale had been added. Bob May used one or possibly two moulds to help him develop the shape of his boat, but half a century earlier she would have been built by eye, with struts and guys, if they were necessary, and clamps and wedges to hold the planks while they were joined to make the shell of the boat (Figure 12).

There is nothing in the boat in the barn that would not have been in her model; that is, nothing that could not have been made locally and cheaply, except the copper rivets with which she is fastened, for the owners of the original salmon net boat, like

12
19ft (5.8m) salmon netting boat under construction at Cotehele Quay, Cornwall, 1968. [*Basil Greenhill*

almost all old style boatmen throughout the world, were poor, and they could not afford to buy anything they could not at a pinch make themselves, even if it were available. They scraped up a living, or more likely part of a living, from the water.

The boat in the barn has thole pins in place of imported iron crutches; the mast is a single piece of solid wood, short enough to be stowed in the boat when not in use; there is no rigging. The mast is kept up by a crutch of iron made years ago in a local blacksmith's shop, attached to the after side of the fore girt. Under her small sprit sail she is usually sailed in the river without the drop keel, but she has a single dagger plate of sheet iron which can be dropped if the wind on the river is uncharacteristically constant.

Each summer the boat is carried down the road to the quay on a pair of wheels, and she is used nowadays not for netting salmon but off the quay for pleasuring up and down the river. Expeditions are arranged to suit the tide. She is pulled and sailed upstream to the tide head on the afternoon flood and back on the evening ebb, six hours of pulling and sailing on the puffs that come down out of the side valleys, downstream on the ebb beyond the bend where the river opens into the mile-wide estuary and into the creeks that lie beyond on the early flood, and then back when the evening flood has grown strong. For this sort of work, with five minutes of fast sailing on a puff, five minutes of pulling and then another puff, the spritsail, so quickly brailed up and set again, is ideal, with a mast which will stow in the boat to reduce windage when the breeze sets in contrary in the narrow river.

The boat is a family boat of the farm, an object held in some affection as a favourite pony or dog might be. But rather more than that, there is something of an overlay of respect for the craftsman's skill of a very special type.

In only one respect does the farm boat differ from her ancestors. Because there are two boats at the farm and it is often necessary to distinguish them in conversation, she has a name, as a big ship must have under the successive Merchant Shipping Acts since 1786. She is not, like the farm boats when the house was built, simply 'the boat' as it might be 'the cart', 'the wagon', 'the barn' or other items of essential everyday equipment which it would never occur to anyone to name.

She is called *Nugget*, a round brown object which is worth much more than might at first appear.

North American lobster boat

The river runs out into the Atlantic. Two thousand five hundred miles away to the west is the coast of Nova Scotia. West of Cape Breton Island is the Gulf of St Lawrence and lying something like a foetus in the womb of the Gulf is Prince Edward Island, once a British colony and now for more than a century a province of the Canadian Confederation. At the west end of the island is Port Hill, a great centre of the island's nineteenth-century shipbuilding industry, which, in the 1880s when the farmhouse in Cornwall was being built, still provided a great many ships, barques, brigs, brigantines and schooners for the expanding British merchant shipping industry. Like the valley upstream of the farmhouse the area was then industrialised but now, like the valley, it has reverted to a deeply rural state. It lies at the back of the great Richmond Bay and off the bay shallow creeks reach far into the land, carrying with them the smell of the tide and evening light of a peculiar clarity.

In one of the creeks Bob Strongman kept his 45ft (13.72m) Cape Islander Northumberland Strait-type lobster boat in the summer (Figure 13). In the winter when the snow blizzards sweep over the island and the sea freezes solid in every bay and creek, the boat was hauled out and propped up high above the tide line (Figure 14).

The boat was narrow for her length and open for the greater part of it, with a short cuddy forward and a steering shelter. Her bows flammed out; that is, they flared so that a choppy sea was thrown back on itself as her 70hp converted Chevrolet automobile engine drove her into it. There were a couple of bunks, a cedar bucket as a seat of ease and a stove in the cuddy, but Bob Strongman rarely spent a night on board. Most of his days in the short two months of the lobster season were spent in the boat on the water, but he slept at home. He drove down the red dirt road to

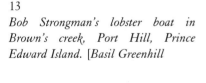

13
Bob Strongman's lobster boat in Brown's creek, Port Hill, Prince Edward Island. [Basil Greenhill

14
Monica Marie, a typical old style Prince Edward Island lobster boat hauled out for the winter at North Rustico. [Basil Greenhill

15

A lobster boat building on Beals Island, off Jonesport, Maine. The wooden trough alongside is the steam box. Filled with steam from a simple boiler the planks are softened in it, if necessary, to make it possible to wrap them around the frames. [Basil Greenhill

Brown's Creek in the big pickup in the early light each morning, pushed the high-sided, flat-bottomed oyster boat which he used as a tender to the big Cape Islander off the red beach into the water and pulled himself out to the grey-painted Cape Islander. He left the dory, as he called the oyster boat without respect for the formal use of terms, on the mooring, and motored out across the bay in the Cape Islander to the narrows of the entrance, where the sand is yellow instead of red, and then out into the Atlantic. Here he hauled his fleet of two hundred or more pots, the long flat-bottomed pots of the North American lobster fishery, then baited and set them again as necessary. It was a hard life but in a good season he could make enough to live comfortably, with a big late model car as well as the pickup and a nicely heated modern house, with the aid of the oyster fishery in the shallow waters of the bay in season and some long-lining for cod out in the Atlantic in the summer.

The Cape Islander was lightly built of cedar, and quite unlike any of the boats so far described. She was a smooth-skinned boat built partly on a skeleton of pre-erected frames, and represented an entirely different kind of thinking about boat-building from the Carolina skiff, or the peat boat or clinker-built salmon boats.

She was conceived, not as a complete shell of planks but as a shape indicated by a series of rib-like formers, frames and moulds, the beginnings of the skeleton of a boat. She was thought of from inside out. Some of these shapes were actual timbers which later were to comprise some of the frames of the boat. Some of them were floors, the lower part of these timbers, which lie across the keel. Some were temporary patterns, or moulds as they are called in boatbuilding, which were shapes made from light timber and removed before the boat was finished. Many of the lobster boat's frames were not made until after some of the planking had been erected around the first frames, floors and moulds, and these later frames were shaped to fit the planks as they had formed up on the basic skeleton. Indeed the majority of the frames in the boat were, in fact, literally pressed into shape by the builders' feet inside the planking, because they were made of flexible narrow flat planks, 'canoe frames', softened by steam so that they could be bent into shape inside the growing hull. But this does not alter the fundamental difference between the lobster boat and the other boats described.

She was built on the mainland of New Brunswick by a full-time boatbuilder whose big shed usually had a Cape Islander under construction for the local lobster fishery of the Gulf (Figure 15). Besides the big boats, he made smaller ones, dories and punts; he made furniture and turned out the local road signs, built wooden sheds and repaired decaying wharves. His approach was modern: he used power tools, ordered his timber in bulk, used glues and laminates and was part of a complex industrial society which interlocks over half the earth.

The boat was brought to Port Hill not by water but on a low-loader across the ferry from Cape Tormentine to Borden and launched into the water for the first time in Brown's Creek. Because of her light construction her working life was limited – she lasted ten or fifteen years. Her shape was very characteristic and a local variation on one common all the way from Connecticut to Cape Breton. The long narrow Cape Islanders began in southern Nova Scotia at Cape Sable and at Jonesport in Maine when motor engines were first used in the lobster fishery in the early twentieth century. The long narrow shape was meant to give speed to low-powered boats. Now with greater power the stern has been widened out and in some versions, like those built in the island and in northern New Brunswick with their flaring bows, a considerable degree of refinement of design has been achieved. To Bob Strongman his boat was strictly a tool, a part of earning his living. He did not regard her as anything special at all. As far as he was concerned, her status was pretty well the same as that of his big Chevrolet pickup which he changed every four or five years. He no more thought of giving her a name than he did the pickup, though most lobstermen do give their boats names.

Bob's grandfather came to the island to be one of the sailmakers for the wooden sailing ships which were built in the next creek to the west. His family came from north Devon and one way or another have been people of the sea for many generations. Bob is no longer alive and most new lobster boats, although moulded to the lines of wooden boats, are now made in plastics.

Norwegian clinker-built pram

The winters in Prince Edward Island are no more rugged than those of Norway, and the winter days are longer in the Gulf of St Lawrence. Nils Andersen has a boat he keeps on an almost tideless inlet off a fjord to the south of Oslo in Norway. She is a pram, a clinker-built boat whose basic structure is quite different from that of any of the other boats described in this chapter.

In calling Nils Andersen's boat a pram I am following twentieth-century British and American usage. Archaeologists tend to use the word to describe a Slavonic type of flat-bottomed, punt-like vessel which was in widespread use in the southern Baltic and the river systems flowing into it from pre-Viking times and which, after the Vikings, spread more widely even into Denmark (Chapter 14).

Nils is a small farmer whose holding is in a valley which runs down to the inlets from the mountains. He does some fishing with the pram, largely for the family's own cooking pot. The boat is built with only nine strakes, three in the flat bottom, three in each of the curved sides. She is long and narrow and her cross-section amidships is like a half circle with the bottom cut off, but despite this shape she is very stable, especially when she has been ballasted down with the weight of two people and their gear. She is also extremely seaworthy and because she has a long skeg aft and a shorter one forward she can be rowed easily. Not every pram has these

16

Nils Anderson's pram. [Basil Greenhill

skegs and those which do not have them are extremely difficult to steer when rowing in a breeze or a rough sea.

The pram has a transom at each end and her planks are brought up in the bow tapering to the bow transom above the water instead of to a stem as all the other boats described in this chapter (Figure 16). She was built in a shed belonging to a pram-builder higher up the fjord; like Nils he was a part-time farmer, and supplied nets and gear to fishermen and bought fish from them. When he built the pram he followed a tradition which his father taught him by example and by a few words of explanation. The boatbuilder's father did not believe it was possible to communicate the ancient mystery of this specialised form of clinker boatbuilding in words, but only by example and trial and error, and then by trial and error again until it was right. Such a method of training, the lack of challenge in the tradition, the unquestioned following of what had been painfully learned before, led not only to a complete absence of innovation but in due course to a positive inability to innovate. The pram was almost exactly like every other pram built in the neighbourhood in the last five generations, and differed from those built by other neighbouring pram-builders only in a few small details which were always the same. She was built purely as a shell with no moulds; not even the transoms were fitted until the shell of planks was complete. The curves of the planks were obtained and held with struts from the floor and from the roof beam of the shed in which she was built. Some local pram-builders used one mould amidships as a guide to the creation of the shape as they planked up. Like the salmon boat in Cornwall, she was fastened with rivets mushroomed over roves.

It has not yet been possible to find positive evidence for the existence of the pram before the second half of the eighteenth century, but it is very probable that the type is much older. There is some evidence in graves excavated near the site of the Norwegian Viking trading town of Kaupang that some people may have been buried in boats which had the basic characteristics of the pram in the ninth and tenth centuries. The use of transoms and upcurving strakes at both ends of a boat seems to represent a logical and sound way of solving the problem of the plank ends – simply by having them all out of the water.

The pram is easier to build than almost any other kind of clinker-built boat. The

17

A 10ft (3.1m) öka at Vestra Simskäla, Wårdö, Åland Islands, Finland. [Basil Greenhill

shed in which it was built measured 25ft by 26ft (7.62m by 7.92m). It had an earth floor so as to keep the atmosphere permanently damp and prevent the pram's timber from drying out in warm summers and splitting and spoiling. The pram was built of unseasoned wood, a single tree of pine which was felled by the boatbuilder and sawn up tangentially to give ten planks, enough for the pram and one to spare. Crook-grown timber was used for the frames and knees, but nowadays they are built with glued laminated frames. Because the building of a pram is less complicated than other kinds of clinker-built boat, builders in the pram tradition were looked down upon somewhat by the neighbours who built the various types of keel boats traditional on the Oslo fjord.

But for all her apparent simplicity, Nils Andersen's pram is, in fact, a highly sophisticated work of engineering in wood. She has the very minimum of frames, made from crooks of branches or visible roots chosen from the tree before it was felled. There is nothing wasted in her. The frames were of course shaped and trimmed to fit the planking after the shell was complete. She too is a work of art as well as a work of engineering.

Nils Andersen occasionally sails the pram under a small spritsail. She has no centre board but she has an outboard motor under which she handles extremely well. She has no name. She is just 'the boat' and the family all regard her as they do the dog, and the pony that lives in the paddock behind the house.

Pram-type boats are in use on the Baltic coasts all the way to southern Finland where a pram is sometimes spoken of as an *öka* in local dialect. They vary in shape according to local traditions (Figure 17) and in Sweden and Finland many are built with steamed inserted frames. *Ökas* are particularly useful where there is floating pack ice since they can easily be hauled out on to the floes when crossing ice-filled waters (Figure 18). One theory has it that the pram developed from logboats cut from the big eastern Baltic willow trees, with their bulbous lower parts. In the late twentieth century prams are being moulded in fibreglass in Finland.

The pram came to Britain because Scandinavian sailing vessels used to load one or two by way of speculation for sale on top of a lumber cargo. The small pram became the standard yachtsman's 'dinghy' before the widespread introduction of inflatable rubber rafts in the 1980s.

Bangladesh boat

Lal Mian lives in Bangladesh. His home is a hut of woven bamboo with a corrugated iron roof and a floor of hard dry mud. It stands under betel nut palms on the corner of a little flat topped hill about 20ft high. All round is a great plain stretching as far as can be seen in every direction. This plain is dotted with little wooded hills, like the one on which Lal Mian lives, each with its cluster of bamboo huts. The plain laps at the foot of the hills like a placid sea, and the analogy is more apposite than it might at first seem, because for four or five months of the year, from June to November, during and after the southwest monsoon, the plain is under perhaps six or more feet of water, and the small wooded hills become islands (Figure 19).

Lal Mian lives in what in Europe and America we should consider to be intolerable poverty. His total income is about £50 or $75 a year. His assets comprise the right to cultivate a bit of land around his mud and thatched hut on another man's wooded island, the use of another tiny piece of land in the flood area near the island, his cooking pots and his hookah pipe and some tiny pieces of jewellery his wife wears, their clothes and the rags the children wear – and his boat (Figure 20).

Most of his money comes through his boat. He operates it rather like a country hire car, taking people to and from the big river where the motor launches run to the district town thirty miles away, carrying small cargoes of rice, jute and pots. The boat was built on the river bank on the outskirts of the district town – on *char*, a stretch of land which exists as dry land for a few months in winter and is submerged for the rest of the year under the flood. The boat is about 30ft (9.14m) long, narrow, round-bottomed, shaped like a slice of melon, but with the raised pointed bow stretching low over the water and the stern curved up higher and more steeply. Her greatest

18
A big pram in use as a ship's boat being worked through the ice in Göteborg harbour, Sweden. [Göteborg Sjöfartsmuseet

19

Lal Mian's home 'stands under betel nut palms on the corner of a little flat topped hill about twenty feet high'. This is a dry season view. In the wet season of the southwest monsoon the water will rise to the foot of the tree-covered hillock. [Basil Greenhill

beam is in the stern. Here she can carry weights, and here Lal Mian lives under a woven bamboo cover called a *chauni* with one of his sons for the six months of the year that the boat operates, when the northwest storms of May and the southwest monsoon in June have drowned the greater part of the countryside.

The boat was built of planks joined edge to edge, half overlapping in 'modified lap', with the edges of the planks rabbeted so that the outer skin of the boat is smooth, to make a great shell which was almost completed before the first floor

20

Lal Mian's boat. She is carrying cattle and their fodder and a flat-bottomed boat which they probably hope to sell. [Basil Greenhill

timbers were shaped to match and fit it (Figure 21). Her conception was the laying of the keel plank along a row of small hardwood logs lying like railway sleepers, side by side at regular intervals. This keel plank was a little thicker than the other planks in the boat were going to be. It was held firm with bamboo pegs and with short lengths of jute cord passed through paired holes drilled in at intervals of about 1½ft (0.47m) and pegged into the ground at either end. The keel plank was shored up at either end with baulks of timber to make a low curve where the bows of the boat were to be and a much steeper higher curve in the stern. To each end of the keel plank *golois* (that is, shaped solid blocks of wood which mark the extremities of one of these Bangladesh boats) were fastened. They were roughly hewn to shape at this stage with adzes and only later cut to their final form.

The shell of the boat was then built up plank by plank. First the garboards, the planks next to the keel, were shaped and fitted and held into place with ropes and wedges and shores (Figure 22). Some of the hardwood planks which were to lie in parts of the boat where they were steeply curved had to be softened so that they could be forced into position. In Europe or America they would have been softened with steam in a rough steam chest like that in Figure 15. In Bangladesh they were charred

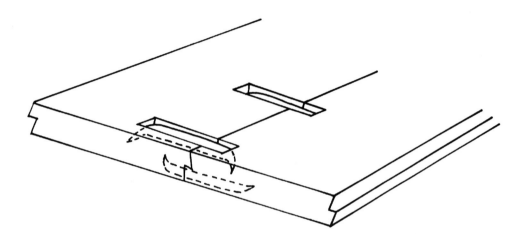

21
The system principally used in joining the edges of the planks in boatbuilding in Bangladesh. [Cicely Hill

22
An early stage in the building of a boat in Bangladesh. [Basil Greenhill

23

Charring a plank on one side to soften it for bending. [Basil Greenhill

24

Fitting a plank at the bow of a cargo boat. [Basil Greenhill

on the side of the plank which was to be the inside of the curve in a shallow trough of glowing shavings (Figure 23).

At the first fitting a plank might show need of a good deal of reshaping. It was then scored with a sharp nail to mark the necessary alterations, removed, cut again, presented again to the boat, removed and shaped again and finally the edges rabbeted with a fine chisel. Then it was fitted again and a difficult curve might call for levers, clamps, guide lines and wedges and the combined strength of all the labourers and *mistris* at work on the boat before it was finally secured in position (Figure 24). Once in position it was held there by a system of guys and wedges and clamps and struts, while shallow slots about ⅛in (0.32cm) deep, 2in (5.1cm) long and ¼in (0.64 cm) wide were cut across the seam at intervals of about every 2in (5.1cm). Into these slots staples were driven to hold the planks together, edge to edge (Figure 21). As

25
The frames were in three separate pieces, . . . they did not even touch one another but overlapped with their ends several inches apart. [Basil Greenhill

soon as a plank had been joined to its neighbour the clamps were removed and the struts and guy lines kept in position while the next plank was fitted and shaped and fastened. The planks were added in pairs, one on each side. This helped to produce the symmetrical hull. A constant check was kept on the hull shape by measuring with a stick from a thin line suspended from the stern *goloi* to the bow *goloi*. The planking was so developed that by the measure of this stick the distance from the centre line to the planking at the same distance from the keel plank at either side was the same. No moulds of any kind were used. The shell of the boat was shaped by eye and the swinging stick, which was in fact a stalk of jute, and as she was built she was surrounded by a forest of struts and guy lines holding the planks in tension. Only

26
The bows of a big cargo boat completed without frames. [Basil Greenhill

when the shell was almost complete were the frames shaped and inserted. Their function was to strengthen the boat and to hold the shell of planks in shape. They were in three separate pieces, not a continuous 'U' shape, but a floor piece to stretch across the keel and join up the planks at the bottom of the boat, a corner piece at the turn of the bilge where the boat's sides turned upward and a rib to strengthen her side. Far from being joined together into a continuous frame, they did not even touch one another, but overlapped with their ends several inches apart (Figure 25).

The building of this Bangladesh boat represented perhaps the purest form of 'shell construction' (that is, the building of the outside skin of the boat first) that can readily be seen in the modern world. The purity of the form is all the more apparent in that although Lal Mian's boat had strengthening frames in three parts, if such they may be called, many big Bangladesh cargo boats, 50ft (15.24m) long or more, have no frames at all (Figure 26). Some have a few floor timbers. As they grow older and weaker they may be framed up with bilge pieces and side pieces but they are not only conceived as shells, they are used and sailed as shells with minimal strengthening frames, if any above the floors, for years on end.

The men who built Lal Mian's boat were *mistris*, itinerant boatbuilders, very simple men, skilled in a trade which they had learned from their fathers and grandfathers. They had learned by copying, by holding the tools and using them in the way their fathers did, with almost no explanation, trying and trying again until, as the years passed, they mastered the complex process of judging and shaping the planks to make the strakes of the boats. Such a method of teaching made for extreme conservatism. Although other methods are used in building boats in Bangladesh, there was little or no innovation in the lives of these men, or in the lives of the smiths who accompanied them and who made all the fastenings for the boat from iron rod and strip in the little smithy they built from woven bamboo under shade trees on a wooded island adjacent to the *char*.

This conservatism among boatbuilders, shown at its extreme among the illiterate and very simple men who build boats in Bangladesh, but paralleled in Norway and Britain and the United States, is extremely important in the history of boats. Because of the methods of communicating the secrets of the trade to future generations, boats have been very slow indeed to change. In many parts of the world, they were still being built until very recently much as they were many hundreds of years ago, sometimes more than one thousand years ago. This means that the evidence presented by boats built in the last years of wooden boatbuilding is relevant to the problems of the evolution of boats; moreover the small boats of recent years often show some of the basic characteristics of the great ships of the period in which they first evolved. A number of examples of this kind of survival will be investigated as the argument in this book develops.

Of course, Lal Mian was not the first owner of his boat. He had found her more or less abandoned, and paid forty or fifty hard-earned rupees to the man who said he owned her and who allowed him to take her away. Lal Mian himself has to have the boat because without her he could not live. He has not enough land to feed himself, his wife and his sons and daughters. If he had he would not go away in the boat, but be a cultivator and stay at home. To be a cultivator on your own land is considered good. Boats are for those who have not got enough land, and to be a boatman is to be a low man on the totem pole.

When he is away in the boat Lal Mian has with him a pot for cooking rice, a small earthenware stove, a frying pan, a plate or two, some bottles and a tin mug. He has one blanket but no change of clothes. He has one hurricane lamp and oil in a bottle and a fishing net. His diet is enriched by fish he catches as he goes along and by wild vegetables, growing out on the *char* land at some places during certain seasons of the year. The secret of Lal Mian's existence lies in an understanding he has with a merchant in the district town who gives him regular cargoes of pots for the homesteads in the area around Lal Mian's own tiny strip of land on someone else's island. Lal Mian delivers the cargoes relatively intact and undamaged and the merchant, to whom Lal Mian is in debt as a result of money needed to marry off a daughter (which took more than a whole year's income) and to finance a small law case both in the same year, is lucky to have this regular work.

However things are changing very rapidly at the end of the twentieth century. The use in boats of simple, reliable diesel engines originally imported from China to work pumps, is revolutionising the lives of the boatmen. Their incomes have doubled and are now greater than those of cultivators. Lal Mian's son will have a very different life and a higher status in his community. His boat will be very different. Locally-built steel flat-bottomed boats have come into use with the diesel engines.

Lal Mian's world comprises the rivers spread over about 3000 square miles of country. He has an intimate acquaintance with almost every yard of the main routes, so that he can find his way along them even at night. He learned the ways and the channels partly when he was working with his father, as his own son is now working with him, and partly by experience since. This world is one of high colour, the continually changing shades of the rivers, the dramatic pageantry of the clouds, the incredible sunsets during the southwest monsoon. It is a very hot and humid world, when at times every living thing seems to gasp for air and the heat strikes at the back of the very eye balls. It is a world of toil at the oar, at the tow rope, at the bamboo pole. It is a noisy shouting sort of a world, with busy waterside markets where boats lie in their dozens, half beached, the crews hawking their wares in strident variations of basic Bengali (Figure 27). But it is also a quiet world of still evenings by lonely islands in great rivers and a leisurely world with little to do sometimes except trim the great bellying squaresail of the boat and to steer her. Lal Mian's boat has no name. It would never occur to him that it was right to give a boat a name. Some of the motor launches which come near his home have names painted on them in garish colours, but this practice is an innovation from another world and has nothing to do with the peasant boatman living on the border-line of existence who will cease to work only

27
A waterside market in Bangladesh.
[Basil Greenhill

because he cannot work any more and so must die. In his way of life Lal Mian is much more typical of the boatman in the history of the world than are prosperous Bob Strongman and Nils Andersen.

The six boats described in this chapter have one thing in common: they were built as tools of work, used to earn all or part of a living. They are not playthings, luxury items, articles of conspicuous expenditure or social prestige. The boat in the barn no longer has to earn her living, though she was built to do so and she lives as if she still had to earn her living. Bob Strongman, with his television, and his pickup and his warm house, and Lal Mian, with his diet of wild vegetables and fish he has caught himself and his one set of clothes, both looked on their boats in the same way, as a means to a living, not in any way endowed with personalities or to be named or otherwise specially regarded among possessions.

All these boats were built with local materials readily available, by men with highly developed special skills which they had learned by example and practice. They were built to be tools and servants, like carts, sheds and trucks, tractors and ploughs. In the history of man as a boatbuilder, most boats have been built in the way that Lal Mian's was, as a job done by very simple men who moved from place to place always doing the same work, always building the same type of boat or group of boats. No element of rent or capital investment was involved, except that made by the future owner in the raw materials of the boat's construction.

These men had something else in common too. They did not use drawings. Nowadays, of course, we think on paper; all planning begins on the drawing board and any big building project, be it a ship, house or factory, requires literally dozens, perhaps hundreds of drawings, without which no one will act. So prevalent has this method of communication of ideas become that even in simple small scale crafts-man's work, drawings are regarded as essential. Now drawings themselves are to some extent being superseded by the computer.

The drawings of course must be accompanied by written instructions, and again so prevalent has communication and training by writing become that, as with draw-ings, we have forgotten that there are other means of conveying information. I have touched once or twice on the significance of the apprenticeship system in its various forms, training without drawings, writing, perhaps even speech, for the development of the boat. We must remember that writing particularly, and to a lesser extent drawing, as a means of universal communication is a very modern phenomenon and it has been largely confined to northern Europe, North America and their spheres of influence. But even there until very recently only a fraction of the population has been able to use these methods of communication. More or less universal adult literacy is really a product of the twentieth century.

Moreover the construction of boats by the development of a shell fabric is a building method which does not lend itself to communication by drawing, or indeed by anything except example; it does not lend itself to innovation. It is only with the development of the skeleton building technique, the lobster boat technique in its various forms, when the shape of the finished boat is dependent on the shape of a skeleton of frames and therefore upon the shape of each individual frame, that innovation becomes readily possible and thinking on the drawing board a practical method of developing design. As far as Britain is concerned it was at the time of the widespread adoption of this method of construction for big vessels in the late 1600s that drawings on paper of ships' hull shapes first begin to appear and probably to have been used.

The examples I have given in this chapter are all except one from the western world. The greater part of this book, because it deals particularly with the development of the boat in northern Europe, Britain and North America, is concerned with the boatbuilding traditions of the western world, and those of the great majority of the rest of the world, including Japan, which are full of parallels and similarities with the traditions of the west.

The boatbuilding traditions of China, however, are substantially different. It has been suggested that the differences may arise in the main from the possibility that a principal influence in the development of boats in China may have been the raft (see Chapters 4 and 5), while in the western world the principal influence very probably was the hollowed-out and shaped log, the logboat. Rafts cannot be used in northern climates at sea because people cannot survive on them; they die of exposure. Rafts can be and are used in tropical seas and they can be and have been used on big rivers in temperate zones. Whatever the reasons the main issues described in the next chapter (shell construction, skeleton construction, edge-joined boats and non edge-joined boats) do not arise in the same way in the Chinese traditions as in the western. Chinese traditions are not therefore discussed in the first part of this book, where we are concerned with general matters, but they are described in some detail in the second part, where we are dealing with some of the evidence in more detail.

Bibliography

BARNES, G W, *Building Your First Wooden Boat*, 1979
CHAPELLE, H I, *American Small Sailing Craft*, 1951
    'The Migrations of an American Boat-type', 1961
CHRISTENSEN, A E, *Boats of the North*, 1968
DE JONG, N J and MOORE, M E, *Shipbuilding on Prince Edward Island*, 1994
GILLMER, T C, *Working Watercraft*, 1972
GREENHILL, B, *Boats and Boatmen of Pakistan*, 1971
JANSEN, E G *et al*, *The Country Boats of Bangladesh*, 1989
JANSEN, E G, *Sailing Against the Wind*, 1992
LOWELL, R, *Boatbuilding Down East*, 1977
LUNT, R K, *Lobsterboat Building on the Eastern Coast of Maine: A Comprehensive Study*, 1975
MCKEE, J E G, *Clenched Lap or Clinker*, 1972
    Working Boats of Britain, 1983
NIELSEN, C, *Wooden Boat Designs*, 1980
WEIBUST, K, 'Holmsbuprammen', 1964
WELLS, K, *The Fishery of Prince Edward Island*, 1986

Shells, Skeletons and Things-in-Between

As I said in the foreword to this book, the archaeology and the ethnography of boats are complementary studies. The study of either enriches the study of the other. The last chapter was mainly ethnographic in content, to aid the broader understanding of boats and boatmen. This chapter also draws partly on ethnographic material.

All but one of the plank-built wooden boats so far described in this book have been conceived, designed and built from the outside in. Their builders have thought of and constructed them as continuous watertight envelopes of wooden planks, shaped so that the submerged parts will pass through the water as easily as possible in relation to the other things required of the boat: its ability to carry goods and people; to provide a stable platform for fishing; to be built cheaply and easily from readily available materials; to meet local requirements for operation – that is, draught, ability to sail or be pulled, seaworthiness in local conditions, and so on. They have built them as a shell of wooden planks, of one shape or another, and then, perhaps as the building has gone forward, or in the case of the Bangladesh boat and the pram at the end of the building process, have added the minimum internal strengthening necessary to keep them permanently in that shape, bearing in mind whatever normal stresses they may have to undergo. These shell-built boats all have one fundamental characteristic in common – their strakes are joined together edge to edge, in one way or another.

One boat, the North American lobster boat, is fundamentally different. She was conceived as a shape around which a watertight skin of planks was to be wrapped, while the other boats were conceived as watertight shells into which strengthening members were to be inserted to fit. The basic difference is that the planks of the lobster boat are not joined to one another edge to edge; the common uniting structure is the skeleton, the framework. There is no physical bond between the planks themselves.

The Carolina skiff, the turf boat, the Cornish salmon boat, the pram and the Bangladesh river boat, for all their very different shapes, ancestry, purpose and environment, have a common link. Their shape was first thought of and visualised as a shell of wooden planks, even though in the case of the skiff the shell began with its

28
Half model of a Maine lobster boat of the 1970s built by Rusty Robinson of Chestnut Street, Camden, Maine. [Basil Greenhill

sides. The shape of the lobster boat was first thought of and visualised as a skeleton which gave shape to planks secured to it, but not to each other, to make a waterproof covering. In fact it is very likely that the lobster boat's first conception was as a model of half the boat, cut down her length amidships, carved out from a solid block of fine knot free pine wood (Figure 28), and from this half model her shape was ultimately derived (see Chapter 20).

Thus it can be said that there are two great general classes of boat in the world. There are boats built of planks joined edge to edge and also usually, but not always, joined to strengthening frames; and boats built of planks which are not joined edge to edge, but only to the supporting framework inside the boat.

In the history of boatbuilding in different parts of the world the great majority of boats in the first category have probably been built as pure shells, their building an act akin to sculpture. Their shaping and symmetry have been made by the simplest of measuring devices, such as the Bangladesh jute stick swung from side to side of a line from the inside of the stem to the inside of the stern to give a very rough symmetry in athwartships section, or by the use of the 'building level', or something comparable to one of the other devices described by Arne Emil Christensen Jr (in *Ships and Shipyards, Sailors and Fishermen* edited by O Hasslöf) or they may have been built by eye alone.

However, many boats built as shells in the last century or two at least have been shaped around one or two temporary frames, called moulds in twentieth-century British boatbuilding practice. Their shape was then basically conditioned by these moulds, though if only one was used, as was the normal practice in boatbuilding in this country in the late nineteenth century, the mould did no more than give the basic athwartships limits of the vessel in the way that her length and the rake of her stem and stern post gave the limits overall. Such boats were built as shells, and their permanent frames cut, or steamed and bent, to fit the shell once it was complete, or nearly complete. Sometimes these moulds were not in position all the time but presented and periodically used in order to check the development of the shape. On occasions they were only half moulds which were swung from side to side and were no more than a general guide to shape and an important aid to symmetry, a development of the basic jute stick of Bangladesh. Certainly they were not often points of stress around which the planks were bent, 'active moulds'; the curvature was usually still obtained by struts from floor and roof if such support was needed. Sometimes, even, the moulds were a general guide to the shape of a vessel actually bigger than that for which they were designed and gave only a general indication to the boatbuilder in developing the shape of the larger boat. At times they played a more active role and the planks of the strakes were bent around them so that they acted as internal props. However the role of the mould was rarely as simple as that. Its assistance might sometimes be needed in the first setting of a plank, but once the plank was fastened to its lower neighbour the shell structure acted as its own prop;

STRENGTH OF PLANKING WHI

A SOFT BACKED BOOK LIKE A TELEPHONE CAN SHOW HOW A ROW OF PLANKS BEHAVE

FIRSTLY
IF YOU LET THE PAGES SLIP FREELY PAST EACH OTHER THE BOOK BENDS EASILY - IT IS ONLY AS STRONG AS THE SUM OF THE INDIVIDUAL PAGES.

THIRDLY
IF BOTH SLIPPING AND PARTING COULD BE S WOULD BECOME RIGID, AND VERY MANY TI

USING SEA TERMS- SEA

WHEN HOGGING
CLOSE NEAR THE SHEER

OPEN NEAR THE KEEL

IF THIS IS ALLOWED TO HAPPEN, NOT ONLY DOES THE BOAT GET WEAK B CAULKING EITHER SQUEEZES OR FALLS

CAULKED PLANKING MUST BE:-
FIRMLY CLOSED BEFORE BOLTING TO TH GIVEN ADEQUATE BUTTING EDGES,— AND THICK ENOUGH TO HOLD THE STOP

TO ENSURE THE EFFECTIVENESS OF THESE MEASURE PROVIDED, WILL MEAN THAT THE SHELL CAN BE UP TO

and the mould relinquished its active role. Now and then the same mould would have an active role for some strakes, act purely as a guide or have nothing but a checking role (the jute stick role) for others. On the whole the mould was a guide rather than an internal prop, its role was passive rather than active. One of the very few contemporary writers with direct personal knowledge of boatbuilding techniques in the nineteenth century (Robert C Leslie, *The Sea Boat, How to build, rig and sail her*, London, 1892) summed up:

> working clinch boatbuilders use few moulds or patterns beyond one midship section, to verify the required width of each plank, and the equal curve of the sides as the boat unfolds herself, plank after plank, from the keel trusting rather for the general contour and model of the boat to a practised eye, and the bend of clean grained wood.

Boats have been built for centuries in some parts of the world by planking up to the turn of the bilge as a shell and then inserting a few frames to fit, then planking up to these frames and then adding more frames made to fit. Sometimes vessels have been built by adding non edge-joined topsides fastened to the upper parts of frames inserted into an edge-joined lower hull. Boats have also been built in other hybrid ways too numerous to describe here in detail. However, always the greater part of their planks have been joined together edge to edge and they have derived a great part of their structural strength from this fact, though in being built they may have derived their shape in greater or lesser degree from the shape of moulds or part frames.

The nature of that structural strength requires some clarification. When a boat or vessel is first launched, when she is pulled ashore, or takes the ground in a tidal berth, or is afloat in waves, she is subjected to certain stresses. When she is pulled ashore or takes the ground these can be very complex, especially if she has a heavy cargo in her. In such conditions even a strong wooden ship built specifically for trades involving these stresses creaks and groans and cracks in a manner alarming to the uninitiated.

A boat or vessel afloat in waves is continuously flexing as she moves through the waves or they move past her. To take two extreme cases: when she is balanced with a single wave amidships her ends are unsupported and they will tend to drop. In this situation the upper strakes are under tension and the seams will be pulled tighter, while the lower strakes will be under compression and the seams will be pushed open. When the wave has reached the stern and the next one the bow, the boat is suspended by her ends with her middle unsupported and the reverse condition occurs (Figure 29). And, of course, rarely is the vessel subject to such simple stresses. Normally, they are much more complex and are continually changing, continually reversing. So as the vessel moves along forces are at work which are continually trying to tear her to pieces. Up to a certain size lightly built, strongly edge-joined structures could deal with this situation very well indeed, and on these grounds alone it is easy to see why edge-joining remained such a universal practice as long as wooden boats and small vessels were built anywhere in the world.

I have, very simply, spelled out the nature of some of the stresses to which a vessel is subject because they were a very important factor and at the same time a great problem in the development of non edge-joined construction. I shall be coming back to them from time to time and particularly in the last chapter of this book.

For lack of evidence the whole subject of how different boatbuilding traditions developed and in what order in different parts of the world is still very controversial. In some areas perhaps shell construction using moulds developed only after skeleton construction itself had separately developed and was in fact a borrowing from skeleton construction into shell construction. This is a subject which can become almost philosophical. Much historical research still needs to be done, and it is here that the finds of remains of ancient boats, perhaps particularly in the Mediterranean

29
Stresses and strains. [Eric McKee

OT EDGE-FASTENED

SECONDLY
IF YOU GRIP THE EDGES
SO AS TO STOP ANY SLIP
THE BOOK GETS HARDER TO
BEND, BUT GAPS APPEAR
BETWEEN THE PAGES ON
THE INSIDE OF THE BEND.

SOME EXTERNAL MEANS THE BOOK
ER THAN IN THE FIRST

KING TRY TO-

WHEN SAGGING
PEN NEAR THE SHEER

LOSE NEAR THE KEEL

FRAMEWORK IS ESSENTIAL, BUT ONCE
RONG AS IF IT HAD BEEN EDGE-FASTENED.

30

This simulation of a nineteenth-century vessel under construction at the shipbuilding yard at Green Park, Port Hill, Prince Edward Island (with the frame sections pinned together instead of scarfed) shows sawn frame sections laid out on the scrieve board before assembly and hoisting into position athwart the keel. [Basil Greenhill

and southern Europe, and the recognition and more intensive study of illustrative material, may make it possible one day to hypothesise and argue on a basis of real evidence. Until then prolonged discussion of what came before which and when and where it came from can be unproductive, particularly as it is at least arguable that the development of the boat happened many times over in different parts of the world.

As Chapters 10 and 11 in this book show, the vessels of classical Greece and Rome and their Bronze Age predecessors back to the fourteenth century BC at least were smooth skinned edge-joined shell-built structures with inserted frames. The strakes were fastened together with stitching (sewn planks construction) or with pegged mortise-and-tenon joints spaced, in later vessels at least, on 12cm centres. By the fourth century AD this was changing. In a wreck of this period excavated off the islet of Yassi Adda on the Turkish coast the mortise-and-tenon joints are smaller and more widely spaced. The shell is less an independent structure and the inserted frames more fundamental to the vessel's strength. A second wreck, found in the same locality and dating from about AD 625, shows this form of construction further developed. Here the mortise-and-tenon joints are so widely spaced and so small that the edge joining contributes little to the vessel's strength and was perhaps used simply to hold the shell together as it was formed and before the inserted frames, fashioned to its shape, which gave the vessel its principal strength, were fitted. Indeed, the upper strakes took their shapes from the upper part of the futtocks and were not edge-joined at all.

The wreck of a vessel of the eleventh century AD was found in Serçe Limani harbour on the Turkish coast in 1973 and excavated by the American Institute of Nautical Archaeology. Her construction as revealed may represent a further step along the road to non edge-joined construction. It was evident that construction after the laying of the keel and the erection of the stem and sternpost had begun with two full frames with floors and futtocks placed more or less amidships. More floors were then fitted and perhaps two more frames. Five strakes a side were then fitted and then upper strakes. She was then framed up to the run of the strakes, none of which was edge-joined. They were spiked to the frames. This is a form of construction very similar to that used in Cornwall 900 years later (see next paragraph). Thus intermediate forms of construction appear to have developed slowly in the eastern Mediterranean in the first millenium AD. It appears to have been several centuries,

31

The ultimate development of fully skeleton built construction, the four masted schooners Charles A Dean, *left, and* Helen Barnet Gring, *right, building at the RL Dean shipyard at Camden, Maine, in 1919. [W J Lewis Parker*

however, before similar intermediate techniques were adopted in northern Europe, where the edge-joined clinker traditions were immensely strong. In due course they developed into full skeleton construction, defined by McGrail (in *Ancient Boats of Northwest Europe*, p 105) as 'full skeleton building with the shape of the entire vessel determined by a pre-erected framework'.

Non edge-joined skeleton built boats and vessels have been built in a variety of ways. In the relatively sophisticated big shipbuilding yards of the late nineteenth century and for a good while earlier, vessels were built by shaping every frame from full-sized plans drawn out on a screive board, or a mould loft floor (Figures 30 and 31). But at the same period, small vessels, coasting smacks and small schooners were built, for instance in Cornwall in the 1870s, by setting up a few frames or even one frame only, approximately amidships, running battens from them fore and aft and deriving the shapes of the remaining frames from the curves of the battens. I think of this as 'intermediate' construction, a halfway house between shell and the skeleton approaches to building as, from what they told me, did the men who adopted these methods.

Just as the builders of complex structures on land, so all ship and boatbuilders have had to solve the problem of how to create the shape of the hull they wanted. Before the use of the half model, then of drawings and now of the computer, they had to visualise mentally the hull forms they were aiming to build. The conservatism which for centuries on end could mark the development of hull forms emerged, at least in part, from this difficulty. The builder could visualise what already existed and then perhaps modify it a little, so that the development of a tradition followed a kind of Darwinian evolution. The developing sub-discipline of nautical archaeology sees the visualisation of hull form as either in terms of the planking (shell) or the framing (skeleton).

It is now increasingly apparent that there was very likely a long period (or series of periods in different cultures) of intermediate ways of building and of groping towards full skeleton construction as defined by McGrail. Of the two gentlemen acknowledged in the author's note to this book, Sawyer Waldron described to me in detail in the mid-1940s relatively sophisticated full skeleton construction as he had worked at it at Appledore in the 1890s and through to 1910. But Sawyer Drew, talking of the building of the ketch *Hobah* at Trelew Creek in south Cornwall in 1879, described an older process of skeleton building in which the master shipwright and his men groped their way forward to the shape of a vessel which in detail depended on what he called 'the natural run of the batten', a series of battens wrapped round one or two or a few frames and run to the stem or sternpost to the shapes assumed by which many of the frames were made. We can get into deep water here and perhaps become too philosophical, but to some extent the shape of the *Hobah* and hundreds of other vessels was never fully visualised, but emerged from a combination of possibilities dictated by the builders' ideas and the physical properties of the available timber. This building process could have interesting results which show how much nature could take over. Thus the ketch *Ulelia*, built near Truro for the trade to Newfoundland in 1877, was not symmetrical. She needed one more deck plank on her port side than on her starboard, yet she worked very successfully for 53 years.

Building on 'the natural run of the batten' might have been a rather extreme form of this man-and-nature shaping, but, again, many variations must have existed and particularly so as full skeleton construction for large vessels in middle and northern Europe slowly evolved in the fifteenth, sixteenth and seventeenth centuries (see the description of the building of the vessel found at Red Bay in Labrador in Chapter 20). But, of course, the strakes of the finished vessels were not edge-joined.

The frames of a transitional or a fully skeleton built vessel, because of the stresses already referred to, had to be either much stronger or more numerous, or both, than the frames of an edge-joined boat or vessel. Strength in a vessel the planks of which were not joined edge to edge was derived also from two other sources. Caulking was driven hard between the edges of the planks into the seams and this driving put the planks under tension which made the whole body of the vessel stronger. Ceiling, a lining of planks, was fitted inside the frames and greatly increased the strength of the whole vessel. More will be said about these strengthening methods in the last chapter of this book. But always the planks were not joined edge to edge, even though in some cases the shapes of some of the frames were derived from the shape assumed by the inside of the planking fastened to frames already erected on the keel.

Among big wooden ships there were some exceptions to this general rule of shell conceived edge-joined and skeleton conceived non edge-joined. Very recent archaeological research in the Netherlands (reported by T J Maarleveld in *Crossroads in Ancient Shipbuilding*) on wrecks found in the polders dating from the period 1600–1650 has shown that average size sea-going mechant vessels were at that time shell-built with the strakes temporarily edge-joined, framing being inserted and shaped to fit. Like the framing of the Bangladesh boats described and illustrated in the last chapter, the frame parts were not interconnected and were made up of timbers of very variable sizes. It appears also that similar methods were used in the construction of larger vessels. Thus these vessels of the period of transition were shell-conceived but not edge-joined when completed. This is an important indication of one way fully skeleton building developed in the period of transition in what was at the time one of Europe's leading shipbuilding communities.

At a much later period some barquentines built of spruce wood in the late nineteenth century at New Bideford and Summerside in Prince Edward Island, Canada, had some of their planks bolted across to one another, edge to edge, to give them greater strength. The same thing was done in some big United States schooners, and in the past there have certainly been other vessels built in greater or lesser degree in the same way in other parts of the world. But in modern times these Prince Edward Island vessels were exceptions, built for a special reason by men who were trained in traditions which did not include the edge to edge joining of planks in wooden ships. They were basically skeleton-built vessels. The records show that both the men who built them and organisations which classified the vessels for insurance purposes had to be convinced of the soundness of such a novel method of construction before it was accepted and used.

We can now refine somewhat the descriptions of the two great categories of plank-built boats and ships in western history, those which are built of planks joined edge to edge and usually, but not always, to strengthening frame timbers inside the shell of planks, and those which are built of planks not joined edge to edge but only to frames. We can say that boats in the former category have historically tended mostly to be shell-constructed, that is, to be conceived as a whole as a watertight envelope of planks into which a strengthening framework deriving its shape from the shell is inserted after the completion of part or the whole of the shell. The majority of such boats and vessels in the past have probably been completed as shells before frames were inserted, but there are many other ways of building them. The latter category tended to be skeleton-constructed, that is, to be conceived as a skeleton of frames around which is wrapped a watertight skin of planks, but again there are many ways of developing the shape, using partly the skeleton of frames and partly the growth of the skin of planks itself. But however blurred the middle ground of building methods may be, the fundamental distinction remains between boats the planks of which are edge-joined and those the planks of which are not edge-joined. As to the order and system of building there may well often be dispute in the cases of individual boats, and as we have just seen during periods of transition temporary edge-joining was used in some cultures, but as to whether the planks were joined together edge to edge by one method or another in the completed vessel there can be no dispute. There are a few types of boat in the world which combine the two categories: the strakes are edge-joined for a distinct part of the structure, not edge-joined over the rest. Such hybrids are rare and each one has to be considered and examined separately. It is possible that hybrids may provide useful evidence as to the local origins of non edge-joined construction.

This basic division of boats into edge-joined and non edge-joined is a new kind of fundamental categorisation, but the evidence of history and the evidence of surviving boats of the old building traditions in the world today strongly suggest its validity. The history of attempts at similar broad classification is interesting. Because most writing on the history of boats has been North European, for a long time there was a widespread tendency to be confused by the clearly defined principal late nineteenth-century methods of building boats in North Europe. Put very simply, these were that boats built with overlapping planks were edge-joined, boats with planks lying flush to one another were not edge-joined. Therefore, the train of thought runs, explicit or implicit, through much writing about the history of boats, all boats throughout the world with planks lying flush were not edge-joined, and only boats with overlapping planks were edge-joined. Even James Hornell, the great British pioneer in the study of the development of boats, was liable to slip into this trap at times, despite his world-wide observation and experience, and in places his thoughts and writing become very confused by it.

A valuable classification put forward very clearly by Olof Hasslöf in *Ships and Shipyards, Sailors and Fishermen*, which remains a most useful working tool, is that which divides boats into those which are shell-constructed and those which are skeleton-constructed. But for reasons given above this cannot be accepted as defining the fundamental differences between the two great categories of boats, because the difference does not at all times and at all places rest in the order and method of construction. It rests in the simple fact of whether the planks of the boat's shell are permanently joined together at the edges or not.

The question is not even as simple as it seems, as we have already seen, for, just as edge-joining and pure shell-construction are not necessarily synonymous, so the absence of edge-joining cannot be taken as evidence for full skeleton-construction, as it has widely developed in the western world in the last 400 years. Here, too, there are intermediate forms. On the banks of the Indus at Sukkur in Pakistan some years ago I watched the construction of a large flat-bottomed river boat. First her two sides were assembled. They were made of planks joined edge to edge with wooden pins driven in holes drilled diagonally across the seams from plank face outside to plank face inside. The vertical columns of cut-off pin-heads are clearly visible in Figure 32. The heads are of oval shape because of the angle at which the pins emerge from the plank face. Behind the complete sides the bottom is being made and is clearly visible in the photograph. A row of floor timbers, like railway sleepers across the dry mud of the river bank, has the planks fastened across it, outside one first, working inwards. The finished bottom is then turned over and the sides fastened to the beam ends. The ends of the bottom are forced up at either end to follow the shape of the sides. Side frames or timbers are then added and then deck beams and decks, the whole making a strong boxlike boat (Figure 33), admirably suited to her environment and purpose, which is to be the great cargo carrier on the River Indus.

Such a form of construction is a mixture both of edge-joining and non edge-joining, of skeleton and shell construction, since the finished boat derives its ultimate shape partly from the shape of shell components and partly from the shape of part of a skeleton. It is interesting to imagine some future archaeologist discovering the bottom structure of such a boat and hailing it as evidence of non edge-joined pure skeleton construction in the nineteenth-century European sense of the term on the Indus in the mid-twentieth century.

In the Peshawar Valley in northern Pakistan a boatbuilder described to me another method of building flat-bottomed river boats which appears to represent another strand in the world's boatbuilding traditions. These boats are essentially skeleton-built on a flat bottom rockered fore and aft.

To build a flat-bottomed double-ended river boat (Figure 34), first the floor timbers are laid out upside down on a stretch of flat river bank. At either end of the boat-to-be the timbers are small, perhaps 6in (15cm) deep, amidships half a dozen timbers may be twice as thick. The keel, a plank of timber 3in (7.6cm) thick, is then fastened over the middles of the floor timbers and then, working outwards from the keel plank the progressively shorter planks of the bottom, each 2in (5.1cm) thick, are fastened on and cut to shape at both ends. The planks of the bottom are laid flat edge

33

A complete flat-bottomed cargo boat worked downstream on the river Indus. The enormous oars, worked with infinite labour, are lashed to thole pins even more complex in shape than the forcola of a boat of the Venetian gondola family. [Basil Greenhill

to edge without edge-joining and without rabbeting, and a caulking of locally-grown cotton is driven between them.

Then the whole bottom of the boat is turned over and the centre part held down by weights, lumps of rock, while the bow and stern are forced up with poles used as levers to give a slightly increased rocker, over and above that given by the shaping of the floor timbers to the bottom of the boat. Then the stem and sternposts are fitted and the side frames, quite straight timbers with no attempt at any kind of shaping, are added, then the beam shelf and deck beams, so that in its next stage of construction the boat is an angular skeleton built up on the finished bottom. Last of all she is planked up in the sides and the decks are laid. This whole process took my informant and his few assistants about twelve days for a large cargo boat and between them he and his family had built forty-four boats in the year before I discussed his trade with him. Despite their apparent weakness these boats wore well in the limited conditions of the river trade.

It is fun occasionally to speculate on very little evidence, providing one does not take the results too seriously, and I suppose it is just possible that the methods of construction could indicate that both the Indus river boat and the Peshawar valley boat have descended ultimately from rafts, rather than from the logboats and to a

34

Flat-bottomed cargo boat on the Kabul river, in the Peshawar Valley, Pakistan. [Basil Greenhill

lesser extent skin boats which appear to have provided the origins of most North European building traditions.

There would appear to be some evidence for a similar tradition of rather specialised building at least in part without edge-joining provided by some wrecks of the seventeenth to nineteenth centuries found in the draining of the Zuyder Zee. The bottom planks of these are not edge-joined and their side frames are not joined to the floor timbers. They, too, may well have been built by laying down the floor timbers upside down, fastening the bottom planking to them, turning the whole over, erecting the side timbers secured to the outermost bottom plank only, and then perhaps fitting such beams as there were and then planking up to the side timbers with or without edge-joining.

There apparently existed in middle Europe a boatbuilding tradition distinct from those of Europe North or South, from Mediterranean traditions as they were in the early centuries AD and from those of North Europe at the same time. This tradition has been variously described as 'Celtic' (by Ellmers in *Keltischer Shiffbau*), as 'Gallo-Roman' and, most recently by McGrail as 'Romano-Celtic' (in *Ancient Boats of North West Europe*). McGrail in a paper published in the *International Journal of Nautical Archaeology* 1994/5 has summed up his reasons as follows: 'the "Celtic" part of this binominal reflects the fact that the spatial distribution of these finds is, by and large, in regions formerly occupied by Celtic-speaking peoples; and the "Roman" element reflects the temporal distribution, first to fourth century AD, and acknowledges the possibility of Roman technological influence.'

The remains of round-hulled boats apparently built in the Romano-Celtic tradition have been found in the City of London at Blackfriars, in the Channel Islands at St Peter Port, Guernsey and in southeast Wales at Barlands Farm in Gwent. The timespan covered by these finds is very limited, roughly the first three centuries of the Christian era. Highly speculative ideas have linked these finds with the British Bronze Age sewn boats (see Chapter 9) at one end of the timescale and with the cog (see Chapter 18) at the other. Less speculative thinking has linked them with the boats of the Veneti, a Celtic people of northwest France, whose vessels were described in detail by Julius Ceasar in *De Bello Gallico* 3.13.

McGrail has summarised the characteristic features of the Romano-Celtic tradition as at present they appear to be as follows:

1. They are built in skeleton-sequence with non edge-fastened, flush-laid strakes. They are essentially frame based or, in McGrail's term, 'frame visualised'.
2. Large iron nails, driven through treenails and clenched by turning the emerging point through 180° to make a hook the point of which is driven back into the timber, are used to fasten the strakes to the frames.
3. The frames comprised relatively massive and relatively closely spaced groups of framing timbers, including floors spanning bottom and bilges, asymmetric timbers spanning the bottom and one side, and side timbers. At any one point all these may co-exist, but they will not be fastened together – they do not comprise a continuous frame.
4. The bottoms of the boats are relatively flat with a plank keel.
5. The mast step, for towing and for sailing, is placed well forward of amidships.

The building sequence of those finds which have been properly recorded and published is still the subject of academic dispute. Some of the characteristics listed above, but not all of them together, were shared with other traditions. Margaret Rule, who excavated one of these finds in Guernsey, considers the vessel's construction to have been 'step wise alternation' between shell and skeleton construction.

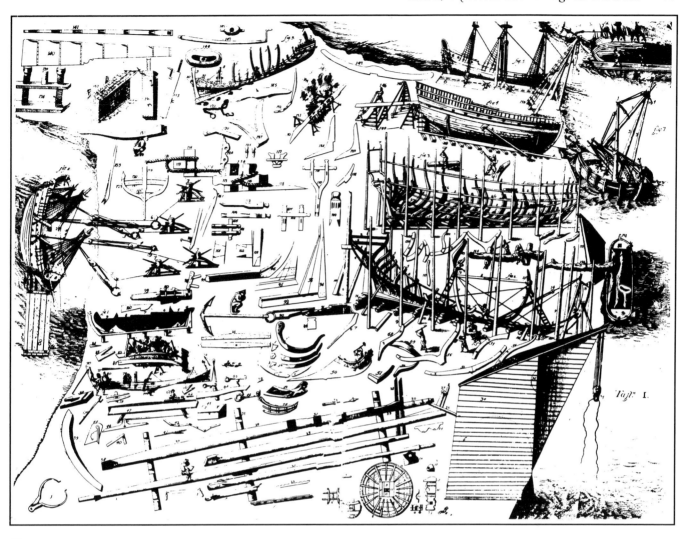

35

A seventeenth-century Scandinavian dockyard. [From Rålamb, Skeps Byggerij eller Adelig Öfnings Tionde Tom, *Stockholm, 1691*

The development of non edge-joined skeleton construction is very clearly illustrated in Figure 35 of a Scandinavian dockyard of the late 1600s when both traditional and transitional methods, as well as the relatively new full skeleton construction, were in use. The vessel number Figure 9 is temporarily edge-joined below to form a shell of the floor of the vessel with upperworks of planks on a skeleton of upper frames, which derive their shape in part from the shell-conceived lower body of the vessel. Thus, of the frames, their lower part is 'passive', their upper part 'active'. This is the 'Dutch' method of building which Landström believes to have been used in building the great Swedish warship *Wasa* of 1628 now restored in Stockholm (see Chapter 20). Figure 4 has a planked-up hull while Figure 3 shows full skeleton construction as already defined. Figure 2 appears to show building from a single midships frame, with ribbands from which the shape of the rest of the vessel will be basically developed. Of the two boats shown at Figure 1, one is an edge-joined clinker-built boat built to moulds, while the other shows the classic 'sculpture', mouldless clinker shell construction. The vessel in the top right-hand corner is deliberately drawn with partly hulk style planking.

The basic reason for the success and general adoption of non edge-joined skeleton construction was very probably economic. Very simply, western man required bigger ships to carry more goods and more people for longer distances. Ships were required which could carry heavy guns to defend themselves and to establish control over the regions with which western man was establishing trade. The skeleton technique of non edge-joined construction is susceptible to far greater development than edge-joined construction could ever be. Vessels can be bigger and new shapes and forms can be readily initiated. Once the problem of providing sufficient strength to withstand seagoing stresses was understood vessels could be built which were large enough and strong enough to make possible the great European expansion of the 1400s and 1500s. The development of the non edge-joined, skeleton-built ship is one of the technical factors which made possible the exploration of the world by western predominance. So this highly complex change in shipbuilding methods is one of the key points in our history.

In the Mediterranean great maritime civilisations developed and died away and the successive generations of Egyptians, Phoenicians, Greeks and Romans ranged far and wide in trading and raiding voyages which played their significant part in setting the pattern of western civilisation for thousands of years. Archaeological and literary evidence suggests that they did so in boats and vessels, the planks of which were joined together at the edges by one means or another. In recent years much further evidence has been obtained from underwater excavations which suggests that Mediterranean vessels of the classical traditions were edge-joined, often by some variations of tenons, mortises, dovetails and so on. John Morrison deals with this subject in detail in Chapters 10 and 11 of this book.

The different techniques of building non-edge joined boats and vessels developed probably at different times and in different parts of the world. As far as North Europe and Britain are concerned, it may have grown up from the thirteenth century or even earlier and it seems to have been gradually adopted with many transitional stages from the late 1400s and early 1500s, but was possibly not fully developed and widely established until the early 1600s, spreading outwards through the Middle East to India (see Chapter 8). But it never supplanted edge-joining for the building of boats and small vessels, even in North Europe, and in the rest of the world thousands of vessels continued to be built with edge-joined planking, and continued to be as long as wooden vessels were constructed. Certainly intermediate forms lingered on in some areas until the late nineteenth century. But gradually in North Europe smooth-skinned boats and ships became synonymous with boats and ships the planks of which were not joined together at the edges, and before very long construction without edge-joining became the standard procedure for nearly all big vessels.

The builder who works in the skeleton tradition works very differently from one who does so in the shell tradition. In shell construction the builder can constantly check and alter his work. If he begins to go wrong he can correct his mistakes. He can take out the plank, change its shape, change the angle at which it is joined to its neighbour. He has plenty of opportunity in fitting and re-fitting the planks to re-work his theme.

A Swedish master shipwright described working in the edge-joined tradition to Olof Hasslöf in 1930: 'When you build clinker, the ship takes shape under your very hands: if it doesn't turn out so well, you can finish it as you want it. Once you get over the bilge the thing is practically done.' A *mistri* in Bangladesh used almost the same phrases to me twenty years later, though he was from a society culturally and geographically utterly remote from Sweden.

But the fully skeleton builder has to make up his frames and put his skeleton together before he can see what his ship is going to look like and, although he can do some correcting by padding out frames and so forth, unless it is going to be the very expensive matter of making new frames, always several at a time, the possibility of changing shapes is very limited. It is not surprising that new methods involving the making of half models of various kinds and later the making of scale drawings on paper, then drawing out the frames full scale on a mould loft floor, began to develop. Nor is it surprising that intermediate methods owing something to older and well understood shell-building traditions were adopted by men faced with the very difficult challenge of full skeleton-building.

It follows from this categorisation of boats and ships into two groups, one old and very big and the other newer and much smaller, the one built of planks joined at the edges, the other of planks not so joined, that some standard definitions which have been widely used are no longer appropriate. As has already been said, because in the late nineteenth century two basic ways of building a wooden boat were predominant in Britain, edge-joined with overlapping planks, and non edge-joined with the planks lying edge to edge so that the outside of the boat was smooth, it was, and still is today, often assumed that only boats built of overlapping planks were edge-joined and that all boats built with smooth skins were and are not edge-joined. For these two types of construction respectively the terms clinker, clenched lap or lapstrake, and the term carvel were generally used, though there never seems to have been general agreement on the definition of carvel. The first of these terms we can still retain, closely defined. The second, carvel, insofar as it has been taken to describe a smooth-planked boat is now meaningless and must be dispensed with altogether since smooth-planking is no indication of whether the boat was built shell, skeleton, or by some intermediate process.

Clinker or lapstrake construction we can define, in the words of Eric McKee in *Clenched Lap or Clinker*, as the method of arranging the strakes of a vessel so that they overlap and are fastened together through the overlap. The term is really appropriate only to boats built in the North Europe traditions of clinker-building in which the planks usually fully overlap for the greater part of their length without substantial thinning of the overlapping parts; there may, however, be considerable local fairing of the overlap in places, for example to produce watertight joints where the ends of the planks are fastened to the stem and stern posts of the vessel. It could be added that the overlap is with the lower edge of the upper plank outside the upper edge of the lower plank. The unqualified term will be used in this book only to mean building in this main North European tradition.

But boats are built in different parts of the world with planks which overlap in other ways and are joined to one another at the edges, and a number of these methods will be described later in this book. It may be useful here to mention three methods of building with overlapping planks other than the method of the main European tradition, by way of example.

As has already been said, the smooth-skinned boats of Bangladesh are built of planks which are cut to a half rabbet at each edge so that they overlap, but the thickness of the skin at the overlap is rarely greater than that of one plank. They are then joined edge to edge with metal lugs. Some Swedish and Finnish big lake boats are built in a very similar way and fastened in a very similar way, but with the plank edges, like those of the dory, faired rather than rabbeted and there is archaeological evidence that this method of fastening has been in use since Viking times. Both of these methods of fastening, so widely separated geographically, are so reminiscent of the sewing methods used in extending some logboats (see Chapter 9) that it is difficult not to believe that the one is a development from the other. The middle west European and northeast North American dory, of which a detailed account is given later in this book, has planks which overlap and which are joined edge to edge, but they are so faired away at the edges as to produce sometimes almost a smooth skin. The term clinker cannot perhaps properly be applied to any of these construction methods. They can only be described in detail as specific building traditions.

The drawing in Figure 36 shows a series of examples of different kinds of

SHELL-FORMING EDGE-FASTENED PLANK JOINTS

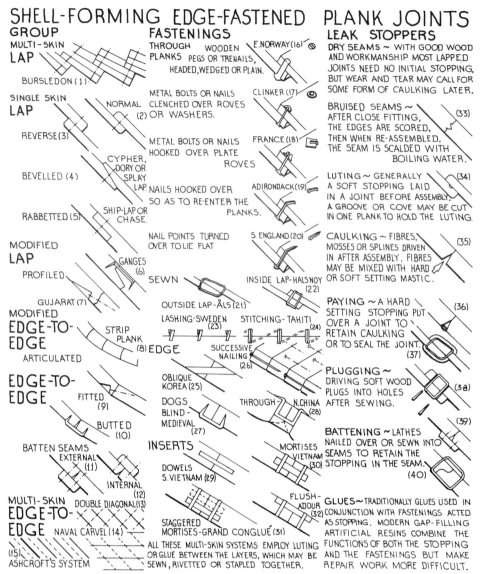

GROUP

MULTI-SKIN LAP
BURSLEDON (1)

SINGLE SKIN LAP
REVERSE (3)

BEVELLED (4)
CYPHER, DORY OR SPLAY LAP.

RABBETTED (5)
SHIP-LAP OR CHASE.

MODIFIED LAP
GANGES (6)
PROFILED.

GUJARAT (7)
MODIFIED EDGE-TO-EDGE
STRIP PLANK (8)
ARTICULATED

EDGE-TO-EDGE
FITTED (9)

BUTTED (10)

BATTEN SEAMS
EXTERNAL (11)
INTERNAL (12)
DOUBLE DIAGONAL (13)

MULTI-SKIN EDGE-TO-EDGE
NAVAL CARVEL (14)
(15) ASHCROFT'S SYSTEM

FASTENINGS

THROUGH WOODEN PLANKS PEGS OR TRENAILS, HEADED, WEDGED OR PLAIN.
E. NORWAY (16)

METAL BOLTS OR NAILS CLENCHED OVER ROVES (2) OR WASHERS.
CLINKER (17)

METAL BOLTS OR NAILS HOOKED OVER PLATE ROVES
FRANCE (18)

NAILS HOOKED OVER SO AS TO RE-ENTER THE PLANKS.
ADIRONDACK (19)

NAIL POINTS TURNED OVER TO LIE FLAT
S. ENGLAND (20)

SEWN
OUTSIDE LAP - ÅLS (21)
INSIDE LAP - HALSNOY (22)

LASHING - SWEDEN (23)
STITCHING - TAHITI (24)

EDGE
SUCCESSIVE NAILING (26)

OBLIQUE KOREA (25)

DOGS
BLIND - MEDIEVAL (27)
THROUGH - N. CHINA (28)

INSERTS
DOWELS S. VIETNAM (29)
MORTISES VIETNAM (30)

STAGGERED MORTISES - GRAND CONGLUÉ (31)
FLUSH - ADOUR (32)

ALL THESE MULTI-SKIN SYSTEMS EMPLOY LUTING OR GLUE BETWEEN THE LAYERS, WHICH MAY BE SEWN, RIVETTED OR STAPLED TOGETHER.

LEAK STOPPERS

DRY SEAMS ~ WITH GOOD WOOD AND WORKMANSHIP MOST LAPPED JOINTS NEED NO INITIAL STOPPING, BUT WEAR AND TEAR MAY CALL FOR SOME FORM OF CAULKING LATER.

BRUISED SEAMS ~ AFTER CLOSE FITTING, THE EDGES ARE SCORED, THEN WHEN RE-ASSEMBLED, THE SEAM IS SCALDED WITH BOILING WATER. (33)

LUTING ~ GENERALLY A SOFT STOPPING LAID IN A JOINT BEFORE ASSEMBLY. A GROOVE OR COVE MAY BE CUT IN ONE PLANK TO HOLD THE LUTING. (34)

CAULKING ~ FIBRES, MOSSES OR SPLINES DRIVEN IN AFTER ASSEMBLY. FIBRES MAY BE MIXED WITH HARD OR SOFT SETTING MASTIC. (35)

PAYING ~ A HARD SETTING STOPPING PUT OVER A JOINT TO RETAIN CAULKING OR TO SEAL THE JOINT. (36)

PLUGGING ~ DRIVING SOFT WOOD PLUGS INTO HOLES AFTER SEWING. (37)

BATTENING ~ LATHES NAILED OVER OR SEWN INTO SEAMS TO RETAIN THE STOPPING IN THE SEAM. (39) (40)

GLUES ~ TRADITIONALLY GLUES USED IN CONJUNCTION WITH FASTENINGS ACTED AS STOPPING. MODERN GAP-FILLING ARTIFICIAL RESINS COMBINE THE FUNCTIONS OF BOTH THE STOPPING AND THE FASTENINGS BUT MAKE REPAIR WORK MORE DIFFICULT. (38)

THE INSIDE OF THE VESSEL IS TO THE RIGHT OF EACH SKETCH
EXAMPLES OF EACH TYPE OF JOINT ARE GIVEN IN A SEPARATE NUMBERED REFERENCE LIST.

36
Some different kinds of edge-joining.
[*Eric McKee*

edge joining and it will be seen that for obvious reasons of strength many systems involve some degree of overlap, whether this is visible on the outside of the finished hull or not. Despite the apparent weakness consequent upon the lack of adequate bearing edges, which might be considered likely to make the vessels less able to withstand the normal working stresses already described, there were many different ways of joining planks lying square edge to square edge. Figure 37 shows a vessel built in this way, the strakes joined together with thick metal pins at right angles to the seams, the shell of a Pakistani *hora* just at the stage when the first floor timbers were about to be inserted.

The term carvel has been given many meanings. It is acceptable for it to be used to signify a building method which involves the use of a single layer of fore and aft strakes closely fitted and fastened to a pre-erected frame work and not joined to one another at the edges. But in this book I shall not use the term at all. It has too unfortunate a history of confusion behind it. The various building traditions which have from time to time been covered by this term will be described separately as they arise.

37
The almost completed shell of a hora *fishing boat at Ibrahim Hyderi in Pakistan. The next stage of construction is the shaping and fitting of floor timbers.* [*Basil Greenhill*

It follows from the preceding paragraphs of this chapter that a boat has been thought of by most boatbuilders in prehistory and history as a reasonably watertight shell of strakes made up from planks joined at the edges and held in shape by such minimal internal reinforcement as may be necessary, given her environment and the work she is to do. It follows also that, since wooden planks are flat, the builders of most boats in history have been successful in part to the degree in which they have been able to acquire the skill to convert flat material into shapes which, when joined together at the edges, will make a hollow object. The shape of that object will depend on the shaping of the flat parts, more than on any other single factor. Men building boats of planks have therefore been concerned more than anything else with the shaping of those planks. To understand the significance of this I can do no better than to recommend *Clenched Lap or Clinker* by Eric McKee, to which I have already referred. This book not only explains the process of deriving the shapes of the planks, it demonstrates it very clearly, by giving the reader a small cardboard half model of a 10ft (3.04m) clinker-built working boat to make up for himself. By doing this one can learn more quickly about the real nature of the problems of wooden boatbuilders and the structure of boats built in the main North European tradition than perhaps by any other means. For the building of larger vessels in the full skeleton tradition equally full and clear explanation is given in the drawings by Sam Manning in *The Evolution of the Wooden Ship*.

The success of boatbuilders in their trade has depended on their ability to foresee the flat shapes which will make up into the three-dimensional curved shapes they want. This is a very difficult and sophisticated skill to acquire, and this difficulty is very clearly demonstrated by the regularity and lack of innovation in the shape traditions that developed in different societies and provided solutions to this problem, and the incredible longevity of some of the successful solutions once firmly established. Thus the Oselver boat, still built to order near Bergen in Norway today, is only slightly developed from the four-oared boat found inside the Gokstad ship and dating from approximately AD 850. It is no wonder that, from time to time in different places, intermediate methods may have developed, designed to simplify the feat of predicting the necessary curves to be given to flat shapes so that they make up into an extremely complex curved three-dimensional object. Yet the art and skill have perhaps been best developed by the least schooled of men, Scandinavians of a thousand years ago, illiterate, itinerant craftsmen in Bangladesh today, who used and use no structural aids to building, but create shells of great efficiency for purpose by eye and swinging stick, or its equivalent, alone.

Since it is the shape of the edges of the planks that principally determines the shape of the boat, it follows that the best way of recording the boat is to record these shapes. This fact has fundamental implications, because it is now recognised that one of the most important tools of the boat archaeologist in recording a boat find, and

38
The four-oared boat found inside the Gokstad ship of about AD 850 as she is displayed today at Bygdøy near Oslo. [Basil Greenhill

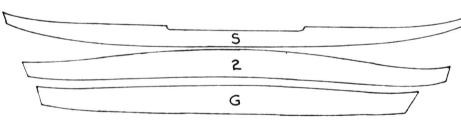

39
Strake diagram of the Gokstad four-oared boat. [Eric McKee

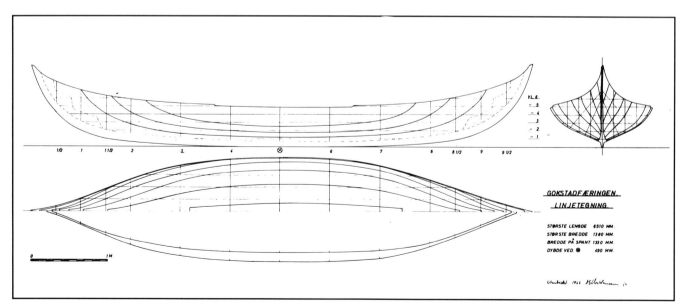

41

A reconstruction of the Gokstad four-oared boat undergoing sailing trials. [*Basil Greenhill*

40

Naval architect's drawing of the Gokstad four-oared boat. [*Universitets Oldsaksamling, Oslo*

◄

then studying and comparing it with other finds, is the strake diagram, that is the drawing of the curved shapes of the planks in the flat. The strakes are the joined-up planks making, in most cases, a complete run from one end of the boat to the other. This tool is proving especially valuable for studying boats in the North European clinker tradition, but it can probably be adapted for use with boats of other traditions with equal success.

The simple examples given in Figures 38, 39 and 40 illustrate the point very well indeed. Figure 38 is a photograph of the four-oared boat, the *faering*, found inside the Gokstad ship burial of AD 850 in Norway. She is a very beautiful Viking boat and is described at length in Chapter 16. Figure 39 is the strake diagram of this boat. These strakes, joined together at the edges and to the keel, stem and stern post, will make up in only one way, that is into the shape of one half of this boat. With a little practice it is possible to read straight off from this drawing the characteristics of a complete boat and by comparing the drawing with strake diagrams of other boats to compare the boats also. It is probably also possible to examine and analyse the structural details and characteristics of the boat herself more easily in the strake diagram than by any other method. Thus the strake diagram has many advantages over conventional naval architects' drawings (Figure 40) with all their difficulties in interpretation, their unreality and their oversimplification. Figure 41 shows a reconstruction of the Gokstad *faering* under sail at Devonport in England.

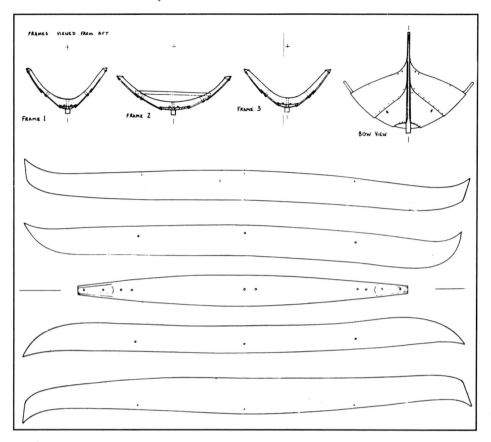

42

Strake diagram of the Årby boat.
[*Owain Roberts*

Figures 42 and 43 do the same job for a possibly even older and certainly smaller boat, the one man (or perhaps one woman) boat found at Årby Farm, Rasbokil, in Uppland, north of Stockholm. Figure 44 shows a reconstruction of this little boat undergoing searching trials. Figure 45 shows the boat under construction. Note the shape of the second strake hanging while awaiting fitting on the left of the building shed.

As a means of recording, comparing and analysing boats, the strake diagram is

44

Owain Roberts at rowing trials in the reconstruction of the Årby boat. [*Basil Greenhill*

43
Construction drawings of the Årby boat. [Owain Roberts

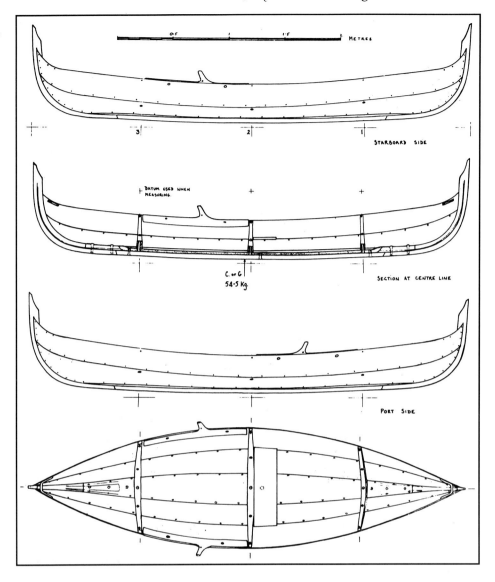

45
The Årby boat reconstruction in Owain Roberts' workshop in Amlwch, North Wales. [Basil Greenhill

likely to be used more and more as a principal tool as the study develops. It was developed in this country by Eric McKee and in Denmark by Ole Crumlin-Pedersen. But it is important to emphasise that in recording and reporting a boat find, it is not adequate to publish only the strake diagram which, when it is derived from incomplete remains, must inevitably be partly hypothetical. Besides the diagram, representing as it will one carefully considered solution to the problem of what was the shape of the whole boat, scale drawings of the strakes and fragments of structure actually found must be published, in order that the reader can appraise for himself the evidence on which the hypothetical solution is based, and form his own conclusions. This has been done in the report on the Graveney boat (see Bibliography).

The reality behind the strake diagram is clearly demonstrated by Figure 46. This shows the thirty-six constituent parts of a small dory built in the Lawrence Allen Dory Shop in Lunenburg, Nova Scotia, and it is obvious that they can make up in only one way. The strakes themselves are slightly shaped to fit at the bevels, but in a classic flat-bottomed boat of this kind only the bottom edge of the lowest strake need in fact be curved, the rest can be parallel-sided stock timber; a single very wide board, perhaps made from two pieces joined end to end as in the Bridgwater flatner; or a sheet of plywood (see Chapter 2).

There is, of course, another relevant factor that worries the boatbuilder. The strakes, be they overlapping or fitting edge to edge, must be bevelled to fit one another. To the boatbuilder working in an edge-joined pure shell tradition, this bevel is fundamental, since he works with stock of indeterminate length, cut to fit at stem and stern only after it has been joined to its neighbour; the angle at which it joins its neighbour, the bevel, is crucial to the shaping of the shell. Thus his tradition may be embodied partly in a series of figures for the bevels of different strakes. But once the strake has been shaped and cut to length it will only fit one way and to one angle of bevel to make one shape of shell. The archaeologists dealing with the finished product should record both the strake shape and the bevel, though the latter is not essential.

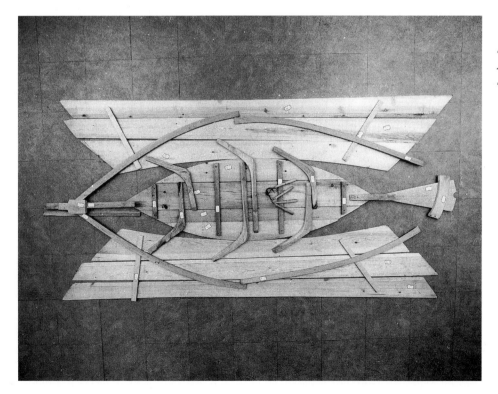

46
The thirty-six constituent shaped timbers of a small dory from the Lawrence Allen Dory Shop at Lunenburg, Nova Scotia. [National Maritime Museum

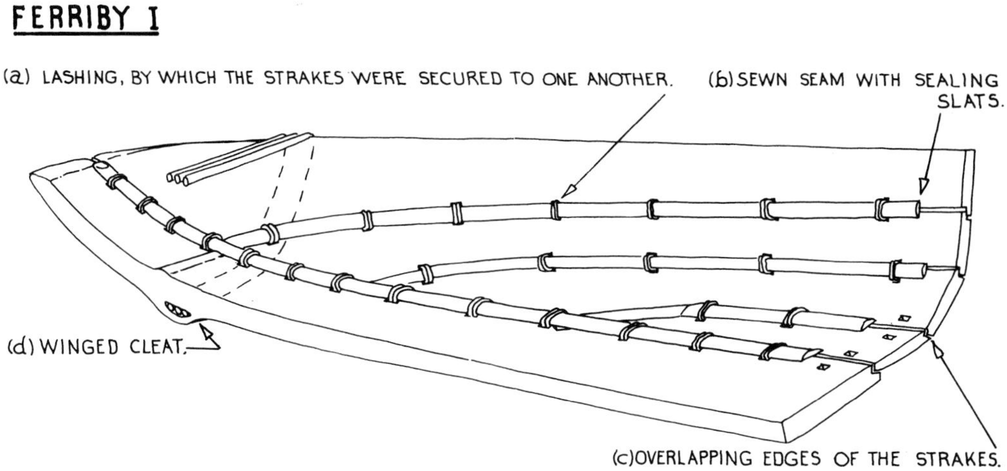

FERRIBY I

(a) LASHING, BY WHICH THE STRAKES WERE SECURED TO ONE ANOTHER.   (b) SEWN SEAM WITH SEALING SLATS.

(d) WINGED CLEAT.

(c) OVERLAPPING EDGES OF THE STRAKES.

47
The plank ends of the first Ferriby boat – an early hypothetical solution. [Eric McKee

There is one further fundamental problem which faces the builder of a plank-built boat, and the solution he adopts is one more detail which does not appear in the strake diagram and which must be recorded to make it possible to assess, appreciate and compare the full boat. This is the problem of the plank ends.

Once the builder has determined the shapes of the edges of the planks which make up his strakes, he has to determine the ways in which he is going to bring these strakes to a conclusion at either end to make his hollow vessel watertight. The shapes of the edges of the strakes determine the general form of his boat; the shapes of the ends and the way they are brought to a watertight conclusion determine the remaining characteristics of the boat. Now, although the problem may at first sight seem obvious and simple, it is in fact very difficult to decide what to do with the plank ends to produce a watertight vessel, and many solutions have been tried in history. Eric McKee prepared a series of drawings illustrating some of the classic solutions.

The first, Figure 47, is an early possible solution, later modified in the light of John Coates' research (see Wright, *The Ferriby Boats*, Chapter 5) to the problem of ending one of the oldest boats, if not the oldest, of which remains have been found anywhere in the world outside Egypt, Ferriby 1 (see Chapter 9). Here, all the parts are shaped from the solid:

(a) is the lashing by which the strakes were secured to one another.
(b) the sewn seams with sealing slats.
(c) the overlapping edges of the strakes.
(d) the winged cleats.

The next drawing, Figure 48, shows the Hjortspring boat of about 300 BC (see Chapter 6). Here are shown:

(a) the sewn seams paid with resin.
(b) the peg tie and strut.
(c) the logboat bottom, extending beyond the hollowed-out stem piece.

The Hjortspring boat may have been built by wood boatbuilders familiar with contemporary skin boatbuilding practice.

In the Björke boat (see Chapter 12), shown in Figure 49:

(a) the plank tapers to an end well above the waterline.
(b) shows the clench overlap fastened with iron rivets.
(c) the logboat bottom providing most of the strength and watertightness of the hull.

THE ALS BOAT

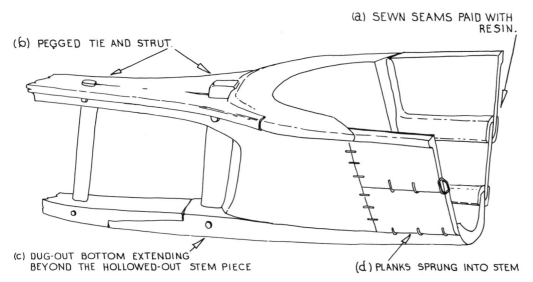

(a) SEWN SEAMS PAID WITH RESIN.

(b) PEGGED TIE AND STRUT.

(c) DUG-OUT BOTTOM EXTENDING BEYOND THE HOLLOWED-OUT STEM PIECE

(d) PLANKS SPRUNG INTO STEM

48
The plank ends of the Hjortspring boat. [Eric McKee

THE BJORKE BOAT

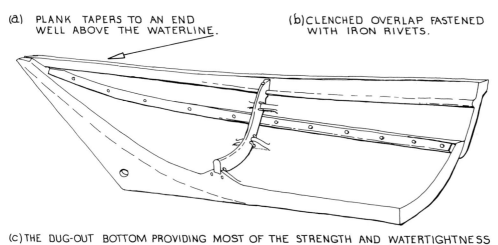

(a) PLANK TAPERS TO AN END WELL ABOVE THE WATERLINE.

(b) CLENCHED OVERLAP FASTENED WITH IRON RIVETS.

(c) THE DUG-OUT BOTTOM PROVIDING MOST OF THE STRENGTH AND WATERTIGHTNESS OF THIS HULL.

49
The plank ends of the Björke boat. [Eric McKee

The next diagram, Figure 50, shows the Gokstad ship (see Chapter 16). This is engineering in wood; massive strength with minimum weight.

(a) shows the raked breasthook, secured by a row of fastenings and which ties the two sides together.
(b) the continuous rabbet with only a few strakes terminating underwater, but these have plenty of edge for fastenings.
(c) the short end planks allow grain to follow the shape of the strake.
(d) the line above which, because of the destruction of that part of the original boat, the drawing is hypothetical.

The Graveney boat (see Chapter 16), shown in Figure 51, dates from about AD 900 and is a cargo vessel, found in Britain, a near contemporary of the Gokstad ship.

THE GOKSTAD SHIP

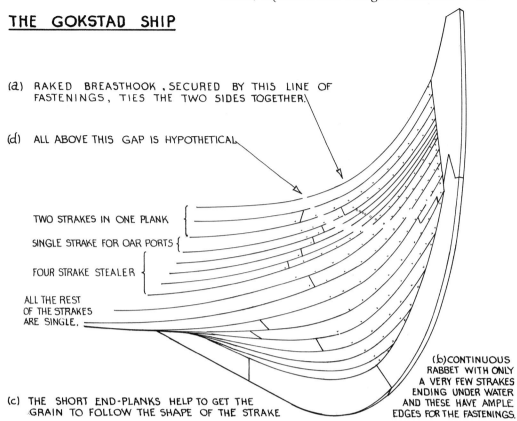

(a) RAKED BREASTHOOK, SECURED BY THIS LINE OF FASTENINGS, TIES THE TWO SIDES TOGETHER.

(d) ALL ABOVE THIS GAP IS HYPOTHETICAL.

TWO STRAKES IN ONE PLANK

SINGLE STRAKE FOR OAR PORTS

FOUR STRAKE STEALER

ALL THE REST OF THE STRAKES ARE SINGLE.

(b) CONTINUOUS RABBET WITH ONLY A VERY FEW STRAKES ENDING UNDER WATER AND THESE HAVE AMPLE EDGES FOR THE FASTENINGS.

(c) THE SHORT END-PLANKS HELP TO GET THE GRAIN TO FOLLOW THE SHAPE OF THE STRAKE

50

The plank ends of the Gokstad ship. [Eric McKee

THE GRAVENEY BOAT

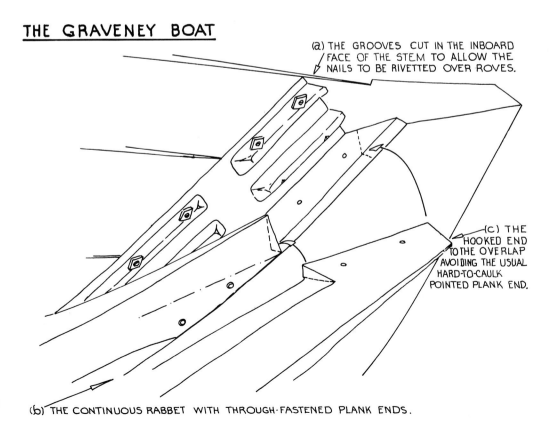

(a) THE GROOVES CUT IN THE INBOARD FACE OF THE STEM TO ALLOW THE NAILS TO BE RIVETTED OVER ROVES.

(c) THE HOOKED END TO THE OVERLAP AVOIDING THE USUAL HARD-TO-CAULK POINTED PLANK END.

(b) THE CONTINUOUS RABBET WITH THROUGH-FASTENED PLANK ENDS.

51

The plank ends of the Graveney Boat. [Eric McKee

THE SKULDELEV WRECK I

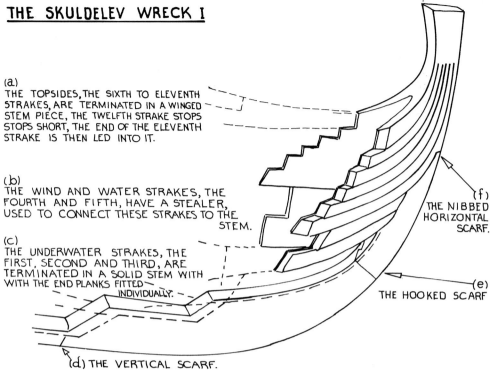

(a)
THE TOPSIDES, THE SIXTH TO ELEVENTH STRAKES, ARE TERMINATED IN A WINGED STEM PIECE, THE TWELFTH STRAKE STOPS STOPS SHORT, THE END OF THE ELEVENTH STRAKE IS THEN LED INTO IT.

(b)
THE WIND AND WATER STRAKES, THE FOURTH AND FIFTH, HAVE A STEALER, USED TO CONNECT THESE STRAKES TO THE STEM.

(c)
THE UNDERWATER STRAKES, THE FIRST, SECOND AND THIRD, ARE TERMINATED IN A SOLID STEM WITH WITH THE END PLANKS FITTED INDIVIDUALLY.

(d) THE VERTICAL SCARF.

(f) THE NIBBED HORIZONTAL SCARF.

(e) THE HOOKED SCARF

(a) shows the grooves cut in the inboard face of the stem post to allow nails to be riveted over roves.

(b) the continuous rabbet with through-fastened plank ends.

(c) the hooked end to overlap, avoiding the usual weak and hard to caulk pointed plank ends.

A century later, Skuldelev Wreck 1 (see Chapter 16 – Figure 52) shows three solutions in one vessel. This is master craftsmanship.

(a) the topside, the sixth to eleventh strakes, are terminated in a winged stem piece, the twelfth strake stops short, the end of the eleventh strake is then led into it.

(b) the wind and water strakes, the fourth and fifth, have a stealer, used to connect these strakes to the stem.

(c) the underwater strakes, the first, second and third, are terminated in a solid stem with the end planks individually fitted. These show:

(d) the vertical scarf.

(e) a hooked scarf.

(f) the nibbed horizontal scarf.

The Norwegian, Swedish or Finnish pram (Figure 53) represents simple efficiency, jogged transom at each end; the central plank is also the keel.

(a) shows the bow narrow with forward overhang, all plank ends are well clear of the water.

(b) iron bands add strength to narrow plank ends which can have only a few fastenings.

(c) the stern is strong, beamy and buoyant.

The next drawing, Figure 54, shows a hypothetical reconstruction of the strake ends of a medieval hulk. The hulk is described at some length later in this book (see Chapter 19). No archaeological remains have yet been identified as those of a hulk.

THE NORWEGIAN PRAM

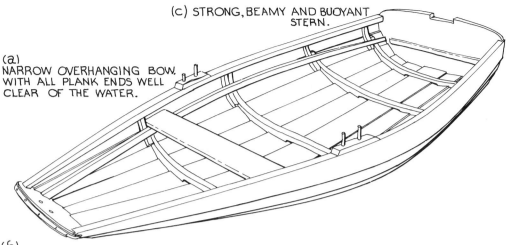

(c) STRONG, BEAMY AND BUOYANT STERN.

(a) NARROW OVERHANGING BOW, WITH ALL PLANK ENDS WELL CLEAR OF THE WATER.

53

The Scandinavian pram. *[Eric McKee*

(b) IRON BANDS ADD STRENGTH TO NARROW PLANK ENDS WHICH CAN NOT TAKE MANY FASTENINGS.

THE MEDIEVAL HULK

(a) NO STRAKE ENDS ON THE PLANK KEEL.

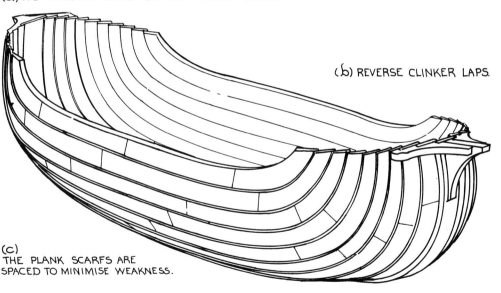

(b) REVERSE CLINKER LAPS.

54

Plank ends of a hypothetical hulk. *[Eric McKee*

(c) THE PLANK SCARFS ARE SPACED TO MINIMISE WEAKNESS.

Like the pram, all plank ends finish above the waterline, but these are cut off on a level plane and not on transoms. This drawing, based on the evidence provided by the carving on the font of Winchester Cathedral dating from about AD 1180 and the ship on the seal of Poole from 150 years later, shows a hulk built in 'reversed clinker', that is, of planks overlapping and fastened together through the overlaps, but with the upper edges of the lower planks outside the lower edges of the upper planks, in reverse of the main North European tradition defined on page 59.

A moment's thought will show that it is very difficult to build in reversed clinker if the plank ends are terminated in any way but those adopted by the hulk, for the simple reason that planks brought up to and secured to stems of any kind are very difficult to fasten if the upper plank lies inside the lower, because the lower planks are positioned first in virtually all building traditions. It has been done. Some medieval cogs were apparently built in this way, although they had the plank ends fastened to straight stem and sternpost and in this century some stem boats have been built in 'reversed clinker' in Sweden. But with the hulk solution to the plank ends it does not matter which way you build your boat of overlapping edge-joined planks and the one tradition is as likely to develop as the other. It is difficult to imagine more range and variety, more different ways of making the ends of a wooden plank-built boat than these drawings and photographs illustrate and they do not include the solution latterly most common, the familiar solution of the everyday wooden boat, one of the most difficult yet one of the most efficient, the straight or curved rabbeted stem with the strake ends nailed, bolted or pegged to it, like the strakes of *Nugget*.

Bibliography

ABELL, W, *Shipwright's Trade*, 1948

ARNOLD, B, 'Gallo-Roman boat from the Bay of Bevaix, Lake Neuchatel, Switzerland', 1975

BASCH, L, 'Ancient Wrecks and the Archaeology of Ships', 1972

BASS, G F, 'Byzantine Trading Venture', 1971

BRONSTED, J, 'Oldtidsbaden fra Als', 1925

CEDERLUND, C O (ed), *The Årby Boat*, 1993

CHAPELLE, H I, *Boatbuilding*, 1947
   American Small Sailing Craft, 1951

CHRISTENSEN, A E, *Boats of the North*, 1968
   'Boatbuilding Tools and the Process of Learning', 1972
   'Lucien Basch: Ancient Wrecks and the Archaeology of Ships. A comment', 1973

CRUMLIN-PEDERSEN, O, 'Cog-Kogge-Kaage', 1965

ELLMERS, D, 'Keltischer Schiffbau', 1969

ELLMERS, D and PIRLING, R, 'Ein mittelalterliches Schiff ans dem Rhein', 1972

GJELLESTAD, A J, 'Litt om Oselverbater', 1969

GREENHILL, B, *The Merchant Schooners*, 1988
   Boats and Boatmen of Pakistan, 1971

GREENHILL, B and MANNING, S, *The Evolution of the Wooden Ship*, 1988

HARDING, A F (ed), *Climatic Change in Later Pre-History*, 1982

HASSLÖF, O, 'Main Principles in the Technology of Shipbuilding', 1972
   (ed), *Ships and Shipyards, Sailors and Fishermen*, 1972

HEIDE, G D VAN DER, 'Archaeological Investigations on New Lands', 1955
   'Ship Archaeological Investigations in the Netherlands', 1970

HOEKSTRA, T J, 'A note on the Utrecht boats', 1975

HORNELL, J, 'Fishing luggers of Hastings', 1938
   Water Transport, 1970

HUTCHINSON, G, *Medieval Ships and Shipping*, 1994

LESLIE, R C, *The Sea Boat. How to build, rig and sail her*, 1892

MCGRAIL, S, *Ancient Boats of North West Europe*, 1987
   (ed), *Maritime Celts, Frisians and Saxons*, 1990

MCKEE, J E G, *Clenched Lap or Clinker*, 1972
   Unpublished study of East Sussex and Chesil Bank beach boats, undated

MARSDEN, P R V, *Ships of the Port of London*, 1994

NIELSEN, C, *Danske badtyper*, 1973

RÅLAMB, A C, *Skeps Byggerij eller Adelig Öfnings Tionde Tom*, 1691

REINDERS, R and PAUL, K (eds), *Carvel Construction Technique*, 1991

ROSENBERG, G, 'Hjortspringfundet', 1937

STEFFY, J R, *Wooden Ship Building and the Interpretation of Shipwrecks*, 1994

TÖRNROOS, B, *Båtar och båtbyggeri i Ålands östra skärgård* 1850–1930, 1968

TRAUNG, J–O (ed), *Fishing Boats of the World*, 1955–67

UNGER, R W (ed), *Cogs Caravels and Galleons*, 1994

WEERD, M D de and HAALEBOS, J K, 'Schepen voor het Opscheppen', 1973

WESTERDAHL, C (ed), *Crossroads in Ancient Shipbuilding*, 1994

WRIGHT, E V *The Ferriby Boats*, 1990

ZACKE, A and HAGG, M, *Allmogebåtar*, 1973

The Roots of Boatbuilding

CHAPTER
4

The Roots of Boatbuilding

Besides the categorisation of boats into those that are built of planks joined together at the edges and those that are built of planks not so joined, it would probably be possible, if we knew the line of development of each separate boat type, very broadly to categorise most boats from their origins into four general groups. Although there is no archaeological evidence, it can be hypothesised that boats began in four principal ways. Boats from each of these four roots developed independently, sometimes several times over in different parts of the world, and in places there was interaction between boatbuilding traditions of the four different origins, so that influences from more than one group affected the shape and structure and development of later boats. Besides these principal roots there were at least two others.

The origins of the boat are, it is suggested:

1. *The raft*

Rafts, sometimes supported on floats of inflated skins, performed some of the functions of boats, but always the raft gains buoyancy, not from being watertight and thus enclosing air so that its total weight equals the weight of water displaced, but from the fact that the material from which it is made is lighter than water, so much lighter that it not only floats itself but has reserve buoyancy to carry people and goods (Figure 55). Nevertheless, as the next chapter will suggest, some boats very probably developed from rafts.

2. *The skin boat*

The skin boat is made by sewing a covering of animal skin or fabric over a framework previously made of wood or bone (Figure 56). The framework can be long and narrow like the Irish curragh, or round like a floating bowl, as in the Welsh coracle.

3. *The bark boat*

The bark boat is made by stripping a continuous cylinder of bark from a suitable tree and then forming a boat shape out of the bark itself. The ends are sealed and the shape maintained by building a strengthening framework of wood, usually of twigs lashed together inside it (Figure 57).

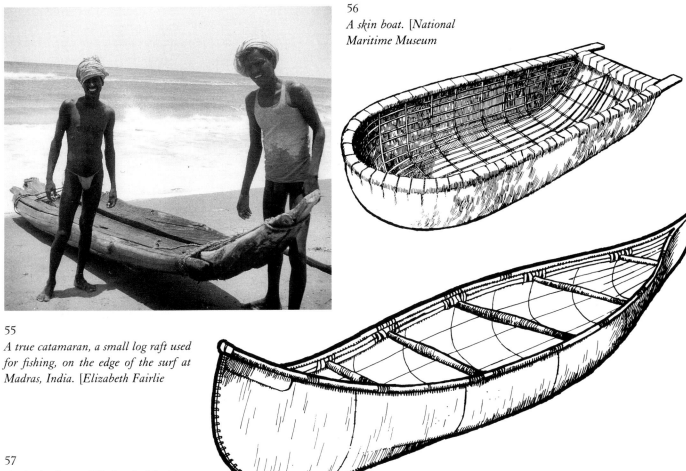

56
A skin boat. [*National Maritime Museum*

55
A true catamaran, a small log raft used for fishing, on the edge of the surf at Madras, India. [*Elizabeth Fairlie*

57
A bark boat. [*National Maritime Museum*

4. *The logboat*

The logboat is made by hollowing out a log and thus producing a basic boat structure, that is, a watertight and more or less boat shape which increases its power to carry burdens by an amount equal to the weight of wood cut out (Figure 58).

Hollowing out a log sounds a laborious and difficult process and it was, but in fact with primitive tools it was a great deal easier than producing planks and joining them together to make a watertight plank-built boat shape. As better tools became available and greater skills were developed planks were added to widen and deepen logboats. In this way the plank-built boat could develop in different parts of the world.

Besides these four main types there were, and perhaps still are, two other boat types rarely but occasionally to be met with. These were: the bundle boat (Figure 59), not a raft but a boat built of bundles of reeds, bark or similar material, perhaps with a light inserted framework and water-proofed with bitumen like the boats of the marsh Arabs of southern Iraq; and the basket boat (Figure 60), which had a basket-like structure, covered with skin or fabric or plastered over with clay or tar to make it watertight.

To make all these different kinds of floating conveyance the only tools needed were axes or adzes, chisels and needles, fire, water, rope and clamps, so all these basic types could be built even at early stages in the cultural development of peoples.

Obviously these roots of boatbuilding were each capable of different degrees of development, determined by the properties of the materials of which they were

58

A simple logboat made from the bole of a salti *palm, and with a plug of mud at its open end, Bangladesh. [Basil Greenhill*

59

A reed bundle boat from Lake Titicaca. [Exeter Maritime Museum

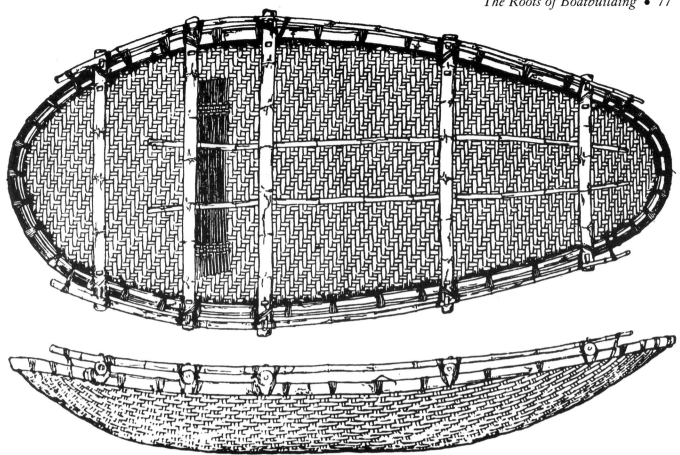

60
A basket boat. [*National Maritime Museum*

constructed. The bark boat was limited in size by the size and strength of the bark and in proportions by its shape. It could not develop far. The skin boat, under ideal conditions of supply of good quality materials, skins, timber and fastenings, could go much further, but again was limited by inherent structural characteristics. The raft could be developed into a watertight vessel (a boat) but to do so meant a great change in the ideas of its builders. Once this barrier was crossed it could have many descendants. The logboat, however, was capable of almost limitless development and had the widest influence on boats in the long run. From this root the greatest variety of wooden boats probably evolved.

In Part Two of this book we shall examine each of these basic types of boat in turn and some of the boat structures that probably developed from them in different parts of the world.

We shall go on to consider the sorts of ship that developed from the boats that began in these ways, and then finally examine briefly how the whole technique of shipbuilding began to change in the fifteenth century to produce a different kind of structure for big vessels in the western world, and particularly in Britain and North America, which continued in use up to the end of the era of the wooden ship, approximately the middle of the twentieth century.

Bibliography

GREENHILL, B, *Boats and Boatmen of Pakistan*, 1971
HORNELL, J, *Water Transport*, 1970
MCGRAIL, S, *Ancient Boats of North West Europe*, 1987
  Rafts, Boats and Ships, 1981
  (ed), *Aspects of Maritime Archaeology and Ethnography*, 1984
THESIGER, W, *Marsh Arabs*, 1978

CHAPTER
5

The First Root, the Raft

In this and the next three chapters I shall describe a few examples of boats represent-ative of each of the main roots of boatbuilding traditions, some in use today, some found in archaeological excavations. Rafts have been widely used in different parts of the world in warmer climates, but floating as they do partly under the water and with the seas continuously liable to break over them, they do not provide sufficient protection for human survival in cold seas, such as those of northern Europe and northern North America, and so they have not evolved in these areas on any scale. They have, however, been used on big rivers in Europe as elsewhere in the world and from them it is possible that a number of boatbuilding traditions may have de-veloped. These building traditions tend to be associated with flat-bottomed boats and vessels.

Rafts are still used in many parts of the world even at the end of the twentieth century, especially in India, southeast Asia and in southern America where they have been very highly developed. An example of what might be called a boat raft is to be seen still in commercial use, though as a tourist attraction, on the rapids of the river Dunajec on the Polish side of the frontier with the former Czechoslovakia (Figure 61). The floats of these rafts formerly comprised narrow flat-sheered logboats. When I made the passage of the rapids in 1980 the floats were plank-built, but I found several logboat floats among the piles taken from rafts dismantled for the winter. The simplest rafts comprise a few logs (Figure 62) or bundles of reeds, or inflated skins (Figure 63), joined together and paddled to a fishing ground. The famous cormorant fishers of the river Li in southern China use rafts made up of five logs perhaps 30ft (9.2m) long. These rafts are of very graceful shape. The most sophisticated rafts comprise a complicated structure of beams and logs, equipped with sails and drop keels (Figure 64), like multiple versions of a sailing dinghy's centre plate and some of them, given crews of men and women brought up to them and their way of life, were capable under ideal conditions, of quite long ocean voyages.

In many parts of the world the raft probably had only slight local influence on the development of boats. The step from a vessel that gained its buoyancy entirely from the nature of the raw material to a watertight vessel gaining its buoyancy from the enclosed air was a very big one requiring an entirely different approach to the whole question of building a floating carrier of people and goods. Boats were much more likely to develop in a society building logboats or one with the materials for skin

61
A boat raft used for running the rapids of the river Dunajec in south Poland. [*Basil Greenhill*

62
A jangada *sailing raft from Brazil. These rafts exist in several different forms and sizes. The base of logs of light wood is pinned together with strong transverse rods of hardwood. The single drop keel is clearly visible in this example at the Mariner's Museum at Newport News, Virginia.* [*Basil Greenhill*

63
An inflated skin raft on the Swat river in northern Pakistan. [*Basil Greenhill*

boats than among raft users. But it has been argued by Hornell, Needham and others that the influence of the raft on the development of Chinese boats may have been wider and stronger than its influence anywhere in the western world, and by others that the raft made of a bundle of reeds may have played a part in the development of the boat in ancient Egypt. In both cases the earliest boats were riverine.

The Lobito Bay boat-shaped raft illustrated here (Figure 65), compared with the accompanying photograph of *sampans* from Bangladesh (Figure 66), a boat type certainly of Chinese origin, illustrates very clearly the way in which the raft may have played a part in the evolution of some Chinese boats and ships. The Lobito Bay boat-shaped raft is one of the relatively few examples of rafts found in Africa. She is built of poles of ambatch wood, arranged in a boatlike shape, but her buoyancy, as in all rafts, is obtained from the sum total of the buoyancy of the individual poles and not from the buoyancy of the hull as a watertight whole. The use of tapering logs arranged in a boat shape with the thicker ends in the stern of the boat (as is obvious since only the thin end can be brought to a pointed stem) inevitably results in a distinctive stern shape. This is clearly shown in the Lobito Bay raft and to be compared with the stern of the Chittagong *sampan*, equally distinctive and generally very similar in shape. The characteristic stern shape, shared by many Chinese boats, has led to the theory that the raft played a larger part in the evolution of boats in China than perhaps elsewhere in the world.

An immense country with rivers thousands of miles long and a coastline of over 2000 miles, China is bisected by the great river Yangtze-Kiang. To the north of its mouth the coastline is low, the seas shallow; to the south the seas are deep, with a rugged coastline and many fjords.

The view has been expressed by Hornell and others that many of the complex patterns of boats on the coasts and rivers of China may have evolved from plank-built copies of rafts of the Formosan type, formerly used on the southern coasts of China, and from where they were probably introduced into Formosa. This highly developed form of raft with its drop keels, rudder and sail was one of the most sophisticated in the world (Figure 64). It was built of bamboo poles lashed together and its shape shows in rudimentary form several characteristics of some Chinese boats and big plank-built Chinese vessels. The early nineteenth-century drawing shown in Figure 67 of a small Chinese vessel, the lower hull of which is made up of half sawn logs arranged raft fashion, lends some weight to this theory.

Professor Shinji Nishimura has pointed out (*Ancient Rafts of Japan*, Tokyo, 1925, in which he describes and illustrates many raft types in use in Asia and elsewhere in ancient times and more recently) that some further evidence of the evolution of the raft into the boat in China was provided by the 'small rafts' of the Kida River, still operating in the early twentieth century. These rafts, as Figure 68 shows, were close to circular in shape and curved up at the sides into a very shallow, beamy, boat shape. Professor Nishimura saw them as a survival of a transition period in which the raft 'gradually evolved into the built up ship'. Certainly the addition of edge-joined sides and two transoms to such a structure would result in a vessel very like a duck *sampan*.

The origins of Chinese boat types and structures generally still await thorough informed study by archaeologists specialising in comparative boat structures. Very valuable work has been published in recent years by J N Green, some of which is conveniently available in his chapter in *The Earliest Ships*, a volume in *Conway's History of the Ship*. At this stage the information available about the multifarious kinds of boat indigenous to China is still inadequate to generalise. It may well be that the raft boat played a larger part in the origin of some later Chinese boat types than it did in the origins of most of the world's boat types, but the flat-bottomed, expanded

64

The sailing rafts of Formosa were up to 35ft (10.67m) in length and 10ft (3.05m) in breadth. This model shows the basic palimped shape, characteristic of most Chinese boats and vessels. [National Maritime Museum

65
*A boat-shaped raft from Lobito Bay, Namibia,
Africa.* [National Maritime Museum

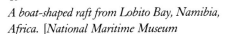

and extended logboat, which played such a large part in the development of boats elsewhere in the world, may have had a strong influence in China too, especially in the north, as it most certainly did in Japan. Thus on the navigable section of the upper region of the Hueng-ho or Yellow River near Shansi, to the northwest of the Wei River where Chinese civilisation first developed, a primitive three-plank boat was relatively recently still used, though it was both curvaceous and sub-divided with bulkheads on the principle of cleft bamboo. The very word *sampan*, used for so many Chinese boats and small vessels, derives from *san* (in the Canton area *sam*) meaning three and *pan* meaning planks.

On the basis of information so far published, despite their variations in outward form the profusion of boat types which existed in China a few years ago all appear to have had certain common characteristics.

1. They were built without keel, stem or sternpost. In the north of China generally

66
Sampans *and logboats on the Karnafuli river, Bangladesh.* [Basil Greenhill

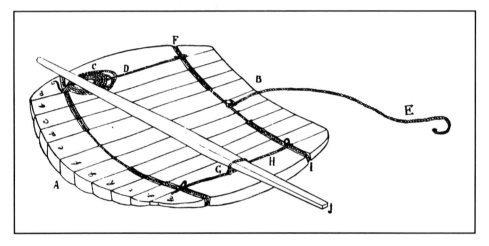

68
Small raft of the Kida river, China. [*S Nishimura*

speaking they were flat-bottomed with a sharp junction or chine between the sides and the bottom – the duck *sampan* (Figure 69). In southern China they tended to be deeper with more curves to them with a rounded turn of bilge where the sides met the bottom – the chicken *sampan* (Figure 70). Almost all Chinese boats and vessels appear to be divisible into one or other of these two classic types.

2. Whether flat-bottomed or slightly rounded, the bottom always has fore and aft rocker and the sides of the vessel do not close in towards the stern but end, leaving a space to be filled in with a transom of planks. In many classical Chinese types, especially in the south, the fore end is equally square ending in a smaller transom bow – the chicken type (Figure 71). In riverine and northern coastal types the ends are often filled in by carrying up the flat bottom structure in steep curves – the duck type. In some ways the general shape can be compared with that of a plywood-built pram dinghy, with its flat bottom, sides curved only in one dir-ection at a time, broad transom stern and small transom bow.

3. In place of the various frames used in most of the world's boats and vessels, the classical Chinese vessels had solid transverse bulkheads of which both the bow and the stern transoms might be regarded as the terminating units. It has been pointed out especially by Needham that this structure resembles that of a bamboo

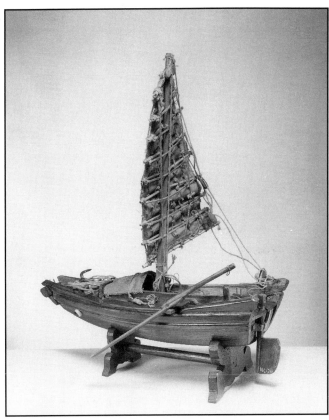

69
Model of a 'duck' sampan *from Wei Hai Wei. [National Maritime Museum*

70
Above right – Model of a 'chicken' sampan. *[National Maritime Museum*

71
Scene in Hong Kong. [Basil Greenhill

stem made up, as it is, of separate cells joined end to end with cell walls between each.

4. On the evidence of the methods used in building a few vessels of traditional Chinese forms in Hong Kong in recent years, coupled with the recollections of David Waters, the historian of navigation who served in China in the 1930s, it would appear that though J N Green has shown that medieval Chinese vessels had keels and stems, in modern times Chinese craft were built by laying a pattern of bottom planks on baulks lying athwartships on the ground. These bottom

72

When in Wei Hai Wei in 1938 David Waters had this model of a Pechili trading vessel made, copying a vessel lying in the harbour discharging cargo. [*National Maritime Museum*

planks were joined edge to edge with nails driven into V shaped slots cut in the outer or upper timber. The lowest parts of the bulkheads, prefabricated nearby, were then secured to the bottom planks and the side planking added, also joined edge to edge. Though for the turn of the bilge the builders perhaps tended to use the lower units of the bulkheads as moulds, the first strakes above them seem to have been shaped and fitted in pure shell style without moulds. With a few fairly easily identifiable exceptions the traditional rule of thumb designs and the method of construction of Chinese craft were not influenced by western practice as long as they continued to be built. Nor is this surprising, for until well after the development of the use of iron and steel for shipbuilding in the west, the interior of China and great stretches of the coast were unvisited by all but a handful of Europeans, and western craft were never seen.

A further characteristic of all Chinese craft is what has been described by David Waters (who has rare first-hand knowledge of the Chinese vessels of the early years

73
This model of a Foochow pole junk was made to David Waters' order as a copy of a vessel lying in Wei Hai Wei in 1938. [National Maritime Museum

of the twentieth century) as their 'palmiped or water fowl shape' which gives them a greater breadth at the waterline aft than forward. In Yangtze and northern vessels, the bow is generally broad and flat. The wedge-shaped bow is more often found in southern vessels and can even develop into a stem post. Most river boats have balanced rudders. In most estuary and coastal vessels the rudder can be raised for beaching and lowered for work to windward, in which it is reported to act as an additional keel.

Figure 72, a model of a Pechili trading junk from north China, illustrates the traditional Chinese form of a large trading vessel very well. The Pechili junk is one of the two oldest types of Chinese seagoing vessel in recent use. She had a flat bottom and could carry up to 400 tons of cargo in numerous watertight compartments separated out by the bulkheads, each compartment a hold on its own, hired out to a different merchant. Big Pechili junks could run up to 140ft or 180ft (42.67m to 54.86m) in length with a beam of 20ft to 30ft (6.09m to 9.14m). The stepping of the masts was unusual, the foremast and the little mizzen were fixed on the port side and the main mizzen less to port of the central line. The general shape shows parallels with the duck *sampan* already illustrated.

Another big seagoing Chinese merchant sailing vessel was the Foochow pole junk (Figure 73), which was also capable of long sea voyages. Indeed one of them, the *Keying*, was sailed from Hong Kong to London in the middle of the nineteenth century. Big Foochow pole junks could carry 400 tons; the huge rudder was lifted when in harbour or in shallow water by tilting it forward and when lowered it was held to the hull by lines running fore and aft and hauled taut by a windlass in the bows of the vessel. Here the general shape shows parallels with the chicken *sampan*.

It is convenient to deal with the boats of ancient Egypt in this chapter because it has been argued that they were ultimately derived, at least in part, from bundle rafts made of stalks of the papyrus plant. The boats of ancient Egypt are, of course, except for one group of British vessels, described in a later chapter, the oldest boats about which we have any very extensive knowledge.

One authority, the Swedish writer Björn Landström, has suggested that the Egyptians may have developed simple flat-bottomed, plank-built wooden boats at a very early date. Such boats developed again in various parts of the world, and their evolution from logboats is discussed in the appropriate chapter of this book.

Some flat-bottomed plank-built boats may have been built in a shape meant to imitate papyrus rafts and some authorities see a strong raft influence in the construction of one of the world's most exciting boat finds, the great river craft called the Royal Ship of Cheops, dating from about 2600 BC, which was found in 1952. She is flat-bottomed and sewn together with ropes. The planks are edge-joined in this way to make a great shell into which the shaped frames were inserted.

Models found in tombs, dated 300 years later, show that the same basic hull form and probably the same construction were still in use. Some models can best be described as punt-shaped, but with a marked sheer higher in the stern than in the bows. Vessels of somewhat similar form with the planks joined edge to edge were in use on the river Indus in Pakistan in the 1950s. They shared with some of the Egyptian ships a remarkable shape of hull in which the bottom turns upwards at a steep angle abaft of amidships.

The Indus punts were very graceful and attractive boats, seen under sail on the great river. They varied from the 16ft (4.88m) or so of a canal ferry or marsh fishing boat to the 50ft (15.24m) or so of large cargo-carrying vessels. The construction, however, appears to have been always much the same. The punt is absolutely flat amidships and the planking of the bottom is bent up at a sharp angle at either end. This bottom planking is made up in one piece in the flat from a hotch-potch of planks of different lengths, re-using planks from old boats which have been broken up, joined together edge to edge with wooden dowels driven diagonally in holes already drilled and cut off at the ends flush with the plank face, so that the outside of the bottom is sprinkled with the oval shapes of the cut-off dowel ends. Across this bottom are laid light floor timbers at even distances, with more substantial timbers where the bottom planks are to be bent up to make the raised ends of the punt. These timbers, like the knees described below, are fastened with iron spikes.

The shaped side planks are then assembled in the same way as the bottom. The shape they are given determines that of the whole boat, where and how much the bottom planks suddenly turn up to make the raised ends and the curve of the sheer. To force the bottom planking up to the shape of the sides, levers are used while the flat midships section is weighted down with stones. The bottom planking is attached to the sides by sawn knees so cut as to give the sides a slight flare. The floor timbers are not shaped at the ends to fit this flare but are cut off square with the edges of the bottom planking, so that their ends do not come into contact with the side planking at all and, as they are laid quite separately from the side frames and are not only not joined to them but do not even touch them, they serve only as a means of holding the patchwork of the bottom planking together, as floor timbers. There is no chine beam and the only caulking in the boats I examined in detail was one of mud applied to the outside of the join between the bottom and sides.

The upward sloping parts of the ends are decked with planks laid fore and aft on beams and the ends of the boat are finished off with bands of planks athwartships, laid across each deck for about one-quarter of its length. The open section of the boat amidships corresponds with the flat run of the bottom planks. There is a heavier beam where each deck ends and the open section begins. The top of the knees are covered with a covering board and boards are nailed to them to act as a form of

74

An Indus punt at Sukkur. [Basil Greenhill

ceiling as far down as the beginning of the curved section of the knee (Figure 74).

The small boats of the canals and marshes, left unpainted and undecorated, were complete as I have described them. They were poled along from the foredeck. The larger, river cargo boat sometimes had a low wooden frame over the open centre section supported by turned posts and covered with bamboo mats. They had as well a long washboard perhaps 2ft high along the outer edge of the hull to give further protection to the open section against spray and the river waves. This washboard was a fixture, and supported by sawn knees. These big punts were steered by very narrow tall rudders and carved downward-pointing tillers. The rudders were hung from a massive framework built out from the bottom planking of the raised stern section (Figure 75). They were propelled with long sweeps pulled by men standing on the foredeck using single carved and turned thole pins to which the great sweeps were secured with ropes, with a massive sculling paddle made from a plank nailed and lashed to the end of a pole over the port quarter and, on occasion, by a *settee* sail set from a long light yard on a forward-raking mast. These big cargo punts were varnished and decorated with carvings, particularly on the planking at the underside of the raised stern and at the rudder head. The model of a punt-shaped Egyptian boat (Figure 76) from the Sixth Dynasty shows a shape startlingly paralleled by that of the Indus punt of the 1950s.

The surviving evidence suggests that Egyptian vessels were almost all flat-bottomed until the Middle Kingdom, roughly for the thousand years 3000–2000 BC. Towards the end of this period round-hulled boats begin to appear in surviving tomb models and drawings and soon after, in the period of the Middle Kingdom (c2045–1780 BC), models of round-hulled boats begin to appear in profusion. The change seems to have been sudden and the flat-bottomed form may have persisted for large cargo vessels.

A new form of construction appears in about 1800 BC in the Dahshur boats, another tomb discovery. The planks were pegged together without sewing and made

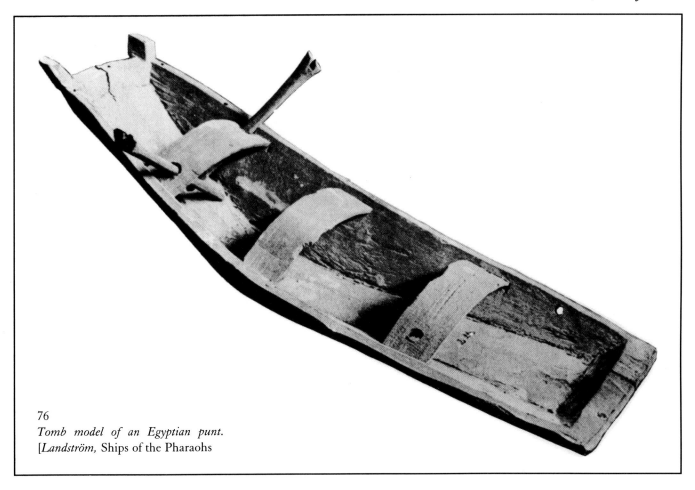

76
Tomb model of an Egyptian punt.
[*Landström,* Ships of the Pharaohs

77
Drawing of one of the Dahshur boats.
[*National Maritime Museum*

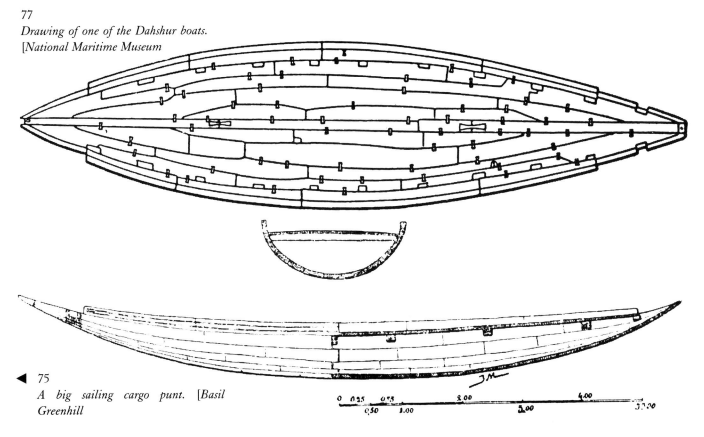

◀ 75
A big sailing cargo punt. [*Basil*
Greenhill

0   025   075   200   400
  050   1.00   200   3000

78
A nuggar *on the Nile in the early twentieth century.* [*National Maritime Museum*

up from very small pieces of odd timber. They have no frames and again their shape appears to have imitated that naturally taken by papyrus rafts. Sewing persisted alongside the new form of fastening right through to the last millennium BC. There are interesting parallels between the Dahshur boats of the eighteenth century BC and the Nile *nuggar* of the present century. The drawing shown here (Figure 77) of a Dahshur boat compares with the photograph of the *nuggar* (Figure 78). The modern vessel was fastened with nails and not with pegs, but otherwise the construction was almost identical.

At this later period very large vessels were constructed for the transport of gigantic obelisks but their form of construction has been the subject of much discussion which has given rise to no general agreement.

Bibliography

ANDRINGA, A J, *Chinese Jonken*, 1970
AUDEMARD, L, *Les Jonques Chinoises*, 1957–69
CHRISTENSEN, A E (ed), *The Earliest Ships* (forthcoming)
HORNELL, J, *Water Transport*, 1970
    Fishing in Many Waters, 1950
LANDSTRÖM, B, *Ships of the Pharaohs*, 1970
MCGRAIL, S and SWITSUR, R, *Early British Boats and their Chronology*, 1975
MAITLAND, D and WHEELER, N, *Setting Sails*, 1981
NEEDHAM, J, *Science and Civilisation in China*, Vol 4:3, 1971
NISHIMURA, S, *Ancient Rafts of Japan*, 1925
PARIS, F E, *Essai sur la Construction Navale des Peuples Extra-Européen*, 1841
WATERS, D W, 'The Antung Trader', MM, Vol. 24, No. 1
    'The Pechile Trader', MM, Vol. 25, No. 1
    'An Exception, The Tong Kung', MM, Vol. 26, No. 1
    'The Hangchow Bay Trader and Fisher', MM, Vol. 32, No. 1
    'The Twaqo' MM, Vol. 32, No. 3
WORCESTER, G R G, *Junks & Sampans of the Yangtze*, Vols 1 & 2, 1947
    Sail and Sweep in China, 1966

The Second Root, the Skin Boat

The Eskimo culture, dependent very largely on what could be won from the sea, developed the skin boat to perhaps its finest forms in modern times. They were an aquatic hunting people in a very hostile environment, lacking in timber but rich in skins, with driftwood and whalebone also available. They developed one of the most specialised of boat types, the kayak, built by making a light wooden framework and sewing seal skins over it. The kayak is a one-man boat, but a bigger skin boat, called in some dialects, the umiak, was used for conveying goods and people. Both types were very safe and seaworthy in skilled hands.

The kayak and the umiaq, its personnel-carrying larger sister, have been the subject of very detailed study and publication, particularly in Canada. David Zimmerly's *Annotated Bibliography of Kayaks* contains 206 references to publications of various kinds. H C Petersen's *Skinboats of Greenland* is an exhaustive and very well illustrated account of both types of Eskimo skin boat. The classical Eskimo boats were built on a framework of driftwood or bone covered with the skins of aquatic animals (Figure 79). Kayaks are widely used in modern Britain and North America by leisure canoeists. Modern kayaks are made of plastic usually in only two pieces, hull and deck, and without frames. They are strong, light, very durable, provide excellent sport if properly used and are based on Eskimo traditions as to dimensions and shape.

Other skin boats have existed very widely and recently were still in use in various parts of the world. They are of two principal kinds, the round coracle type shaped like a floating bowl only slightly longer than she is broad and still used in Wales (Figure 80), Shropshire and in other parts of the world at the end of the twentieth century and the curragh type, a long narrow structure, a boat form in its own right also still in use recently in Ireland and elsewhere (Figure 81).

It is likely that the skin boat was an important means of transport in Bronze Age Europe, and possibly later. It may also have been in use much earlier. Detlev Ellmers has indeed seen it as the beginning of water transport in northern Europe and has suggested its use as early as 9000 BC in the colonisation of Norway. There are fragments of evidence about the use of skin boats in Britain in prehistory, some of which have been gathered together here.

80
Coracle from the river Teifi in south-west Wales. [*National Maritime Museum*

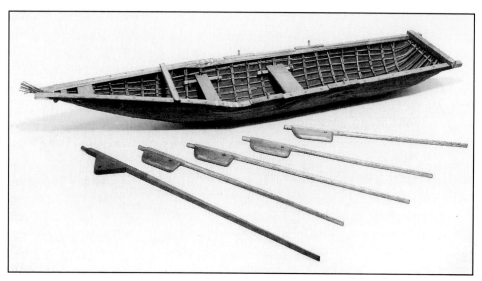

81
A model of a curragh from Mulroy Bay, County Donegal, Ireland. Note the narrow bladed balanced oars. [*National Maritime Museum*

But, of course, by very definition, unlike logboats and round-hulled plank-built boats like the massive Bronze Age structures which survived in various places in Britain for nearly 3000 years (see Chapter 9), skin boats with their short-lived covering and light flimsy skeletons simply do not survive to provide archaeological evidence, though one piece of wood believed to be part of the gunwale of a skin boat has been discovered in a burial mound at Ballinderry in Ireland and dated from the tenth century AD. A shaped piece of reindeer antler discovered in Schleswig-Holstein dating from 9000 or so BC may, Detlev Ellmers has suggested, have been part of a rib of a skin boat. Archaeologists have long argued over the significance of the skin boat as a factor in the origins of wooden boat types. It is a simple and obvious basic boat form, but it could only develop in areas where a hunting people had both sufficient suitable skins and sufficient and suitable timber for the framework. It was unlikely to develop where people had both the available timber and the tools to make logboats, which in their extended forms are far more durable, of greater capacity and at their best more seaworthy than skin boats. It should also be remarked that there is a time dimension. Logboat size trees were not available in northern Europe until the Mesolithic period, c8000 BC.

At about the same period, c8000 BC tools of sufficient size and strength to cut out a

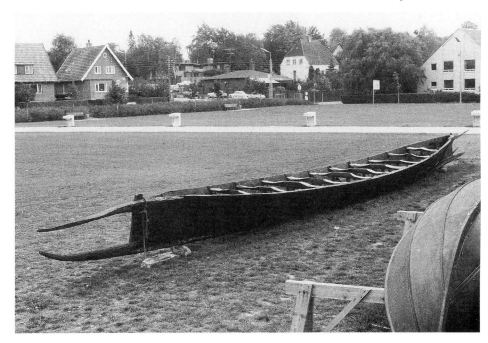

82
This rather rough reconstruction of the Hjortspring boat at Roskilde in Denmark gives an adequate general impression of her probable general appearance when complete. [Basil Greenhill

logboat developed. Logboat making can be easier than might at first seem. With the aid of fire a great deal can probably be done, given a good deal of time, with very simple tools. But there have to be tools of a reasonable size and archaeological evidence suggests that some peoples who do not appear to have had such tools nevertheless conducted maritime trade. Paul Johnstone suggested that the maritime trade which appears to have existed in the eastern Mediterranean as early as the later part of the seventh millennium BC may well have been conducted in, or on, reed-bundle rafts, and there is good local evidence for this in some specific cases. But where the right conditions suited them, much later in the development of man, the skin boat probably played a large part in commerce over water in different societies at different periods and without necessarily always influencing the later development of wooden boats, when materials, tools and skills became available. It is likely though that the individual boats did not last very long.

For several reasons then, it seems likely that the skin boat perhaps played only a marginal role in the history of the development of most later wooden boat types, which, particularly in northern Europe, appear to have evolved principally through that of the logboat; this argument is developed extensively in succeeding chapters of this book.

The skin boat probably particularly influenced the development of boats in those areas where conditions were such that skin boatbuilding peoples and logboat boatbuilding peoples came together, as they may have done in parts of Scandinavia in prehistory. Indeed, it has been argued by Eric McKee that the skin boat, although not a main stream of development, had a vital part to play in the improvement of efficient internal stiffening of edge-joined plank-built boats and could account for the apparent superiority of Scandinavian framing in the Viking Age (see Chapter 15). It is argued by some archaeologists that the rock drawings found at many places in Norway and Sweden represent Stone Age and Bronze Age skin boats and that the Hjortspring or Als boat (Figure 82), a wooden boat dating from about 300–350 BC, is a wood-built imitation of a skin boat made by a wood boatbuilding people, already far advanced beyond the simple logboat; copying for some reason an earlier boat form or a boat form used perhaps by a conquered enemy, or for ceremonial purposes.

83
Rock carvings at Norrköping, Sweden.
[*Postcard*

The rock carvings at Norrköping, Sweden illustrated here (Figure 83) have been dated to the Bronze Age and they are considered by many authorities to represent skin boats. In 1971 Professor Marstrander of Oslo University and Paul Johnstone organised the building of a hypothetical reconstruction of one of these boats (Figure 84) and established that the boat was manoeuvrable, seaworthy and could carry a substantial load in calm water. The experiment did not prove that the rock carvings represented skin boats, or even boats at all. But it did show that it was possible to build effective boats with the materials available in the Bronze Age and much earlier. The boat was not however subjected to prolonged trials, laden, in rough water.

The Hjortspring boat is the earliest known plank-built boat found in Scandinavia.

86 ▶
The Caergwrle bowl. [*National Museum of Wales, Cardiff*

87 ▶▶
The Bantry Boat. [*National Maritime Museum*

84
Experimental skin boat. [*Paul John-stone*

85
The gold boat model from Broighter. [*National Maritime Museum*

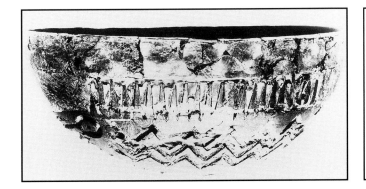

It is a round-bottomed boat made of five overlapping timbers, stitched together, edge to edge. But the particular interest of the boat rests in its stem and stern. These comprise solid blocks carved out to form bows and stern, with the bottom plank projecting outside the boat proper at either end almost like a runner, so that the general appearance is not unlike that of the rock carvings, though the boat herself is a wooden clinker-built craft, plank-built with a slightly hollowed bottom and with the end blocks in what appears to be an early form of the Scandinavian tradition. It may well be that she represents a mingling of boatbuilding traditions. Carbon dated at 350–300 BC, she has been the object of a great deal of research and reconstruction. About 30 per cent of the original boat is now (1995) to be seen in a very elegant display in the Danish National Museum in Copenhagen. A skeleton of slender steel pipes supports the surviving timber and indicates the approximate original shape of the whole.

The evidence for the existence of the skin boat in Britain is very limited. A gold boat model found in 1891 near Limavady in the north of Ireland was part of a horde or votive deposit (Figure 85). It is believed to represent a skin boat with oars and a mast and it has been dated at the first century BC. The model is only 7½in (19cm) long, 3in (8cm) in the beam and lacks any details of construction, though there are details of propulsion and steering. The Caergwrle bowl, a shale bowl found in a bog near Caergwrle Castle, Flintshire, in 1823 and now in the National Museum of Wales at Cardiff (Figure 86) is even less evidence, though it is generally considered to represent a Bronze Age skin boat formalised in the limitations of its bowl function. It measures 8in (20cm) across its largest axis, the gold band around the rim includes twenty sun disks, a Bronze Age decorative feature, as are also the *occuli* in the 'bows'. The vertical triangular cuts are believed to represent oars and the three horizontal zigzags the sea, but all this is rather hypothetical. Better evidence is provided by a carving on an eighth century pillar near Bantry in County Cork (Figure 87) usually considered to represent a skin boat of generally curragh form.

Coracles have been the subject of detailed study by Geraint Jenkins of the National Museum of Wales. They are very simple skin boats made in latter days by stretching fabric over a rough framework. They were used in the late twentieth century on the river Teifi for salmon fishing and elsewhere in Wales at least partly as a tourist attraction.

Bibliography

ADNEY, E T and CHAPELLE, H I, *Bark Canoes and Skin Boats of North America*, 1964
ARIMA, E Y, *A Contextual Study of the Caribou Eskimo Kayak*, 1975
BARNWELL, E L, 'Caergwrle Cup', 1875
BRØNDSTED, J, 'Oldtidsbaden fra Als', 1925
CHRISTENSEN, A E (ed), *The Earliest Ships* (forthcoming)
ELLMERS, D, 'Keltischer Schiffbau', 1969
HANSEN, K, *Umiaq*, 1980
JENKINS, J G, *Nets and Coracles*, 1974
JOHNSTONE, P, 'A Medieval Skin Boat', 1962
    'The Bantry Boat', 1964
    'Bronze Age Sea Trial', 1972
MCGRAIL, S (ed), *Aspects of Maritime Archaeology and Ethnography*, 1984
MARSTRANDER, S, *Østfolds jordbruksristninger: Skjeberg*, 1963
PETERSEN, H C, *Skinboats of Greenland*, 1986
ROSENBERG, G, 'Hjortspringfundet', 1937
WESTERDAHL, C (ed), *Crossroads in Ancient Shipbuilding*, 1994
ZIMMERLY, D W, *An illustrated glossary of kayak terminology*, 1976
    An Annotated Bibliography of Kayaks, 1978
    Hooper Bay Kayak Construction, 1979

The Third Root, the Bark Boat

With the bark boat we are back in the boatbuilding tradition of shell construction, for despite a superficial resemblance to the skin boat the bark boat is in fact of completely different origin. In the skin boat the skin is a watertight cover. It is usually skeleton-built, and derives its shape from the frame around which it is wrapped. Although in recent times framing has sometimes been used to determine the shape of the bark 'skin', the simple bark canoe is shell-built, the bark being the main strength member determining the shape of the boat and only supported by an internal framework made to fit it. Perhaps the terms skeleton-built and shell-built can be applied most accurately to many skin boats and bark boats. Working bark boats required constant maintenance, particularly if they were employed in running river rapids when laden.

The bark canoe is particularly associated with the Native Americans. Certainly these people developed it to its most perfect form, particularly in the Ottawa valley region, but it also existed elsewhere in the world: Australia, South America, Africa, Siberia and Indonesia. Even Native American canoes varied greatly in shape and structure. The Ottawa valley canoe (Figure 88) was made by lumbermen at the beginning of this century and is an excellent and rare example of the Native American bark canoe in her most developed form. Her framing bears little resemblance to the complex structure of twigs used by the Native Americans before they adopted the methods of their European contacts, but its shape is still determined by the bark shell and the frames have been carefully made to fit. This canoe was probably made by Sarazin of the Algonquin Reserve in Ontario. Sarazin's son was still building bark canoes in the 1960s. The raw materials of the canoes he built were spruce roots, cedar wood, ash wood, spruce gum, bear grease, moose hide and the bark of the white or canoe birch tree, though spruce bark and other barks could be used.

The white birch was preferred because the bark is more waterproof than that of most substitutes. It was gathered in the largest available pieces in the early summer when the sap was flowing. Roots of the black spruce which lie close to the surface were collected at the same time. From the black spruce also came the spruce gum

88
Ottawa Valley bark canoe. [National Maritime Museum

89
Inserting the ribs in a bark canoe. [Canadian Geographical Magazine

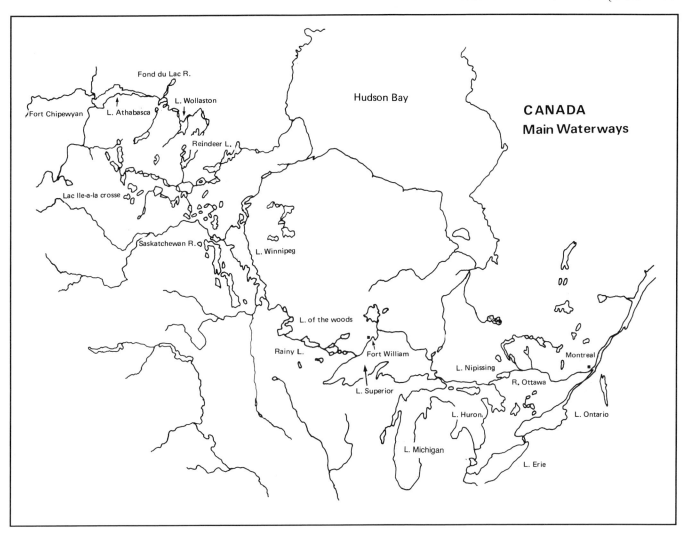

Fond du Lac R.

L. Wollaston

Fort Chipewyan L. Athabasca

Reindeer L.

Lac Ile-a-la crosse

Saskatchewan R.

L. Winnipeg

L. of the woods

Rainy L.

Fort William

L. Superior

Hudson Bay

CANADA
Main Waterways

L. Nipissing

R. Ottawa

Montreal

L. Huron

L. Michigan

L. Erie

L. Ontario

90

The fur traders' canoe route across Canada. [National Maritime Museum

used to cement the seams in the bark and this also was gathered in the first warm May weather after the April thaw.

Sections of bark were stripped from the white birch trees for the hull; white cedar wood was used for the ribs, gunwales and sheathing; ash (or possibly maple) for the thwarts. There was perhaps an element of 'frame-thinking' in that a flat wooden pattern weighted down by stones was used to shape the steamed bark and temporary stakes kept the sides of the bark vertical.

Steamed gunwales were then fitted and the bark allowed to dry in shape. At bow and stern pieces of birch bark were sewn together with spruce roots, subsequently sheathing was fitted under tension inside the bark and U-shaped ribs forced into position to tauten the bark shell. Latterly these ribs were often thin flexible planks several inches wide, very like the 'canoe'-framing of the lobster boat (Figure 89). The gunwales were temporarily secured by nailed planks, thwarts were fitted and finally the seams in the outer bark caulked with the spruce gum. In a booklet by Camil Guy, published by the National Museum of Canada, there is an excellent detailed account, copiously illustrated, of the building of the very beautiful type of canoe that used to be used by the Weymontaching Band in Quebec Province. These canoes were further strengthened by an integral sheathing or ceiling of long strips of wood perhaps only ⅛in thick which lie between the birch bark and the ribs. Properly handled, the bark canoe could stand up to hard wear and it was a vehicle of serious transport, on inland waterways, not only of human beings but in its larger forms of

91

A canot de maître, *or Montreal canoe, shooting rapids, an oil painting by Mrs E M Hopkins.* [*Public Archives of Canada*

heavy goods, and big bark canoes played a major role in the development of Canada.

Half the fresh water in the world is to be found in Canada. There are as many miles of inland waterway as there are in all the other countries combined. You can put a canoe in the water in any Canadian city and paddle to the Atlantic, Pacific, Arctic Ocean or through the United States to the Gulf of Mexico. This fantastic pattern of natural water routes was the highway of the bark canoes of the *voyageurs*, mainly French-speaking, who opened up the trade of the northern part of the continent. There was a regular east-west trade across Canada thirty years before settlers in the United States had crossed the Mississippi. The greatest of the bark canoe trade routes was the '*Voyageurs' Highway*' of the fur trade, 3000 miles of canoeing from Lachine near Montreal to Fort Chipewyan on Lake Athabasca (Figure 90). Only with the coming of the railways in the 1880s did this route cease to be the fastest way of crossing Canada. The fur trader's canoe was larger than the usual Indian canoe; it could be up to 36ft (10.97m) in length (Figure 91). Its reign was from the seventeenth century to the early part of the nineteenth century, and it played a fundamental part in the development of the North American continent.

These Native American bark canoes were very sophisticated craft. Bark canoes used in Australia, South America and Africa were often simpler. In some cases a long piece of bark was peeled off a tree and the ends in turn placed over a fire. They became soft and pliable and the edges were doubled over and secured with skewers of wood; light pieces of timber were then placed between the edges of the bark to prevent the sides from collapsing. In many of the Australian bark canoes a few stretchers were present but no frames. Most of these primitive bark canoes were made from a single piece, but more sophisticated builders from northern Australia developed techniques of joining together wide strips of bark, extending the sides with bark weatherboarding and using gunwales and frames made of mangrove stick.

Bibliography

ADNEY, E T and CHAPELLE, H I, *Bark Canoes and Skin Boats of North America*, 1964
GUY, C, *The Weymontaching Birchbark Canoe*, 1974
MCGRAIL, S, *Rafts, Boats and Ships*, 1981
MORSE, E W, *Canoe Routes of the Voyageurs*, 1962
    Fur Trade Canoe Routes of Canada, Then and Now, 1968
SHACKLETON, P and ROBERTS, K G, *The Canoe: A History of the Craft from Panama to the Arctic*, 1983.

CHAPTER 8

The Fourth Root, the Logboat

More types of boat and vessel in the world probably owe their remote origins to a hollowed-out log than to a raft, skin boat or bark boat, for the hollowed log is susceptible to almost limitless development while the very nature of the structure and materials used in rafts, skin boats and bark boats restricts their development in varying degrees. The lines of descent from the logboat are extremely complex, starting and stopping again at different times in different parts of the world, interrelating in some areas, developing in other places without any apparent influence from other areas. The greater part of the remainder of this book will be taken up with an examination of some of the complex lines of descent traceable back to logboats of one form or another.

McGrail has shown in his most comprehensive study of the logboat, not only in Britain but internationally, that in England and Wales alone the remains of over 170 ancient logboats have been recorded, which means that very many have been discovered and either not recorded or not recognised at all for what they are. Of those recorded about half survive in various museums in different states of disintegration. There are records of more than another 150 discoveries of ancient logboats in Ireland and Scotland. Probably every country in Europe could add its quota. Most of these logboats have not been excavated scientifically, nor have they been published adequately; indeed many have not been published at all. The oldest examples of logboats we have today are several thousand years old. Radio-carbon dating shows that logboats were used in England and Wales from at least 1500 BC to about AD 1400. In fact they were probably used both earlier and later. Logboats were still being made in the last quarter of the twentieth century in Europe (in Poland), in Asia, Africa and North and South America for everyday use as working boats. They varied in shape and structure from hollowed logs, so crudely made that they derive most of their buoyancy from the lightness of the wood used rather than from the air they envelop, to light graceful structures with shells so thin that they are indistinguishable from plank-built boats (Figure 92). Indeed, as I have seen in Bangladesh, it is often difficult to tell whether a particular boat has been carved out from a single hollowed log or built up of planks, especially when she has been much repaired with planks and her sides extended.

The undertaking of making a logboat is a considerable one. Suitable trees must be available near to the water, and the community concerned must have a great deal of

92
A logboat is poled on a small tributary of the Brahmaputra in the Garo Hills, Assam, India. [Basil Greenhill

time available for this kind of specialised work, for making a logboat frequently takes more time than building houses, or cattle pens or fencing fields. It is a kind of large scale capital investment requiring a sufficient surplus of food production to enable the logboat makers to give the considerable amount of time demanded by the work. They must have reasonably efficient tools. It follows that to make such a big investment the community must be a prosperous one in a certain stage of technical development.

In 1973 I watched a big logboat being made in Brazil (Figure 93). The men who made her did so as a normal job, for these vessels were still being cut out for use in beach and river fishing, and could then still be seen lying on the beach beneath the expensive hotels on the fabulous foreshore at Copacabana in the southern suburbs of Rio.

Very similar square-ended logboats were used in the Casubian Lake District of northwest Poland and one is preserved in the Kartuzi folk museum. From them were ultimately derived the long, narrow, double transomed plank-built boats in use still on the lakes in the 1980s (Figure 94).

By way of contrast, the lovely little logboat in Figure 95 was in use, with many others, in 1980 in drift fishing on the river Bug in central eastern Poland. Plastic substitutes had been tried but found too heavy and liable to fracture and the domestic cutting out of these boats from the huge Polish willows was continuing. Mr Zalewski, her maker, owner and user, demonstrated the technique he had used with a broad-bladed adze in hollowing out the log (Figure 96) and then showed us the nets and the long paddle used to manoeuvre her in the rapids (Figure 97).

Low relief transverse bands inside similar canoes have been taken by some authorities, including Hornell, as evidence of the influence of skin boat-building techniques on the dugout. A more probable explanation for their presence is to provide a toe-hold and prevent the crew slipping on the wet wood.

A well-made logboat from a small log can be efficient, light and seaworthy. In her bigger versions inevitably, because of the dimensions of the tree from which she was made, she is long and narrow. She derives her stability from her length and is admirably suited for use on rivers and lakes and as Figure 98 shows, she can be a very beautiful structure. Figure 99 shows an altogether more primitive logboat of comparable dimensions. This logboat was a working cargo-carrying vessel which in the calm winter weather regularly crossed the upper part of the Bay of Bengal.

The efficiency of a larger logboat was greatly improved by softening the sides with fire and water and then forcing them apart with wooden struts. This treatment:

(a) made the sides curve into a boat shape; and

94 ▶
Plank-built double transom boats derived from logboats at Kartozy-Sianowo in the Cashubian Lake District of Poland. [Basil Grenhill

95 ▶▶
Mr Zalewski and his logboat at Kanienczyk, Poland. [Basil Greenhill

96 ▶
Mr Zalewski demonstrates how he cut out his logboat. [Basil Greenhill

97 ▶▶
The equipment used by Mr Zalewski drift fishing on the river Bug. [Basil Greenhill

93
Adze work on a new logboat in Brazil. [Basil Greenhill

(b) made the ends of the logboat lift so that they were higher than the middle thus giving the logboat 'sheer', the characteristic curve of a traditional wooden boat in profile.

Ole Crumlin-Pedersen's diagram (Figure 100) derived from practice in northern Finland, shows one way in which a logboat can be made.

The result was a shape still to be met with in many parts of the world. If the solid ends were shaped away at the bottom and sides a graceful logboat canoe could result. The third and fourth boats down from the top in the wall display in the Mariner's Museum at Newport News (Figure 101) correspond almost exactly with stages two and three in Figure 100.

Where the tools and skills existed to make planks from logs, and once a logboat had been expanded, it could be made more efficient still by extending the sides with planks. These were fastened to the sides of the logboat, and when metal fastenings were not available the planks were sewn on with natural fibres, or pegged with wood pins. A second and a third plank could be added to make a seaworthy boat. This process was applicable even to the largest logboats and some expanded and extended boats still in use in Bangladesh in the 1960s were seagoing ships 70ft (22.86m) long, carrying many tons of cargo (Figure 102).

It must not be assumed from the foregoing that this process of development was inevitable. The great majority of logboats were quite adequate for the limited requirements for which they were made, without expansion, extension, or, indeed, much shaping. Once again the logboat must be judged by the purpose for which she was made. For use on a lake, small river or sheltered arm of the sea a simple log will do. Sometimes logs were extended without expansion. The great majority of logboats

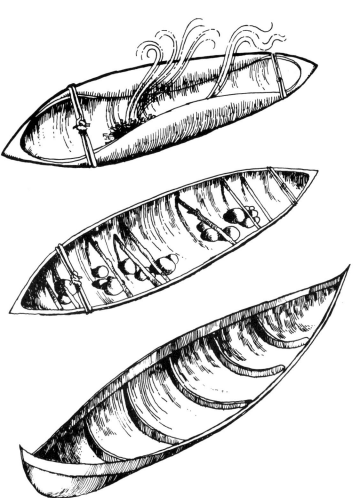

101
Above right – Logboats in the Mariner's Museum at Newport News, Virginia. [Basil Greenhill

102
A balam, *an expanded and extended logboat, deep laden in the Bay of Bengal, 1959.* [Basil Greenhill

surviving in Britain do not appear to have been expanded, although some were probably extended.

But it is from this root, that of the expanded and extended logboat, that many different types of boat developed in different parts of the world; in particular most European edge-joined boats and vessels, including those in the northern European and British clinker tradition.

The planks could be joined to an expanded logboat and to each other in several ways. They could be joined flush, edge to edge, so that the outside of the boat presented a smooth surface. They could be joined to overlap one another at the edges, clinker-style, so that the outside of the boat had the ridges of the plank edges running along its length, or they could be joined to overlap one another with a bevelled edge on each plank or a half rabbet on each plank. Such boats, although the planks may in fact overlap quite as much as in the second form, may have smooth skins. The four different methods are shown very clearly in Figure 103.

Though until very recently both simple and expanded and extended logboats were still widely used in many parts of the world, at the same time plank-built boats were developed. The process depended on the availability of timber and tools to make planks. Depending on the tools used (splitting wedges, axes, adzes or saws) the planks that resulted lent themselves to being used in different ways, and this influenced the types of boat that developed.

In some societies early plank-built boats were deliberate copies of the lighter and better-shaped types of logboat. Indeed, in some parts of the world this process of copying still goes on; the planks are always joined to one another to make a wooden shell as in the original logboat and perhaps afterwards strengthened with frame timbers, cut to fit. Thus the logboat determines the shape of the final boat. Figure 104, drawn by Kurt Kuhn for Dr Wolfgang Rudolph, shows a boat made on a logboat base which can easily be converted into a keel plank and thus a round-hulled, plank-built boat evolves. It is one of the processes of such evolution, and appears to be that of at least some local boats in northern Europe, in Bangladesh (Figure 105) and in many other places.

Japanese seafarers and boat- and shipbuilders were by deliberate administrative decision isolated from outside contacts for more than two centuries. It is not surprising, therefore, that the history of Japanese boatbuilding traditions demonstrates the development of the logboat and evolution from it in a very pure form, without significant outside influences. Apart from a few logboats found in fresh water environments no discoveries of ancient boat remains have been made in Japan. But there is an outstandingly rich field of detailed contemporary illustrations of boats and ships from the fourteenth century onwards. From these, from the detailed legislation enacted in the late nineteenth century designed to discourage the building of large traditional vessels, and from the evidence provided by small vessels built to the old traditions in recent years, it is possible to reconstruct the evolution of Japanese traditions with a reasonable degree of confidence – perhaps more confidence than with any other vessels except the Viking ships.

Despite the great influence of Chinese culture in many ways in old Japan, traditional Japanese boatbuilding seems to have owed nothing to China, a phenomenon that has been the subject of much speculation. While, as we have already seen, the raft is generally accepted to have played a large part in the evolution of Chinese boats and ships, it appears to have played no part in the development of those of Japan. Illustrations of the fourteenth century show highly developed logboats built in three parts: a central hollowed-out log with two more hollowed logs joined to it, one at each end, and set at an angle to the basic log to give a sheer to the whole structure, usually higher in the stern than in the bows. The photograph of an undated but

104 ▶

Plank-built boat on a logboat base. [Kurt Kuhn

105 ▶▶

Plank-built boat on a logboat base in Sylhet district, Bangladesh. [Basil Greenhill

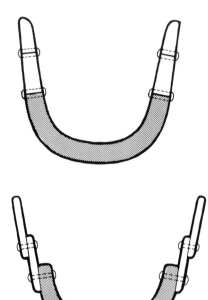

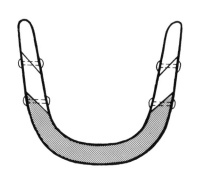

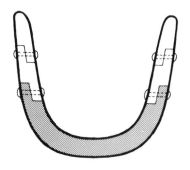

103

Methods of edge-joining the planks of an extended logboat. [Kurt Kuhn

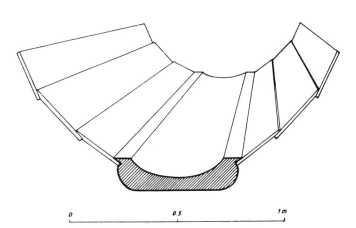

106

Model found in a tomb, undated, of an ancient Japanese three part logboat. [*Basil Greenhill*

ancient tomb model in Figure 106 shows the general shape of these vessels.

The basic logboat appears never to have been expanded but only extended. An entirely plank-built, completely frameless, edge-joined tradition, copying the three log form, was apparently developed in the sixteenth century, after which time no more illustrations of big logboats appear. This frameless plank-built tradition, the *Yamato-gata*, Japanese-style, was to persist for 300 years with relatively little development. This persistence was the product of Japanese political history. In the 1630s the Tokugawa Shogunate prohibited foreign voyaging and, apart from very restricted entry to designated ports, prohibited visits by foreign ships. At first a restriction was imposed forbidding the building of vessels over approximately 50 tons gross, and though this was soon lifted for merchant ships, the embargo on foreign trade was very rigorously enforced. It was at roughly this period that the big Yamato-gata vessels were perfected for the trades round and among the Japanese islands and, in the absence of any foreign contact, the tradition persisted in detail for big ships until Japan was opened up in the last quarter of the nineteenth century, and it survived into the early twentieth century.

Yamato-gata is best represented by a strake diagram (Figure 107) and a photograph of a model (Figure 108). The diagram shows an edge-joined vessel without frames built of broad strakes. She has no keel but a massive hog. Crossbeams just below deck level were a long-term characteristic of the tradition in all sizes of boats and vessels. One of the relatively few contemporary models surviving, that shown in Figure 108, has been dated by Professor Satoru Matsuki as of the very early nineteenth century. Later in the century as cargoes became bigger the lines were changed a little with greater beam and higher sides.

After the Meiji Restoration in 1868 the building of big *Yamato-gata* vessels was progressively discouraged by government policy and the introduction of a degree of framing was encouraged in small vessels. In 1887 the building of *Yamato-gata* vessels

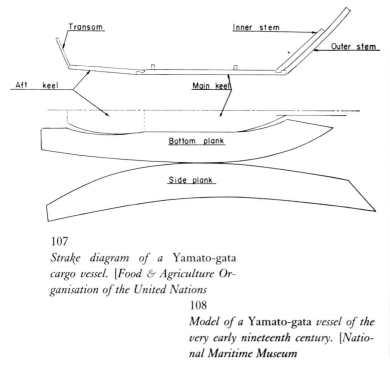

107
Strake diagram of a Yamato-gata *cargo vessel.* [*Food & Agriculture Organisation of the United Nations*
108
Model of a Yamato-gata *vessel of the very early nineteenth century.* [*National Maritime Museum*

of over 50 tons was again forbidden and the last big traditional cargo vessels vanished before 1930. The goverment's object was, of course, the encouragement of work in traditions which would permit the building of much bigger wooden vessels. Since there was no restriction on small vessels the old tradition lingered on among the beach-fishing boatbuilders. The extra strength needed to withstand the stresses imposed by the semi-diesel engines adopted after the First World War forced fishing boatbuilders to adopt variations of skeleton-construction even for small vessels, though edge-joining was retained.

For some types of fishing, however, motors had still not been adopted even by the late 1950s or were specifically forbidden in the interests of conservation (as they were in the Maryland oyster fishery of Chesapeake Bay and in the Truro river oyster fishery in Britain). In these circumstances almost completely traditional vessels survived; indeed I was able to examine and record an almost pure *Yamato-gata* vessel built as late as 1957. She was a seine-net boat working off the beach of Kenada-wan at the mouth of Tokyo Bay (Figures 109 and 110). Thus it was that in Japan, more clearly perhaps than in some other parts of the world, the boats and small vessels of the twentieth century were the true descendants of the big vessels of previous centuries.

The photographs that follow show local, contemporary, models of logboats from different parts of the world. Figure 111 shows a type of logboat in use in recent years by the Miccosukee groups of Native Americans in the central area of the Everglades in Florida where this model was made. Cut from a cypress trunk these logboats were most often poled in the shallow water by a man standing on the solid after deck, and they appear to have been remarkably stable for their size.

The model of a sophisticated logboat in Figure 112 comes from the bayou areas southeast of New Orleans in Louisiana. Logboats, locally called *pirogras*, of this type were still in use in the late twentieth century by, amongst others, the Cajuns, the remote descendants of the French expelled by the British from Nova Scotia in 1755 who found their way to Louisiana and settled there. The model was made by Adam Billiot at Cut Off, Louisiana, in 1990.

109
A mid twentieth-century Yamato-gata *fishing vessel.* [*Basil Greenhill*

110
An inboard view of the vessel in Figure 109. [*Basil Greenhill*

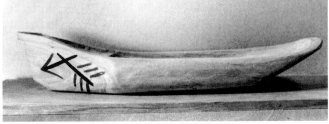

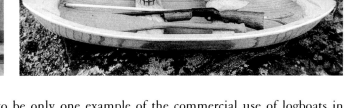

111
Model of a logboat from the Florida Everglades. [*Basil Greenhill*

112
Above right – Model of a logboat from the bayous of Louisiana. [*Basil Greenhill*

There is believed to be only one example of the commercial use of logboats in northeastern North America. This was the canoe hewn out from two logs joined together which was in use in numbers in the salmon fishery on the Miramichi River in New Brunswick, Canada, until the middle twentieth century.

The model shown in Figure 113 shows clearly the first stage in the evolution of the plank-built boat from the logboat. The boat has a single strake sewn (see Chapter 9) on to the bulbous logboat base to give it more length and free board. These boats were in use in great numbers for inshore fishing off the coast of Sri Lanka in the mid-twentieth century before the introduction of cheap, reliable, outboard motors. The boats themselves were quite as roughly built as the models, which were made for tourists.

I have already referred several times, especially in Chapter 2, to what in the mid-twentieth century was probably the richest boat culture surviving in the world outside China, that in Bangladesh in the valley of the Brahmaputra and its tributaries, where even late in the twentieth century there were still thousands of rowing and sailing cargo boats on which the economy and society were entirely dependent. The majority of them were variations on the same basic types, of different shapes and proportions but of the same construction. They were round-hulled boats built of edge-joined planks, in different ways, sometimes with the lower plank laid outside

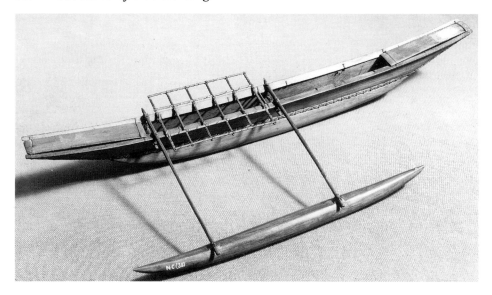

113
Model of an extended logboat from Sri Lanka. [*National Maritime Museum*

the upper, in the reverse of the main European tradition (see Chapter 19), more frequently built in this way but with the planks half rabbeted so that the outside of the vessel presented a smooth skin (Figure 114), sometimes built in ordinary northern European clinker style. The vessels were built in purest shell tradition without formers, moulds, or any aids to the eye of the builder except the swinging of a stalk of jute on each side of a line rigged from stem to sternpost. All, or almost all, of the hull shell was complete before the frames were shaped to the shell and inserted. Some boats are never framed at all except for a few floor timbers. The evidence suggests that the boats of this great floating world developed from expanded and extended logboats. Indeed, it was still possible to see boats at every stage of development from the logboat (so light and so similar to small plank-built boats as to be distinguishable from them only on close examination) to the sophisticated plank-built boat. All had the solid block ends, characteristic of some types of boat of logboat origin (Figure 115). The planking of most of these boats coming up to the gunwale at bows and stern instead of into the bent-up keel plank, shows a solution to the problem of the plank ends adopted in few places in the modern world. This solution resembles a form of

114
The sterns of two smooth skinned cargo boats of Bangladesh. [*Basil Greenhill*

115

The sterns and bows of most river boats of Bangladesh end in a solid block — the goloi. *Here the stern* golois *of beached cargo boats stretch out over the water like the sterns of Viking ships in Figure 227.* [*Basil Greenhill*

planking shown on pictures of European vessels which were called hulks in the fourteenth century (see Chapter 19).

Besides the round-hulled boats there were flat-bottomed vessels, some of the largest of which, with sides clinker-built in European style, resembled the cogs of medieval Europe which will be discussed in a subsequent chapter.

For years in the second half of the twentieth century the vast community of watermen and their boats was in slow decline with the development of roads, improved railways and motor launch services. But two things happened late in the century to arrest that decline. A local type, the *korsha*, a flat-bottomed chine-built structure, rather like the *bateaux* once used by lumbermen in Maine (see Chapter 18), still constructed in shell tradition and edge-joined, which is cheaper and easier to build than the complex shapes of the many types of round-hulled boat, came into general usage. It was easily copied by local metal-working shops in thin steel strip, which was cheaper to maintain and a cheaper building material than wood. At the same time, simple, cheap, Chinese-made diesel engines became available with reasonable service back-up. Thus the weeks' long toil at the oar in the intense humid heat of this country (Figure 116) slowly became a thing of the past and the result was a revival of water transport and of boatbuilding – and a change in the social status of the boatmen, who are much more prosperous than before.

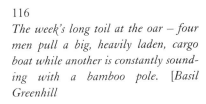

116

The week's long toil at the oar – four men pull a big, heavily laden, cargo boat while another is constantly sounding with a bamboo pole. [*Basil Greenhill*

A baggala *type vessel from the Persian Gulf lying in Karachi, 1953.* [*Basil Greenhill*

118
The stern and starboard quarter gallery of the baggala. [*Basil Greenhill*

When Europeans first penetrated the Arab trade routes in the late 1400s using their non edge-joined skeleton-built, or semi skeleton-built, big ships to give them the necessary range and fire power, they found the great Arab trade of the Indian Ocean was conducted in highly developed plank-built boats and ships, the planks of which were sewn together edge to edge. Such vessels were not gimcrack affairs but strong and seaworthy, provided they were well maintained – which usually meant rebuilding them each year.

Under European influence Arab vessels rapidly developed to copy features of contemporary European hull forms, like the ornate stern of the sixteenth-century European traders. But shell construction, the strakes edge-joined, the frames shaped to the shell, and with metal fastenings, seems to have remained very widespread in the seafaring Arab world until the demise of the sailing vessels in the later twentieth century though eventually in some places the shell-constructed vessels gave way locally to partly skeleton-built or entirely skeleton-built non edge-joined vessels. At the end of the twentieth century a thriving trade is still conducted in Arab vessels little different in general shape from some of those the first European travellers met with 500 years ago, but they are driven by simple diesel engines.

The three photographs in Figures 117 to 119 show a transom-sterned *baggala* from the Persian Gulf and an Indian vessel of the same type with three masts. Both these merchant vessels are types which until the third quarter of the twentieth century ranged far and wide in the Arabian Sea. The principal long-range vessels were based at Kuwait. The *baggalas'* quarter galleries still show the influence of seventeenth- and eighteenth-century European merchant ships, though I took these photographs in the early 1950s.

Figure 120 shows a pointed sterned *bhum*. The *bhum* is a derivation from the double-ended, edge-joined, plank-built sewn vessels and examples of similar types survived in use until comparatively recent years. A dozen or so models are known to exist of one of these types, the *mtepe*. The *mtepe* was built in the Lamu Archipelago of east Africa and was a surviving example of a large wooden sewn ship with many parallels with early Arab vessels. As the photograph (Figure 121) of a model clearly shows the strakes were sewn together with coir twine, pegs were then driven into the stitch holes from the inside to secure the stitches and to prevent leaks. The exposed twine was then cut off flush with the outside of the boat. Frames were subsequently inserted and stitched direct to the strakes and beams provide athwartship strength.

119

A three-masted transom-sterned Indian vessel off Bombay, 1950s. Note the painted ports, a form of decoration copied from British merchant vessels of the nineteenth century. [Basil Greenhill

120

A bhum *type hull in Karachi, 1953. [Basil Greenhill*

As I have already said, clear evidence of a probable origin in an expanded and extended logboat is provided when a boat type has solid or block ends to a planked hull, in place of a stem and sternpost or transoms or any other of the terminations described and illustrated in Chapter 3. These block ends represent of course the solid ends of almost all logboat structures. There are groups of boats of this type in the southern Baltic, a distinctive environment where the raw material available, the technology used and the function of the boat have all remained much the same for many centuries. Thus early boat types have survived to the present day and provide authentic first-hand evidence for boat historians and archaeologists. These boats have been studied by Dr Wolfgang Rudolph who has pointed out that in this region the principle of shell-construction being given by the logboat model, the progressive evolution of the technique led to craft of higher quality being developed along two different lines:

(a) by way of the extension of expanded logboats, which became in the end no more than bottom shells
(b) by way of three or five part bottom plank boats which were shaped so as to

121
A model of a mtepe. [*National Maritime Museum*

resemble closely the form of the logboat, and in the building of which the use of hollowed-out massive baulks of timber for the boat ends was a favourite solution to the problem of the plank ends.

Bottom-shelled boats developed at Rostock around the mouth of the Oder and around that of the Vistula, while the longitudinally-laid bottom plank boat with block stems developed around the lower Oder, the east Pomeranian lagoons and at Rügen among other places. There is an excellent display of boats of this type in the Polish Fisheries Museum at Hel at the mouth of Gdańsk Bay.

Big logboats were in commercial use in the United States, for instance in the Long Island Sound oyster fishery, as late as the beginning of the twentieth century. Perhaps the most remarkable logboat originated vessel in use in the modern world was developed in the United States. She was the Chesapeake Bay log bugeye (the origin of the name is uncertain) used in the oyster fishery on the eastern, that is the Maryland, shore of the great bay. She was the more remarkable in that she was a

122
A Chesapeake Bay log canoe under construction. [Marion Brewington

nineteenth-century development of the logboat and at the same time one of the largest types of logboat-based vessel to be developed anywhere in the world.

After the War between the States the Maryland oyster fishery, rich from several years of no fishing and with prices sky-high, faced a period of great potential prosperity. The fishery had been carried out by scraping with tongs from canoes and small sailing vessels. Now a change in Maryland legislation allowed the dragging of dredges to scrape the oysters off the beds. To drag these heavy dredges bigger and more powerful sailing craft were needed, but there was little capital available. To build a non edge-joined skeleton vessel was a shipwrighting job; the building traditions of the oystermen were traditions of edge-joining. Canoes had developed from Native American logboats and were made up by bolting together shaped logs to create a massive frameless boat, the main part of the shaping of which was done with the axe or adze from the solid mass of timber bolted together (Figure 122).

123
The very late Chesapeake Bay log bugeye Sanxton Hubbard *of Cambridge, Maryland, built at Solomons, Maryland, in 1891.* [Marion Brewington

The situation in the oyster fishery was met by the development of the log bugeye in the late 1860s. In the words of their historian, Marion Brewington: 'Some person added a couple of extra wing logs, put a deck on his logboat, and with that the bugeye was born.' In fact they had massive solid edge-bolted beams (the bolts were ¾in (1.9cm) thick iron) of shaped logs with no floor timbers, frames fastened to the made-up bottoms which were planked up in the ordinary way, and ordinary decks and low bulwarks. In an entirely separate development, an ocean and two millennia apart, they had parallels with the Romano-Celtic boats already described (see Chapter 3). They were very distinctive vessels in appearance with clipper stems and long trailboards and a very simple two-masted rig with jib headed sails which anticipated much of modern yachting practice (Figure 123). They ceased to be built in the 1890s. The big logs needed to make them soon became difficult to obtain and many vessels were built of the same form and appearance but of conventional non edge-joined skeleton construction. But the log bugeye, while she lasted, was a most remarkable American ultimate development of a simple logboat.

Bibliography

ANON, *Oman, a seafaring nation*, 1979
BREWINGTON, M V, *Chesapeake Bay Log Canoes*, 1937
    Chesapeake Bay Bugeyes, 1941
CRUMLIN-PEDERSEN, O, 'Skin or Wood', 1972
GREENHILL, B J, *Boats and Boatmen of Pakistan*, 1971
HADDON, A C and HORNELL, J, *Canoes of Oceania*, 1936–8
HAWKINS, C W, *The Dhow*, 1977
HOURANI, G R, *Arab Seafaring in the Indian Ocean in Ancient and Early Medieval Times*, 1951
HOWARTH, D, *Dhows*, 1977
JANSEN and BØSTAD, *Sailing Against the Wind*, 1992
JANSEN, DOLMAN, JERVE and RAHMAN, *The Country Boats of Bangla Desh*, 1989
JEWELL, J H A, *Dhows at Mombasa*, 1976
MCGRAIL, S, *Logboats of England and Wales*, 1978
MACKEAN, R and PERCIVAL, R, *The Little Boats. Inshore Fishing Craft of Atlantic Canada*, 1979
PRINS, A H J, *Sailing from Lamu*, 1965
RUDOLPH, W, *Inshore Fishing Craft of the Southern Baltic from Holstein to Curonia*, 1974
VILLIERS, A J, *Sons of Sinbad*, 1940

PART THREE

Aspects of the Evolution of Boats and Vessels in Europe, North America and Asia

CHAPTER
9

The Sewn Plank Boat

In times before the ready availability of iron fastening material, in societies that for one reason or another, geographical, economic, perhaps even traditional, did not have ready access to iron forms suitable for use as boat fastenings, wooden plank-built boats have been fastened by wooden pegs or dowels and also, in combination with them or entirely, by sewing, binding and lashing the constituent parts together using locally available materials and techniques developed over long periods of experience. Sewing was frequently used in association with wooden trenails for fastening floors, plank ends and so forth. The practice of sewing and binding the structures of boats together has been virtually worldwide and has been followed from prehistory, through classical times and through subsequent history to the present day when it is in use in a few local areas in widespread parts of the world. It is also used in the building of some small boats and rowing skiffs by 'stitch and glue' methods.

The subject of sewn plank boats, of the different techniques and materials used, of the distribution of the practice geographically through prehistory and history, and of the conditions in the societies that used the techniques, is immensely complex and one in which archaeology and ethnography are perhaps even more closely related than they are, as this book surely shows, in the study of the development of boats generally. This fact is brought out very clearly in the major publication on the subject, *Sewn Plank Boats* edited by McGrail and Kentley, which is published as the British Archaeological Record International Series No 276, 1985. Here the papers deal with examples of the sewn plank built boat widely separated geographically and in time.

There were presentations by Lipke on the Royal Ship of Cheops, by Patrice Pomey on Mediterranean sewn boats in antiquity, by Marco Bonino on the sewn boats of Italy from 900 BC to the present day, on the sewn boats of Sweden by Christer Westerdahl and of Finland by Henry Forssell, on Estonian sewn cargo vessels of the twentieth century by Carl-Olof Cederlund, on sewn craft of the nineteenth century in the European parts of Russia by Jerzy Litwin, and a whole section on the sewn plank-built boats of the Indian Ocean, Asia and Oceania comprising papers by Robert Adams, Eric Kentley, Pierre-Yues Marguin, and R H Barnes. This selection of papers gives some idea of the depth and breadth of this subject and of its time-span. In addition there is *A Handbook of Sewn Boats*, London, 1986, a monograph of A H J Prins, which is a most comprehensive survey of the subject and its problems.

Specialist local studies include Christer Westerdahl's *Et sätt som liknar them uti theras öfriga lefnadsart*, Umeå, 1987, which deals with the sewn boats of the Saamish (Lapp) people of northern Scandinavia and their influence on the development of the Scandinavian boatbuilding traditions and Carl Olof Cederlund's *Ett fartyg byggt med syteknik*, which describes a large (50ft, 15m) clinker-built vessel structure excavated in Stockholm, which was sewn and had many non-Scandinavian features. She probably dates from the very late 1600s and may well have been Russian.

Inevitably archaeologists and ethnographers working in this field have concerned themselves greatly with the details of methods of stitching, binding, lashing, caulking and so forth used at different times in different societies and geographical locations. Of all the multitudinous sewn plank boats, in this short chapter of this introductory study I shall confine my descriptions to three important examples. These are: 1. The sewn plank boats dating from the Bronze Age which have for many years been associated with Ferriby on the Humber river in Britain but are now known to have been more widely distributed in Britain and possibly in Europe; 2. The logboat-based sewn vessels which until very recent years were in widespread use as cargo carriers and fishing boats at the northern tip of the Bay of Bengal which I had the opportunity some years ago to study at first hand; and 3. The sewn plank boats of the Saamish people and their possible role in the evolution of the Finnish lake boats of the end of the twentieth century.

The British Bronze Age sewn plank boats

These are the oldest known plank-built boats in Europe. The first three to be found and excavated, at North Ferriby on the Humber river, have been carbon-dated to circa 1300 BC. The most complete of these three finds comprises much of the three great oak planks which comprised the bottom of the boat which is estimated to have been some 52ft (15.35m) long when complete. There is also one sidestrake surviving. The planks were stitched together with bindings of yew and she was caulked with moss held in position with oak laths. Cleats were left proud in each plank and holes cut through them. Through the holes transverse timbers were passed, connecting the bottom planks together laterally. It follows that the logs from which these planks were cut out must have been massive. E V Wright who discovered and excavated these boats and hypothesised over a lifetime a number of possible forms their complete structure may have taken calculated that the log from which the bottom planks were fabricated must have had a diameter of at least 3⅖ft (1.1m).

These boats appear to have been flat-bottomed with a minimum two side strakes. The ends were closed with watertight transoms. Figure 124 shows E V Wright's reconstruction dated 1988 which appears in his publication *The Ferriby Boats*, London, 1990. This book reports on a life's work and records to the highest standards the excavation of these boats and their subsequent study. This is very important because it has been recognised for years by those involved with the archaeology of the boat that the Ferriby finds are the most important made in northwest Europe until the end of the 1980s, because of what they reveal of the sophistication of the woodworking techniques of 3300 years ago and of the sort of boat which could be built and her possible capabilities.

Their importance has been resoundingly confirmed at the end of the twentieth century by discoveries which appear to indicate that they were by no means unique. In August 1990, a substantial plank fragment was discovered during excavation of a late Bronze Age site in the grounds of Caldicot Castle in Gwent, south Wales. Here, as at Ferriby, there appears to have been a shipping and boat place of a type found in Scandinavia and Finland as well as in Asia; for instance I have seen sites of this kind

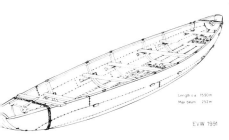

124

E V Wright's 'hypothetical reconstruction' of a complete boat of the Ferriby find. Dated 1991 this is the latest of a series of hypotheses. [E V Wright

in Bangladesh where boats are regularly landed and rebuilt annually to renew the sewing and lashing of sewn plank boats. The find was of a fragment of plank 13ft (3½m) long and 1⅗ft (over half a metre) wide which had been worked in a manner strongly reminiscent of the Ferriby finds and of the Brigg boat (see below). This important find is dated to the mid second millennium BC and demonstrates that in the Bronze Age sewn plank boats of somewhat similar type were not confined to the Humber river system. This supposition was confirmed in the summer of 1992 when further plank fragments, worked in a way which indicate that they were re-used Bronze Age boat material, were found at the nearby site of Goldcliff east of the mouth of the Usk. Caldicot and Goldcliff are both on the north shore of the Severn estuary.

The next find is so recent that at the time of writing, early 1995, no substantial publication has yet appeared. In September 1992 substantial remains of a boat structure, initially carbon-dated as around 1350 BC, were found during the construction of a new road in the heart of Dover. A substantial part, about 30ft (9.5m) estimated as half to two-thirds of the boat's full length was recovered and is at the time of writing in water tanks awaiting conservation. Such examination as has been possible indicates a structure of similar type to the Ferriby boats but with differences of structural detail. Found where she was in an ancient course of the river Dour, her probable use, seaworthiness and capacity must await detailed study in due course.

There is further evidence of highly developed boatbuilding traditions at an early date in Britain. At Brigg in north Lincolnshire a boat structure was found in 1888 and re-excavated in 1974 under the supervision of Professor McGrail (Figure 125). What was found was the bottom of a flat-bottomed boat in general form not dissimilar to a Polish *galar* (Figures 126 and 127). As Figure 127 clearly shows the *galar* herself is an edge-joined structure. The Brigg boat had sewn oak planks with moss caulking and longitudinal laths at the plank seams and transverse timber through cleats left proud of the planking. These features appear to relate her to the traditions represented by the Ferriby boats, but she is carbon-dated around 800 BC, roughly 500 years after Ferriby.

The existence of these discoveries in Britain of large boat structures of three and a half thousand years ago and the difficulties of assessment, examination, and especially of conservation, to which they have given rise, has once again exposed the absence of a point of focus in Britain for this kind of specialised archaeological work. The extraordinary decision of the trustees of the National Maritime Museum to disband their Archaeological Research Centre in 1986 and close down the conservation facility, with all the expertise which had been built up there, has left Britain with no such point of focus. These are the most important finds of the remains of ancient boats found in Europe. In Scandinavia, Germany, the Netherlands, Greece, Poland and on the coasts of North America they would have been a major commitment of a museum or national organisation with qualified staff and equipment. Through the museums' educational facilities their significance would be interpreted to the public and they would become objects of national pride – indeed international, for there are indications that the traditions they represent may have been coexistent in Europe.

The sewn plank boats of Bangladesh

In the second half of the twentieth century the possibility of watching expanded logboats being developed into extended logboats by the stitching or binding of planks along their sides, not as an archaeological experiment but as a normal task for working fishermen who would use the boats as working tools, was extremely remote. I was indeed fortunate therefore in the late 1950s to stumble, by sheer chance, on a group of men doing just this on a grassy bank of the Karnafuli river in Bangladesh. The boats on which these men were working were some 30–35ft (9–11m) overall on a logboat base of about 25ft (7.8m). They were used for dipnet and other fishing during the cool, calm, weather of winter inshore in the Bay of Bengal.

Fortunately the *mistris* working on the boats had no objection to the camera and I was able to take a series of photographs (Figures 128 to 132), which illustrate the process of construction very well.

The basic expanded logboat (I was unable to witness or determine the methods used to expand the logboats) is prevented from closing again by massive irregularly spaced sawn floors, nowadays usually fastened with iron spikes. It is pierced down the gunwale at intervals of about 6in (say, 15cm). A 1in (2½cm) plank which has been shaped on its lower edge, as is clearly visible in Figure 129, is then held in position with clamps for a few feet down the gunwale. It is drilled at intervals corresponding with the holes in the logboat base and lashed into position with one or two turns of the split bamboo through a few of the pared holes. The seam between plank and logboat is then caulked with teased-out old rope and the whole packed on both sides with a seal of grey mud. Over this mud strips of the broad green leaves of palms are laid, and over these in turn tightly bunched long coarse grasses. On the outside of the boat the whole seam is finished off with a protecting cover of split bamboo strips. The whole is held in position, and plank and logboat held together with a tight sewing of split bamboo, the strips being crossed diagonally between the pared holes inside the boat, but not on the outside. The holes are then finally plugged and the bamboo stitching, so that it will work as little as possible, is jammed with teased-out old rope, driven in hard.

To support the side planks 'against the blows of the sea', as the builders put it, half a dozen short round spars, often roughly cut and still with the bark on them, are bound tightly into position with their feet against the side of the logboat just below

128
An expanded logboat lies on the water's edge. On the mud above her lie three other logboats, each extended with a single plank each side. [Basil Greenhill

the seam inside. Over these, and at the level of the seam, two bamboo stringers are lashed into place with split bamboo binding, which is passed through the seam holes at intervals of about 2ft (0.61m). The vertical and horizontal spars are not lashed to one another. The heads of the vertical spars are secured to the upper edges of the plank by lashings passed through holes drilled in the plank. Occasionally a narrow second plank is added, nailed roughly into position. The whole structure is clearly visible in the photographs reproduced here, including the two transoms, one at 45 degrees, the other vertical, with which the ends of the boats are closed above the solid blockends of the basic logboat.

The largest of these sewn fishing canoes which I examined measured 32ft (10m) by 6ft 2in (2m) by 3ft (0.86m). They were dismantled each year, when the great seas of the southwest monsoon make sea fishing impossible, and the basic logboat is used as a river fishing boat. In November at the beginning of the cooler, calmer weather, the planks are sewn on again and the boat, equipped perhaps with a spritsail, but propelled mainly with paddles, goes back to use in the open seas. I was told that a logboat made of good timber lasted about twenty years of this work, but towards the end of that time so many pieces of timber would have been used to repair her that she would have become almost a plank-built boat.

The methods used in building these small fishing boats has been described at length because the same principles are used in constructing the great cargo-carrying sewn *balams* which are no more than greatly enlarged versions of the simple structure I have described.

The Chittagong Gazetteer, a reference book of the early years of the twentieth century, defines four types of cargo-carrying plank extended logboat, the *ad balam* with one plank each side, the *balam* proper with two planks a side, the *gadu*, which has three planks a side and needs thirteen men to work her, and the *jalyanao* with four planks a side. *The Gazetteer* adds that the *jalyanao* was used for deep-sea fishing. In experience during our field work we found the word *balam* used indiscriminately by the boatmen to describe all three types and the number of planks seemed to depend more on what timber was available at the time of the vessel's construction than upon the size of the vessel; this may be merely an indication of the decline in timber resources in the course of the twentieth century. Morever, a *balam* did not always have the same number of planks on each side. The greatest number of planks a side I saw was five, and the vessels concerned, which were between 60ft and 70ft (19m and 22m) were not of the very largest kind.

These large sewn *balams* are wonderful and impressive vessels (Figures 133 and 134). Seagoing boats, they are quite without iron in their whole structure, except possibly for the use of iron spikes to secure the floor timbers in the basic logboat, though in the *balam* built in the classic tradition trenails were used for this purpose. Above the turn of the bilge the framing was a complex of light vertical spars and stringers. The vertical and horizontal spars of this framing were separately lashed to the planking and not secured to each other. This framing provided a strong but flexible stiffening to the planking which could work in a moderate sea without coming to any harm. There were no fixed decks and a crew of up to fourteen men lived on top of the cargo under the bamboo *chauni* and rowed the boat from loose planks laid in the bow (Figures 102, 133 and 134).

At the after end of this temporary foredeck is stepped the mast, usually in a tabernacle made from a very heavy log with a deep notch cut into it. From a yard on this mast the single squaresail is set. The *balam* is a seagoing boat with her long narrow hull and well cut sail she can make some sort of a showing to windward in the expert hands of a good crew (Figure 134). I once saw one with a long thin spar, almost certainly a bamboo pole, its foot secured in the bulwark to leeward slightly

◄◄ 129

A new first plank being fitted to an old logboat. The shaping of the lower edge is very obvious, but the plank has not been shaped finally. This is a trial fitting. [Basil Greenhill

◄ 130

Both extending side planks have been shaped, fitted and fastened to this logboat base. [Basil Greenhill

◄◄ 131

A few light props to act as side supports, stringers, and a shallow topstrake on one side are added to complete the expanded and extended logboat. The massive sawn floor timbers are to prevent the expanded logboat from closing again. Co-existent with this relic of the dawn of the plank-built boat is the sophisticated sampan, *from another age and another culture, landing men on the shore.* [Basil Greenhill

◄ 132

Two of the Karnafuli expanded and extended logboats completed and equipped with dipnets for fishing. [Basil Greenhill

133

A large sewn balam *on the Karnafuli river. The vessel was about 60 ft (18.5m) and, as far as could be determined, no metal had been used in her construction.* [*Basil Greenhill*

134

A large partly metal fastened balam *under sail and apparently making some way to windward. Note again the co-existent* sampan *under a settee sail in the background.* [*Basil Greenhill*

abaft the mast, its head thrusting forward the luff of the squaresail about a third of the way down from the head, much in the way the *vargord* used to be used in Cornish luggers in the nineteenth century, before the introduction of the high peak lug with a short luff made their use unnecessary. Some Viking ships were equipped with a similar device, the *beiti-ass*, the tacking spar. Skuldelev 1, the big cargo ship now on display at Roskilde in Denmark, was fitted with such a tacking spar. Many *balams* carry a short second mast from which a lateen sail is set. This second sail no doubt helped a great deal in sailing to windward and may make it possible with an experienced crew to go through the wind. *Balams* so rigged have a distinctly medieval appearance.

As I have said, the small planked fishing logboats end at bow and stern in tall tapering transoms, which occupy the space between the plank ends above the block end of the basic logboat. Many big *balams* have bow and stern shaped in the same way. Others have shaped stem and sternposts of heavy timber lashed into place instead of the transoms. I have even seen one sewn *balam* with a clipper bow, complete with trailboards. There is also a type of sewn boat, locally called a *murina* in Chittagong and constructed in the same way as the sewn *balam*, which has

135

The structure of a murina, *the logboat, the two extended planks sewn with grass caulking protected with split bamboo, the stitching and the decorated stem, together with the thole pins, are clearly shown in this photograph.* [*Basil Greenhill*

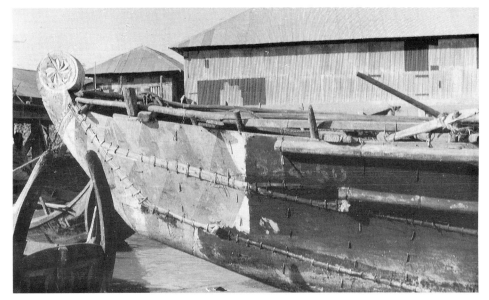

136

A heavily laden murina, *Chittagong, 1952. This expanded and extended logboat was of largely sewn construction. Note that the* sampan *in the foreground is rowed facing forward with crossed oars.* [*Basil Greenhill*

137

The 'framing' of a murina. *Balams were framed with the same pattern of small branches and laths.* [*Basil Greenhill*

pointed ends, the stern rising to a rounded head ornament (Figures 135, 136 and 137).

The survival of the sewn *balam* into the second half of the twentieth century can perhaps be explained by certain advantages. She had a degree of structural flexibility, ease of repair and economy of heavy frame timbers, over iron-fastened boats. In one single convoy of eight of these floating coelacanths, each laden with firewood, we

once met in the Sunderbans, the delta of the great river Brahmaputra, seven were big sewn boats of different forms. And this was in 1959.

The sewn plank boats of Fenno Scandia

Sewn plank boats have existed in Fenno Scandia (Denmark, Norway, Sweden and Finland) since prehistory. Reference has already been made to the Hjortspring boat of approximately the late fourth century BC. Fragments of sewn boat structures have been found in Norway dating from about 600 years later. Finds have been made also in Norway of sewn plank boats of pre-Viking, Viking, and slightly later dates. The earliest of these finds is the Bårset boat, where the sheerstrake is sewn, though the rest of the boat is iron-riveted; she has been dated at roughly AD 700. Several other fragments with indications that they came from sewn plank boats of roughly this period have been found. At Tuna in Badelunda in the northeast of Lake Mälar in Sweden a boat has been excavated by Stenbergen, Nylén and Schönbäck which Bengt Schönbäck has described to me as an expanded logboat extended with two strakes a side, the whole sewn together with withies and trenailed to the frames and with a trenailed external keel. The boat has been carbon-dated at the mid AD 600s, that is, early in the Vendel period. Boat graves excavated in the Åland Islands, notably at Karböle in Jomala community, contained remains of similar structures. Several boats of similar construction, that is, sewn 'five piece' boats have been found and excavated by Henry Forssell and others in Finland in the late twentieth century and carbon-dated from the mid thirteenth to fourteenth centuries. At Suojoki in Keuruu in central Finland Forssell, Vilkuna and Taavitsainen and others before them have excavated an ancient boat harbour (Figure 138). The boat remains found have been of sewn five part structures comprising an expanded logboat keel, two side strakes and elements at the bow and stern which are carved out, rather than bent, curved planks. The sewing is described as of roots. One of the boats has been carbon-dated at the late AD 1200s.

The location of Suojoki underlines one of the difficulties of the study of development of the sewn plank boat in Fenno Scandia – and indeed, more especially of the development of the boat in Finland itself. Keuruu was an area of contact between the trader-peasants of the settled areas to the south and the Saamish members of the wilderness, foraging culture of the interior of Finland. Suojoki may have been a Saamish site, a trading meeting place of farmers and people of the interior, representatives of two economically different cultures. And it is perhaps significant that in the nineteenth and early twentieth centuries a Saamish trade item with the settled areas comprised parts of boats.

138

Above left – an international group at part of the Suojoki excavations, left to right Henry Forssel (Finland), Christer Westerdahl (Sweden), Professor Seán McGrail (UK), Leena Sammallahti (Finland), Professor Christoffer Ericsson (Finland) in black beret, Ann McGrail (UK), Harry Alopaeus (Finland), Janne Vilkuna (Finland), Anne Giffard (UK), John Hackman (Finland). [Basil Greenhill

139

Above right – a working wooden fishing lake boat at Tolpanniemi, Kuusamo. The boat appears to be one of the local types described by Itkonen as Kainuu boats. [Basil Greenhill

140

Above left – the modern popularity of the lake boat in Finland is shown by this photograph taken before the start of a race for wooden boats used for leisure at the great annual Sulkara Rowing Regatta. [Postcard

141

Above right – the birth of a modern wooden lake boat, Savonlinna, 1983. Ideally the stem and keel should be in one piece with a natural crook. Active moulds are used in modern construction. [Basil Greenhill

Sewn plank-built boats from the north, from Norway, Sweden, Finland and Russia west of the White Sea, have been generally attributed to Saamish boatbuilders and there are a number in museums in northern Norway. They were studied and recorded by Faerøyvik and, in addition to his book in English edited by Arne Emile Christensen, there is an extremely valuable archive of his plans of boats of the North in private hands in Bergen.

As Arne Emile Christensen has pointed out, boats are mobile objects. Just as very recent research described later in this volume has shown that not all the classic Viking ships were built in Scandinavia, so ethnic, cultural and geographical borders do not correspond in the north of Norway, Finland and western Russia, and the cultural origins of boat finds are not always clear. One of the most interesting questions is, perhaps, the possible role played by Saamish sewn plank boats in the origin of the ubiquitous Finnish lake and river boats (Figures 139, 140 and 141) in their very many local variations, which were very important vehicles in the history of the development of a country better endowed with navigable waterways than almost any other in Europe and not well endowed with roads until the present century. T Itkonen's paper 'Suomen Kansanomaiset veneet' published in Helsinki in 1926 remains the best general description of all the multitudinous local forms taken by these clinker-built boats. Lake boats in both wood and plastic are now used in vast numbers for recreational purposes: you can buy plastic ones at many filling stations.

Much research is still needed into the sewn plank boat in northern Europe and its possible wider influence. I would like briefly to draw attention to two examples of Saamish sewn plank boats which exist in museums, because they share a common, important, structural feature which has, perhaps, not been widely noted.

In 1908 Gustaf Hallström, a Swedish anthropologist, made an expedition to the Kola Peninsula just east of the Finnish border in Russian territory. Here he found sewn plank boats being built. He used one on a passage of the River Tuloma to Kola and was greatly impressed both with her performance in rapids and her carrying capacity. As with all the sewn plank boats Hallstrom saw in the Kola Peninsula area in 1908 the strakes were stitched together with rope made from raffia (some Saamish boats were sewn with reindeer sinews) but the floors and the junctions of the stems and the planks were fastened with iron nails.

Hallström made a measured plan of his boat which is reproduced here (Figure 142), which originally appeared in his report of his expedition in the Swedish journal *Fataburen* in 1909. The boat measured 14ft (4.4m) by 3ft 9in (1.2m) and had a floor

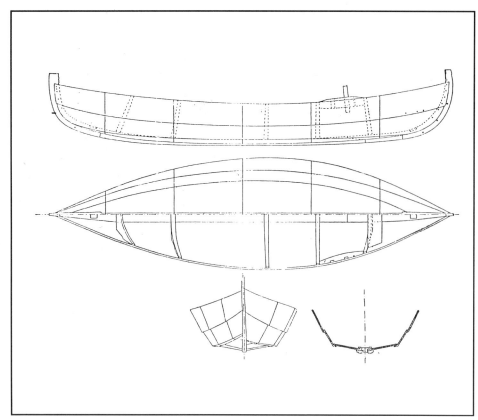

142
Gustaf Hallström's drawing of his sewn boat from Russian Lapland. Note the structure of the chine seam. [Nordiska Museum, Stockholm

144 ▶
The Saamish sewn plank boat in the National Museum, Helsinki. [Basil Greenhill

145 ▶
The bottom of the National Museum's sewn plank boat. [Basil Greenhill

width of 2ft 3in (0.7m). It will be noticed that she has a peculiar characteristic, at the chine, the junction of the first and second planks. The second plank is, in fact, a shaped timber hewn out of a log leaving a longitudinal fillet of about 1$\frac{7}{10}$in (4cm) which projects under the first plank, the edge of which therefore rests effectively in a groove or mortice, something of the kind of the chine log of some west European and American flat-bottomed boats. Such a method of construction, while solving the difficult problem of the sewn chine joint in what is in fact a V-bottomed boat, indicates an excellent supply of good timber and very skilled boatbuilders. This feature is clearly visible in the photograph of a model of the boat made from Hallström's drawing (Figure 143). Apart from the chine log construction the form of this boat, I am told, is close to that of some modern lake boats built for racing.

In the Finnish National Museum in Helsinki there is on public display a rather roughly built sewn-planked boat (Figure 144). The museum's documentation of her

146 ▶
This close up clearly shows the very unusual structure of the chine seam of the Saamish sewn plank boat. [Basil Greenhill

143
This photograph of a model made by Kenneth Britten from Hallström's drawing clearly shows the overlapping at the chine seam. [Basil Greenhill

147

Top right – *'Women from the neigh-bourhood coming on visit', Petsamo, Finland, c1933.* [National Museum of Finland

148

Middle right – *Old Saamish boat at Ristilä, near Kemijarvi, 1992.* [Basil Greenhill

149

Bottom right – *similar boat in current use at Ristilä, 1992.* [Basil Greenhill

is rather slight. It records her acquisition by T Itkonen and her purchase by the museum on 2 February 1910. She is believed to have come from the Lake Inari region of Arctic Finland, not far removed to the west of the Kola Peninsula. The boat is recorded as having been built for the museum's purposes as an example of the sewn plank building methods of the area. She is entirely sewn and trenailed and is of much the same construction as the Kola boat, being V-bottomed and having exactly the same feature, clearly visible in the photographs (Figures 145 and 146) at the chine. In her case the second plank is a relatively massive object and must have been hewn out with great skill. The boat measures 10ft 3⅓in (3.15m) by 3ft 6in (1.2m) by 10⅔in (0.27m) and is very similar in general appearance to the boats photographed at Petsamo in 1933 (Figure 147) though these were almost certainly wood and iron fastened.

150

Tenojoki boat at Utsjouki, 1992. Note the squatting board, a recent development as outboard motors have become more powerful. [Basil Greenhill

At Ristilä, south of Kemijarvi, in August 1992 I came across a very old boat, derelict and half buried in reeds; which, though larger, metal-fastened and with the majority of her frames steamed, was very reminiscent of the boat in Helsinki (Figures 148 and 149). Nearby lay a modern version in current use (Figure 149). These boats appear to be of the type described by Itkonen as 'south Lapland' and to be in use over a very large area north of Kainuu to the rivers of the far north which flow into the Arctic ocean. In 1992 this pattern of distribution still seemed to hold, though some of the boats were of plastic, evidently moulded from wooden boats of this general shape.

The month before, on the Tenojoki at Utsjoki in the extreme north of Arctic Finland, there was a whole fleet of salmon fishing boats in operation, six plank boats distinctly reminiscent of enlarged versions of the Kola boat in general form (Figure 150). Itkonen says of these very interesting boats:

> The so-called river Lapp boat of the Tenu and Utsjoki river valleys can be regarded as a modification of the Lappland (Perapohja) boat. It is even narrower than the original Finnish form, but the stems are slightly more upright. The development of this boat has apparently had its first inspiration from those eighteenth-century settlers who moved in large numbers from the valleys of the Torniojoki and Kemijoki rivers to Norwegian Lappland and to the Tenojoki river valley where part of them became gradually absorbed by the Lapps.

Bibliography

CEDERLUND, C O, *Ett fartyg byggt med syteknik*, 1978
  (ed.), *The Årby Boat*, 1994
COLES, J, FENWICK, V and HUTCHINSON, G (eds), *A Spirit of Enquiry*, 1993
FAERØYVIK, B and O, ed. by CHRISTENSEN, AE, *Inshore Craft of Norway*, 1979
ITKONEN, T, 'Suomen Kansanomaiset Veneet' *Suomen Museo* XXXIII, 1926
MCGRAIL, S *Ancient Boats of North West Europe*, 1987
  (ed), *Aspects of Maritime Archaeology and Ethnography*, 1984
MCGRAIL, S and KENTLEY, E (eds), *Sewn Plank Boats*, 1985
PRINS, A H J, *A Handbook of Sewn Boats*, 1986
WESTERDAHL, C, 'Et sätt som liknar them uti theras öfriga lefnadsart', 1987
  (ed) *Crossroads in Ancient Shipbuilding*, 1994
WRIGHT, E, *The Ferriby Boats*, 1990

CHAPTER 10

Ships and Boats of the Mediterranean from 3000 to 500 BC

1. *The Times* of 20 March 1995 reported that Dr Bob Brier of Long Island University New York with colleagues from the University had made a seven-foot model of the Cheops ship out of pine and glue and tested it in a tank at the Webb Institute in Glen Cove N.Y. After pulling it through the water several hundred times under different conditions he concluded that it would have served perfectly well as a river boat. 'It is', he said, 'an elegant, beautifully designed craft, with wonderful properties in the water.'

In the Neolithic period the use of seagoing craft of some sort is to be inferred from the presence in the Peloponnese of obsidian flake available only in the island of Melos and from the colonisation of the island of Crete from the mainland; they were probably reed craft, but no representations of them survive.

The Cheops ship: 2600 BC

In the cedar timbers of the Cheops ship, well preserved in an airtight 'grave', the methods of the Egyptian builders of large Nile ships can be clearly and comprehensively seen (Figure 151). There is no keel. The planks (12–14cm thick) of the nearly flat bottom are joined edge to edge by mortice and tenon fastenings. There are no pegs to reinforce the joint (Figure 152); but instead cords are passed from side to side through pairs of holes in each plank making a V-shaped passage. Twelve frames are

151

The ship reconstructed from parts found in 1954 in a ship grave near the Great Pyramid at Giza in which the Fourth Dynasty Pharoah Cheops was buried.

152

The bottom planks of 151. They are of cedar and 13–14cm thick, joined side by side by mortice and tenon joints reinforced by a system of ropes threaded through holes and meeting in pairs on the inside. They are joined end to end by hook scarfs.

fitted at intervals to the hull planks (which are scarfed end to end) and bound to them with cords.

The ship is 43.4m long and 5.9m in the beam and displaces 40 tons. A spine (or shelf), also scarfed, runs down the median line and is supported by stanchions bound one to each of the twelve frames. The deck beams are let into the top wales and lashed to holes in them. Subsidiary spines (or shelves) on each side of the ship are let into the deck beams. On deck there is a long structure. The result is a river ship of great elegance and fine lines.[1]

Six pairs of oars (varying from 7.8m to 6.8m) were found in the 'grave'. Landström thinks that they were all used to steer the ship, since as a royal ship she would have been towed. But it may have been thought that oars provided a more royal progress.

Egyptian sea-going ships

After 2600 BC Egyptian texts in the Old Kingdom describe voyages both commercial and military to the Levant, the former for the import of timber and metals unavailable in Egypt. Such ships are depicted in a relief (Figure 153) in the temple of Sahure (Fifth Dynasty) at Abusir. These ships also made voyages to Punt (probably Somalia) for myrrh, electrum and ebony and to Sinai for turquoise. The ship in Figure 153 shows seven oars (eight in another ship in the relief) on the port side, recognisable as such by the shape of the blade:[2] lancet shaped as opposed to paddles which had egg-shaped blades. A similar number on the starboard side is implied. The ship has three rudders all shown on the port side. By the time of the Fifth Dynasty of the Old Kingdom passenger ships on the Nile were rowed, with occasional exceptions, rather than paddled. The much lighter Nile ship under oar (Figure 154) shows eleven oars on the port side and two rudders. It has a canopy and no sailing equipment. By contrast the seagoing Sahure ship in addition to its heavier build and additional rudders has a massive double mast shown unstepped with sail, yard and boom invisible, a hogging truss of two ropes twisted together, stressed by a

153

A relief found in the tomb of the Pharoah Sahure of the Fifth Dynasty of the Old Kingdom (c2450 BC). It shows the departure and return of seagoing ships probably to and from Syria.

2. Landstrom (1970) p55

154

Detail from a relief from the tomb of Ti of the Old Kingdom (Steindorff: Das Grab des Ti: Leipzig 1913).

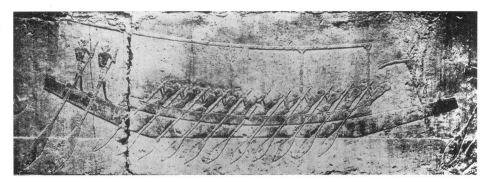

155

A relief from the temple of Queen Hatshepsut at Deir el Bahari c1500 BC showing seagoing ships returning from Punt (Somalia).

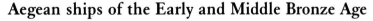

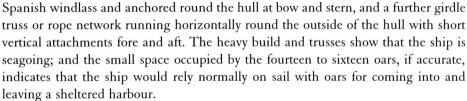

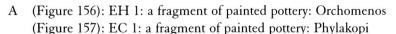

156

A fragment of pottery from Orchomenos on Lake Copais. It shows an early Bronze Age longship.

Spanish windlass and anchored round the hull at bow and stern, and a further girdle truss or rope network running horizontally round the outside of the hull with short vertical attachments fore and aft. The heavy build and trusses show that the ship is seagoing; and the small space occupied by the fourteen to sixteen oars, if accurate, indicates that the ship would rely normally on sail with oars for coming into and leaving a sheltered harbour.

Nearly a millennium later in the New Kingdom (c1500 BC) the ships that Queen Hatshepsut sent to Punt (Figure 155) are similar in their main features but have fifteen oars a side and a single mast.

Aegean ships of the Early and Middle Bronze Age

The following examples of ship portraits and models from the islands and mainland of Greece belong to this period. (Early Helladic/Early Cycladic I = 3000–2500 BC, Early Minoan/Early Helladic II = 2500–2200 BC, Middle Minoan/Middle Helladic III = 1700–1600 BC). They fall into three groups:

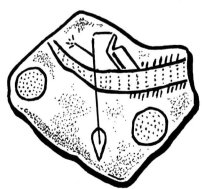

157

A fragment of pottery from Phylakopi on the island of Melos showing an early Bronze Age longship.

A   (Figure 156): EH 1: a fragment of painted pottery: Orchomenos
     (Figure 157): EC 1: a fragment of painted pottery: Phylakopi
     (Figure 158): EC 1: Naxos lead model: plan view
     (Figure 159): EC 1: Naxos lead model: side view

B   (Figure 160: a, b, c, d, e, f, g and h): EH 11: the Syros fans
     (Figure 161): EM 11: clay model: Palaikastro

C   (Figure 162): EM III: seals
     (Figure 163): MH/MM III: painted fragments from Iolkos

158
Plan view of a lead model of an early Cycladic longship (from before 2500 BC) in the Ashmolean Museum at Oxford.

159
Port view of the same.

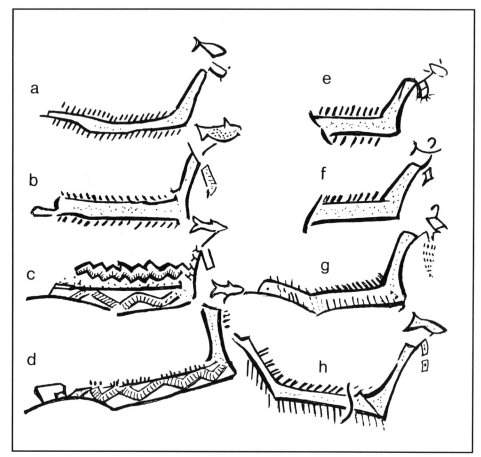

160
Aegean Bronze Age longships shown on eight fan-shaped terracottas from the island of Syros, dated after 2500 BC (EH 11).

161
A rather crude model of an early Bronze Age (EH 11) longship from Palaikastro in Crete and now in the Heraklion Museum. It emphasises the high stern and low forefoot.

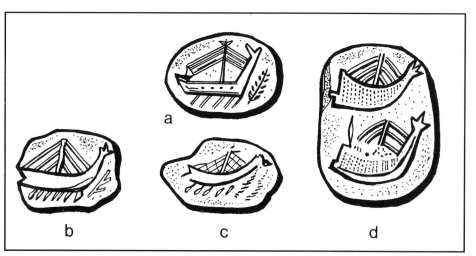

162
Minoan seals (EM 111–MM 11) showing longships of the asymmetrical type under sail.

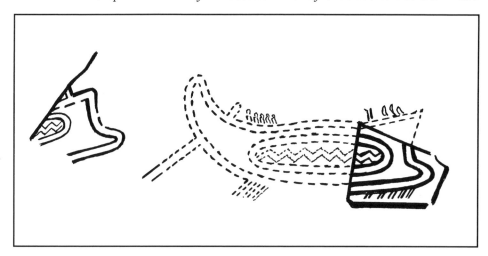

163
Fragments of coloured pottery (MH III) from Iolkos at the head of the gulf of Pagasai. They show parts of two longships the main feature of which is the forefoot strongly shown. The stern is identified in one by part of the rudder.

The first group, A, from the period 3000 to 2500 BC, consists of the Orchomenos and Phylakopi fragments and the lead models from Naxos.

The Orchomenos fragment shows what may reasonably be taken to be a long ship with markings above the hull indicating thirteen paddles or oars. One end of the ship stands high; the other end (which appears to be incomplete in the picture) rises slightly and the keel line is longer than the topwale.

The Phylakopi fragment shows the upcurving end of a longship recognisable as the stern by the rudder and tiller. The rudder has a pennon attached to it (streaming aft) and may be held by a roughly indicated and partly preserved figure (forward). Forward again on both sides of the hull are marks indicating oars or paddles (seven 'above' and thirteen 'beneath').

Of the four roughly similar lead models from Naxos, three are in the Ashmolean Museum, Oxford, and one in the Merseyside Museum, Liverpool. They were identified by Renfrew[3] as representing early Cycladic longships. The best preserved of the Ashmolean examples (Figures 158 and 159) is presented by Basch in three photographs including one showing the ship in plan. The Museum gives the measurements as 40cm long, 2.2cm high amidships, and 3.5cm broad, giving a ratio of beam to length of 1:11.4 (comparable to the ratio of dragon boats 1:10–1.14).[4]

The models were simply made from three strips of lead, one for the bottom and one for each side of the model; but, as Basch[5] observed, the shape of the hull has been worked very carefully. The midships part, about half the total length, is on an even keel (apart from slight hogging which may be accidental) and would have been devoted to the oarsmen or paddlers and the median gangway. The two ends rise gently to about an equal height, 6.2cm. Towards each end, beyond the area of propulsion, the hull tapers; but at one end the hull broadens again, while at the other it narrows nearly to a point as the bottom lead strip rises, narrows and bends vertically. The end where the hull broadens and where the gap between the side pieces is filled by the still wide bottom strip is likely to be the stern. Room had to be made there for one or two passengers (furthest aft) and the commander and helmsman (forward of them). The other end, pointed and rising above the water, is certainly the bow, narrow and pointed so that it cannot obstruct the view of the helmsman aft. If anything, the end now identifiable as the bow is the higher, but only very slightly. The identifiable stern in the Phylakopi fragment (Figure 157), allowing for some exaggeration of the rise aft, would fit the symmetrical Naxos ship, whereas the Orchomenos fragment (Figure 156) presents a different, unsymmetrical, type.

The next group of representations, B, consists of the Syros fans (Figure 160: Early Helladic II) and the Palaikastro model (Figure 161: Early Minoan II). The most

3. Renfrew (1967)

4. Wachsmann (1995) p19

5. Basch (1987) = B 153–156

164

The Medinet Habu frieze. It is a triumphant record by Ramses II of the defeat in 1186 BC of a raiding party of the Sea Peoples by an Egyptian sea patrol aided by strong land forces.

striking characteristics of the ships portrayed on the eight Syros fans are the following:

1. with one exception (f) they resemble the Phylakopi fragment in showing what appear to be oars or paddles above and below the hulls;
2. their high-rising end makes a right angle (or nearly so) with the keel;
3. their lower end rises at a (in some cases much) wider angle from the keel, so that they are far from symmetrical and in a general sense resemble the ship of the Orchomenos fragment;
4. their lower end, like the Orchomenos ship (in all cases except where the ship shown is incomplete) terminates in a projection.

If these characteristics are taken into account it would seem that the Syros fan ships belong to a type (foreshadowed by the Orchomenos ship), the main characteristics of which are that it is unsymmetrical and has a projection at the lower end.

These two characteristics are roughly expressed, with no other refinements, by the Palaikastro model (Figure 161).

The third group, C, consists of later Minoan seals (Figure 162 a–d), and the painted sherds from Iolkos (Figure 163: Middle Helladic III).

The Minoan seals show ships with an indication of oars and sail rigging. One end is high and bifid or trifid, the other lower surmounted by a structure at which one side of the mast rigging ends. The answer to the much debated question which end of these ships, and hence of the ships of the unsymmetrical type in general, is bow and which stern is offered by potsherds from Iolkos (Figure 163: Middle Helladic: c1600 BC). Put together, the two sherds show the identical ends of two ships one behind the other and between them part of the rudder of the ship in front. The presence of the rudder identifies the ends of the two ships, each showing a projection, as bows (cf the symbol from the Phaistos disc which shows the same forefoot[6]).

The reason for this bow projection must be considered. Later, sheathed in bronze (the fastening of the sheath indicated by a semi-vertical line) it became an effective ram, but the longship at this early stage was a means by which warriors could take themselves to a scene of action rather than a weapon in itself for confrontation at sea, which is not shown until much later (Figure 172). In the Minoan seals (although the keel of ships there represented is often unrealistically rockered) and in the Iolkos fragments the projection is at waterlevel. It appears to be a continuation of the keel as a cutwater into which, aft of its end, the stempost has been stepped. As such it would

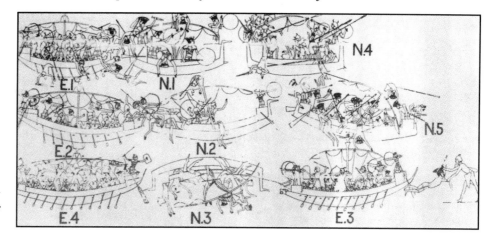

165

A selective presentation of 164 demonstrating the chronological sequence embodied in its design.

have hydrodynamic advantages. In the Syros fans, however, the forepart of the ship is set at an angle to the keel and appears in some examples to rise well above waterlevel. This feature is particularly puzzling because the oar or paddle markings continue most unrealistically, indeed impossibly, into the rising bow even in one extreme example of it (Figure 160 h) (though not into the rising stern). In the Minoan seals the keels of ships represented are often rockered to an unrealistic extent to fit the ships into the circular space available. It may be that the natural rise of the keel at the bow was actually angled rather than curved in the ships portrayed, but that the height or the rise has been exaggerated to accommodate the ship in the space available on the circular face of the fan. This exaggeration need not however have taken place in the stern where the oar/paddle markings do not occur aft of the angle.

Over the wide temporal span of the early and middle Bronze Age it seems that two types of ship were in use. The symmetrical type appears first in the Early Cycladic I Naxos models and later in some Middle Minoan seals. The asymmetrical type appears first possibly on the Orchomenos fragments, certainly in the Early Cycladic II Syros fans, and later in the Middle Minoan seals and the Middle Helladic Iolkos fragments.

The Medinet Habu battle frieze (Figures 164 and 165)

The Sea People were active in the Levant as sea raiders from the fourteenth century BC up to and probably after their battle with the land and sea forces of Ramses III in 1186 BC at the entry to the Nile Delta. The battle was presented in detail in a surviving painted frieze which shows accordingly the ships used at the time by the Sea Peoples in their raids and those of the squadron that Ramses III deployed against them.

Shelley Wachsmann[7] has given a valuable summary of the textual evidence for these maritime activities. These texts speak of battles at sea between ships of the Hittite king Shuppiluliuma II and the ships of Alasiya (Cyprus), and in the reign of Ramses II between the ships of the Shardanu and Egyptian naval forces. They are evidence for the first warships recorded as engaging in battles at sea as distinct from longships rowed by fighting men to the scene of engagements on land.

The various tribes of the Sea Peoples are compared by Wachsmann to the Vikings, whom they closely resembled, making raids in small parties of ships on the towns and cities of the Levant coastline and getting away before the coastal powers could react effectively. He concludes that they must, like the Vikings, have used small oared ships to carry out these tactics successfully with some but not a great deal of room for booty. The relief gives, perhaps with some patriotic exaggeration, an occasion on which they were not successful. A small naval patrol seems to be

6. Casson (1972) = *SSAW* Pl55

7. Wachsmann (1981)

engaging the raiders just offshore, and large land forces are at hand to provide support for the naval patrol.

Five ships of the Sea Peoples (Figure 165: N1–5) are shown without oars and with their sails brailed up to the yard. The four Egyptian ships (E1–4) are shown with eight, ten and eleven oars a side and with sails brailed up. It is reasonable to regard them as twenty-oared ships. All the Egyptian ships have a single rudder, two of the raiders' ships have two rudders (N1 two on the same side, N4 two one on each side). Nelson (1943) was undoubtedly right in regarding the four Egyptian ships as forming a temporal sequence and at least three of the raiding ships (N1, N2 and N3) doing the same. But it is not to be concluded that battle was between only one Egyptian ship and two or three raiders. The squadrons are likely to have been composed of a small number (at least five or six ships).

166
Drawing of a typical Egyptian warship shown in 164.

167
The best preserved of the bigger ships in the procession of ships depicted in the miniature frieze of the West House at Thera (before 1628 BC).

The Egyptian warships (Figure 166)

The four Egyptian ships, shown in profile, are roughly symmetrical with the tapering stern rising a little higher than the lion-headed bow (cf the Theran ships in Figure 167). In general shape they are similar to the smaller Theran ships, but in size larger. Their dimensions may be roughly estimated. If ten oarsmen a side are taken as the type manning, the horizontal rowing area with an interscalmium of 1m is 10m giving an overall length of about 15m. Beam for the extent of the rowing area is not less than 4m with 1.5m for each of the oarsmen port and starboard and 1m for the central gangway/deck accommodating the fighting men and the two sidescreens protecting the oarsmen, giving a ratio of 1:3.75; but, more importantly for speed under oar, about 1:4.7 on the waterline.

There are bow and stern structures giving in the stern a seat for the helmsman who holds the loom of the single rudder in his right hand and in his left the tiller (absent in the relief in its present state but indicated by the helmsman's gesture and hence probably painted, as Wachsmann suggests). The structures also provide station for the archers, while the fighting men stand in the gangway. The masts have a manned 'crow's nest' with lifts for the yard but no visible halliards. Ropes (single lines) run from points where the sail is brailed to the base of the mast. The absence of a boom at the base of the sail, regular in Nile boats and Egyptian trading ships and occurring in most of the Theran ships, is to be explained by the function of these ships as warships in which a boom would give additional weight, and in the case of the collapse of mast and yard in battle (N3, 4 and 5) additional danger.

Since the Egyptian ships seem to have moved in to attack the raiders beached on shore the oars are shown manned although the engagement has become stationary. The oarsmen's heads are seen over the top of the protective sidescreen while the oars emerge from beneath it and over the topwale. An Egyptian soldier is to be seen leaning well outboard over the topwale, implying that the screen is a necessary distance inboard of it. This arrangement is possible, longitudinally if as in this case the oars are not being pulled, and laterally if the oar's loom is long enough, not less than 1m (i.e. with a gearing of 1:3 in a 4m oar). The oars of the Cheops ship (p.132) were 7.8–6.8m long. It seems clear from the (as usual) rather outsize fighting men portrayed that inboard of the oarsmen's seats on both sides and probably slightly higher there was a fore-and-aft gangway or deck, but no high canopy-deck such as appears in later oared warships (p.144). This deck is seen giving standing room for heavily-armed fighters while the archers took up positions of greater vantage on the bow and stern structures.

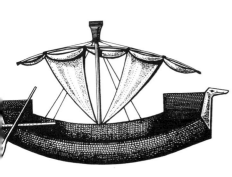

168

Drawing of a typical ship of the Sea Peoples.

The longships of the Sea Peoples (Figure 168)

The raiding party consisted of four 'peoples', the Peleshet, Ijeker, Denyen and Skeklesh.[8] The men of N2 and N4 are distinguished from the others by their horned helmets and in the case of N4 their use of very long spears and poles. The other three, N1, N3 and N5, have 'brush' helmets. All have round shields except in the case of the capsized ship (N3) where shields have understandably been thrown away.

The ships of the raiders are, like those of the Egyptians, of a single type. The two types are dissimilar in profile but effectively much the same. They are shown as of the same size and hence of the same rating as twenty-oared ships, but whereas the Egyptian ships curve upwards gently at bow and stern, the raiding ships have stem and sternposts stepped into the keel at bow and stern making a right-angle joint. The stem and sternposts terminate in birds' heads with long beaks, one facing forward in the bow and the other facing aft in the stern. In two cases, N4 and N5, there is a very small projection in the stern. Other such projections are shown in models and vasepaintings; but in proportion to the ships from which these project they are so much larger that the function for them and for the minute projections in N4 and N5 can hardly be the same. For the latter the only explanation can be a practical preference for stepping the sternpost a few centimetres forward of the end of the keel.

The parallel horizontal lines above the keel in the raiders' ships may, with the exception of N3, be explained, as in the case of the similar lines in E1–4, as defining the topwale and the upper edge of a protective sidescreen which is set up sufficiently far inboard to provide space for a man to stand, when the oars are not being pulled. In N1 and N4 two levels inboard of the sidescreen are required for fighting men to stand, and that is provided by the oarsmen's seats (lower level) and by a gangway/ deck (upper level). Since the oarsmen's heads are not visible, it is reasonable to suppose that the oarsmen's seats are vacant, and that the oarsmen have joined the fighters.

N3 is a different matter. As the fighting proceeds through N1, N2, N4, N5 and N3, the ship is being pulled over apparently by means of its mast. (The reverse process is often used by yachtsmen to right a capsized boat.) In N1 the ship is upright, in N2 it is leaning, in N4 it leans more, and in N5 still more until in N3 the mast is broken as a result of the force on it and the ship is lying over on its starboard side (and showing its port side). Whereas before the ship was seen from the starboard side, from keel line at the bottom to the 'crow's nest' at the top of the picture, now the ship and the surface of the sea are shown in plan.

At the top the curving keel is seen, and converging slightly with it, the topwale. The sidescreens, not surprisingly, have disappeared in the melee.   The stump of the mast emerges from behind the topwale (1) beside two ropes each shown by double lines which curl round the broken off part of the mast to the yard in the foreground around which it is bound, and (2) beside the foot of a (drowned) man under the other side of the hull. Along the sole of his foot runs a double line which by comparison with the double-lined ropes attached to the yard must also be a substantial rope. Further towards the foreground and parallel to this rope there is a single line which, traced to the right and beyond N3 to the bow of the Egyptian ship E3, ends in both hands of an Egyptian man and must be another, less substantial, rope (cf the brailing ropes similarly shown). It runs right through the ship to what is probably the prow and it may *faute de mieux* be recognised as a towrope. It would seem that N3 represents the final stage of the battle, E3 showing the prisoners being taken away in an enemy ship. If this explanation of N3 is right the raider ship shown is similar to the other raider ships and *mutatis mutandis* to the other Egyptian ships.

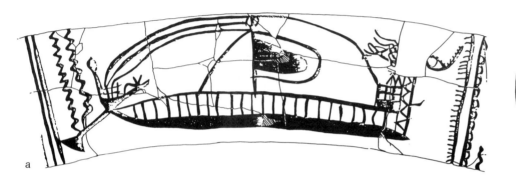

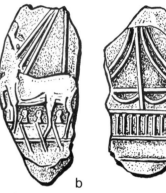

169

a. The late Helladic longship depicted on a clay box from the Pylos-Tragana tomb (1200–1100 BC).
b. Cretan seal (c1400 BC) showing part of the port side of an oared ship.
c. Similar Cretan seal with oarsmen's heads replaced by uprights.

The Pylos-Tragana ship

The impressive realism with which the symmetrical (crescentic) Theran ships of the West House wall paintings (Figure 167) and the warships of the Medinet Habu battle scene are represented is in strong contrast with the crude Cycladic examples of the asymmetrical type of longship with its high stern and forefoot. However, the ship of the twelfth century BC painted on the Pylos-Tragana casket (Figure 169) shows that the asymmetrical type continued to exist in Mycenaean fleets. The starboard side of an asymmetrical longship is shown there (partially restored) exhibiting a mixture of realism in detail with a primitive convention of perspective in representing the ship as a pentecontor with accommodation for twenty-five oarsmen a side. (The area restored is within the dotted lines.)

The realistic details of the Pylos ship comprise the up-curving stern with its emphasis through enlargement on the rudder and tiller; and the bow structure and forefoot. The unrealistic elements are the twenty-three vertical lines from the starboard topwale to the horizontal line of the port topwale, indicating thwarts (*zyga*: on which the oarsmen sit), and the pair of zig-zag but in general vertical lines indicating by a similar convention of perspective the wash made by the rudder (or rudders). On this interpretation the Pylos ship is the first illustration of a pentecontor, the Homeric warship. The Pylos 'rower' Linear B tablets produce some evidence for the use or triacontors in Mycenaean cities at about the same date.[9]

Two fragmentary Cretan clay seals (Figure 169b and c) dated about two hundred years earlier than the Pylos-Tragana box pose clearly the problem of its interpretation. They are provocatively placed side by side by Casson.[10] In (b) a horse stands in front of the port side of an oared ship in which the heads and shoulders of four oarsmen (in three cases with oars) are shown rowing over the top wale. The bottom wale is shown, and above the oarsmen's heads what is either the deck or the far (starboard) topwale. A mast and lifts are visible but the yardarm and brailed-up sails are masked by the horse's body.

In (c) mast, lifts, yardarm, brailed-up sail and brails can be seen above double

9. Wachsmann (1995) p25

10. *SSAW* Pls 52 and 53

(a)

(b)

170

Two fragments of two Attic kraters of the Geometric period showing the prows and part of the rowing area of longships.

parallel horizontal lines as in (b); but below them instead of oarsmen as in (b) there are ten pairs of vertical lines, and below the latter a pair of horizontal parallel lines and still lower a further pair of horizontal parallel lines i.e. the bottom wale or keel. The ten pairs of vertical parallel lines in (c) seem rather too close together to represent thwarts. On the other hand the artist may have wished to represent the common type of twenty-oared ship (*eikosoros*: ten a side), but found that there was only room across the face of the egg-shaped seal for ten thwarts if they were packed closely together. The same explanation can be given if the ten pairs of parallel lines represent deck-stanchions normally marking off oarsmen's rooms. The third possibility is that they represent a sidescreen but the sidescreen is indicated in the early period by hatching (cf Figure 170a and b) or a plane surface (Figures 164 and 165). In both the first two cases the pairs of verticals would be modes of indicating the oar system short of showing actual oarsmen and oars.

The same two alternatives face the interpreter of (a), the Pylos-Tragana box, but there the whole ship is shown, and the unrealistic height of the bow structure makes a point in favour of the interpretation of the horizontals above the verticals as representing the far side rather than a deck of the ship, the verticals then representing the thwarts. It cannot be said that (b) and (c) solve this vexed question but at any rate they offer objects of reflection.

Longships of the Geometric period

The asymmetrical longship appears next most notably on Attic Dipylon kraters in the late Geometric style of 760–735 BC (Figure 170a and b). The Dipylon krater fragments, like the Pylos-Tragana casket, show ships with a mixture of realism and primitive perspective. Unfortunately no picture of a whole ship has survived among them but the fragments in Figure 170a and b depicting two prows illustrate the painter's style and corroborate each other. In these the forefoot is a marked feature showing no trace of a metal sheath to make it an effective or a more effective ram. There are also three slight but rather enigmatic projections forward from the stem. Aft of the stem, which is elegantly curved, there is a symbolic circular eye.

The foredeck has a railing and the *akrostolion* makes an even more elegant curve forward and then aft. Above the upper edge (i) of the black hull continuing horizontally from the black bow there is a horizontal line (ii) through which at regular intervals rise vertical lines (iii) (dim in (b) but strongly marked in (a)) which rise to cross a thin line (iv), then a thick black band (v) and then another thin line (vi) above which they project. Between these verticals there are at regular intervals hooks, recognisable as tholepins, for which the Greek word is *kleis* meaning 'hook'. A number of human figures are shown all of size disproportionately large: in (a) a man stands beside the forefoot, three men stand on or more probably (since it is unquestionably a railing) behind line (ii) and two in the space *in between* (ii) and (iv). In (b) one man stands on the foredeck and two *in between* the upper and lower edge of (v).

Many different interpretations of these fragmentary pictures have been given. The interpretation of the Pylos-Tragana ship offered above is based on the assumption of a primitive perspective which may reasonably be applied also to the Dipylon vase ships. While line (i) must undoubtedly be taken (because of the tholepins it carries) as the topwale port side, (v) in that perspective becomes the topwale starboard side with its railing. The vertical lines (iii) become, as in the Pylos-Tragana ship, the thwarts (on which the oarsmen sit) and as, in the picture, they continue upwards the uprights of the starboard railing (vi). Then by implication lines (iii) at their lower end also do duty as the uprights of the railing port side. The fact that two of the human figures stand definitely, and two more probably, in between (ii) and (iv) and two in between the upper and lower edges of (v) militates very strongly, it would seem, against the interpretation of (v) as a deck or gangway *above* (i). It seems much more likely that (v) is the topwale starboard side with (vi) and the continuation of (iii) as its railing. It is perhaps too much to expect that the painter of (a) would have inserted tholepins in (v) (if it was a topwale) at the top right hand corner, when the painter or (b) omitted them much more blatantly on both topwales.

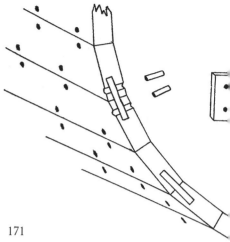

171

A diagram showing the shell method of ship construction as described in Odyssey 5 243–261.

Odysseus's ship: eighth to seventh century BC

In the period from the beginning of the eighth to the end of the seventh century BC the *Iliad* and the *Odyssey* were being put together. They describe a society in which because of its geographical conditions seafaring played a central role. Characteristics of oral poetry are formulae reciting common procedures and detailed descriptions of common objects, both often repeated. These in the case of the omnipresent ships have given a more exact knowledge of them and their navigation than at any other time in antiquity. These are set out at length in *GOS* Ch 3.

The longships themselves may be envisaged as the Geometric vasepainter saw them, the round ships as very roughly shown by a clay model in the Heraklion museum. For the method of building, which applies to both, there is the account in the *Odyssey* of the ship which Odysseus built on Calypso's island.[11]

Calypso tells Odysseus 'where tall trees grow, alder and poplar and pine, dry long ago, well seasoned'. 'He then set to, cutting the planks, and quickly got on with the job. He dragged out twenty felled trees, and adzed with the bronze. He cleverly planed them and made them straight to the line. Then Calyso brought drills, and he bored holes in all the planks (i.e. mortises) and fitted them to each other. He hammered the hull together with tenons (*gomphoi* = 'teeth') and *harmoniai* (pegged mortise and tenon joints). As broad an *edaphos* 'rounded hull' of a beamy merchantman as a man skilled in carpentry will round out, so broad an *edaphos* did Odysseus fashion for his wide ship'. This 'shell' method of construction (Figure 171) by building up the sides of the hull without ribs has been found in the wrecks of merchantmen on the sea bed of the Mediterranean dated from the Bronze Age to the classical period. Odysseus's ship has no keel.

After completing the hull Odysseus turns to the superstructure, the *ikria*, a raised poop where the helmsman and important passengers sat. Such a poop is also a

11. For the model in the Herakleion museum see *GOS* Pl.1f: Odyssey 5.243–261

172

The Aristonothos vase: Attic black-figure style probably of west Greek origin. It gives the earliest picture of an armed confrontation of ships at sea. The two ships shown are of different design, the one on the left Greek and the one on the right probably Etruscan.

feature of longships. The side view above shows uprights and a longitudinal rail, together forming a short railing on each side of the platform or seat on which the helmsman sits. So Odysseus 'sets up and fashions the *ikria*, fitting it with many uprights, and completes it with long *epenkenides* [i.e. horizontal timbers].' In the ship he also made a mast and a yard fitted to it. He made a rudder as well to steer with.

Odysseus also gives his ship wattle screens to keep out the spray in rough weather and 'spreads much brushwood'. Brushwood has been found under the cargo in a Bronze Age wreck and in one case specially cut to fit between the frames. It seems then that its function was to serve as dunnage, a springy layer to protect cargo and also to protect the planking. Odysseus had no cargo in prospect but he seems to be describing the usual fittings of a cargo vessel. Calypso then brought cloths out of which to make sails: 'these as well he fashioned cleverly'. He rigs the ship with three kinds of rope: *huperai*, *kaloi* and *podes*, the last being sheets attached to the lower corners of the (square) sail, the second being the brailing ropes for shortening or furling sail, while the first (upper ropes) are braces attached to the ends of the yard and used for bringing it round. Finally, he pulled the ship down into the sea with levers.

There is no reason to think that the method of construction of the longship differed fundamentally from that of the broad merchantman. Homer's longships are usually pentecontors, ships of twenty-five oarsmen a side with two officers. In the Catalogue in the fifth book of the *Iliad*, of the ships that went to Troy, one of the latest parts of the Homeric poems, the Boeotians are first mentioned and in addition to the usual record of the number of ships (in this case fifty) the number of men in each (120: not specified as oarsmen) is added. Since double-manning oars is unknown at this date and the development of two levels of oars without reducing the length of the ship is improbable (but not impossible), the most likely explanation is that a spare oarcrew was carried (as happens in a play of Euripides[12]) in a fifty-oared ship.

Pentecontors were probably about 30m long and had a mast of at least 11m. They had a substantial keel. When Odysseus's pentecontor broke up in a storm he lashed keel and mast together and rode on them. The use of the word *steira* which means the forepart of the keel indicates that it is the keel projecting forward of the stempost and forming what is called the forefoot. At a later date a warship with ram above the waterline was called *anasteiros*.

There is some evidence that the edge to edge joints of the early longships were reinforced by cord lashings in the manner of Egyptian ships. In the *Iliad*[13] it is said that after nine years at Troy the planks of the Greek ships had become rotten and the cords had worked loose.

Other structural features of the early longships are the substantial cross-timbers projecting at each end on each side of the hull fore and aft, in addition to the twenty-five internal thwarts on which the oarsmen sat and under which they stowed gear and cargo. The after cross-timber, the 7ft *threnus*, may be so called (since the word can mean a footstool) because the helmsman's foot rested on it; but in the sixth-century model of a longship[14] the projection is too far aft for that explanation and it is more likely that when the ship was beached the projection was of a convenient

12. Euripides *Helen* 1530–1614: *GOS* p200

13. II 135

14. *GOS* Pl27b

height to use as a step when going aboard, and thus acquired its name. In the later, larger longships a stern ladder was used for boarding and regularly carried.[15]

The Aristonothos vase (700–650 BC) (Figure 172)

Whereas the Dipylon vases showed beached ships and men fighting from them or on land as they did in Homer, the Aristonothos vase half a century later showed a confrontation between ships at sea. The two ships involved are of very different types. The ship on the left (moving right) is of the Greek asymmetrical type with five men (disproportionately large) at the oar on the starboard side, probably implying five more on the port side, possibly representing symbolically a larger file on both sides. The oars are shown unrealistically with the looms in the oarsmen's hands and the shafts and blades discontinuously below the ship. There is a pronounced forefoot but the state of preservation of the painting makes it impossible to say whether there are or are not fastenings for a bronze sheath converting it to an effective ram. In addition to the outsize oarsmen there are three even more outsize armed men on a canopy-deck over them. The ship on the right pointing left has a mast and crow's nest. It is largely symmetrical but the bow terminates in a high downward pointing forefoot not apparently metal-sheathed. There are three armed men on deck but no other crew although a helmsman is implied by two rudders with tillers, and the canopy deck is supported by ten stanchions (one merging with the mast in the picture) which mark the oarsmen's rooms in between (p.145). A twenty-oared ship (*eikosoros*) is implied.

Confrontation at sea appears to have effected a revolution in longship design and started a series of modifications of which the first is the canopy (non-structural) deck in place of the keel-line gangway which accommodated the fighting men in the ships of the Medinet Habu frieze. For the vasepainter this feature ruled out the conventional perspective by which he had shown the further as well as the nearer topwale of the longship. This development has proved confusing for the modern enquirer since the earlier conventional perspective of thwarts and further topwale and the later realistic rendering of stanchions and canopy deck produce very similar results. Fortunately the men in the former apparently standing in mid-air and the armed men in the latter firmly placed on deck serve to distinguish the reality behind each.

Development of the longship

Evolution of the longship answered the need for a better power:weight ratio in warships when the ram became the main offensive weapon in confrontation of ships at sea. The first of the new types was the pentecontor with two files of oarsmen at different levels on each side of the ship (the 'two' or bireme). The second was the three or trireme (*trieres*) with three files of oarsmen a side at different levels. This latter type was evolved in two forms, one in Phoenicia of the eighth century BC without an outrigger (the survival of this type three into the fifth century BC is by no means certain) and the other in mainland Greece (Corinth) with an outrigger. Threes and occasionally twos were used as first-line ships in large numbers at the beginning of the seventh, in the sixth, fifth and the greater part of the fourth centuries BC; in the latter part of this period their function changed to some extent.

The invention of the ship with two levels of oars is attributed to the Ionian city of Erythrae by the historian Damastes of Sigeion, writing in the late fifth century BC.[16] Such ships were first shown in a group of fragments of vasepainting from the Late Geometric (735–710 BC) and Early Archaic (700–650 BC) periods, and identified as showing ships of two levels of oars by R T Williams.[17] They appear shortly after-

15. *GOS* Pls 11, 12b, 13, 15a and b, 20a

16. *FGrHist* 5f6

17. R T Williams (1958): *GOS* Geom.42–44 and Arch.1: Pl7d,e,f and 8a

18. Morrison and Coates (1986)=*AT* Pl47

173 and 174
Fragments of the Nineveh relief preserved in the British Museum. This relief was carved as a decoration of Sennacherib's palace at Nineveh to celebrate his invasion of Phoenicia and the evacuation of Tyre to Cyprus by its ruler King Luli in 701 BC.

173 (top) shows some of the round (symmetrical) fleet auxiliaries (ker-kouroi) carrying passengers on deck and

wards in the relief from the palace of Sennacherib at Nineveh depicting the evacuation of Tyre in 701 BC in a fleet composed of longships (with armed forefoot) and auxiliaries (symmetrical) both rowed at two levels. The vertical line (in one case the vertical band) indicates the termination of the metal (iron or more usually bronze) sheath of the forefoot. This line or band is absent in Geometric but occurs regularly in Archaic vasepaintings, e.g. most clearly on the early fifth century red figure painting of Odysseus and the Sirens.[18] The first secure appearance of the effective ram simultaneously with the multiple-level oarsystems in the warships of the Nineveh relief confirms the suspected causal relationship of the former with the latter.

Fragments of the Nineveh palace relief (a) and (b) (after 701 BC) and (c) a fragment of Geometric vasepainting (735–710 BC)

(a) Detail showing fleet auxiliaries (Figure 173)
(b) Detail showing an oared warship (Figure 174)
(c) Fragment of Geometric pottery from the Acropolis: Athens National Museum 265: (Figure 175)

The relief in Sennacherib's palace at Nineveh showed the evacuation in 701 BC by King Luli, under threat from Sennacherib's land invasion, of people from Tyre and Sidon by sea to Cyprus. The ships of the evacuation fleet are under oar and of two distinct types, but with certain common features. All are rowed at two levels en echelon. The uppermost oars are worked over the topwale, the lower through oarports in the sides of the lower hull. Oarsmen, disproportionately large, are visible at the upper oars in the open-sided 'rooms'. All the ships have a canopy deck to accommodate *epibatai* with a substantial bulwark hung with shields outboard, over which appear the heads and shoulders of disproportionately large human figures.

rowed by oarsmen at two levels, an upper level of oarsmen visible in open 'rooms', a lower level working oars through oarports in the hull. 174 (bottom) shows the best preserved of the (asymmetrical) warships recognisable as such by their forefoot sheathed in (metal) ram. They are shown rowed at two levels in the same way as the auxiliaries while a third level is left unmanned.

175

Three fragments of Attic vase paintings. They indicate the way in which the different levels of oarsmen were depicted (a and b) in the Geometric and (c) in the early Archaic style. They are of importance in enabling the warships in the Nineveh frieze (eg 24) and in the Persian seal (44) to be recognised as threes.

One type of ship, shown in (a) (Figure 173), is upward-curving in the bow as well as in the stern. Being fleet auxiliaries designed to keep up with oared warships they like them have a two-level oarsystem which sacrifices some cargo-carrying capacity for greater power and a short hull.

The other type, shown in (b) (Figure 174), also shows oars worked at two levels, but here the bow is sharply pointed at waterlevel and the forefoot is armed with a [bronze] sheath. These ships, identified by their rams as warships, also stand higher than the other type, having a course of rectangular hatched areas alternating with open spaces below the bulwark with its shields and above the stanchions rising between the visible upper oarsmen's rooms. The puzzling additional course visible in this Phoenician warship is fortunately explained by the near-contemporary group of Late-Geometric fragments of vasepaintings mentioned above, which have been shown to depict un-decked longships with two-level oarsystems. The most important of these is shown in (c) (Figure 175). It depicts a similar course of alternate hatched areas and open spaces but with the difference that the open spaces there are the 'rooms' of visible oarsmen.

The otherwise inexplicable additional course of open areas alternating with hatched areas appearing in the warship is shown then to be the unmanned upper-most oar-level of a Phoenician three. It is unmanned since the qualities, speed and manoeuvrability which characterise the three would have been thought unnecessary in an operation (a voyage of about 27 nautical miles) where no naval challenge was expected (Sennacherib having no fleet) and speed would have been restricted to that of the two-level auxiliaries. Furthermore the topweight of the large number of deck passengers may have made an unmanned uppermost oar level desirable, possibly even necessary. Further, it is likely that in such an emergency trained oarsmen rather than ships were in short supply.

The two features, the ram and the additional course leading to greater height above the waterline, which distinguish from each other the two types of ship shown in the relief, in fact express the difference between a bireme fleet auxiliary and front-line three.

If this interpretation is correct, it appears that in the late eighth century BC there was a Phoenician type of decked three with *no outrigger*, with *two* open side courses (at the zygian as well as at the thranite level as distinct from Greek type of furze which has only one) and with thalamian oars rowed through ports in the hull. This three-level oarsystem, as will be seen, by the fifth century was superseded in Phoenicia by another which may be called Corinthian or Greek, but re-appears in the late fourth century with the development of the five. Its occurrence in Phoenicia in the eighth century explains the hitherto puzzling attribution by Clement of Alexandria[19] of the invention of the three (*trikrotos naus*) to the Sidonians. Clement is a late and perhaps not very reliable witness but he is likely to have derived his information from the *Inventions* of Philostephanos of Cyrene who lived in the third century BC and was a pupil of the poet Kallimachos.

The Spartan ivory plaque: 650–600 BC (Figure 176)

The plaque represents the starboard side of a longship carefully and, within the usual limits, realistically. The sharply-pointed forefoot is in strong contrast to the blunt boar's head forefoot of Attic black-figure ship portraits (Figures 177, 178 and 179). The sharp forefoot and in particular the row of round shields along the ship's side are Phoenician characteristics. The ship is shown at the point of arrival, beached stern first with a man disembarking greeted by a woman. The scene presumably illustrates a story, in which the large bird (?*kokkyx*, cuckoo) observing the greeting with interest may have some significance.

176

The ivory plaque found in the temple of Artemis Orthia at Sparta (650–600 BC. The word orthaia *written right to left on the bow of the ship depicted is an indication of the plaque's dedication to Artemis (cf. GROW Ch.5.13: the similar inscription of ISIS on a ship named* Dioscuros).

19. *Stromateis* I.16.76

177

Theseus's return depicted on the François vase by the Kleitias painter. The exaggerated size of the human figures make it difficult to decide the type of longship shown. If the section of eight 'rooms' represents about half the ship it is a triacontor (fifteen oarsmen a side), if it represents about a third it is a pentecontor (twenty-five a side).

There are nine men shown aboard. In the stern facing forward the helmsman sits at two rudders, one raised the other down. Facing him and seated are two figures one behind the other and behind them two figures standing on either side of the mast on the median gangway and with their hands on the halliards. Forward of them there is a seated figure wearing a helmet and forward of him a figure standing with his hands on the forestay. On the bow platform a squatting figure with rod and line is playing a fish and on the forefoot another squatting figure is relieving himself (and possibly indicating a function of the forefoot as the primitive heads).

The process of arrival is shown with an Homeric particularity. The ship has been rowed to the beach stern first and the oars shipped, the sails have been furled (with brailing ropes hanging down) and the sailyard is about to be lowered by letting go the halliards. Then the mast will be lowered by letting go the forestay. There is also a hint of the backstay.

The great exaggeration of the size of the figures and the suggestion by the single helmeted seated figure that the three seated figures represent a larger number both of oarsmen and fighting men make it difficult to guess the type of longship the artist is showing in shorthand. The five shields and the five oarsmen's 'rooms' in the post and rail course on the ship's topwale may also stand for much larger numbers. Nevertheless as it stands the plaque gives much more information about an open seventh-century longship and its navigation than would have been given by an attempt at greater realism in so small a space.

Longship portraits of the sixth and fifth centuries BC

The portrayal of the longships with one level of oars reached a peak of realism in the Attic black-figure vasepainting of the sixth century. Kleitias's *volute krater* of 570–560 BC (Figure 177), found in incomplete fragments, showed an Athenian oared warship

178

One of five careful portraits of a long-ship on the inner rim of an Attic black-figure dinos by the Antimenes painter (530–510 BC). Apart from the exaggerated human figures it is realistic. The 'room' of each of the fifteen oarsmen is entirely taken up by his head. The oars are rowed through oarports below the topwale.

bringing Theseus home. One fragment shows the bow decorated as a boar's head. A mouth line and two vertical strap-like markings (as in the warships of the Nineveh relief) indicate the fastenings of the bronze sheath of the ram. A low bow screen has a rail above which extends forward of the high stem post. Other fragments put together show the stern and eight 'rooms' of the sternwards section of a light undecked longship. The eighteen crew members shown are exaggerated in size so that it is difficult to guess whether a half or a little less than a third of the rest of the ship is shown. Assuming that three or four of the figures are ship's officers not oarsmen, in the first case the ship is a triacontor, in the second a pentecontor. On general grounds a pentecontor might be expected of Theseus but there may not be space for seventeen rooms between the two fragments.

The helmsman is seated in the gently upcurving stern with the usual stern railing of two horizontal and two vertical bars on each side. Forward from the stern railing on each side there runs a slightly lower hull railing with regular uprights marking the oarsmen's 'rooms'. Below the topwale a lower wale is shown. The oars have been shipped.

The finely drawn longship on the inner rim of the black-figure dinos by the Antimenes painter of 530–510 BC (Figure 178) is certainly a triacontor. In it the human figures having to be accommodated at sea are more nearly proportionate to the ship. The helmsman is seated aft of the massive stocks of the two rudders. The

179

A ship portrait on the inner rim of an Attic black-figure dinos by Exekias (550–530 BC). The artist intended to represent a long ship with twenty-five oarsmen a side working their oars through oarports to gain, like the ship in 28, the greater protection given by a higher topwale. The oars however have been carelessly shown as coming quite unrealistically over the topwale and leaving the oarports unmanned. A ship with fifty oarsmen a side is unknown.

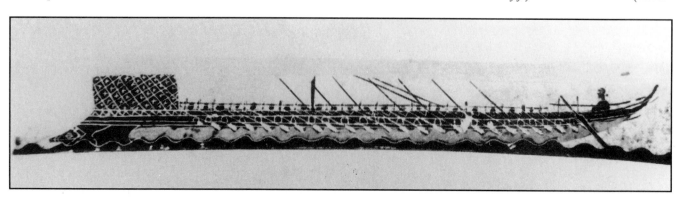

180

Two fragments of a sculpted panel (metope) from the Treasury of Sicyon at Delphi. The scene shows the bow of the Argo *with two horsemen (the Dioscuroi) standing in front of it. Since the Argonauts number fifty the ship is a pentecontor.*

fifteen oarsmen on the starboard side are seated so that their heads appear in the room-spaces of the hull rail and their oars emerge unrealistically high from semicircular oarports between the top and lower wales. The bow has a screened foredeck and a boar's head forefoot on which the bronze sheath fastenings are apparent. The mast is stepped, and the sail, too high to be shown, is certainly brailed up to the yard.

With this picture of a triacontor the very similar picture of a pentecontor on the inner rim of an Attic black-figure dinos by Exekias (Figure 179) may be compared. The helmsman sits rather far aft of the rudder looms. The heads of the twenty-three (for twenty-five) oarsmen on the port side are shown in a more realistic size than in Figure 178 in the 'rooms' marked by the uprights of the side rail; and below the topwale but realistically in relation to the heads in the 'rooms' there is a course of twenty-four (for twenty-five) oarports. The oars, however (twenty-three for twenty-five) have been inserted carelessly (? by another hand) as if they were all worked over the toprail, the oarports being neglected. Since a ship fifty oars a side is not known, it cannot be the case that this is a two-level ship (with the lower level unmanned).

*   *   *

In the late Geometric period (735–710 BC) fragments of pottery show that ships with oars at two levels, said to have been invented in Ionia at Erythrae, were known in mainland Greece; and, as has been seen, at the beginning of the seventh-century BC longships of three levels appear in a Phoenician fleet with round ships of two levels as fleet auxiliaries. The first realistic representation of a two-level *longship* is shown in a relief, which survives in two fragments, of the bow of the *Argo* in the Delphi museum dated in the second half of the seventh century BC (Figure 180). In the first fragment the ship is plainly beached with a horse and rider standing across the forefoot. Aft from the forefoot a wale of three timbers runs aft. The second fragment shows the triple wale as the lowest wale above the keel and between it and a second wale above it a space in which there are two oarports, one the space of an interscalmium aft of the other. Above the second wale and between it and the topwale en echelon is another oarport. The position of these oarports is exactly confirmed by a detailed portrait of the stern of the *Argo* (Figure 181) (as always a pentecontor since there were fifty Argonauts) shown as a two-level ship. The fact that

181
A scene depicting the stern of the Argo *engraved on an Etruscan bronze casket from Ficoroni in the Villa Giulia museum in Rome and dated towards the end of the fourth century* BC. *Like the sculpted panel at Delphi (30) the casket shows the* Argo *as a longship (a pentecontor) rowed through oarports at two levels.*

both ships represent the *Argo* is an irrelevant coincidence, evidence only for a tradition, perhaps started by the *metope* exhibited at Delphi, that the *Argo* was a two-level oared ship. The importance of the two portraits is that they demonstrate that the second level of oars was placed in the longship en echelon *below* the original single level and not as some have argued above it with an outrigger.[20] There are other less realistic two-dimensional portraits of two-level longships in black-figure vasepaintings dated towards the end of the sixth century[21] which do not quarrel with the conclusions reached.

The reason for the development of two levels of oars must lie in the area of the longship's efficiency as a warship and be closely connected with the development first of a deck to enable a warship to engage an enemy ship at sea and secondly of the ram as the principal offensive weapon. In the first recorded battle at sea involving oared ships equipped with the ram, the Phocaeans fought a combined fleet of Carthaginians and Etruscans off Sardinia (535 BC).[22] The Phocaeans won, but lost sixty ships and had another twenty made useless from losing their rams. If they were using the pentecontors in which they had taken themselves and their families to the west a few years before under the threat of Persian invasion, these would have been ships of a single oar level with plenty of room under the thwarts for gear, victuals and baggage. Consequently they would have been slow in acceleration and manoeuvre and thus unable to ram the enemy from the most favourable angle. It seems more likely at that date that they had built the new two-level pentecontor and had learnt their first lesson in the tactics of ramming. This subject engaged the attention of naval tacticians for the next century.

Once the longship was armed with a bronze ram, development was directed towards the best possible power:weight ratio. By sitting a longship's fifty oarsmen in two files on each side, and at two levels instead of one, there was a sacrifice of space below the thwarts where gear, booty, etc, was normally stored, but a great gain in the reduction of weight with a much shortened hull. The asymmetrical fleet auxiliary (*kerkouros*) would become less efficient as such by sacrificing to speed space for cargo and passengers, but that would be reckoned less important than the ability to keep up with a fleet of twos or of threes rowing as twos. A fleet had to have more of them.

20. In particular H T Wallinga (1993) and (1995)

21. *GOS* p109–112, Arch.85–89, Pls 19–20, Figs 28 and 29. There is a relevant passage in the *Cyclops* of Euripides (perhaps before 438 BC) which has not yet been brought into the discussion. Odysseus has succeeded in escaping alone from the Cyclops' cave. He is planning with the chorus of satyrs to rescue his companions and get away in his 50-oared longship. In lines 466–468 he offers to take the satyrs with him: 'And then, when I have embarked you, your friends and the old man, into the hold of the black ship (*neōs melainēs koilon embēsas skaphos*), I shall take you away from this country with twice as many oars (*diplaisi kōpais*) [as those with which I came]'. He does not say how he will get the oars, but Odysseus *polumēchanos* could be trusted to find them somehow.

There are three passages which confirm that *neōs..koilon skaphos* means the hold of a ship. Herodotus 8.119 'to send down the passengers from the deck (*ek tou katastrōmatos*) into the *koilē naus*'; Xenophon *Hellenica* 1.6.19: 'changing the position of the decksoldiers (*epibatai*) from deck to the *koilē naus*'; and in particular Demosthenes 32.5: 'Hegestratos . . . at night went down into the *koilē naus* and made a hole in the bottom of the ship (*edaphos*: see p12 above)'. In the 'under the thwarts (*zuga*)' on which the oarsmen sat Alcinous stowed the presents he was sending back with Odysseus on the Phaeacian pentecontor (Od.13.21). In a two-level four swamped at the battle of Mylae the *zygioi* escape by breaking through the deck and the other level of oarsmen (plainly the *thalamioi*) are drowned (see Ch.X p18). There can be no doubt that the second file of oars was added below and between the original oarsmen seated on the thwarts (*zuga*), it in the hold.

22. Herodotus 1.166.12

The Warships of the Mediterranean 500 to 31 BC

The three: historical background

During the period of colonisation by Greek and Phoenician settlers of large areas of the Mediterranean and Black Sea, Athens, becoming prosperous and populous, was sending out her surplus people, as Thucydides wrote[1] 'to Ionia and most of the islands' (of the Aegean); and Miletus, an equally prosperous Greek city of Caria, was founding colonies on the coasts of the Black Sea and establishing with Corinth a trading post at Naucratis in Egypt. Corinth at the same time was sending colonists first to Corcyra and then to Italy and Sicily. The Greek settlers met competition in the east from the Phoenician cities of the Levant and in the west from Tyre's colony of Carthage and from the Etruscans. This competition, leading to engagements at sea, resulted in the development of the longship, as has been seen, into a vessel first equipped with a deck for fighting men and with a ram and then shortened and rowed more efficiently by oarsmen at two levels.

Thucydides covers these centuries in a few sentences. After speaking of the period of colonisation he says that with the acquisition of wealth the Greek cities began to build fleets and rely on sea power. Corinth, well known for her wealth, led in this respect. 'She was the first city in Greece where threes were built' and the Corinthian shipwright Ameinocles 'appears to have built four ships for the Samians'. Thucydides proceeds to speak of the first sea battle (dated about 664 BC) as having taken place between the Corinthians and the Corcyraeans' implying the use of threes in it. It would then appear that the Corinthian three was built at about the same time as, or not long after, the type built in Phoenicia. Pharaoh Necho (610–595 BC), who was known as a philhellene, having close ties with Corinth and Samos as well as with Phoenicia, is said by Herodotus[2] to have built a fleet of threes on the Nile for service in the Mediterranean and on the Arabian Gulf for service presumably against piracy in the Indian Ocean. It is significant that Thucydides gives 'cleaning up piracy' as the next achievement of Corinth's new fleet after the sea battle against Corcyra. 'The Ionians also' he says, 'later possessed a numerous fleet' at the time of the Persian kings Cyrus and Cambyses (559–529 BC) and 'for some time took control of their own seas against Cyrus' whose ships would have been Phoenician. He

1. 1.13.3
2. 2.159.1

151

mentions Polycrates, ruler of Samos (572–540 BC),[3] as possessing a strong fleet (certainly containing threes) and concludes his list of 'the most powerful fleets' with the statement that the Phocaeans when colonising Massalia (600 BC) defeated the Carthaginians in a sea battle. He continues: 'even these, it appears, . . . employed only a few threes and were still equipped with pentecontors and [other] longships. It was only a short time before the Persian wars and the death of Darius that the autocratic rulers in parts of Sicily and the Corcyraeans had threes in great numbers. In fact those (that I have mentioned) were the last considerable fleets to be built before Xerxes' expedition'.

The story of the three's slow rise to its dominating position in the fifth century is understandable. Development of the three-level oarsystem was in pursuit of the same aim as that which had produced the two-level system, achievement of a power/weight ratio more favourable to good acceleration and manoeuvrability. The Nineveh relief appears to show three-level warships but its trustworthiness in the matter of the number of oars in each file is doubtful. If, however, it is to be taken at face value and there actually were eight in each of the lower files as Figure 174 shows and eight or nine are to be inferred in the uppermost level which is not manned, it would appear that the designer had followed the precedent of the two and divided twenty-five, the number of oarsmen in each file of the pentecontor, into three rather than two, producing a ship with files of eight, eight, nine or eight, eight, eight. The resulting ship being under-powered embodied an idea which clearly needed further development; and the necessity for a period of development explains the length of time before it became at all widely adopted. It would also not have been much more expensive to build than a two level pentecontor and is, therefore, not the ship which Thucydides said that only the richest states could afford.

The three ultimately developed, no doubt by experiment in Phoenicia and mainland Greece, and adopted in Athens by the fifth century was a much bolder application of the three-level oarsystem in a much larger ship with more than three times the number of oars which had been worked in a pentecontor. It is not therefore surprising that this design took some time to evolve, and when evolved was only built and employed in small numbers, since it demanded skilful and expensive building and skilful and expensive operation. However, these ships proved extremely successful: under skilled handling by Athenian officers and enthusiastically rowed, they saved Greece from conquest by Persia and enabled Athens to establish a naval hegemony in the Aegean which lasted for more than a century. It remains to examine such evidence as there is for its evolution. By a most unfortunate coincidence the black-figure style of vase-painting, in which ships were often represented for their own sake on the inner rim of a *dinos*, was abandoned at the moment when the three became a regular part of Athenian life. The red-figure style, which tended to present mythical scenes, took its place. The single really informative red-figure painting of the stern of a three is accordingly another anachronistic presentation of the *Argo* (Figure 187).

182

A coin struck by Sidon, the leading maritime city of Phoenicia, in the last half of the fifth century BC. At this date the longship portrayed can hardly be other than a three although no oars are shown.

183

A coin struck by Sidon in the early fourth century. The innovation of a 'bank' of oars below a longship's hull is unrealistic but by the use of triple 'stepping' the three levels of oars are indicated, at this date at Sidon only of a three.

The three in Phoenicia and Athens

Sidonian fifth-century coinage (Figures 182 and 183)

In the fifth century BC the Phoenicians and the Palestinian Syrians were the leading naval powers in the eastern Mediterranean and provided the largest contingent, 300 threes, for Xerxes' invasion fleet in 480 BC. The next largest, 200 threes, was the Egyptian. In Phoenicia,[4] Sidon was the leading naval city with Tyre in second place. Herodotus[5] related that Queen Artemisia of Halicarnassus (in Caria, another important naval province) rated her ships in Xerxes' fleet second only to the Sidonian, and her reputation at the end of the century was no less.[6] Evidence of Sidon's pride

3. See *AT* p40 n.3

4. Herodotus 8.67.2, 7.44; Diodorus 10.44

5. Herodotus 8.99.1

6. Euripides *Helen* 1451–4, 1530–4

184

A coin struck by Sidon in the early fourth century. The double 'stepping' of the oar bank in this coin shows that the longship portrayed has two levels of oars. It is unlikely but not impossible that the ship shown is a four, an innovation which Sidon might wish to advertise, but there is no other evidence of fours in Phoenicia at this early date. The ship is perhaps more likely to have been a two-level pentecontor.

185

A crudely designed fifth century coin of Arados, an island city like Tyre off the Phoenician coast. The ship shown must be a three.

7. *LSRS* Pl32a and b

in her ships, of which the best were threes and thus most likely to be exhibited, is shown by their appearance on almost all the coins minted before Alexander came on the scene in 332 BC. These coins provide the only extant representations of them.

The sharp profile of the Nineveh Phoenician ships is repeated. In the last half of the fifth century the Sidonian ships portrayed, which can only be threes, appear without oars. They show (e.g. Figure 182) a deck hung along its edge with shields in the Phoenician manner and a large 'eye' aft of the ram, a bow ornament and a *stylis* placed across the upward curve of the stern. Below the line of shields there is an open space divided into 'rooms' by the stanchions supporting the canopy deck. Below the topwale there is a line which may indicate the lower edge of an an outrigger for the uppermost file of oarsmen. There is no sign of oarports for the middle file of oarsmen below that line or of oarports for the lowest file between the two narrow parallel wales running fore and aft lower still. Oarports are a small detail which a coin engraver might reasonably omit.

The Sidonian coinage of the early fourth century (e.g. Figure 183) shows a marked change. Oars are now shown in the pictures of ships: they do not emerge realistically or semi-realistically from the ship's side, but are placed quite unrealistically (yet as a formalised row of oars) under the keel. There they are 'stepped' in three rows to show a three-level ship (at this date certainly a three) and in two rows (Figure 184) to show a two-level ship. (For 'stepping' to indicate three levels of oars see the Pozzuoli reliefs[7] of a much later date, first century BC–first century AD).

Arados coin (Figure 185)

Arados was a city of Palestinian Syria, on a small island off the coast, like Tyre, and proud of her warships. Her coin gives a crude and conventional representation of a three. The deck is hung with shields and supported by stanchions dividing a recessed area into 'rooms'. The stanchions stand above three horizontal courses, the lowest of which is a wale terminating forward in a ram. Above this wale there is a recessed slit in which are a number of short uprights, probably brackets supporting the outrigger which is indicated by the two horizontal lines above them. The stanchions butt onto the upper of these horizontal lines which terminates forward in the 'eye'/*epotis*.

The Vienna fragment of an Attic red-figure cup (Figure 186)

This fragment, which is in the Vienna University Museum, is about contemporary with the fifth century Phoenician coinage. It shows part of the side of a Greek three. The deck-rail is not hung with shields and the deck stanchions curve to suggest perspective and a narrow deck. The stanchions appear to butt onto two strongly marked horizontals which are likely to indicate an outrigger (but with no detail added of uprights or tholepins). Below are two sets of parallel wales framing courses of oarports for the two lower files of oars. The lowest oarport gives an indication of an *askoma*. The vertical lines seen inboard of the deckrails and continued in the space between the deck stanchions may be ropes hanging down from the yard and through a slit in the deck above the gangway running fore and aft. On the hull below the wale there is a decoration of uncertain kind.

The Ruvo vase (Figure 187)

An Attic red-figure *volute krater* by the Talos painter dated at the end of the fifth century shows the port side of the stern of a three. The human figures are greatly exaggerated to portray a scene in the story of the Argonauts. The deck of the ship has a low rail. Beneath it, as in the ship of the Vienna fragment, the deck stanchions curve down and inboard of the outrigger butting onto a middle wale which runs fore and aft below the course of oarports of the upper (zygian) file of oars. Straight

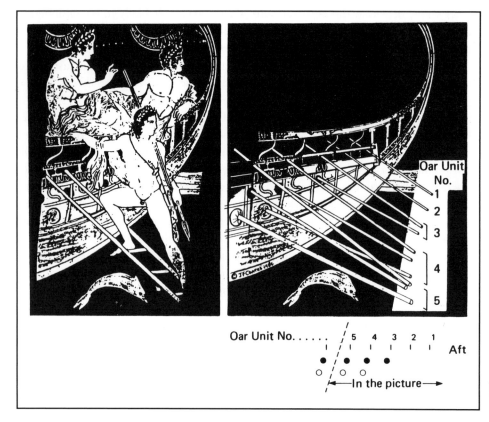

Oar Unit No.
1
2
3
4
5

Oar Unit No. . . . . . / 5 4 3 2 1
Aft

In the picture

187

◄◄ *The Furtwangler drawing of the scene painted on an Attic red-figure volute krater by the Talos painter in the Jatta collection at Ruvo in Apulia. It is dated at the end of the fifth century and includes a detailed picture of the stern of the* Argo, *shown, anachronistically, with a three-level oarsystem. At this date the system can only be that of a three.*

◄ *The system shown is clearer if the human figures, greatly exaggerated in size, are removed and the implied oars are added.*

brackets support the outer face of the outrigger (on which the ladder rests) butting onto the lower wale indicated by a pair of doubled parallel lines. The single larger oarport for an oar of the lowest file (thalamian) shows what must be an indication of the leather sleeve (*askoma*) with which it is known to be regularly equipped.[8] The outer face of the outrigger shows a short vertical (merging with the after of the two deck stanchions) connecting the parallel horizontals and a tholepin. The details of this stern are carefully indicated but with a somewhat puzzling method of perspective. They are corroborated precisely, but with a different method of perspective and with oarsmen and oars, in the Lenormant relief fragment.

The Lenormant relief (Figure 188)

This relief found on the Acropolis at Athens and now in the Acropolis Museum is dated like the Ruvo vase to the end of the fifth century BC. In its completed state the relief would have been coloured making the oarsystem easier to envisage. It shows a section of the starboard side of an oared warship which in view of its date can only be a three. On the deck, which appears to have no rail, there are traces of reclining figures. Seven of the uppermost file of (thranite) oarsmen are visible between the deck stanchions which are shown curving aft, partly as perspective and partly to fit the oarsmen's curving backs. Their oars are near the beginning of the stroke, slightly forward of the tholepin (seen as a vertical post connecting the horizontal timbers of the outrigger face), to which they would have been secured with a leather strop. There are other vertical posts in the outrigger face, which stands in higher relief than the wales. The stanchions may also be seen as they stretch down to butt onto the upper wale of the hull's side. From beneath the outrigger the middle file of (zygian) oars (needing colour to show the oarports) may be seen to emerge and reach the water forward of the thranite oars. Forward of the zygian oars and shown as slanting in harmony with them there is a bracket supporting the outrigger and butting onto

186

A fragment of an Attic red-figure cup of about 450 BC. It shows part of the (?port) side of a three.

8. *AT* p169–170

188

The Lenormant relief in the Acropolis Museum in Athens, dated like the Ruvo vase to the end of the fifth century BC. It shows a midships section of the starboard side of a three-level warship; and at that date, like the Ruvo vase, it can only be a three. Unlike the Ruvo vase it does fortunately show oars at three levels; and it is demonstrable that the two representations (187 and 188) share the same oarsystem. They have provided the basis on which, helped by information from literature and inscriptions, a reconstructed three has been built and operated (see p.169).

the lower wale as in the Ruvo vase stern. Forward of the bracket the lowest (thalamian) oar emerges above the lower wale. Colour would have been needed to show the thalamian oarport and *askoma*.

Apart from the departures from realism occasioned by the attempts at perspective the Lenormant relief and the Ruvo vase picture are sufficiently realistic and in harmony for a reconstruction to be based on them and on such other details as archaeology and contemporary literature provides (see p.169 below). The most important of the former are the dimensions of a three required by the remains of the Zea shipsheds, and information relating to threes concerning the great variety of gear and about the number and length of oars in the three categories.

This reconstruction is not out of harmony with the Vienna fragment although the latter is much less informative in details of the oarsystem. It does however show the deck rail which is a feature of later threes as shown on coins and probably the narrow deck which, Thucydides says,[9] still characterised the Athenian ships at Salamis.

It is of greater importance that this reconstruction does not quarrel with the representations of threes on contemporary Phoenician coins. Although, not surprisingly in the case of coins, the outrigger is never plainly attested in them, and oars either not at all or by an unrealistic convention, the conclusion is that the three-level ships in Phoenicia of the fifth century BC followed what might be called the Corinthian design, influenced probably by the eastern Greeks. This may be the significance of Thucydides' remark, in the context of building the first threes in Greece at Corinth, that the Corinthian shipwright Ameinocles 'made four ships for the Samians'.

From the three to the thirty

Three-level longships in the Nineveh frieze design (Figures 189–191)

In the fourth century BC a type of three-level ship resembling the threes of the Nineveh frieze undoubtedly appeared in Phoenician cities. The first and clearest pictures of this type of ship are shown on coins of Arados dated 350–300 BC (Figure

189

Coins of Arados struck in the years 350–323 BC. They show ships with shields hung over the deck rail (the top line) and beneath them two open side courses. No oars are shown.

190

A coin struck in the Phoenician city of Byblos 340–333 BC. It shows armed men of exaggerated size on the deck of a ship with a guard rail. Beneath is an open course of oarsmen's rooms, a course of shields and a lower open course of rooms.

191

A gem from the Phoenician city of Amathus in Cyprus. The ship shown has the head and shoulders of three armed men unrealistically (even if sitting) on deck. Over the edge of the deck and covering the open oarsmen's rooms below it (cf 42) is a course of shields. Below the upper course of rooms there is a lower course of rooms above the topwale. The oars are shown in the Sidonian manner, triple stepped below the keel.

9. Thucydides 1.14.3

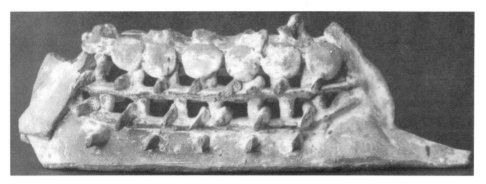

192
The Erment model of a ship with three levels of oars: 350–300 BC. This model gives three-dimensional confirmation to the interpretation of the Amathus gem given above. The stubs of oars are in the positions indicated, rowed at the lowest level through oarports and at the higher two levels over the sills of open rooms. The edge of the deck is hung with shields. In the floor of the deck are holes in which the missing figures of armed men could have been slotted.

189). The stern curves up sharply and is crossed by a *stylis* of the usual kind. They show the usual Phoenician row of shields hung over the deck rail, and below them an open space divided into 'rooms'. Below them there is a horizontal line and below it, unlike the fifth-century coin of Arados described above, a second open space divided into 'rooms'. The representation of the hull is minimal and the bow in both cases has been much worn.

A Byblos coin from the reign of Ayimel (Figure 190: 340–333 BC) shows three armed men on a deck with a railing. Below it deck-stanchions divide the open space into 'rooms' at the bottom of which there is a course of larger shields, and below them again stanchions dividing a lower open space above a bulging but shallow hull. With slight differences the oarsystem shown seems to be the same as that on the Arados coin above.

A similar oarsystem appears in a ship depicted on an engraved gem of Amathus dated 340–330 BC (Figure 191). The two courses of open 'rooms', as in the ship on the Byblos coin, have no row of shields above them; and the three fighting men, greatly out of proportion with the ship, are rendered only with heads and shoulders.

If these three ship portraits represent threes they must indicate a revival of the system shown rather crudely in the warships of King Luli's evacuation fleet more than four centuries before. Such a revival is unlikely, since Sidon at any rate had apparently employed threes with the Corinthian oarsystem very successfully for two hundred years. It is more likely that these portraits represent a new three-level ship to be advertised, the five. In 351–350 BC there was a short-lived Sidonian fleet employing threes and fives. In 332 BC at the siege of Tyre the Tyrians, and in Alexander's fleet the Cypriot and Phoenician kings (including probably the king of Amathus), but not the Sidonians, had fives. The appearance of the new kind of coin-portrait and the new kind of ship in Phoenicia at much the same time is a significant coincidence.

In the Erment model (Figure 192) dated 350–300 BC, there is strong, three-dimensional, corroboration of the existence of the oarsystem with two courses of open rooms. It was bought 'in the Egyptian market' and its date is accordingly imprecise and its provenance uncertain. The model represents a warship with a pronounced forefoot acceptable as a ram and with an aft-curving stem. The stubs of oars survive at three levels: the top and middle levels are open and the oars are rowed over sills. At the lowest level they are rowed through oarports. There is no outrigger. There is a deck, and a bulwark with a row of shields hung over it in the Phoenician manner. The six holes in the deck surface (visible from on top) are likely to be slots into which figures of six disproportionately large soldiers (as shown in the Byblos coins and the Amathus gem) were probably fitted. There can be little doubt that the model is Phoenician and that it shows a Phoenician type of ship, possibly a three, most probably a five, of the last half of the fourth century BC.

193, 194

Seal impressions from the treasury of Persepolis dated widely from 520–331 BC. Though the impressions are imperfect and much damaged 193 (left) may be recognised as representing a three-level ship in the Greek design with an outrigger and a single open course of rooms; and 194 (right) as representing a three-level ship of the Phoenician design (a three or a five).

The Persian seals ([a] Figure 193, [b] Figure 194)

Among the seal impressions found in the treasury of Persepolis there are two of particular interest. Their dating is very wide, between the building of the treasury in 520 BC and its destruction on Alexander's invasion in 331 BC. Both show oared warships.

(a) In this impression the ship has a high curving stern, a seated helmsman and two large rudders. On a deck and continuous foredeck there stand four soldiers of exaggerated size recalling those on the Byblos coins, the Amathus gem and probably on the Erment model. There is a mast, a sail loosely brailed up and rigging. The die appears to have been twisted slightly when the impression was being made resulting in two positions for the mast and distortion of the lines on the hull. The deck line shows no shields and there appears to be a sidescreen masking the greater part of the deck stanchions in the open space below the deck. Below the open space there is an outrigger, its lines distorted by the twisting. From the outrigger oars slope downwards and aft and are continued beneath the hull. They are stepped at their extremities to show, as Casson observed, that the ship has a three-level system. The hull has a sharp forefoot in Phoenician style and a slight indication of fastening for the ram sheath. It may be safely identified as a three of the 'Corinthian' design probably of the fifth century BC.

(b) An impression from another seal shows a warship with oars in the Sidonian style placed symbolically all under the ship. The damage to the bottom of the impression makes it impossible to say whether the oars are stepped indicating that it is, as seems likely, a three or five. There are four soldiers of exaggerated size on the deck. Under the deck there are wide vertical structures alternating with open spaces above a wale. Under them there is a second course of the same kind above another wale very close to the keel. The impression is much damaged in this area but it does nevertheless appear that there are two open courses of rooms in which the rooms are separated from each other by vertical structures. There is no sign of an outrigger. There could be a row of shields at the edge of the deck but the damage makes it impossible to say so with any certainty.

It is remarkable that these two seals, as with some difficulty interpreted, contrast (a) the Corinthian type three with (b) a type which may be either a late sixth-century Phoenician three or a Phoenician five of a date after 351 BC.

The polyremes

In the naval history of the ancient world the fourth century BC was the great age of innovation set on foot by the introduction of the polyreme at the beginning of the fourth century BC in Syracuse by Dionysius I. The word polyreme is a convenient modern term for oared warships rowing more than one man to an oar. The five was a natural development of the three by double-manning the two upper files of oars. The four was invented, Aristotle said,[10] by the Carthaginians and as the natural development of the two-level oar system by double-manning at both levels was a less ambitious and probably later step.

Dionysius was planning to drive the Carthaginians out of Sicily. By 399 BC[11] he had started to acquire the necessary armaments to engage 'the most powerful people in Europe' . . . 'assembling by decree craftsmen from the cities he ruled and attracting them with high wages from Italy and even from territory ruled by Carthage. He planned to manufacture a great quantity of arms and missiles of all kinds and, in addition to them threes and fives, although a ship of the latter type had not at that time been built'. Later Diodorus repeats himself probably quoting from a different source:[12] 'In fact the catapult was invented at this moment in Syracuse, when the best craftsmen had been brought together into one place. As a result the craftsmen brought a spirit of competition to their work which was unsurpassable, and invented many new missiles and original devices of great potential usefulness. Dionysius also began to build threes and ships of the five type, being the first to devise this latter type of warship (this statement may imply that his previous fleet consisted of pentecontors). The fact was that Dionysius was aware that a three had been built first in Corinth and was keen to increase the size of warships built in Syracuse which had been colonised from Corinth'.

Dionysius's naval building programme does not seem to have gone ahead very fast. In 398 BC Dionysius sent a five, the prototype, to Locri to bring back as his bride the daughter of a distinguished Locrian. Eight years later in an attack on Rhegium with fifty ships his flagship was a five and there is no mention of any others. At the siege of Motya in 397 he had 'a little less than 200 warships' with no mention of threes or fives. After the fall of Motya, where the catapult was employed successfully from the land against ships. Dionysius sent his fleet commander Leptines to lie in wait for the expected Carthaginian invasion fleet[13] which when it arrived the following spring numbered 400 ships. No Syracusan fleets with more than 100 threes are mentioned until the end of Dionysis's reign in 367 BC when he had assembled for an attack on Carthaginian territory in Sicily a large army and 300 threes. No fives are there mentioned by Diodorus. But Aelian[14] speaks of Dionysius II 'having his rule well fortified by the possession of not less than 400 ships, sixes and fives'. It is inconceivable that Dionysios I could have left his son 400 sixes and fives. Aelian, in the second and third centuries AD, may have seen evidence that Dionysius II had fives and one or two sixes in the fleet he inherited and envisaged, through his Roman conditioning, something like e.g. the Roman Republic's fleet at Ecnomus which consisted of fives with a six for each of the consuls (p.168). Since Pliny[15] quotes Xenagoras as authority for the invention of the six in Syracuse, it may well be accepted that at the end of his life Dionysius returned to his old ambition to assemble a strong military and naval force against the Carthaginians in Sicily and designed one or two sixes as flagships with an oarsystem double-manned at all three levels. When later (256 BC) the Romans built a fleet of fives to invade Carthage each of the two consuls had a six as flagship. Dionysius's invention of the five was important, but perhaps more important for its effect on naval warfare was the invention of the catapult and its use against ships from shore and subsequently on ships against enemy ships.

The design of the Syracusan five and six

Warship types acquired their names from the number of files of oarsmen (or alternatively from the number of oarsmen to each 'room') on each side of the ship. This is

10. Frg 600 Rose

11. Diodorus 14.41.2

12. Diodorus 14.42.1

13. Diodorus 14.53.5

14. *Var.Hist.* 6.12

15. Xenagoras in Pliny *NH* 7.207–8

the only clue to the design of the Syracusan five and six, but it is at least reasonable to assume that both were modifications of the three with the use of double-manning at two and then three levels, in both cases therefore retaining the outrigger. They would then both, from a side view, appear similar to the three in their main external features, the necessary internal alterations to accommodate the additional oarsmen being invisible. No depictions of Syracusan three-level ships are however preserved.

It has been mentioned that ships with the name *pentērēs* (five) are recorded with threes in the fleet of Sidon in 351 BC. Unfortunately in the period of Tennes's reign 357/6–348/7 BC the standard of coining declined: Betlyon (1982) speaks of 'the lack of definition and poor workmanship' and the oars are shown as a single unstepped bank providing no clue to the Sidonian fives. In the earlier reign of Abd'astart I (372–362/1 BC) oars are shown but stepped at two levels, suggesting that the type of which Sidon was then proud was the double-manned four which by that time may have been invented in Carthage and imitated in Phoenicia.

Fives are also mentioned at Alexander's siege of Tyre in 332 BC as flagships of Phoenician kings and also as belonging to Alexander's Macedonian fleet.[16] There is mention of 'the fives he had with him' as well as the 'royal five' (a five belonging to one of the Phoenician kings) in which he led the first approach to the city from Sidon. Fives and fours[17] are also mentioned as in the Tyrian fleet. Seven fives and fifty fours are listed in the Athenian naval inventories of 325/4 BC.

The success of Alexander's naval operations on the Indus and of Nearchos's return voyage to the Persian Gulf, both albeit in ships no bigger than triacontors, encouraged him on his return to conceive ambitious naval plans.[18] 'Vessels of every sort were built for him at Thapsacus (a Syrian city on the Euphrates) and seamen and pilots were recruited from all parts'. Arrian[19] says that he sent a Greek, Herakieides son of Argaios, to Hyrkania at the southern end of the Caspian sea 'taking with him shipwrights, with orders to cut timber in the Hyrcanian mountains and build long-ships both aphract and cataphract *on the Greek model*. For he was seized with a longing to learn about the sea which is called Caspian and Hyrcanian, with what sea it is joined'. Arrian also quotes Alexander's contemporary Aristoboulos[20] as saying that when Alexander entered Babylon he found his fleet there 'made up partly of ships brought from Phoenicia', two fives, three fours, twelve threes and thirty triacontors. Arrian's phrase 'on the Greek model' is gratuitous and should be noted. It implies that there was, as has been seen, a distinction between the Greek and the Phoenician model at this time, and in the case of the cataphract types, threes to sixes, this distinction will become important.

Before his death in June 323 BC Alexander had further naval plans in mind. Curtius[21] gives details of a fleet for the circumnavigation of Arabia and Africa: timber was to be felled in the Lebanon mountains and brought down to Thapsacus where the keels of 700 ships, all sevens, were to be laid down. In his memoranda read after his death were plans 'of which the greatest and most memorable' was to build 1,000 ships 'larger than threes' for a war against Carthage. Pliny[22] attributes the invention of the ten to Alexander. Later in this chapter when it has been possible to distinguish the Greek from the Phoenician/Carthaginian type of five it will be seen that for practical reasons only the Greek type was capable of development into the warships of larger denominations than six, while the Phoenician type of five was not. This may account for Alexander's specification of the Greek model. It has been seen that in the case of the three the Greek model was in fact adopted by Phoenician cities in the fourth century BC and it will be seen that sevens and larger ships were built there towards the end of the century under Macedonian orders and later under Roman orders necessarily by imitation of the Greek model.

16. Arrian 2.22.2ff, Curtius 4.3.11

17. Arrian 2.21.9

18. Plutarch *Alexander* 68

19. Arrian 7.16.1

20. Arrian 7.19.3

21. Curtius 10.1.17

22. Pliny *NH* 7 207–8

The fleets of the successors

The period between the death of Alexander in 323 BC and the recognition of Roman sea power in 198 BC (although until 66 BC still ineffectually challenged) saw the competition for power fought out at sea, first between the fleets of Alexander's successors and finally between Rome and Carthage and Rome's allies and Macedon.

The news of Alexander's death aroused Athens to reassert her independence. A plan to assemble by means of a new Hellenic League a fleet of 200 fours and forty threes was adopted in a mood of patriotic optimism. Antipater, who had been left in charge of affairs in Macedon, was besieged at Larisa near the head of the Malian gulf where 100 threes supported him. There was an unsuccessful attempt by an Athenian fleet of 170 ships to defeat the 100 threes before the main Macedonian fleet guarding the Hellespont could join them: and Athenian hopes were finally ended in defeat by the combined Macedonian fleet at Amorgos.

Of the elder Antigonus, to whom the satrapy of Phrygia had been allocated, Tarn said[23] that he, of all Alexander's successors, 'showed the firmest grasp of the meaning of sea power and the firmest resolution to win it'. His principal rival was Ptolemy, whose province was Egypt and with it the opportunity, which he took without delay, of occupying as much as he could of the area of the Mediterranean essential to sea power: Phoenicia, Koilë Syria, Cyprus, and the maritime cities of Asia Minor. Antigonus's first step was to invade Phoenicia and set up shipyards there, to capture Ptolemy's naval base at Tyre with its warships and to persuade Rhodes to build ships for him. By 315/4 BC[24] he had assembled a fleet of 240 longships made up of ninety fours, ten fives, three nines and ten tens. There were also thirty cataphracts. It must be assumed that the balance of ninety-seven cataphracts were threes. Antigonus seems to have inherited (and later passed on to his son Demetrius) Alexander's interest in the larger cataphracts, necessarily (see p.159) 'on the Greek model'.

This catalogue makes it clear that the four, which the Athenians had clearly favoured in 323 BC, was of the new types the warship of the day. Among the bigger ships after them tens equalled fives in favour.

Cyprus had remained in Ptolemy's possession, first under his ally Seleucus with 100 ships, and later, when Seleucus returned to his province of Syria, under his brother Menelaus, with whom in 315 BC he was able to send there a force of 10,000 men and 100 ships. In 306 BC after much movement and counter-movement on both sides Antigonus decided that the moment had come for him to consolidate his naval power in the eastern Mediterranean ordering his son Demetrius[25] 'to proceed to Cyprus [from Athens] and finish the war with Ptolemy's generals as soon as he could'.

After collecting men and ships in Caria and Cilicia[26] Demetrius crossed to Cyprus with 15,000 soldiers and 400 cavalry and a fleet composed of more than 110 'fast threes' and fifty-three of the heavier stratiötides as well as troop and cavalry transports. The phrase 'heavier stratiötides' distinguishes the bigger ships, fours and upwards, from 'threes which were not fast but carried troops. None of the latter was present at Salamis. The heavier stratiötides in Demetrius's fleet were: seven Phoenician sevens, ten sixes, forty-five fives (including the harbour guard) and thirty Athenian fours. On this battle plan he would have included seventy-eight of his fast threes in the line.

Demetrius drew up his eventual line of battle of 160 ships outside the harbour of the city of Salamis into which Menelaus had withdrawn with his fleet of sixty ships. Ptolemy was approaching from Kition along the coast with his fleet of 140 ships 'of which the largest was a five and the smallest a four' (thus all 'heavier stratiötides), intending to join forces with Menelaus and his sixty ships and thus outnumber the

23. *Antigonus Gonatas* (1913) p72
24. Diodorus 19.62.7–8
25. Diodorus 20.46.5
26. Diodorus 20.47.1
27. 5.203c
28. Theophrastus *Characters* 25.2, Arrian 3.2.4
29. Appian *Mithridates* 92
30. Diodorus 16.61.4
31. Arrian 6.18.2
32. Diodorus 19.65.2
33. Polybius 5.101.2, 16.6.1
34. Appian Punic Wars 8.75
35. See *SSAW* p131 n121
36. Morrison and Coates (1995) = *GROW* 5.11

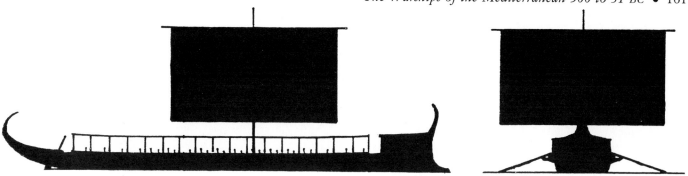

195, 196

Silhouettes of reconstructions by Coates of the hēmiolia and trihēmiolia, the latter as represented in 197, 198, 199, 200 and 201.

enemy. Demetrius however took his ships into position outside the harbour at nightfall on the day before Ptolemy's fleet was expected, stationed a guard of ten fives at the harbour entrance; and prevented the two enemy forces from joining up.

Ptolemy's fleet was defeated and the reason given was that his ships by and large were lower and thus more vulnerable to missiles and less well placed for boarding the higher ships. The battle marks the end of the four's popularity.

Ptolemy II Philadelphus who succeeded Ptolemy I Soter in 283 BC and reigned until 246 BC pursued a very different naval policy, deciding to imitate and compete with the Antigonids in building the larger cataphracts. Athenaeus[27] gives a list of the biggest ships in his dockyard, probably derived from an official document: two thirties, one twenty, four thirteens, two twelves, fourteen elevens, thirty nines, thirty-six sevens, five sixes and seventeen fives while the ships from the four to the *tri-ērēmiolia* (elsewhere termed *trihēmiolia*) were double these in number. It is interesting that most numerous and hence presumably the most useful type among the 'heavier stratiōtides' is the seven with the nine a good second and the five and eleven third and fourth.

It will be convenient here to discuss the ships with the puzzling names of *hēmiolia* and *trihēmiolia* (Figures 195 and 196).

The *hēmiolia* first appears in the fourth century as a pirate craft[28] and it is mentioned in a list Appian gives[29] of ships used by pirates in the first century BC. But as early as 346 BC it appears as a respectable naval type,[30] and Alexander found it useful in his Indus fleet where it appears as a one-level triacontor[31] and Agathocles also used it a few years later.[32] In the next century *hēmiolioi lemboi* occur in Philip V's fleet of 217 BC and later the *hēmioliai* at the battle of Chios were presumably cataphract.[33] An invasion fleet sent to Utica by Rome in the third Punic war consisted of fifty fives and 100 *hēmioliai* both apparently cataphract.[34] The only clue to the oarsystem lies in the name indicating one and a half files of oarsmen a side. Coates in *Greek and Roman Oared Warships* has explained his arrangement as neatly taking advantage of the greater beam amidships of the fine-lined hull of a fast type of ship to add half a file on each side to a ship with one level of oars, and producing an oarsystem in which half the oars (those amidships) could have been double-manned. There is no recognisable iconographical evidence.

The idea of using the midships beam to accommodate an extra half file of oarsmen appears to have been used in a larger ship recognised as a more economical variety of the three and hence called a *triērēmiolia* or *trihēmiolia* for short.

The *trihēmiolia* was, like the four, a favourite type at Rhodes. It was used for commerce raiding during Demetrius's siege. As well as appearing in Ptolemy II's list, evidence for its use there occurs in papyri. Inscriptions show that the type was in use in the Athenian navy at the end of the third and in the first century BC.[35]

The Lindos prow (Figure 197)[36] can safely be taken to represent a *trihēmiolia*. On the lateral face of the oarbox, where oarports would otherwise have been shown, there is an inscription of which a good deal remains. It can be seen to have contained

197

Stone blocks found on the Acropolis at Lindos and reconstructed as a prow (265–260 BC). An inscription on it relates to the crews and commanding officers of two trihēmioliai.

a. The prow on which the Victory of Samothrace (200–180 BC) stands in the Louvre, Paris.

◄ 199a & b

b. Detail showing oarports en echelon as they appear on the lateral face of the outrigger on both sides of the prow.

the names of 288 men who served in *trihēmioliai* together with their commander and two trierarchs. It is possible that the 288 names formed the crew of the two *tri-hēmioliai* of which the trierarchs are named. If that is so, allowing twenty-four men for the hyperesia (compared with thirty of a three and forty-five of a four) and supposing files on each side of the ship of 24 + 24 + 12 = 60, 120 + 24 all told would be the complement of each ship.

There are four ship portraits which resemble the Lindos prow in respect of the oarbox. The first is the Lindos relief (Figure 198)[37] which represents the stern of a ship which from its position is likely to be a *trihēmiolia* but shows no oarports or oars. The second, third and fourth all have oarports or oars or oarports en echelon. They are: the prow on which the Victory of Samothrace stands in the Louvre (Figure 199),[38] probably dedicated by the Rhodians between 200 and 180 BC, a warship shown on the Palazzo Barberini mosaic of the early first century BC (Figure 200),[39] and the Hellenistic Palazzo Spada relief (Figure 201).[40]

In the *trihēmiolia* as reconstructed by Coates two full files of oarsmen work their oars through an oarbox with their oarports en echelon, as seen in the second, third and fourth representation above; and as in the *hēmiolia* there is a further lower half-file of oarsmen taking advantage of the wider beam in the midships section of the ship. In representations where oars are shown (e.g. the Palazzo Berberini mosaic: Figure 200) the presence of the half-file is masked by the two full files. In the

37. *GROW* 5.21

38. *GROW* 5.20

39. *GROW* 5.26

40. *GROW* 5.36

41. *AT* p126

42. Diodorus 20.92.5

43. Theophrastus *Historia Plantarum* 5.8.1

44. Pliny *NH* 16.203

45. Plutarch *Demetrius* 32.2

◀ 198

A relief (190–180 BC) on rock beside the ascent to the Acropolis at Lindos probably representing the stern of a tri-hemiolia. This photograph was taken by A S F Gow before 1914 and before the relief was damaged by an earthquake.

200

Detail of a mosaic in the Palazzo Berberini, Palestrina (early first century BC) showing a trihemiolia in an Egyptian river scene. Two levels of oars en echelon mask the midships half file below them.

201

The Palazzo Spada relief of the first century AD believed to be based on a Hellenistic original. It depicts a trihemiolia, the third half file masked as in 50.

Samothrace monument only the prow and the oarports there are shown. The *tri-hēmiolia* unlike the *hēmiolia* may not, then, have been a polyreme since it may not have used double-manning.

The conquest of Cyprus led immediately to Antigonus's decision to invade Egypt at the head of a large land force with Demetrius bringing 150 warships and 100 supply transports. Bad advance planning and intelligence led to the expedition's withdrawal. The account of the naval aspect is nevertheless informative. The threes ('the fast ships') were employed to tow the supply ships, a function which can be observed of Athenian threes in the mid-fourth century BC[41] in relation to corn-ships and probably in relation to Alexander's army across the Hellespont in 334 BC and Demetrius's to Cyprus in 307 BC. The strongest of Demetrius's ships were able to reach Kasion in bad weather of which three, named as fives, were swamped there at anchor. It appears then that for such a voyage Demetrius left his sixes and sevens behind, took 100 threes to tow the supply ships, and fifty threes, fours and fives; and that the seakeeping qualities of the five were superior to the threes and in particular to such of the thirty Athenian fours in his service as were still in commission. This information supplies another reason for the five's popularity. Here as nowhere else there is a vivid description of the hardship suffered by the crews of the ships at anchor off Kasion for lack of drinking water.

In the course of his narrative of the siege of Rhodes which followed the Egyptian expedition, Diodorus[42] notes that it was after the siege and the death of Antigonus that Demetrius launched the largest warships, Theophrastus[43] adding that his control of Cyprus and the resources of long timber there gave him the opportunity to build larger ships. An eleven[44] and a thirteen[45] are attributed to him, the latter before Antigonus's death. Plutarch also mentions an unidentified occasion much later when his enemy Lysimachus stood on the shore admiring his fifteens and sixteens as they moved past.

The Romans get onto the sea

In 264 BC the Romans decided to intervene in Sicily against Carthage, which was allied to Hiero, the ruler of Syracuse, in support of a group of mercenaries who had seized Messana on the Sicilian side of the strait. Twenty years before, the Roman consul Cornelius had toured Magna Graecia with a squadron of ten cataphract ships, probably threes and belonging to their 'naval allies', Greek cities with which they had relations by treaty. In 264 BC Polybius[46] says that not only did they have no cataphract ships but no warships of their own, not even a *lembos*. So on this occasion as well they borrowed fifty-oared ships and threes from the Greek maritime cities of Tarentum, Locri, Elea and Naples and sent their men across in them. The Carthaginians attacked and one of the Carthaginian cataphracts in hot pursuit ran aground and was captured by the Romans. Later, when the Romans succeeded in capturing Agrigentum (*Akragas*) their ideas enlarged and they decided 'to get onto the sea' and took steps to build 100 fives and twenty threes. 'As their shipwrights were completely inexperienced in building fives, since ships of this kind had not been used in Italy, they had difficulty' and 'used the captured cataphract (which by implication was a five) as a model'.

The reason Polybius gives for the Romans' use of a Carthaginian model for her new fleet of fives is very difficult to believe, when fives at this time were in common use in Macedonia, Greece and Egypt. The Romans could certainly have hired Greeks, as they did in other matters, to instruct their shipwrights if they had wanted fives of the Greek design. It is possible but not very likely that Dionysius's inventions of the five and the six in Syracuse were unknown in the Greek cities of southern Italy, Rome's naval allies to whom she would turn for the skilled craftsmen she needed. But much more recently in 280 BC Pyrrhus, King of Epirus, and a protegé of Demetrius, when invited to Tarentum made the crossing in a flagship which was probably a seven and his army was transported by the Tarentines in a large fleet, 'many horse-transports, cataphracts and carriers of all kinds'. It is difficult to believe that Pyrrhus's own ships, in view of his connection with Demetrius, did not consist of some bigger cataphracts in addition to his flagship even if the Tarentine cataphracts were, as is rather unlikely at this date, no bigger than threes. A more likely reason for the Roman adoption of the Carthaginian model was a hard-headed assessment of the merits of the Syracusan/Greek type as inferior to the Carthaginian/Phoenician. It is perhaps significant that the fleet Agathocles of Syracuse had assembled to invade Carthage just before his death in 289 BC consisted of fours (as scouts) and sixes (as ships of the line). The Romans adopted sixes, which were necessarily of Greek design, as flagships, but their fives were built on the Carthaginian model. They did not proceed to build, as the Egyptians and Macedonians did in their period of naval rivalry, ships bigger than fives for their front line or bigger than sixes for their flagships. This Roman policy was maintained even in the Civil Wars at the end of the first century BC. Octavian's fleet at Actium had no ships bigger than sixes, but Antony's fleet gathered from the eastern Mediterranean and Egypt ranged from sixes to tens in the front line. His defeat ended the age of the big ships.

Selected iconography of warships from the four to the ten

In the remainder of this chapter a selection will be made from the considerable number of existing representations of those which illustrate best the polyreme types most in use from the fourth to the first centuries BC. A full iconography is to be found in *GROW* (Chapter 5).

The four is unique insofar as it is illustrated by a graffito labelled *navis tetreris longa* (Figure 202). The graffito naturally is a very rough portrait and much detail has been omitted. The absence of deckrailing, oarbox, oarports and stern ornament (*aphlaston*) does not mean that a four was without them. The most must be made of what has been included, of the Latin/Greek label in particular.

202
The graffito at Alba Fucentia of the first century BC to the first century AD. This representation of a four is unique as the only picture of an ancient ship labelled as to type. The representation omits much and is very rough; but the wickerwork course divided into rooms below the deck gives an important clue to the oarsystem.

46. Polybius 1.20.13–14
47. Appian *Civil Wars* 5.107
48. Cicero *In Verrem* 2.5.88
49. *GROW* 5.10
50. *GROW* 5.27
51. *GROW* 5.29

203

A coin issued by Demetrius Poliorketes (300–295 BC) to advertise his power at sea after his father Antigonus I had fallen at the battle of Ipsos in 301 BC. It is then likely to represent a ship larger than a three.

204

A Praeneste relief in the Vatican Museum in Rome: second half of the first century BC. This ship portrait represents in some detail a large Egyptian warship, at least a nine.

Beneath the wale marked by a line running forward to end in an upper ram (*proembolion*), there is a rectangle probably indicating the *parasemon* identity symbol usually on the termination of the oarbox forward in the *epōtis*. Forward of, and lower than, the *epōtis* there is a blunt ram. Beneath the deck, aft of and continuing the sidescreen of the forecastle, there is the main feature shown, a course of latticework divided into twenty-two 'rooms'. This latticework course is a very common feature of polyremes, taking the place of the open side of the three divided into rooms by deck stanchions. It was presumably a permanent sidescreen resulting from the greater use of missiles.

The twenty-two 'rooms' may be taken as a clue to the number of oarsmen in the file. The name *tetrērēs* indicates that there were four files a side. That these were at two levels is shown by a passage in Appian's account[47] of the battle of Mylai between Sextus Pompeius's fleet under Papias whose ships were shorter and lower than their opponent Octavian's fleet under Agrippa. Agrippa's flagship 'smashed into Papias's at the *epōtis*. Of the oarsmen, the thalamians were all trapped but the others (*hoi heteroi* = the others of two categories) broke through the deck and swam away'. The description of an incident in the Second Punic War in which decksoldiers from two Carthaginian fours were unable to board the higher Roman five confirms that the four was lower. With four files of oarsmen at two levels of oars, necessarily double-manned, and twenty-two men in each file, there would have been eighty-eight oars and 176 oarsmen in each four.

Coates calculates the height above the waterline of a four so manned at 2.2m. The ratio of the height above waterline to the length of the rowing area calculated at 22 × the interscalmium of two Roman cubits of 0.444m is then 2.2:19.5, 1:888. The same ratio in the graffito is 7:58, 1:8.3. If the larger Doric cubit is used the ratio is 1:9.8. It seems at any rate that the eye of the graffito artist was not very far out.

The attempt by the Athenians and Antigonus I to use the four as a frontline ship instead of the three was a failure, but Ptolemy I and later the Romans used the four as a fast and manoeuvrable complement in conjunction with the five. It has been noted (p.163) that in Demetrius's fleet in the Egyptian expedition which contained threes, fours and fives in a storm only the last succeeded in getting through to Kasion. The fours were driven to dangerous moorings at Raphia. As the flagship of a Roman fleet commander in Sicily in 73–71 BC the four is described as appearing like a floating city (*urbis instar*) to the pirates against whom she was operating, but under sail as having 'an incredible turn of speed'.[48]

The five to the nine

There are two ship portraits which may represent the five of Greek design: the portrait on the coins of Demetrius the son of Antigonus I (300–295 BC;[49] Figure 203) and the Isola Tiberina monument (100–50 BC:[50] Figure 205). However, the boxing-in which came to be the rule of the bigger ships in the third century BC makes separation from each other of fives, sixes, sevens and eights virtually impossible. The two ships named are both quite unlikely on historical grounds to be threes, cannot be fours since they both have outriggers which is the mark of the uppermost oar-level of the three, and of the types developed from the design of the three. Both are distinguishable from the type with the deep oarbox showing three levels of oars emerging from it, which will here be called the Carthaginian/Roman design. It seems likely on practical grounds that ships larger than eights were rowed at two levels; and the Praeneste relief (50–1 BC: Figure 204)[51] will be discussed as such.

Demetrius introduced a series of coins after his father's defeat and death at the battle of Ipsos and five years after his victory over Ptolemy at the battle of Cypriot Salamis. The series showing on the reverse the prow of a warship was plainly 'to

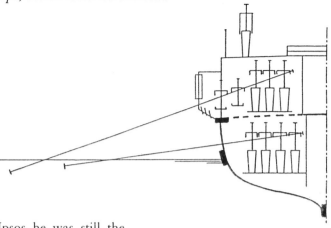

remind his rivals as well as his subjects that in spite of Ipsos he was still the unchallenged master of the sea'. The coin is likely therefore to remind them not of one particular ship or type of ship but of the 'heavier stratiötides' in general on which his sea power was based. The information which the prow gives is likely to relate to any or all of these bigger ships.

Aft of the idiosyncratic, unevenly bifid, stubby and slightly retroussé stempost there is a gap; and then the screened foredeck runs aft and continues as the main-deck, but over an open side to the edge of the die. Beneath the foredeck sidescreen the topwale continues forward to the upcurving stempost. Right forward below the topwale there is a large eye-panel below which runs aft the middle wale (composed of two narrow slats containing zygian oarports when it is below an outrigger), from the *proembolion* under the *epötis* to the edge of the die. The *epötis* terminates the outrigger (*parexeiresia*) on the lateral face of which are in some cases indeterminate markings (?of oarports; cf Figure 197). Below the middle wale the thick, decorated bottom wale runs forward to the ram. On the foredeck stands a winged figure with *stylis* in her left hand and a trumpet (the signal at sea for close encounter) in her right hand.

The solidly built outward projecting *parexeiresia* is the mark of a bigger ship than a three, and its open side a mark of its early third century date.

The Isola Tiberina monument (100–50 BC) (Figure 205)[52]

This impressive monument on the downstream end of an island in the Tiber has been dated from the stone of which it is made to the last half of the first century BC. It is the remains of a ¾ scale replica of a big Roman warship to greet the eye of the traveller coming up the river from Ostia. If a five was intended it would have been of the Carthaginian/Roman type. For its prestigious position a six at least, as a consular flagship, is likely, for which the Carthaginian/Roman design is unsuited. Coates has reconstructed it as a six in the Greek design. It is also possible to reconstruct it as a seven in that design. The special feature it shares with other late Republican ships is a horizontal *parodos*, a side-gangway along the top of the *parexeiresia*.

The Roman five

The appearance of the first Roman fives, built on the model of the captured Carthaginian cataphract, is given in a series of coins (Figure 206) of that date showing the bow section of a warship. The oarbox is deep and has a pair of horizontal slats on its lateral face which provides a longitudinal opening through which three levels of oars could be worked. This is a trivial variation of the deep oarbox with three longitudinal rows of oarports set quincunx fashion, appearing later (250–180 BC) on

205
Left – the Isola Tiberina naval monument: 100–50 BC. A large scale model of a Roman warship, important in view of the monument's site and probably a six in which consuls raised their flag.
Right – an oarplan by Coates of a six.

52. *GROW* 5.27
53. *GROW* 5.18.1
54. *GROW* 5.15
55. *GROW* 5.35
56. *GROW* 5.43
57. *GROW* 5.41

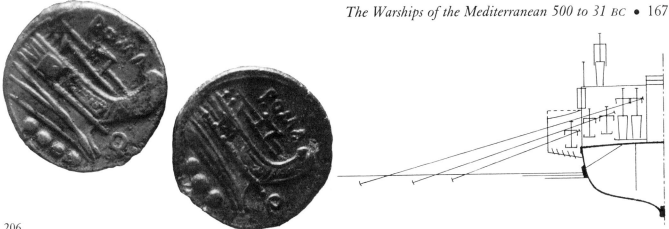

206

Top left – two examples of the 'prow series' of Roman Republican coinage: 264/3–241 BC built on the design of a Carthaginian cataphract ship.
Top right – an oarplan by Coates of a five of the 'prow series'.

207

Below left – an example of a Calenian dish: c275–175 BC. It gives an unusual picture of a number of similar warships massed together without oars. They may be captive Carthaginian fives.

208

Below right – a Carthaginian grave stele. It shows a ship with the deep oarbox of the ships in 56 and 57.

the Calenian dishes (Figure 207)[53] which there is ground for believing represent Carthaginian ships. There is a number of other representations of this oarsystem: the Carthaginian grave stele (Figure 208)[54] third century BC, the Ostia (Poplicola) frieze (Figure 209)[55] shortly after 20 BC, and the Shipshed fresco from Pompei AD 54–68.[56] All have been reconstructed by Coates as representing workable three-level oarsystems which cannot however be further extended, as the oarsystem of the Greek five demonstrably can.

It seems reasonable to see this system as a descendant, through Tyre, which was Carthage's mother city and maintained close ties with her, of the Phoenician five which was a development of the Phoenician outriggerless three of the late eighth century BC. This Phoenician three seems to have been largely, but perhaps not entirely, displaced by the Greek design in the fifth and fourth century BC. It did however serve as the model for the Phoenician five invented in the fourth century BC at about the same time as Dionysius was inventing his five by extending the Corinthian three. The main difference between the two designs was that in the Corinthian system there was an outrigger for the thranite oarsmen, while in the Phoenician/Carthaginian/Roman system the oars emerged from the ship's hull at the same distance from the median line through a flat oar-panel.

The Amandus fresco (AD 54–68)[57]

This fresco from the House of the priest Amandus in Pompeii depicts a three-level ship of the Greek design. She could be a three, or a five.

A high foredeck with a high bulwark leads aft to a maindeck with a waist-high bulwark hung with shields, the latter crowded with armed men. Below the deck the

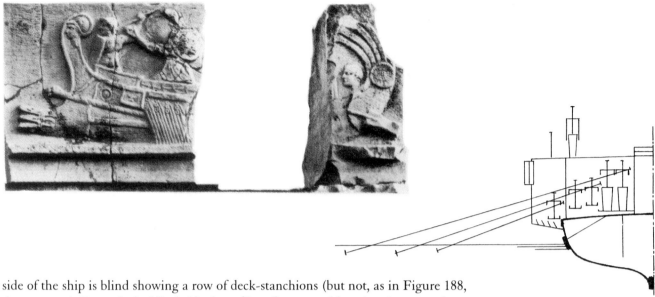

side of the ship is blind showing a row of deck-stanchions (but not, as in Figure 188, the oarsmen). Beneath the blind side three files of oars roughly painted emerge from an oar panel.

There are three other similar ships in a fresco of the Casa del Atrio Corinzio in Herculaneum carrying towers manned with spearmen. These are unlikely to be threes. It seems most likely that the Amandus ship like them is a five, one of the 'heavier stratiötides', and showing a blind side not even with stanctions below the deck level. The blind side must be interpreted as a course of permanent screening as was used in the larger cataphracts. Fives were rare in the contemporary Roman fleets. The scenes of naval warfare, however, which the Pompeii and Herculaneum frescos depict in any case must reflect 'battles long ago'.

The nine

For ships of larger denomination than eight practical considerations require two levels of oars rather than three. Dr Coates has reconstructed a nine from the ship portrayed (port side) in great detail in the Praeneste relief (Figure 204)[58] 50–1 BC. The detail is not however matched by equivalent realism. The human figures are as usual of size disproportionate to the ship, and length of the ship is disproportionate to its height. It has lost by damage only the end of the ram and the stern. The crocodile symbol on the wale in the bow forming a *proembolion* has been taken, probably rightly, to indicate that the ship is Egyptian, a more likely provenance than Rome. In the prow there is a fine forward and then aft curving stempost against which leans the foremast with sail furled. There is no foredeck but instead a well in which the foremast and a man stands. Behind him is a tower, which is regular battle equipment in such a ship; and in front of him is the framed *para-sëmon* which illustrated the ship's name. Armed men stand on the deck behind a planked bulwark with shields (or possibly shield decoration) on its side. In front (outboard) of the bulwark there is a *parados* (cf the Isola Tiberina monument above) on which two armed men stand. The *parodos* is made possible by the projection from the hull of a *parexeiresia* (for the upper of the two files of oars) on top of which is a course of louvres (recognised as such by Casson).[59] The upper file of massive oars are equipped with leather sleaves, *askömata*: thirteen are visible, making twenty-five or twenty-six a side but there may have been more before damage. The lower file of oars is visible packed closely behind the upper file. As a nine the ship would have had four men on the oars of one and five men on the oars of the other level.

209

Left – a relief on a funerary monument set up shortly after 20 BC on the Ostia seashore to commemorate the naval career of Cartilius Poplicola. It shows a deep-oarbox three-level warship which can only be a five.

Right – an oarplan by Coates of the Ostia ship as a five.

58. *GROW* 5.29
59. *SSAW* p145

210
Olympias *under sail on her trials in 1987.*

The reconstruction of the three and the trials 1987–90

On the basis of the evidence assembled by the writer for the three of the fourth and fifth centuries BC, direct and indirect, from archaeology, epigraphy and literature, John Coates developed a design[60] which was accepted by the authorities of the Greek government. An agreement was reached between them and the Trireme Trust (UK) that a three should be built in Greece at Greek expense to the specifications and designs of John Coates. It was also agreed that the Trireme Trust should be permitted to carry out trials of the completed vessels. The ship later named *Olympias* and built by the Greek Navy in Piraeus under the supervision of John Coates was

60. Coates *AT* Chapter 12

launched on 27 June 1987. The Trireme Trust brought out in the following July a crew of 200 for the first trials (Figure 210) at Poros on the east coast of the Saronic Gulf; and trials organised by the Trust and made possible by the generous cooperation and help of the Hellenic Navy were carried out in 1988, 1990, 1991, 1992 and 1994. In July 1993 *Olympias* was brought to the Thames through the generosity of two Greek shipowners to celebrate the 2,500th anniversary of the birth of democracy. The Trireme Trust (USA) cooperated from 1988 to 1993. Reports on the trials of 1987 and 1988 and a survey of the experience gained 1987–1990[61] have been edited by Timothy Shaw and published by Oxbow Books, Oxford. The following (with some small omissions and alterations) are concluded in that survey to have been the lessons learned from the trials:

A   *Oarsystem*
1. Oars of equal length are workable together from three levels simultaneously and after a relatively short period of training.
2. Damage to oar blades by clashing together was minor and avoidable.
3. An interscalmium of two attic cubits of 0.444m (i.e. 0.888m) is too short to enable the acceptable maximum power to be reached.
4. The position of the hull beams in *Olympias* caused the thalamians' stroke to be too restricted for high-powered rowing. Given a longer interscalmium of 0.98m, now thought to be correct (from recent archaeological discovery[62]) that restriction could be avoided in any further reconstruction.
5. The oar gearing required in fast threes is a high one, about 2.8 ie the ratio of the length from the centre of pressure of the blade to the thole to that from the thole to mid-hands.
6. Oar straps of tanned leather stretched in use (oars being forwards of their tholes) cause too much lost motion in oars, particularly those working through oarports. If straps are to be of leather (as attested in antiquity) they must be of rawhide, a material hard and unyielding, provided that it is dry, true of most circumstances in such ships in the Mediterranean, but certainly not in open oared craft in northern European waters where oars have usually been worked aft of the thole. JTS adds (4.4.95): We are not now in a position to be certain about the use of rawhide as against tanned leather. As laced up hitherto, both have proved rather unsatisfactory, but a new knot with which we are experimenting may change that.
7. Sustained lubrication of oars and *askōmata* is essential for higher-powered rowing.
8. An oar blade area of 0.08m[63] is sufficient, owing to the high gearing of the oars.
9. Oars must be as light as they can be made without becoming too flexible, if high powers and rates of striking are to be reached, irrespective of consequent fragility and risk of damage in battle.
10. The longest attainable oarstroke is necessary to develop the maximum power.
11. Maximum power is achieved at a striking rate of about forty-five strokes per minute.
12. Modifications to the oar rig in *Olympias* that are needed to enable the required oar power to be reached in a sprint (raising maximum power by 25–30 per cent and speed to 9.5–9.7 knots) have been established clearly enough to make building and testing a modified ship a worthwhile experiment.
13. The same modifications are expected to enable the ship with a good oarcrew to maintain 7½ knots all day continuously as attested for a three in antiquity.
14. Cushions on the seats of oarcrew (as attested in antiquity) are necessary for repeated sustained periods at the oar, not merely a comfort.

61. Shaw ed., *The Trireme Project*, 1993

62. Morrison, 'Ancient Greek Measures of Length in Nautical Contexts' *Antiquity* Vol. 65, No. 247, June 1991

63. See footnote 2

15. Oarcrew must be protected from the sun.

16. Ventilation for the lower oarcrew is barely adequate in *Olympias*.

17. In hot weather each member of the oarcrew needs about one litre of water per hour while working hard. Dehydration is a real danger for oarcrew: the need, on the other hand, to urinate is minor.

18. (JTS adds [4.4.95]): In hot weather each member of the oarcrew needs to drink *at least* one litre of water per hour while working hard. On a long journey this should be supplemented by easily-digestible foods such as grapes, figs and honey to keep the concentration of sugar in the blood from falling too far. Some salt should also be taken. The heat severely restricts the power output of the rowers.

B *Ship*

1. Oarports near the waterline of the ship when loaded with crew are safe if provided, as attested in antiquity, with *askōmata* to prevent entry of water.

2. A hull constructed with the same arrangement of timbers and the same scantlings as were found in the Marsala ship is satisfactory for a three.

3. If hogging is to be prevented the plank tenons must fit tightly in the longitudinal direction. This has been indicated to be a critical aspect of the construction of longships built in the ancient Mediterranean manner.

4. Side winds do not cause the ship to heel over enough to affect performance under oar except when also under sail.

5. No undue vertical oscillations of the ship are developed at high oar power or at low ones.

6. The ship is easily steered and turned under both oar and sail, rudders being effective and light to handle.

7. No ballast is required for stability or to bring the ship to her correct waterline when fully loaded. In antiquity, since longships did not sink when holed, they cannot have carried ballast.

8. The resistance and drag of the quarter rudders when fully immersed is high, strongly indicating that in antiquity it would have been the practice to have as little of blade and stock immersed as expected demands for manoeuvrability allowed, rudders being readily adjusted to meet circumstances.

9. The torsional stiffness of the open hull (undecked) is adequate owing to the cross-bracing fitted between the hull beams which are also clamped to the middle wales by lodging knees (which are horizontal). Without such bracing the torsional stiffness would have been very much lower, leading to resonance in torsion with oar strokes at higher rates of striking.

10. The height of the centre of gravity of *Olympias* has been established by experiment, the only way to do so accurately. The metacentric height when fully manned is between 0.88m and 1.1m depending upon the load and disposition of variable and moveable weights.

11. (JTS adds [4.4.95]): The tension in the hypozoma (or the sum of the tensions in the hypozomata) should be 13½ tonnes force. (In *Olympias* it has been unintentionally limited to about 6 tonnes because the anchorages as built (but not as designed) are inadequate.

C *Sail*

1. The ancient Mediterranean rig, of which there had been no practical knowledge in a longship, has proved to be effective, handy and weatherly, enabling the ship to make way pointing 60 degrees into the apparent wind with only 7 to 10 degrees of leeway.

2. The area of the mainsail, 95m,[64] could be increased a little by lengthening the main yard.

3. Spars (of the yards) were made unnecessarily heavy.

4. The mainmast tabernacle is not secured by beams and floors strongly enough to give confidence of its safety in supporting an unstayed mast.

D *Navigation*

(In antiquity engagement with an enemy, for which the ship was built, was always under oar.)

1. The main means of propulsion over long distances, as a usual practice, has been shown to have been by sail, oars being used generally when necessary on account of urgency, safety or the need to come into or to clear the land.

2. On passage, oars can usefully supplement sails (motor-sailing as it were) but only in light breezes astern or on the quarter, raising the speed under sail from about 4 to 6 or more knots, without drawing on the physical reserves of the oarcrew to any significant extent. Such combined use of sail and oar has been found to be less useful in beam winds owing to interference in working oars due to heel of the ship. However, if the beam wind is steady, and not too severe, its heeling effect can be offset by stationing spare crew members on the windward side of the canopy.

3. The capacity of an oared ship to reach shelter, to claw round a headland or to keep clear of a lee shore under oar and against head winds has been tested. This is a most important factor in making navigational judgements and in keeping in mind reserve courses of action on passage in this type of craft. *Olympias* has made good 3 knots against a head wind gusting to 25 knots and waves of up to one metre in height for 70 minutes. The oarcrew had by then become exhausted, a reminder of a state of affairs which, for thousands of years, captains of oared ships had to keep in mind constantly irrespective of whether their oarcrews were of free men, convicts or slaves.

4. The wind resistance of the hull in a head wind has been found to be 1/30 of the water resistance of the hull at the same fluid speeds past the ship. In beam winds the ship drifted at 1/26 knot sideways per one knot of wind speed.

Bibliography (selected) of Chapters 10 and 11

BASCH, Lucien, *Le musée imaginaire de la marine antique*, Athens, 1987

BETLYON, J W, *The coinage and mints of Phoenicia in the pre-Alexandrian period*, 1982

CASSON, Lionel, *Ships and Seamanship in the Ancient World*, Princeton, 1972 (reprinted 1985) = *SSAW*

GRAY, Dorothea, 'Seewesen' Archaeologia Homerica I G Gottingen 1974

KIRK, G S, 'Ships on Geometric Vases', *Annual of the British School at Athens*, 44 93–153

LANDSTROM, Bjorn, *Ships of the Pharaohs*, London, 1970

MORRISON, J S, *Long Ships and Round Ships*, London 1980 = *LSRS*

MORRISON, J S and COATES, J F, *The Athenian Trireme*, Cambridge, 1986 = *AT*
  Greek and Roman Oared Ships, Oxford, 1995 = *GROW*

MORRISON, J S and WILLIAMS, R T, *Greek Oared Ships*, Cambridge 1968 = *GOS*

RENFREW, C, 'Cycladic Metallurgy and the Aegean Early Bronze Age' *American Journal of Archaeology* 71 (1967) 1–20

WACHSMANN, Shelley, 'The Ships of the Sea Peoples' *International Journal of Nautical Archaeology* 10.3 (1981) 187–220. Additional Notes *IJNA* 11.4 (1982) 297–304
  'Paddled and Oared Ships before the Iron Age', *The Age of the Galley* 10–35, London 1995

WALLINGA, H T, *Ships and Sea-Power before the Great Persian War* Leiden 1993
  'The Ancestry of the Trireme: 1200–525 BC' *The Age of the Galley*, London, 1995

WILLIAMS, R T, 'Early Greek Ships at Two Levels', *Journal of Hellenic Studies* 78 (1958) 121–130.
  Addenda: *JHS* 79 (1959) 159–160

64. Coates, *AT*, p222–225

The European
Clinker-Built Boat
Before the Viking Era

The rest of this book deals with the development of boats in northern Europe and North America, particularly between the beginning of the Saxon migrations in the fourth century AD and the development of the various skeleton-building techniques, which gradually became standard practice for the building of big ships from the early or middle 1400s onwards. After this date no new strands come into northern European wooden boat and shipbuilding traditions until the development of plywood and wood reinforced plastic in the mid-twentieth century. Big ships were skeleton-built, while boats continued to be built in the traditions which had evolved in the preceding 900 years and which are described in the following chapters. Some small ships continued to be built in these traditions also. Thus it was in boats and a few small vessels that the ancient traditions were still very apparent in northern Europe in the first half of the twentieth century, just as they were in Japan.

As has already been said, one of the types of boatbuilding which developed from the logboat was clinker or lapstrake, with planks overlapping, lower edge of upper planks outside upper edge of lower, or much more rarely, the other way round. Though this technique of boatbuilding occurs elsewhere in the world, it was in northern Europe that it achieved its greatest development in the various kinds of Saxon and Viking ships. Clinker-building, with planks fully overlapping, became the main tradition in Britain, Scandinavia and northern Europe generally as long as wooden boats were built, and although lapstrake was never the central tradition it was more widespread in North America than is generally realised. Among the northern European boatbuilding traditions described in Part Three of this book, therefore, the history of clinker-building is dealt with in special detail.

As a reminder of what is meant by clinker-building in this context, Figure 211 shows fully overlapping clinker planking. The persistence of the tradition is shown in Figure 212 of a clinker-built fishing lugger from Beer in Devon photographed in 1936 when such boats were still commonplace.

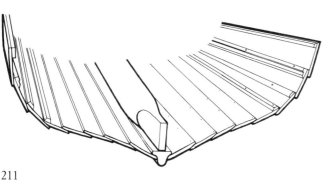

211
Clinker or lapstrake construction.
[National Maritime Museum

212
Clinker-built lugger from Beer, Devon,
1936 [Basil Greenhill

This is perhaps the stage at which to ask: why clinker? Why did overlapping edge-joined techniques develop in some places and smooth-skinned edge-joined traditions elsewhere? We have seen that the question is misleading because of the various different ways in which the planks of smooth-skinned boats were joined edge to edge with varying degrees of overlap to produce a strong and (when the wood was saturated) reasonably watertight join (see Figure 36). Since classical times it has been perhaps a minority of the world's edge-joined boats in which the planking has lain with only the squared-off edges in contact.

As to why the fully overlapped tradition in two forms developed in widely separated areas of Bangladesh and in Uttar Pradesh hundreds of miles away in India (see pp.232 and 254) might be worth some further study. As far as Bangladesh is concerned it is most unlikely to have been a European innovation, not only because this was unusual and indeed very difficult at the level in rural society at which the boatbuilding *mistris* operate, but because the forms of the traditions in Bangladesh are essentially alien to those of Britain. Moreover, the tradition is to be found in the most basic forms, in the extension of the simplest expanded logboats with fully overlapping clinker-planking in, for instance, the valleys of the wild border mountains between Assam and Bangladesh, and it runs right through the boatbuilding of the most eastern parts of Bangladesh to large sophisticated cargo boats.

There may be some special reason why fully overlapping planking developed in northern Europe. The use of cleft planking (see Chapter 16) was widespread, and cleft planks in their untrimmed state are triangular in section. The originators of boatbuilding traditions were using planks of which one edge was materially thicker than the other. Flush-joining edge to edge with such material was very difficult indeed and it could be that the natural solution, a full overlapping of the edges, followed from this historical situation.

Because the remains of many ancient boats have been discovered in Scandinavia and elsewhere in northern Europe, in bogs and marshes, old harbours from which the sea has long receded and been excluded, and in burial mounds, as well as underwater in the Baltic there is quite a lot of evidence from which to follow the development of the northern European clinker-built boat through more than 2,000 years of history. In particular, the development of boat-building within 250 miles of the Skaw (see map at Figure 213) over the period AD 800 to 1200 is now well covered by archaeological finds.

But it is extremely important to remember in considering the evidence provided by these archaeological finds that each gives information only about itself. Though similar features in the boats can be compared, these similarities do not mean that a later boat is necessarily, or even possibly, a direct descendant of an earlier one. The

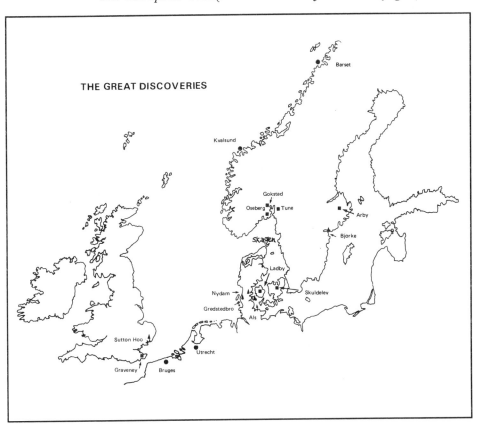

THE GREAT DISCOVERIES

213

Some of the principal discoveries of remains of clinker-built vessels of before the Viking period made in northern Europe. [Basil Greenhill

finds are still far too scattered both in time and place to enable us at this stage to come to even tentative conclusions about the general evolution of more than one or two particular boatbuilding traditions of the many in northern Europe in the past two millennia, and only the most tentative conclusions covering very short periods of these. Despite all the progress which has been made in the late twentieth century the study of the archaeology of the boat has still a long way to go, even in this one part of the world, and just as in parts of Asia today very primitive boats still co-exist with very sophisticated local vessels, so much the same thing very probably happened in Europe at the time of the Saxon and Viking migrations, indeed it continued to occur with boats right down into the present century.

As more archaeological finds come to light, so the history of the clinker-built boat in northern Europe is being more accurately and completely understood. Even so at the present moment a great deal of what follows is still conjecture. This fact and the study of the clinker tradition is of particular interest in Britain, because the clinker-building technique is our own strongest boatbuilding tradition and persisted until a few years ago as the normal method of boatbuilding in this country.

The accompanying map (Figure 213) shows the location of an important few of the most complete of the hundreds of remains of ancient clinker-built boats which have now been found in northern Europe. There are more than 420 graves in which a boat was buried known in northern Europe and Iceland. Many of these and other finds have never been fully published, and in very few have the boat remains been fully studied.

In recent years many new finds have been made. A number of them have been well researched and published, others have not yet been fully published. Nevertheless, the selection of classic finds which follows is still sufficiently representative for the purpose of this introductory study.

I shall be describing some of the principal finds and the evidence they provide in detail, and it will therefore be convenient to list them. In rough chronology, the finds date from:

pre AD 700:	*AD* 700–1100:
1. Hjortspring	8. Utrecht
2. Björke	9. Oseberg
3. Nydam	10. Gokstad
4. Sutton Hoo	11. Tune
5. Gredstedbro	12. Ladby
6. Kvalsund	13. Graveney
7. Bårset	14. Årby
	15. Skuldelev finds

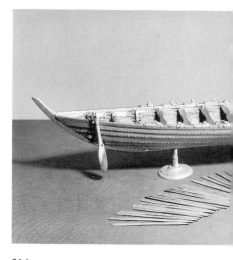

214
Model of the Nydam oak boat as originally reconstructed. [National Maritime Museum

It may be useful to recapitulate the basic facts about the clinker-building tradition. The shell of edge-joined planks is built first. The ribs or frames, such as they are, are added afterwards and shaped to the shell of planks. It is the planks, not the frames, which first determine the shape of the boat. In clinker work in its purest form the builder builds by eye alone, that is, he forms the shape with the planks without the use of any patterns or moulds.

This was the primitive skill of this kind of boat and shipbuilding. It was very difficult, given in particular the ways in which knowledge of boatbuilding traditions was conveyed from generation to generation, for the boatbuilders to innovate and experiment with new forms. Traditions of boat form and shape, therefore, tend to persist for many hundreds of years where these non-innovative techniques and traditions existed. This fact is demonstrated perhaps most clearly in the boats of Norway. But nevertheless major developments could take place rapidly at times, as it is possible they did in southern Norway in the ninth century.

Hjortspring

This find has already been described in Chapter 6.

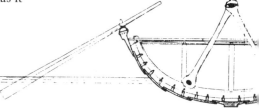

Björke boat

A very early logboat-based clinker-built boat found in northern Europe, the Björke boat, 23½ft (7.16m) long, is attributed to about AD 100. It was discovered on an island west of Stockholm.

It is a simple boat comprising a log hollowed out to leave a very thin and gracefully-shaped shell to which two planks have been added, one on each side (see Chapter 8). They are fastened to the basic logboat with iron rivets and laid fully overlapping, clinker style. The planks, like the logboat itself, have been cut with lugs or cleats left outstanding on the inner surface. Holes have been worked in these cleats and strong natural grown frames, six in number, have been lashed to them with withes. At the top of the planks the timbers have been fastened to the plank direct with iron rivets. The long broad planks are each in one piece and with the cleats, which make them twice as thick, very few planks can have been obtained out of the tree from which they were made.

The boat, inevitably from its construction, is long and narrow, her proportions dictated by her logboat base and the planks used to extend it. The logboat was never expanded. The evidence which leads to the widespread agreement that the North European clinker-built boat evolved from the expanded and extended logboat rests elsewhere, in the method and order of construction of early clinker-built boats and in the archaeological evidence provided by boat graves and expanded logboats fished up

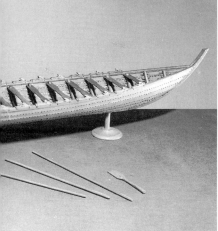

from the sea off the Swedish coast. The argument was brilliantly summarised by Ole Crumlin-Pedersen in 'Skin or Wood', his contribution to *Ships and Shipyards, Sailors and Fishermen*.

Nydam oak boat

Four extremely important boats have all been found in areas associated with the migrations of Saxon peoples to Britain and date from the general period of these migrations, about AD 300–600. They are not, however, all necessarily Saxon boats. The Björke boat was a relatively small vessel, but some of the same general characteristics occur in the big clinker-built boat find, the Nydam oak boat, dated in the early fourth century AD. She was found in southern Jutland near the present Danish/German border and is thought to represent the type of ship that brought the Angles and Saxons to Britain. Two oak-built boats were found on the same site, but the first had been chopped to pieces. The second was more or less intact.

The second boat is entirely plank-built of oak but has the proportions of a logboat-based vessel, long and narrow, and the relevant shape athwartships (Figure 214). She is built of broad planks, only five on each side scarfed together in places, with double cleats each twice the thickness of the planks themselves. Such a system of building was prodigiously wasteful of wood and labour, since here again only a relatively few planks can have been made from each tree. The boat was the product of a well organised society rich in both timber and time. The materials used strictly limited its shape to something like that of a logboat.

The bottom of the Nydam oak boat is really nothing more than an extra heavy plank shaped to take the garboard strakes and thickened in the middle to take the strains of beaching on sand. This plank is joined to the stem and stern posts by a shallow horizontal scarf at each end. The overlapping planks are joined to one another with iron rivets, and grown timber frames are lashed to the cleats with withes. She is thought to be the type of vessel that introduced clinker construction with iron fastenings into Scandinavia.

The vessel is constructed entirely of oak. She was a rowing boat with curved wooden single thole pins to which the oars have been secured with twisted withes. Thus with the Nydam oak boat, a rowing boat, pulled not paddled, appears for the first time in the archaeological evidence of the remains of an actual boat in northwest Europe.

There is much controversy about the details and indeed about the real shape of the Nydam boat. She was originally reconstructed in the form shown in the model in the National Maritime Museum (Figure 214). This model shows a hull form which would require much ballasting. The Swedish authority Harold Åkerlund suggested that she may have been wider and rounder than was at first thought. He suggested that she may have had a fuller midships section (Figure 215) and may have been strengthened by a rope truss running fore and aft – an idea now not generally accepted – and that the stem and stern posts rose more steeply than is shown in the model. It may also be that what has previously been taken as the stem was in fact the stern, and *vice versa*. The study of the remains of ancient boats is likely increasingly to give rise to controversy of this kind in which the assumptions of earlier eras, often based on suppositions and deductions inadequately recorded, are coming under a new challenge.

The reconstructed Nydam oak boat is now on display in the Archaologisches Landesmuseum in Schleswig, northern Germany and an intensive programme of study of the site of the find and further excavation was initiated by the Danish National Museum working with the Landesmuseum in 1989. This is continuing at

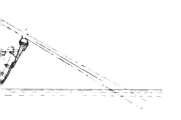

215
Harold Åkerlund's reconstruction of the midships section of the Nydam oak boat. [Harold Åkerlund

the time of writing (1995). It has already revealed that the oak boat was built from trees felled between 310 and 320 AD. A new plan for the structure of the vessel is being drawn up. The Nydam site is likely to provide much fresh information.

Nydam pine boat

With the Nydam oak boats was found substantial fragments of another built of soft wood. All three boats were found in a bog, probably formerly a lake, in which they had been sunk perhaps as ritual sacrifices of the captured property of an enemy. This third boat has been dated from about AD 400. She was smaller than the oak boat and appears to have differed from her in several important respects.

1. She was built of more and narrower planks.
2. She had a 'T'-shaped keel, which is the earliest keel of this type, as opposed to the keel plank, so far known to have been discovered in actual boat remains in northern Europe.
3. The stem and sternposts were joined to this keel with a different form of scarf from that used in the second Nydam boat, the one built of oak. This scarf form may have developed from the Björke boat form. It has been suggested also that the Nydam soft wood boat may have had a much more developed form of stem than the boats of earlier periods so far discovered – but the stem and stern post have not at the time of writing been discovered in the new excavations.

This third Nydam boat perhaps shows structural characteristics (keel, stem and stern posts, narrow and numerous planks) which were to survive into the Viking Age and show a possibly later and certainly different tradition from the keel plank boats described in this chapter. Built as she is of different material, she may well have originated in Norway. Indeed neither the Nydam oak boat, nor the pine boat, despite the location in which they were found, were necessarily built by Angles. Like the Hjortspring boat found nearby, they may well have been vessels from some other area lost in a raid on Angle country or captured by Angles; just as the pine boat may have come from Norway, the oak boat may have come from North Germany and represent a different local tradition. It would be unwise at this stage to assume an evolutionary connection between these two; all three, with the Björke boat, may represent units in the complex of a North European tradition in which boats co-existing in simple and sophisticated forms showed in their construction the influence both of the expanded and extended logboat and, to a lesser extent, possibly the influence of skin boats.

At the time of writing in 1995 the site of the find of the pine boat is being re-excavated by the Danish National Museum.

Gredstedbro boat

Although only a few fragments were recovered, the next boat find, the Gredstedbro boat, also discovered in southwest Jutland near the Danish/German border, gives vital evidence. The three fragments preserved are the most important parts for learning about the structure of the boat. They are a frame and pieces of the keel and a stem or stern post, joined to the keel by a shallow horizontal scarf. These fragments of timber have been dated by radio-carbon analysis at AD 600–650. The boat has a broad keel plank, much worn on the underside, thus showing she was frequently pulled ashore, and a horizontal scarf of post to keel very much like the scarf of the oak-built Nydam boat.

216
A general view of the impression of the Sutton Hoo ship taken during the first excavation in 1939. [British Museum

But she also shows several very important developments on (but by no means necessarily from) the Nydam boat.

1. She has eight narrow planks on each side, in place of the five broad planks of the Nydam oak-built boat.
2. The planks are smooth without cleats and the framework which survives was secured direct to them with wooden pins (trenails) as the frames of a modern clinker-built boat were fastened direct to the planks.

This is a completely different form of construction from the lashed frame cleat construction of the Nydam boats. Less flexible, in some ways less durable, but far simpler, quicker and more economical both in timber, time and labour, it is a great step forward in boatbuilding. It is possible that the cleat and lashed frame form of construction of Nydam and some later boats may represent boatbuilding craftsmen's allegiance to the logboat origins of the boats they built. Although in some societies logboat hulls were and are pierced while the logboat is being made in order to measure thickness, in some primitive communities possibly the custom was that the precious logboat made with such labour must not be pierced. It is easy to leave cleats in the basic logboat to lash the frames to when they are inserted. The tradition died hard in the plank-built boat but the obvious advantages of the hull-piercing trenail won completely in the long term.

Sutton Hoo ship

In 1939 an Anglo-Saxon burial mound was excavated at Sutton Hoo near Wood-bridge in Suffolk. Buried in it with a hoard of magnificent treasure had been a great boat, about 88½ft (27m) long. The timber had all rotted away, but the imprint of the hull and of the long rows of iron rivets remained in the sand (Figure 216). Through careful excavation in 1939 and again between 1965 and 1970 it became possible to see that the boat had the same kind of shallow horizontal keel scarf as the Gredstedbro boat, a keel plank of similar cross section and nine strakes a side. There appear to have been no cleats. The frames were secured to the planks with trenails, the strakes were narrow and ran beautifully up the gently rising stem and stern posts. Like the Nydam oak boat they are each made up of several lengths of timber scarfed together. The Sutton Hoo ship is broader than the reconstructed Nydam oak boat and would generally appear likely to have been a better sea boat, even if the Nydam boat is reconstructed in a manner which makes her broader, more full-bodied and more seaworthy than she is thought to have been in the past (Figure 217).

Although the Sutton Hoo ship burial is dated by the accompanying finds at about AD 625 is seems probable that the ship was actually built around the year AD 600, or perhaps a little earlier, as several patches of repair work suggest a fairly long working life. She represents a great development in the broad tradition of which the Nydam oak boat is another representative.

This fact suggests once again that, as has occurred throughout history, boats of widely differing sophistication existed together in Dark Age northern Europe. The Sutton Hoo ship may represent a main stream of the migrants' boatbuilding techniques at the time of the invasion of Britain by the Angles, Saxons and Jutes, even though she may represent it in one of its most refined and luxurious forms, and these traditions may have persisted for many centuries.

Graveney boat

This theory perhaps receives some further support from chronologically the next important boat find made in England, the Graveney boat, discovered near Faversham in Kent in the autumn of 1970 and excavated jointly by the National Maritime Museum and the British Museum. This very important find, dating from about AD 900, is described in exact sequence in Chapter 16 of this book.

The last two boats described, Sutton Hoo and Gredstedbro, and possibly the two Nydam finds as well, may represent variations on the boatbuilding traditions of the peoples who invaded Britain from North Germany and Denmark in a migration which lasted for approximately 200 years, from AD 400–600, the so-called Anglo-Saxons, families of Angle, Saxon, Jute and Frisian origin.

None of the four boats described may be typical. The Nydam oak boat may already have been obsolete when she was built. The Sutton Hoo ship may have been an exceptional Royal vessel. But these boats show that the people who made the

217
This model of the Sutton Hoo ship is based on early assessments of her probable form, but gives a good general impression. [*British Museum*

218
Model of the larger Kvalsund boat. [*Norsk Sjøfartsmuseum*

migration could construct very well-built clinker-built open rowing boats which were seaworthy and could be very big. At least two types of boat may have developed, a long narrow vessel of war, or royalty, and a slower, wider, more stable type which would be better able to carry many passengers and goods in general seafaring.

Such boats brought family and village groups, young and old, women, children and animals. It has been argued that they cannot have crossed the North Sea direct from Schleswig and must have made long circuitous journeys in shore of the Frisian islands. Such journeys must have taken months and many boats which started out no doubt never arrived. The hardships in such journeys can be imagined. Only the fittest even of these people, who had already lived through the rigours of infancy and childhood in the Dark Ages, can have survived to reach Britain and form a strand in the ancestry of many British, American, Canadian, Australian, and New Zealand citizens today.

Kvalsund and Bårset boats

The next major North European boat finds, in chronological order of probable date of construction, comprise the finds at Kvalsund in western Norway. Their date has been much disputed, but the two boats are usually thought to have been built around AD 700. The planks of the larger boats are narrow and the frames are secured to the upper strakes with trenails and iron spikes, to the lower planks with lashings to the cleats. In the smaller boat the frames are fastened with trenails throughout. As the model in the Norsk Sjøfartsmuseum, Oslo (Figure 218) shows, these boats are long and narrow and the larger of the two has seven narrow strakes on each side of a keel rather like that of the Nydam pine boat, that is, of a very shallow T-section. The boat is built of oak and is about 50ft (15.24m) long, with its softwood frames in one piece. The hull is quite full-bodied and could have been sailed, but there is still no evidence at all of a mast or sail and the boat was rowed with single tholes with withy lashings to secure the oars.

Another boat dating from the same period and found in northern Norway is the Barset boat. As has already been said in Chapter 9, her uppermost strake is sewn to the next, the rest are fastened together, clinker fashion, with iron rivets.

By AD 700, therefore, there is still no positive evidence of the appearance of the sail in the North European wooden boatbuilding traditions, as represented by the finds described in this chapter. The boats (long, narrow and varying in depth, keel structure and cross section in a manner which suggests adaptation to use in shallow or deep waters, involving beaching or lying to moorings afloat) are rowing boats, apparently increasingly efficient for this purpose, both in the open sea and in more restricted waters.

It can be argued that the adoption of the sail in the development of the boat tends to happen as necessary. When larger numbers of people have to be carried for reasons of transport, as in migrations, or warfare as in raiding parties, or fishing, they can provide predictable and reasonably reliable motive power, and under these conditions a rowing boat is more efficient and usually safer than a long, narrow, squaresailed sailing boat and there is no cause for the adoption of sail. Sail comes when it is necessary to propel large boats with few men, or for great distances, under conditions when sails can be used favourably. The fishermen of Shetland, operating ninety miles offshore, did not adopt the sail until early in the nineteenth century. It may well be that the sail was not widely used in the great northern Norwegian fisheries until much the same period. When the use of the boat is considered and the economic and social background to that use, the fact that the utilization of the sail in northern Europe may not have developed on a large scale until widespread seafaring began at the onset of the Viking Age is not so surprising as it might otherwise seem.

Bibliography

ÅKERLUND, H, *Nydamskeppen*, 1963
BRØGGER, A W and SHETELIG, H, *Viking Ships, their Ancestry and Evolution*, 1951
BRØNSTED, J, 'Oldtidsbaden fra Als', 1925
BRUCE-MITFORD, R L S, *Sutton Hoo Ship Burial*, 1968
   The Sutton Hoo Ship Burial, Vol. 1, 1975
CHRISTENSEN, A E, *Boats of the North*, 1968
COLES, J, FENWICK, V and HUTCHINSON, G (eds), *A Spirit of Enquiry*, 1993
CRUMLIN-PEDERSEN, O, 'Cog-Kogge-Kaage', 1965
   'Gredstedbro Ship', 1968
   'Skin or Wood', 1972
EVANS, A C, 'The Sutton Hoo Ship', 1972
   The Sutton Hoo Ship Burial, 1986
GJESSING, G, 'Båtfunnene fra Bårset og Øksnes', 1935
HAYWOOD, J, *Dark Age Naval Power*, 1991
HUMBLA, P, 'Om Björkebaten fran Hille socken', 1949
MCGRAIL, S (ed), *Maritime Celts, Frisians and Saxons*, 1990
ROSENBERG, G, *Hjortspringfundet*, 1937
WESTERDAHL, C (ed), 'Crossroads in Ancient Shipbuilding', 1994

13

The Round-Hulled Boat
Before the Viking Era:
A Different Tradition

The Utrecht boat was discovered in 1930 in a dried-up former bed of the Rhine. She is dated from the twelfth century AD. As Figure 219 shows, she comprises a great logboat made from a long narrow tree so that its proportions are near to those of a massive keel plank. This logboat in fact comprises a hog, that is a member to accept the garboard fastenings, rather than a keel, which by definition is the principal longitudinal strength member of a vessel. The natural upward curve at either end of the logboat is carried on by huge extension pieces scarfed onto the rising end. Two planks and a wale made from half a log extend on each side of the boat, the planks laid overlapping, clinker-style and fastened by trenails except at the ends where they are fastened with iron nails to small transoms. She has massive floor timbers, which extend only a short way above the sides.

The structure is a larger and more sophisticated version of one currently in use in Bangladesh in areas where the narrow straight trees available reduce the logboat base of the local boats to little more than a keel plank, or hog, as shown in Figure 220.

The Utrecht boat was perhaps an inland waterway vessel herself, like the Bangladesh boat illustrated, and she may well be an example of an early and primitive form, co-existing in the Europe of the twelfth century with much more sophisticated vessels in the same tradition. Certainly conditions in the Low Countries in the second half of the first millennium were such that this type of vessel would have been suitable for trading in the great areas of marsh, fen and tidal inundation and on the great rivers of this part of Europe. She has the marks of wear on her bottom consistent with her having taken the ground on sand or gravel beaches.

A recent example of a not dissimilar shape would appear to be a type of barge used in Norfolk in the nineteenth century, and her general form may owe something to the building traditions which influenced the construction of the Utrecht boat. Another nineteenth-century boat in the same tradition but developed in the direction of the flat-bottomed boat may be seen in Figure 221, a flat-bottomed boat preserved at

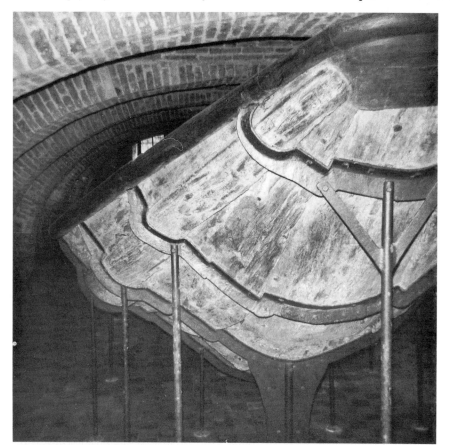

219
The Utrecht ship in her cellar in Utrecht. [*Basil Greenhill*

221
Flat-bottomed boat at Ketelhaven Maritime Archaeological Museum. This type of boat has been in widespread use in the Netherlands as a tender to working vessels. In the twentieth century construction has usually been in iron. [*Basil Greenhill*

220
A clinker-built extended logboat in Sylhet district, Bangladesh. [*Basil Greenhill*

the Ketelhaven Maritime Archaeological Museum of the Northeast Polder in Holland, showing parallels of shape with the Utrecht boat. She may well demonstrate a persistence of similar building traditions in the same general area for more than a thousand years. It has been suggested that the Utrecht boat may be an ancestor of the medieval hulk. But there is nothing to connect the two very widely differing hull structures (see Chapter 19).

Bibliography

CRUMLIN-PEDERSEN, O, 'Cog-Kogge-Kaage', 1965
MCGRAIL, S, *Ancient Boats of North West Europe*, 1987
PHILIPSEN, J P W, 'Utrecht Ship', 1965
VLEK, R, *The Medieval Utrecht Boat*, 1987

CHAPTER
14

The Flat-Bottomed Boat Before the Viking Era

Once planks were available at a price a boat need no longer have a logboat base, but could be built simply with broad planks making a bottom and sides. Such a simple flat-bottomed boat is the Somerset turf boat, described and illustrated in Chapter 2. Here a logboat origin is perhaps indicated by the massive block ends which may reproduce the solid ends of the original basic logboat structure. It is of interest that Itkonen mentions, but without date or reference, the discovery of two flat-bottomed boats in peat bogs in Karelia in Finland.

The turf boat represents a very old boatbuilding tradition on the Somerset levels and illustrates the simplest form of plank-built flat-bottomed boat extremely well. To recapitulate, the block ends, locally 'nosers' (there is no differentiation between bow and stern) are kept as low as possible so as to minimise the effects of local winds on the boat and make it easier to pole. It was poled with a special pole, locally known as an 'oar'. The floor timbers were called in local dialect *hrungs* (which appears to be a variation of the old Scandinavian *hrong*, floor timber) and the side frames *drashels*, which word was used also in the local dialect for a flail.

From the simple logboat beginnings both the flat-bottomed boat and the keel plank round-bottomed boat could develop. The drawings by Kurt Kuhn for Dr Wolfgang Rudolph reproduced here of nineteenth-century boats of the German Baltic coast show examples of how these two different lines of development could grow (Figures 222 and 223).

A number of examples of flat-bottomed boats in Romano-Celtic tradition have been found in the Rhine region and in the Thames at London. These finds are dated to the first and third centuries AD. Fragmentary remains of boats of the same type and period have been found in Bruges and in Avenches in Switzerland. Beat Arnold, who excavated vessels of this tradition in Lake Neuchâtel in Switzerland described them as neither shell nor skeleton, but of 'bottom based' construction. Accepting this definition McGrail sees the crucial difference in whether the angles of the side planks added to the flat bottom were governed by pre-placed frames or by the bevel put on the outer edges of the bottom. There may be seen a not totally different situation with two widespread North American flat-bottomed boatbuilding traditions. The skiff, the

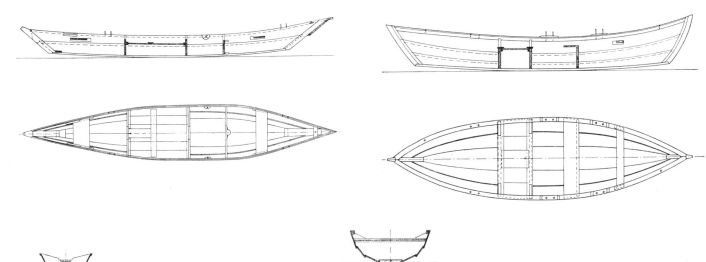

222
Above – a flat-bottomed clinker-built boat of the German Baltic coast. [Kurt Kuhn

223
Above right – a round-hulled keel plank boat from the same coast. [Kurt Kuhn

building of which is described in Chapter 2, can be regarded as essentially shell-conceived, the dory as of skeleton construction.

The history of the flat-bottomed boat has been generally neglected and it is only very recently that the type has begun to be recognised as an important and very old strand in the development of the boat in northern Europe and North America. Recognisable remains of simple flat-botttomed boats are less likely to be found than those of round-hulled vessels, which are more likely to remain intact and on discovery to be recognised as obviously parts of ships or boats. Round-hulled ship fragments are also less likely, because they have been extensively and characteristically worked in a way which makes the timber hard to adapt to other purposes, to be torn apart and used again for purposes not associated with boatbuilding. This is only too likely to happen to the flat and relatively unworked boards used in simple flat-bottomed boat construction. For in some forms of flat-bottomed boat, including the Somerset turf boat and the whole vast international tradition of boats of similar form and varying degrees of sophistication, there need be only four curved edges in all the planks of the boat: the curves of each side of the flat bottom and the curves of the lower edge of the bottom strakes which fit them.

This simple fact is fundamental to the appreciation of the history of the flat-bottomed boat. In its simplest forms it was the boat which presented the fewest problems of construction, because it has the fewest and simplest curves to the plank edges. In Chapter 3 I said that historically a boat has been thought of as a reasonably watertight shell of strakes made up from planks joined at the edges, and held in shape by such minimal internal reinforcement as may be necessary. I pointed out that since wooden planks are flat, boatbuilders have been successful to the degree in which they have been able to convert flat material into shapes which, when joined together at the edges, will make a hollow object of the shape of the sort of boat they are trying to build. The formation of the boat will depend on the shape of the edges of the planks more than anything else. The success of the boatbuilder depends on his ability to foresee the flat shapes which will make up into the three dimensional form of the boat he wants.

I went on to point out that this skill of judging the shapes of the plank edges is an extremely difficult one to acquire, and that this difficulty had played its part in the history of the development of boats again and again. Just how complex the shapes of planks can be even in a very simple boat is shown by the strake diagram of the Gokstad *faering* in Figure 39.

In Chapter 2 I showed that in flat-bottomed boats, like George Adams' skiff, the

224

An 'exploded' banks dory built at the Lawrence Allen Dory Shop, Lunenburg, Nova Scotia, and on display at Mystic Seaport, Connecticut. [Basil Greenhill

great problem of the boatbuilder was reduced to its very simplest terms. George Adams had to know the bottom curve of his sides, and almost nothing else presented him with any difficulty. Boats in the tradition of the Somerset turf boats give their builders an even easier time. Here the only curve to worry about is even simpler: Figures 39 and 46 show the contrast between the complexity of the strake shapes of the Gokstad *faering* and those of a banks dory, a relatively sophisticated flat-bottomed boat.

Given this relative simplicity it is little wonder that the flat-bottomed boat has had its own building traditions, probably for at least 2000 years in northern Europe and for much longer in Egypt. Even in its most complicated forms, where the sides are curved as in the medieval cog and the nineteenth-century Bridgwater boat (Chapter 18), its construction requires much less of the boatbuilder's peculiar skill than does that of a round-hulled vessel. I do not think this fact can be illustrated more clearly again than by the photograph in Figure 224 of an exploded banks dory. Here are all the component parts of a classic flat-bottomed boat, another fisherman's dory from the Lawrence Allen dory shop in Lunenberg, Nova Scotia (bigger and more complex than that in Figure 46), set up so that you can see how they are shaped and where they fit together. And the only complex shape is in the bottom edge of the lowest strake. Yet within certain limitations and for certain purposes this boat form is efficient enough. I shall have a lot more to say about the origins, characteristics and development of the banks dory in Chapter 18 of this book. No wonder the basic form has persisted for centuries and is still in use all the way down the east coast of North America and in Portugal and was in use very recently in northwestern France. Very similar craft are still to be found on the sea coasts of Somerset and Dorset in Britain, in Holland, in western Germany, and in Denmark, and on the coast of the southern Baltic and in southern Gotland among many other places. However the parts of a boat of this kind are only too likely to be utilised for other purposes once the boat

225

Two stone pictures from Gotland.
[Gotlands Historical Museum

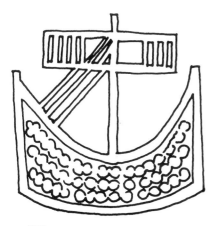

226

Ships on coins from Birka and Hedeby.
[Nordiska Museum, Stockholm

they have comprised is finished with, so flat-bottomed boats are unlikely to make archaeological finds.

The absence in the Low Countries and western Germany, where the flat-bottomed boat type appears to have developed most in Europe, of the boat burials and sacrifices which have proved such a valuable source of information on some other North European vessels, also means that little is positively known of these 'Frisian' boats of the centuries before the Viking era. But on the evidence of place names, the visual evidence of ships represented on coins found in Scandinavian trading centres and on stone carvings on the Baltic island of Gotland from the pre-Viking era, and in view of information coming to light on the probable trade routes of the people of western Germany and the Low Countries at the same period, it is now beginning to be thought possible that big Frisian vessels of the flat-bottomed type traded as far north and east as the vicinity of Stockholm, until the Viking expansion at the beginning of the ninth century made such long range trading far too dangerous because of piracy.

Two stone pictures from the island of Gotland reproduced here (Figure 225) and dated about AD 700 are among the earliest illustrations of sailing ships in Scandinavia. They show the sharp transition between keel and stem, characteristic of the flat-bottomed boat and later to be characteristic of the cog (see Chapter 18). The two early ninth-century coins from Birka and Hedeby (Figure 226) also show ships with straight stem and stern posts.

These vessels appear clearly to have used sails, and it was possibly from these ships that Scandinavians learned to use the sail. It seems likely that the flat-bottomed Frisian vessels were more suited to sailing than the early boats in the Scandinavian clinker tradition can have been. All the illustrations reproduced here show angular projections at the junction of the stem and stern posts with the bottom structure of the vessels. These projections would certainly increase the directional stability of the ship and thus improve her sailing characteristics. Ole Crumlin-Pedersen believes that this stem feature, known in Danish as the *barde*, may have been incorporated in ships and boats of the Scandinavian clinker tradition when sail was first introduced. Certainly something very like it appears in the Graveney boat (see Chapter 16) which provided the first archaeological evidence of the existence of this feature, which appears in a number of drawings of ships from widely different parts of northern Europe over a long period. Subsequent improvements in shipbuilding methods made the *barde* unnecessary in the later Norse ships, though, as we shall see later, it is probable that their sailing virtues always lay in certain specific directions.

Quite apart from the rowing characteristics of vessels in the North European clinker-building tradition, the use to which they were put and the economic and social background against which they operated, it may well be that the early use of the sail by the Frisians and the later use by the Scandinavians may have been conditioned partly by the availability of suitable fabrics for sail-making in the two areas. I shall have more to say about the history of the development of the squaresail in northern Europe later.

The Slav traditions

The coasts of the southern Baltic, of Poland and northern Germany and of the Russian enclaves between Poland and Lithuania, are quite different from those of the north shores, of Sweden and Finland. There is no multiplicity of deep creeks and fjords and sheltering archipelagoes. The shore is shallow far out to sea and exposed and there are few large bays.

The settlements tended to develop at the heads of the estuaries of rivers of which two, the Oder and the Vistula, are great arteries connecting the Baltic with the whole of its southern hinterland.

In this area, inhabited at different times by a shifting complex of peoples, equally complex boatbuilding traditions developed, traditions of the old inhabitants of Prussia, of the Balts, of the Goths, and increasingly over time, of the Slavs. These traditions were indigenous to the peoples of the area and co-existed with the developing boatbuilding of Scandinavia and western Europe. In Poland by the beginning of the 1990s thirty wrecks of plank-built boats and numerous fragments of boat structures had been excavated. Some of these have been published in Polish and German and a convenient brief summary by the late Dr Przemyslaw Smolarek was published as 'Aspects of Easy Boatbuilding in the Southern Baltic Region' in *Crossroads in Ancient Shipbuilding* in 1991.

The boats of this region over the centuries from the eighth century onwards to the post-Viking period tend, as might be expected from the geographical situation, to be flat-bottomed, the vessels of the coast often having small keels and mast steps. The true pram, the punt-like structure of the great rivers and the bays, flat-bottomed, sometimes with fore and aft rocker, the flush laid planks of the bottom edge-joined, with flared sides and usually with chine logs (see Chapter 17) at the turn of the bilge, was widespread in south Baltic Slavonic boatbuilding. Its ends were usually raked, punt-like, so that when it reached the shallow shore the cargo and people could easily be discharged, but sometimes the bow end was pointed.

Dr Smolarek identifies other general types of flat-bottomed boats indigenous to the south Baltic shores and rivers, some of them seagoing. With these vessels, quite different from the Scandinavian traditions, the south Baltic peoples conducted trade and warlike activities from at least the eighth century AD until after the decline of the Viking expansion. Then the Slavs, Balts and Estonians became a threat to Scandinavia. The Danes in particular had to create a whole system of defences, including the very blockages of waterways which have given us the Skuldelev finds – the beginning of the modern study of the archaeology of the boat. There were, it seems, Slavonic settlements in Denmark and Sweden, and at Fribrodre on Falster in Denmark a boatbuilders' yard dating from the tenth century has been excavated which appears to have been operated by west Slavonic people.

Also in *Crossroads in Ancient Shipbuilding*, Wladyslaw Filipowiak, in writing of shipbuilding at the mouth of the Oder, finds archaeological evidence for the development locally of the plank-built boat from the logboat. By the ninth century AD a clinker building tradition had developed which appears to be quite distinct from the Scandinavian, with a shallow rounded keel, a different frame structure, and with the strakes fastened with trenails (because the high grade local oak used would have corroded iron very quickly). Iron fastenings were used only where the edge bevels of planking made the use of trenails too difficult, and at the hood end-stem fastenings.

Bibliography

BASS, G F (ed) '*A History of Seafaring Based on Underwater Archaeology*'
CRUMLIN-PEDERSEN, O, 'Cog-Kogge-Kaage', 1965
GARDNER, J and MANNING, S F, '*The Dory Book*', 1978
GREENHILL, B and MANNING, S F, '*The Evolution of the Wooden Ship*', 1988
GUTHORN, D J, '*The Sea Bright Skiff*', 1971
HAYWOOD, J, '*Dark Age Naval Power*', 1991
ITKONEN, T, 'Suomen Kansanomaiset Veneet', 1926
MCGRAIL, S, '*Rafts, Boats and Ships*', 1981
  (ed), '*Maritime Celts, Frisians and Saxons*', 1990
  '*Romano-Celtic boats and ships*', 1995
NYLÉN, E and PEDERHAMM, J, '*Stones, Ships and Symbols*', 1988
RUDOLPH, W, *Inshore Fishing Craft of the Southern Baltic from Holstein to Curonia*, 1974
WESTERDAHL, C (ed) *Crossroads in Ancient Shipbuilding*, 1994

CHAPTER 15

The Viking Age

In the years immediately before the onset of the Viking Age in the late eighth century AD it appears, from the available evidence already described in this book, that the Scandinavian and some other North European round-hulled boats had the following general characteristics:

1. They were clinker-built with the strakes laid with the lower edge of the upper outside the upper edge of the lower.
2. Their timbers were each in one U- or V-shaped piece cut to shape.
3. The strakes of entirely plank-built boats were by now narrow and made up of several planks joined end to end.
4. The timbers could either be fastened direct to the strakes or secured with ties to cleats left upstanding on the strake when they were cut out. There are a number of examples of both nailed and lashed timbers from pre-Viking remains, besides those that have already been described in this book. On the whole the indications are that cleats had become obsolescent, if not obsolete, south of Norway by the beginning of the Viking period.
5. They had no permanent beams, though even early Viking ships were to have permanent beams at every frame.
6. Two traditions seem clearly to have emerged: the keel plank boat, associated with the shallow waters of the rivers, creeks, waterways and coastal seas between northern Denmark and the north of France; and boats with T-shaped keels, some of them very small, associated especially with Scandinavia.
7. Within the family of keel plank boats different traditions had developed which were to give rise to different types of boats and ships.
8. Round-hulled boats were rowed with oars worked on single thole pins with lashings of thongs or withes. Sails were already used.
9. These boats were steered with a side rudder, perhaps sometimes with a steering oar.

These in very broad terms seem to have been the vessels, as far as is at present known, of the peoples of Scandinavia before the Vikings, and the vessels with which the trade, commerce, travel and raiding of the peoples of what is now north Germany, Holland, Belgium, northern France and Britain were carried on about the year AD 800. There almost certainly have been many other types, or developments from the types described above. Fresh archaeological discoveries are now frequently adding to our knowledge.

It may well be that the Scandinavian tradition was a specialised one on the edge of a wider tradition, rather than being its principal branch. It may be that remote influences from skin boatbuilding traditions played a larger part in the Scandinavian than in the main European developments of the period and led to the development of this special family of sensitive, aristocratic boats, boats associated with the activities of a very energetic and virile people well recorded in the vivid poetry of the sagas, and sufficiently alien from the modern world to grip the imagination today.

The Viking Age is of irresistible interest to many people in Britain and in North America. It was a period of great, almost incredible, expansion by the Scandinavian people which resulted in the settlement of large areas of the British Isles by peoples of Scandinavian origin, so that there is a very good chance that any reader of this book whose mother tongue is English has an element of Scandinavian in his or her ancestry. It resulted in the settlement of Iceland and of Greenland, and in the discovery of North America, followed by the establishment at L'Anse aux Meadows, on the northern tip of Newfoundland, of a short-lived base for exploration and the repair and maintenance of the ships (for which work there were good facilities), and with accommodation for about 100 people, including women. From this base the Gulf of St Lawrence was explored and 'Vinland' discovered, probably in the area of the Miramichi in what is now New Brunswick. But the risks and costs of this operation were too great and its returns too small to justify its continuation at a time when the Scandinavian population of Greenland itself was only some 600. Greenland Viking interest therefore turned to trading with the Eskimo even as far north as Ellesmere Island.

This age is thought of as one of plunder, piracy and violence. In fact, these were commonplaces of the times. The Scandinavian expansion, though it contained these elements, was also an era of colonisation, settlement and of trade as peaceful as the circumstances of the times allowed. The Scandinavians sailed to Newfoundland in the west, and into the Mediterranean and through the great rivers of Russia down to the Black Sea in the east, for purposes of trade and exploitation of natural resources as well as of piracy and war.

We know today more about the evolution of the ship within 250 miles of the Skaw between AD 800–1200 than about the development of almost any other kind of ships and boats until modern times, thanks, largely, to the rigorous efforts of the Danish National Museum, centred at Roskilde. The large number of archaeological boat finds that have been made in Scandinavia (forty in south Scandinavia alone by 1989), the finds of Scandinavian ships elsewhere, and other evidence, notably in literary sources, have been studied more intensively and more ably perhaps than the evidence of the development of any other boats except for the Athenian trireme. The fact of the physical survival of the remains of their vessels has served the memory of the Vikings well. But the story is still incomplete. The results of much work still await publication and many of the conclusions that have been reached must still be regarded as tentative.

Because of the widespread Scandinavian influence in Britain, the Scandinavian tradition of boatbuilding during the Viking Age is part of the British heritage, and is particularly and obviously so in some areas of the country more than in others. But it is only a part of our heritage, and many boatbuilding traditions in Britain probably spring from other sources, some of which may be partly influenced by Scandinavian traditions.

Our own clinker-built boatbuilding traditions were, such evidence as we have suggests, highly developed at the time of the Viking invasions. We still know very little of them, but the discovery of the Graveney boat in 1970 revealed a boatbuilding tradition as developed as the Scandinavian but quite different in many ways. Moreover, the Scandinavian traditions about which we know so relatively much, probably paralleled and sprang eventually from the same roots as the traditions indigenous in Britain and elsewhere in Europe at the time of the Viking expansion. We have begun to learn a little about the origin of these traditions, with the Sutton Hoo and Graveney finds and other evidence, but much more is needed before any but the most tentative conclusions can be formulated.

For all these reasons it is justifiable to examine what we know of the development of the Scandinavian boatbuilding traditions at the time of the Viking expansion in some considerable detail. They are part of our heritage and parallel the development in this country of earlier traditions which in turn form part of our heritage of boatbuilding traditions, but about which we still know very little.

Viking ships, that is vessels constructed generally in the traditions revealed by the Scandinavian evidence for the period, were certainly built in the British Isles. A new, unused stem piece for quite a large boat was found many years ago on the island of Eigg in Scotland which suggests the possibility of boatbuilding. The great longship, 30m overall, found in Roskilde fjord in Denmark and known to archaeologists as Skuldelev 2, was, it is now known from study of her timber, built from material of Dublin origin and most likely in Dublin itself. McGrail suggests, in his report on the vessel remains found during excavations on the Dublin waterfront, *Medieval Boat and Ship Timbers from Dublin*, p.98,

> During the Viking period and up to the mid-twelfth century . . . the evidence is thus overwhelmingly that the Dublin ships and boats were in the mainstream of the Viking tradition, in their sequence of building, in their form and structure, and in their method of propulsion (and probably also steering) . . . The Dublin wood working techniques are in the mainstream, with little, if any, sign of regional variations.

Bibliography

ADDYMAN, P *et al* (eds), *The Vikings in England*, 1981
ANDERSEN, B and E, *Råsejlet-Dragens Vinge*, 1989
BANG-ANDERSEN, A, GREENHILL, B and GRUDE, E H (eds), *The North Sea*, 1985
BRØGGER, A W and SHETELIG, H, *Viking Ships, their Ancestry and Evolution*, 1951
BRØNSTED, J, *The Vikings*, 1967
CLAUSEN, B L (ed), *Viking Voyages to North America*, 1993
CRUMLIN-PEDERSEN, O and VINNER, M, *Sailing into the Past*, 1986
CRUMLIN-PEDERSEN, O (ed), *Aspects of Maritime Scandinavia*, 1991
FOOTE, P G and WILSON, D M, *Viking Achievement*, 1970
GEIPEL, J, *The Viking Legacy*, 1971
HOLMQUIST, W, *The Swedish Vikings*, 1979
INGSTAD, A S, *The Discovery of a Norse Settlement in North America*, 1977
INGSTAD, H, *The Norse Discovery of America*, 1985
JONES, G, *A History of the Vikings*, 1968
LAMM, J P and NORDSTRÖM, H–A, *Vendel Period Studies*, 1983
LOYN, H R, *The Vikings in Britain*, 1977
MCGRAIL, S, *Ancient Boats of North West Europe*, 1987
    Medieval Boat and Ship Timbers from Dublin, 1993
NYLÉN, E and LAMM, J P, *Stones, Ships, and Symbols*, 1988
SAWYER, P H, *Age of the Vikings*, 1971
VEBAEK, C L and THIRSLUND, S, *The Viking Compass, Guided Norseman first to America*, 1992
WILSON, D, *The Vikings and their Origins*, 1970

CHAPTER
16

The Viking Ships and the Graveney Boat

In the late AD 700s Europe was entering the 250 years of Scandinavian expansion, the years of the Vikings. This was the period when kings and earls, local chieftains and merchants and bands of villagers from what are now Denmark, Norway and Sweden, using the clinker-built boat as the chief tool and agent of their expansion, colonised, traded and raided from southern Russia to North America. They settled in Iceland, Greenland, northern France, Britain and Ireland, and worked their great open boats into the Mediterranean and much smaller boats down the great rivers into the Black Sea.

The story is complex; trading on long established routes, colonisation and raiding went on all at the same time. But in very simple terms the Danes' sphere of interest was northern Europe, including eastern and southern Britain, where they appear to have settled extensively, leaving a legacy of place names, words in local dialect and a strain in the ancestry of some people who come from those parts of Britain. The Swedes penetrated the great rivers of Russia to the Black Sea. The Norwegians occupied the Scottish Isles, parts of western Britain, the Isle of Man, Ireland, Iceland and Greenland from where they made voyages to the North American mainland. The map (Figure 227) shows the approximate routes taken by the Vikings. The dotted lines show routes which are conjectural. In central Europe when moving from river to river the Vikings are assumed to have transported their boats overland across watersheds – which limits the size of the vessels which can have been used in regular trade.

The regular maintenance of this kind of deliberate open boat sailing often in rigorous climatic conditions is one of the most remarkable, perhaps the most remarkable, of seafaring achievements in the history of European man. Until the voyages and colonisation of the sixteenth and seventeenth centuries no people from European homelands ever spread so far by sea as the Scandinavian peoples during the Viking Age. As to the size of their fleets, a carving on a rune stave dating from the thirteenth century (Figure 228) found during the excavation of the old quays at Bergen in Norway shows the stems of a great Viking fleet of forty-eight ships. In the light of knowledge as it now stands of Scandinavian shipbuilding of the period, it is

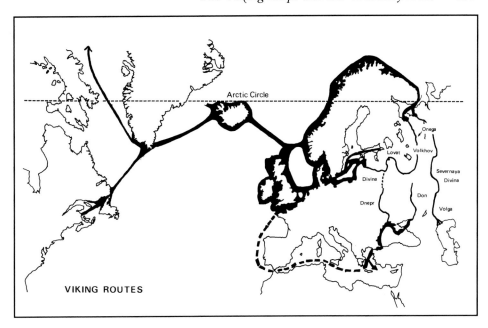

227

The Viking expansion. [Basil Greenhill

possible from this rune stave to identify several of what are thought to have been the basic types of Viking ship.

Some of the ships associated with the period of the Scandinavian expansion which still survive today in greater or lesser degree of completeness will be described. These, and numerous other finds, many of them not yet excavated or, if excavated, not yet fully published, most of them more fragmentary, give clear evidence of the scale and sophistication of Viking shipbuilding. These ships were the principal technical achievements of the people who built them. In the words of the Danish historian Johannes Brønsted in his book *The Vikings*:

> The ships of the Vikings were the supreme achievement of their technical skill, the pinnacle of their material culture; they were the foundation of their power, their delight, and their most treasured possession. What the temple was to the Greeks, the ship was to the Vikings; the complete and harmonious expression of a rare ability.

There is no generally accepted explanation of the origin of the word 'Viking', though the Danes themselves were using it in the eleventh century. It has become synonymous with an expansion which was to affect most of Europe and the North Atlantic islands. The reasons for the sudden outflowing of the Scandinavians beginning in the late eighth century are still a matter of speculation, but amongst them may have been the development for the first time in the north of the use of the sail, allied with significant improvements in shipbuilding. Probably partly in search of new land to settle, or for political reasons, or in pursuit of trade, or as pure raiders and pirates, or as mercenaries in the service of other powers, the Scandinavian peoples moved outwards for over two centuries.

228

This carving on a rune stave of the 1200s found in Bergen shows the stems of a great fleet of Viking ships. [Bergens Sjøfartsmuseum

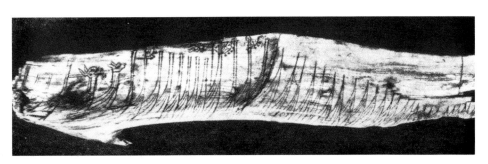

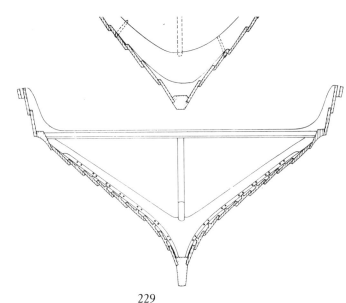

229
Above left – model of the Oseberg ship.
[*National Maritime Museum*

231
Above right – section of the Oseberg ship. [*Ole Crumlin-Pedersen*

Oseberg ship

In 1905 the richest and most magnificent of all Viking archaeological finds was made on Oseberg farm near Tonsberg in Norway. This was the grave of a rich woman and the find comprised a cart, sledges, beds, household utensils, all inside a magnificently decorated clinker-built vessel. Recent carbon dating has shown that the vessel was built around 820 AD and buried about fourteen years later. Dating from the beginning of the age of the Scandinavian expansion, she represents the greatest single find of the art of the Vikings – vigorous, highly skilled surface decoration with its roots deep in the Scandinavian art of the preceding centuries and with influences from Europe to the south.

The ship was taken from the burial mound and when reassembled was found to be of a form which, it has been suggested, probably represents an early Viking *karve*, a ship on the whole intended for service in relatively sheltered waters. The model illustrated here (Figure 229) was made in the workshops of the National Maritime Museum and it illustrates the general form of the ship very well. The sail and

230
The Oseberg ship. [*Basil Greenhill*

rigging, which did not survive in the burial mound, are highly conjectural, based on contemporary rock scribings found on the island of Gotland in Sweden and are, in the light of recent research into Viking sailing (see later in this chapter) anachronistic for the Oseberg ship.

Though the ship probably was of a type meant for service in fjords and the network of sheltered waters in southern Norway and Sweden, this one was evidently very special, used as a family boat for a chieftain or chieftainess. She is exceptionally elaborately decorated and as she was recovered almost in her entirety, it is possible to see the full shape of the vessel and her bow and stern without so much speculative reconstruction as in some other cases. Today she stands reassembled in the Viking Ship Museum of the University Museum of National Antiquities at Bygdøy, outside Oslo, and although there is no detailed record of the work done and the assumptions made in reassembling her, she gives a very good impression of what she must have looked like when in use (Figure 230).

This remarkable structure is now early 1200 years old. Her construction is of great interest. The strakes are narrow and numerous, the frames are secured to them with lashings to cleats. There is a fully developed T-shaped keel. The ship had a mast and evidently had a squaresail. For the first time there are permanent beams joining the heads of the frames. These beams are a great characteristic of the Viking ship; their development is one of the possible keys to her evolution.

But the most important feature of the Oseberg ship is that the boat is really in two distinct parts. The timbers are in one piece and at their heads amidships, where the gunwale of a pre-Viking ship would have been, is a strong L-shaped plank. This was called the *meginhufr* in old Norse, that is, the strong middle plank of the three plank strake. Thus, it can be argued that there is a complete boat of pre-Viking shape, something like the Nydam fir boat but with a more highly developed T-shaped keel, below the *meginhufr*. Above the *meginhufr* and at a sharp angle to the lower strakes, are two more strakes, supported by knees secured to the *meginhufr* and the beams above the frame heads. The shape is very clearly shown in the drawing (Figure 231) by Ole Crumlin-Pedersen. Thus a basic boat shape has become the bottom of the boat and the extra strakes the sides. To put it very roughly, there are two boats, one above the other. And thus, in terms of archaeological finds, the Oseberg ship represents a distinct and clearly demonstrable development, a landmark in the evidence for the history of the Scandinavian shipbuilding traditions. A more recent find, the Klåstad ship in Norway, Arne Emil Christensen tells me, apparently shows an even more complex structure of the same kind from about the same period (Figure 232). She appears to have been a merchant ship and she was laden with a cargo of whetstones.

Gokstad ship

A vessel like the Oseberg ship, for all her beauty, must have been uncomfortable and dangerous if she ventured on North Sea crossings, particularly with heavy cargo and her hull form was such that she could become suddenly unstable when sailed beyond a certain speed which she was quite capable of attaining in a strong breeze. The Gokstad ship, shown in Figure 233, was also found south of Oslo, but in 1880, twenty-five years earlier than the Oseberg ship. Recent radio carbon dating has shown that she was built seventy-five years or so after the Oseberg ship. She was built around 895–900 AD and buried only ten years later. This was a time of intense maritime activity for the Vikings when in the first flush of their expansion some of them were raiding the coasts of England, Ireland, Scotland and France almost annually. The Gokstad ship, for all that she is still probably a vessel intended for trading within a relatively restricted area of sheltered water, also certainly the boat of

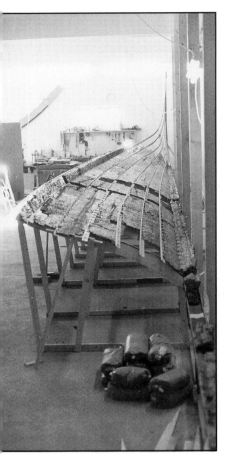

232
The Klåstad ship undergoing reconstruction. The meginhufr *is clearly visible above the topmost strake.* [Basil Greenhill

233
The Gokstad ship. [Basil Greenhill

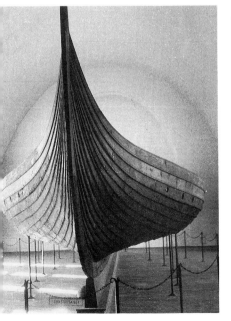

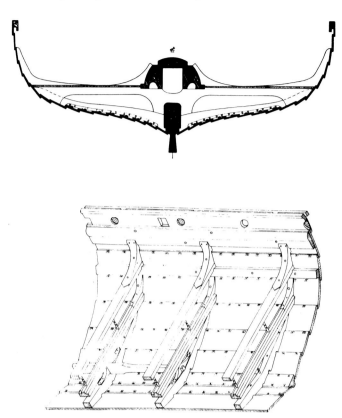

236
Above left – Skuldelev Wreck 5 – midships section. [Ole Crumlin-Pedersen

a very prosperous family and not necessarily a vessel close to the types used on the raiding or colonising voyages, shows a really considerable development on, but by no means necessarily from, the Oseberg ship. She is a fine seaworthy vessel, superbly constructed as far as can be told from the vessel as she is to be seen today.

She still shows her ancestry. The *meginhufr* dividing the lower boat from the upper planks is still there, though in a much less obvious form than in the Oseberg or Klåstad ships and the imposition of one ship on top of another is not at all so obvious, the change in shape of the structure at the critical point being far less acute. The floor timbers are still in one piece, secured by lashings to cleats on the planks of the lower boat. The beams are secured to the timber heads but the sides are higher and the strakes above the beams are secured to the knees with metal fastenings. The whole structure is clearly seen in the diagram (Figure 234), by Ole Crumlin-Pedersen. There is thus a difference of structure between the lower boat and the upper, but the basic boat is a less significant part of the structure as a whole and the beams are nearer the floor. The basic boat is built like the Nydam boat, the top part in a newer and more economical style. The Gokstad ship perhaps represents the ultimate development of an old Norwegian and north Swedish tradition, already obsolescent when she was built, in which radially split oak planks with cleats were used. Perhaps (one can speculate) the men who built her did so in what may already have been to them an old-fashioned way, with cleats and lashings instead of trenails securing the frames directly to the strakes, because she was a vessel belonging to a powerful family.

The hull has more body to it and the vessel is altogether more seaworthy than the Oseberg ship. For the first time there was found a *beitiass*, a wooden bowline or reaching spar, which is believed to have been used to thrust the luff of the squaresail out to the wind, and this has been taken as clear evidence that attempts were being made to improve the windward qualities of the sail – several 'reconstructions' of the

◄◄ 234
Section of the Gokstad ship. [Ole Crumlin-Pedersen

◄ 235
The reconstruction of the Ladby ship landing horses. [Ole Crumlin-Pedersen

Gokstad ship have been built and subjected to exhaustive trials on different voyages at sea. The type has been shown to be extremely seaworthy if handled properly and, though she does not by any means necessarily represent the type of vessel used in Viking transatlantic voyages, to be fully capable of such work.

It could be that the expansion of the Viking seafaring activity which did actually take place in the fifty years between the Oseberg and Gokstad ships is sufficient to account for the tremendous improvement in design represented by the latter. On the other hand the improvement may have been responsible, at least in part, for the expansion in voyaging. More likely, they were just two separate special purpose vessels, the one archaic, the other incorporating some of the current features of vessels built in the middle of the ninth century for long-range voyaging.

Ladby ship

Neither the Oseberg ship nor the Gokstad ship, magnificent structures though they are, fully represent the ordinary run of vessels in which the Vikings made their long voyages overseas either to raid, trade or colonise. These were probably very different. The raiding vessels were long narrow ships, and a number of representatives have been found in the Danish peninsula, notably at Skuldelev and Hedeby. One, the Ladby ship, was excavated on the island of Funen in Denmark in one of the four boat graves that had been found to date in that country. She is long and narrow, 67½ft (20.6m) long and only 9½ft (2.9m) broad. Smaller than the bigger longships she probably represents the smaller type of vessel in which the Danish Viking raids on eastern Britain were carried out. Similar vessels dating from about AD 1000 have been identified in the Skuldelev finds in Roskilde fjord, only a few miles from Copenhagen. But these long, narrow, lightly built vessels were not peculiar to Danish and North Sea waters. One of them, at least, Skuldelev 2, as has already been said was built in Ireland. Others are illustrated in the Bayeux Tapestry, which shows the transports of the Normans (five generations removed Norwegian Vikings) who invaded England in 1066.

A reconstruction of the Ladby ship (Figure 235) was built in Denmark and subjected to some informal sea trials. She proved to be seaworthy and easy to row and sail in good conditions downwind. She could be run ashore very easily in the right conditions. The Ladby ship, like the Sutton Hoo ship, was found as a ghost in the sand and little detail could be learned of her construction, although she is now under re-assessment by a team from the Danish National Museum. But Skuldelev Wreck 5, the smaller of two longships found in Roskilde fjord and raised in the early 1960s, has the same length/beam ratio of the Ladby ship of about 7:1 and sufficient of her was recovered to show her midships cross-section (Figure 236).

The Bayeux Tapestry scene illustrated here (Figure 237) shows horses being transported in vessels very similar in general appearance to the Ladby ship. The experiment was tried of embarking horses on board the Ladby ship reconstruction and putting them ashore again. This was completely successful on the shallow, sheltered, non tidal coasts of the Danish islands.

It is convenient now to compare the midships sections, insofar as they can be reconstructed with varying degrees of conjecture, of some of the principal vessels so far discussed. The drawings here (Figure 238) show the conjectural midships sections of the Hjortspring and Nydam boats, and the Oseberg, Gokstad and Ladby ships. In considering the proportions of the Ladby ship it should be borne in mind that she is nearly as long as the Gokstad ship, but half the breadth and depth; a long, narrow, fast rowing and sailing vessel reminiscent perhaps in her proportions of the twentieth-century Finnish church boat from Petäjävesi of which a photograph

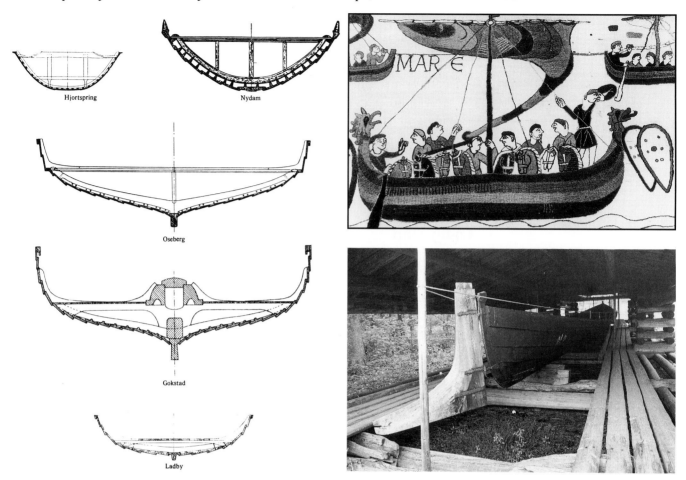

appears in Figure 239, and, when bereft of the fanciful head and stern ornaments given to the reconstruction, somewhat similar to the church boat in general appearance – though the church boat's structure was different in some fundamental aspects. It will be noted that the Ladby ship had the same extra heavy strake, this time number four, like the *meginhufr*, so clearly demonstrated in the Oseberg ship and to a much lesser extent in the Gokstad ship. The shadow of the strakes in the sand clearly showed this *meginhufr* and from its existence it has been assumed that the Ladby ship, like her two Norwegian contemporaries, was something of a mixture of building traditions though in this case, as in the Gokstad ship, in a very refined form.

It will be noted that the beams in the Ladby ship are a feature of the upper boat, holding its bottom together and secured to the heads of the timbers of the lower boat. As the two become merged into one another, the lower boat gradually assumes the status of simply the bottom of the boat, and the beams tend to sink lower and lower in the structure. This tendency is demonstrated even more clearly in one of the most important finds of vessels of the period of the Scandinavian expansion ever made and the find that really started the modern study of the archaeology of boats and ships, also made in Denmark: the Skuldelev find.

Skuldelev find

The Skuldelev find, one of the most important of all archaeological boat finds, was made in Roskilde fjord, twenty miles west of Copenhagen, in the late 1950s. Parts of five vessels, a fishing or ferry boat, two longships, two cargo ships, all dating from

239
The church boat of Petäjävesi in central Finland in her boathouse. These boats were used to take whole communities by water to attend church in parts of Sweden and Finland. Often an overnight stay was involved for which accommodation in huts was sometimes provided. [Basil Greenhill

◀ 237
Scene from the Bayeux Tapestry, from Bayeux Tapestry *by F Stenton.* [*Phaidon Press*

about AD 1000 were found blocking a shallow part of the fjord. They had been deliberately sunk to make an obstruction against maritime raids, probably by the Wens, the Slavic inhabitants of northern Germany, who were attacking southern Denmark at this time.

One of the longships (Skuldelev 2), of which only fragments survive, built in Ireland, perhaps represents the principal Danish Viking raiding vessel type, about 92 ft (28m) long with twenty to twenty-six pairs of oars. This may have been the kind of ship in which a further Danish invasion of the British Isles took place in about the year 1000, a successful invasion which led to the rule in England of King Canute of Denmark. The other longship is of the type found at Ladby and already described.

The first cargo ship (Skuldelev 3) was the most complete of all the finds. She represents a small vessel, and the model (Figure 240) is based on reconstruction from the wrecked timber by Ole Crumlin-Pedersen. Not too much significance should be attached to the sail of the model.

This small Skuldelev cargo ship is a vessel of great interest. She is about 40ft (13m) long and 10ft 3in (3.2m) in beam, primarily a sailing vessel with provision for seven oars as auxiliary power. She was light enough to be hauled overland for short distances when empty of her cargo, shallow enough to be used in rivers, yet with enough keel to be an effective sailing vessel by the standards of Viking ships. She could carry about 4.6 tons of cargo and retain a safe freeboard. She was, perhaps, a farmer's boat to carry him and his men to market with their products.

Her construction shows a further development and is in the tradition which employed trenails to secure the frames direct to the strakes. There are no cleats with lashings and the two boats one above the other have at last become faired into one. The frames are no longer in one piece with knees above them; there are separate floor timbers. The beams are even lower than in the Gokstad ship. The stem and stern post comprise carefully carved sets of plank ends – on the lines of the solution to the plank end problem illustrated in Figure 50. The strakes of the Skuldelev vessel are not brought to the stem and stern post as in almost all the other boats so far described, and as in most full-size clinker-built boats of modern times, but the upper sections of both the stem and the stern post are cunningly carved to provide the ending for several strakes together.

The Scandinavian peoples of the Viking period colonised large areas of the British Isles and established settlements in Iceland and western Greenland, and for over two centuries sent a series of expeditions to Canada, which continued as expeditions to

◀◀ 238
Midships sections of northwest European clinker-built boats. Ole Crumlin-Pedersen is now of the view that the Ladby ship had a further strake above those shown here. [*Ole Crumlin-Pedersen*

240
Model of the small Viking cargo or farmer's ship, Skuldelev Wreck 3. [*Basil Greenhill*

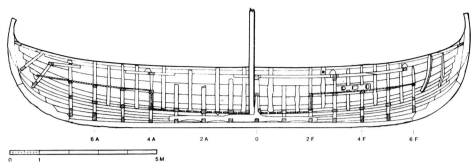

6A   4A   2A   0   2F   4F   6F

0   1   5M

241
A Viking knarr *of moderate size, Skuldelev 1, a preliminary reconstruction of longitudinal section.* [*Ole Crumlin-Pedersen*

collect timber. They transported small armies which harried France and Britain; they traded in the Mediterranean. In the course of this great maritime activity they moved many hundreds of men, women and children, horses and cattle, tools and agricultural equipment, trade goods, weapons and timber cargoes.

Though there is dispute about the early Greenland voyages in particular, and on economic grounds some authorities suggest they may have been made in local vessels of a type developed in Iceland, these great movements of peoples and goods were not made in longships like the Ladby ship, or in *karves* like the Gokstad and Oseberg ships, or coasters like the small Skuldelev cargo ship. The great ocean voyages to Iceland, Greenland and Canada are unlikely to have been made in these vessels either, despite the proven seaworthiness of the Gokstad ship. A lot of them must have been made in vessels with greater cargo-carrying capacity, relatively short, broad, sailing cargo ships of the type referred to in the sagas as *knarr*. The big cargo ship found at Skuldelev, usually referred to as Skuldelev 1, built with pine planking, probably in Norway, perhaps represents an example of a small vessel of this general type.

She is 54ft (16.5m) long and nearly a quarter as broad as she is long, very strongly built and a burdensome vessel with full round stern and bows. The bows of the *knarr* were so characteristic that in one or two places in the sagas, the prose poems of the Viking peoples written down in Iceland long after the events they purport to record, some Icelandic women are called *knarr bringa* (*knarr* breasted).

Constructed with a shell of narrow strakes, strengthened by timbers, separate futtocks and knees and beams at the timber heads, the massive *knarr* still shows a sudden change in the run of planking above the fifth strake up from the keel. Thus, perhaps, the influences at work in her ancestry can still be seen. Like the Oseberg ship she may be a development of the basic plank-built boat shape of an earlier age. She is also herself one of the ancestors of some of the wooden sailing ships of the Middle Ages. The *knarr* has few oars, her sailing efficiency under her squaresail appears to have been dependent partly on her beating spar. Like all the Viking ships so far described she was steered with a side rudder.

242
Skuldelev 1 as she is displayed in the Viking Ship Museum at Roskilde. [*Basil Greenhill*

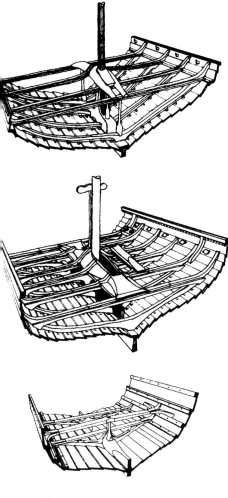

243
Comparative structures of Viking ships, AD 800–1000, top to bottom, Oseberg, Gokstad, Skuldelev 3. [Ole Crumlin-Pedersen

Ole Crumlin-Pedersen made a preliminary reconstruction (Figure 241), showing a longitudinal section. Today this vessel is as fully re-erected as she can be in the Viking Ship Museum by the shores of Roskilde fjord in Denmark, and Figure 242 shows her as she is now, with a framework of black metal to indicate the likely shape of the complete vessel.

She could, it has been calculated, carry 24 tons of cargo on a safe freeboard for sailing with a minimum crew of five. By the standards of trading in the Viking age this seems to have been a very considerable cargo. An even larger vessel of the same type but eight metres longer and with about double the cargo capacity has been found and partly excavated at Hedeby in Schleswig in an area which was Danish for many centuries. Another from a century or so later found at Lynaes north of Roskilde was evidently of similar type and size while the cargo ship found at Bergen and described in Chapter 17 was 85ft (36m) long and nearly 30ft (11m) in the beam.

It may be helpful at this point to summarise in very general terms the changes which appear to have taken place in the development of Scandinavian shipbuilding traditions over 200 years between AD 800 and about AD 1000. In a simplified way this can perhaps best be done by the three diagrams reproduced here which have been drawn by Ole Crumlin-Pedersen (Figure 243). They show the midships sections of the Oseberg ship, with its sharp transition of the *meginhufr* above the lower hull, the basic boat and the upper structure with the high beams at the top of the lower hull. Transition is far less marked, though still present, in the Gokstad ship, the lower hull less significant, the beams lower in the vessel. In the Skuldelev small cargo ship, the lower hull has become the bottom of the vessel. The upper structure has grown to be at least half the side of the ship. The beams have sunk to just above the floor timbers and additional beams have come in above them. It is the inside structure which reveals the apparent development of the tradition.

Graveney boat

There is plenty of evidence that during the two centuries the Vikings came to Britain as raiders, traders and colonisers they met with a great deal of opposition, some of it at sea. There must have been in Britain highly developed boatbuilding traditions, perhaps almost as highly developed as those of the Scandinavians, sharing some common ancestry.

But until the 1970s there was only shadowy evidence as to the nature of these traditions. Rather more information has become available through the discovery in 1970 in a tributary of the Thames in marshes near Faversham, Kent of the Graveney boat, which has been dated as from the early tenth century AD. She is no grand great chief's ship, like the Oseberg or Gokstad ships. The parallel is more with the two workaday Skuldelev cargo boats and she is between the two in size, clinker-built with a plank keel, or hog, instead of the T-shaped keel of the Scandinavian finds. The stern post, which survived, and the way the ends of the planks were fastened to it is quite outside the Scandinavian tradition as are the massive floor timbers and the apparent absence of cross-beams. Her great beam and sturdy framing distinguish her as a carrier of bulky cargoes. The massive frames are joined straight to the strakes with trenails. Her stern post has a sharp projection at the foot which appears to provide the first archaeological evidence for the *barde* (see Chapter 14), a feature which has been seen in various forms in contemporary illustrations of Scandinavian vessels. She is probably a boat which had an everyday job of work to do. A coaster, perhaps operating between creeks and rivers of southeastern England, occasionally across to the Low Countries, it may well be that the highly developed clinker tradition which she represents had roots in what is now Holland and Belgium and

southern Germany. The Graveney boat's structure has been the subject of more thorough examination and report than any comparable boat find made previously in Britain, and few boat finds anywhere in the world have been more thoroughly researched and published. But the full signficance of the find will only be assessable in the light of further discoveries of this period.

The hypothetical lines of the Graveney boat prepared by Eric McKee have been the source of hydrostatics prepared by Burness Corlett and Partners, the naval architects. Analysis suggests that the vessel was intended to be a moderately fast carrier of heavy concentrated cargoes, such as stone or salt. For this purpose the design is good and there is little to fault. She is seaworthy, reasonably fast and capable of making seagoing voyages under sail carrying six or seven tons of cargo, though in these conditions she will have had a tendency to ship water amidships. Her seagoing qualities are much in excess of those required for a vessel for service only on the river. It was hoped to put these conclusions into practice in due course by trials with a full-sized reconstruction which the National Maritime Museum planned to build. This would have served not only for the trials, but also to show the problems which faced the original builders. As has been demonstrated in Denmark in recent years this would have been an excellent way to press even further the detailed study of the structure of this very important vessel. But this project was ended by the closing down of the Archaeological Research Centre, and the ending of all archaeological work at the Museum. A half size (eighth size by volume) model of the boat has been privately built and sailed by Dr Edwin Gifford.

The three photographs are an admirable illustration of boat archaeology in action, since the Graveney dig was one of the most difficult, because of the conditions in which the boat was found. The first, Figure 244, shows the boat after its initial excavation, indicating her position relative to the Graveney Marsh dyke. The second, Figure 245, shows dismantling in process, a joint operation carried out by National Maritime Museum and British Museum staff, and the third, Figure 246, the site at dusk. In order to recover the boat before the drain was flooded work had to be carried on far into the nights.

Eric McKee spent over a year examining and recording the timbers and with the aid of a ¹⁄₁₀th scale model made by himself arrived at a preliminary hypothetical

245
The Graveney boat being dismantled.
[National Maritime Museum

246
The pressure of time meant that work
on the Graveney site had to go on far
into the night. [National Maritime
Museum

247
A working tool model reconstruction of
part of the Graveney boat. [Eric
McKee

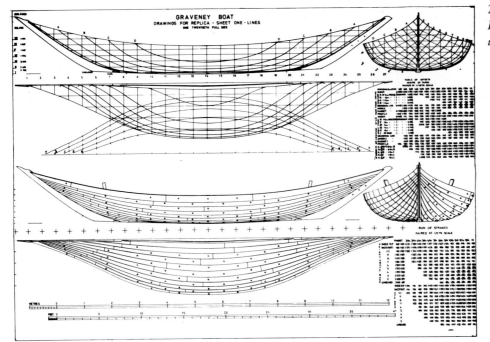

Lines of the Graveney boat – the conventional drawing. [Eric McKee

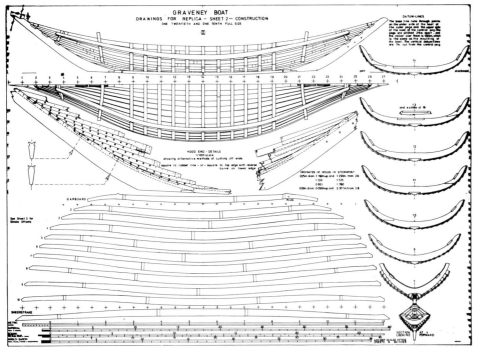

Structural drawing and strake diagram of the Graveney boat. [Eric McKee

reconstruction of the whole boat which gained widespread acceptance. The scale model, which gives a general indication of the possible full shape of the parts which were found, but which is no more than a working tool, is shown in Figure 247. Working drawings (Figures 248 and 249), both in conventional naval architects' and strake diagram form, indicate the generally agreed hypothesis of the form of the minimum boat. In this way much has been learned from the substantial timbers found 8ft (2.44m) under the blue clay of the Graveney marshes in the cold October of 1970. The original builders would indeed be very surprised to know of the money and effort spent to learn from their work as much as possible of the traditions which conditioned them.

Årby boat

In an era of nationally popular small boat sailing the question is often asked, what were the small boats of the Vikings like? Surely, it is said, they must have developed fast rowing and sailing boats which, within the limitations of their traditions, were of quality comparable with that indicated by the big ship finds which have been described here. They did indeed. Fragments of a number of small Viking boats have been found in Scandinavia and in Dublin the remains of boats of the size and type of the Årby find. Among the principal finds are those at Vendel, Valsgärde and Tuna in Badelunda, all north of Stockholm, the parts of boats found inside the Gokstad ship and the boat found at Årby near Upsala in middle Sweden. Her date is uncertain. It has been put very roughly at between AD 850 and 950 but she may well be earlier. She is a nicely shaped, simple little structure, about 13ft (4m) long made of a keel plank with two strakes on each side – a five plank boat. She has three timbers, each in a single piece, fastened direct to the shell with trenails. She was rowed by one man or woman who sat amidships and pulled the oars against two single thole pins, cut out of planks secured to the upper strakes on each side. The oars were secured with grommets. She was equipped also with a paddle. She had no gunwale and was a light canoe-like craft (Figures 42 to 45 in Chapter 3) of very pretty shape.

In the early 1980s this boat was the subject of a joint Anglo-Swedish reconstruction and trials project fully published by the Museum of National Antiquities in Stockholm, in 1993. Owain Roberts was in charge of the trials and he summed up the scientific results in the following general terms,

> The trials showed that the boat from Årby was probably ideally suited to the [local] conditions which are believed to have existed when she was in use about a thousand years ago. Her construction was light but strong so that she could withstand the strains of work and yet be beached without the need for great strength.
>
> She could be propelled with little effort over the distances one might expect in a lake. The boat is small and suitable for one person only – a personal means of transport. She would have given great satisfaction to her owner both from her ease of handling and her versatility. Indeed, for a lake-side dweller this little boat may have represented the same convenience and capability as one would these days expect of a bicycle.

Gokstad boats

The boats of the Gokstad find were larger. The smallest, the *faering* or four-oared boat, has three strakes on each side. She also has three timbers secured direct to the plank shell, together with inclined frames at the bows and at the stern, where a miniature side rudder may have provided the means of steering her. She has winged carved stem and stern posts like the Skuldelev finds and parts of the Gokstad stem, that is the plank ends are carved out of the solid and are in one piece with the stem itself.

The smallest of the three boats (Figures 38, 39 and 40, Chapter 3) has thole pins similar to those of the Årby boat. She is 20ft (6m) long, and is also light, very easy to row and will take three people in comfort. She is rowed by two men but one can handle her well enough. She is most beautifully shaped and built of very thin planking, so finely constructed as to be almost a work of art in her own right.

We do not know for certain what considerations were made by those who reconstructed her from the planks found in the Gokstad ship, for no detailed record was left. Nor can we be absolutely certain what new work was put into her. The boat as she is today in the Viking Ship Museum at Bygdøy therefore, is herself an approximation, but so right for her purpose as a fast rowing boat that she is probably fairly

close to the original form. More than one replica has been made of her including the one built at the National Maritime Museum, Greenwich (in order to gain experience for the work on the aborted Graveney boat replica), which was subjected to extensive sea trials, including sailing trials. The building and trials of this boat have been published in the Museum's Maritime Monograph Series (see Chapter 3).

Oselver boat

It is probable that these two small boats from Sweden and Norway represent types which had already been developed for several centuries when they were built in approximately AD 850 and AD 1000. The type has continued to be built down to the present day and can be seen in its modern form in the *oselver* from the Hardanger area of Norway near Bergen. The *oselver* has correctly been described as the boat of a thousand years. She is a perfect example of a simple boat built with overlapping strakes which has changed scarcely at all in that time. The *oselver*, illustrated here (Figure 250), was built in Norway especially for the National Maritime Museum's Archaeological Research Centre to represent a type of boat used in Norway from Viking times until today, and exported in large numbers to the Shetlands, from where it influenced boat construction and shape in the north of Britain and gave rise to the very similar *fourern* used by Shetland fishermen into the second half of the twentieth century. While few strakes make for relatively easy building and flexible strength for low weight, her shape is restricted to an almost straight V-section. Built without moulds with frames fitted after planking, the boat demonstrates two points very clearly. The first is the tendency of small wooden boats built by people in remote communities to continue to show the basic constructional characteristics of their very remote ancestors. The second is the importance of size in the longevity of boat design. In the larger examples of this constructional method the desirable quality of flexibility in a small boat becomes a weakness in a ship, and the method was replaced by designs using heavier structures, fuller sections and more and narrower strakes. The building of small boats in wood represents a deep folk culture. Bigger vessels came and went, but the world of small boats remained indissolubly bound up with the life of humble watermen. Though big ships changed out of all recognition in the fifteenth and sixteenth centuries, all over the world small boats continued, as long as they were built of wood, to show the basic constructional characteristics of their remote ancestors – the big ships of eight or more centuries ago.

Sailing the Viking Ships and Boats

A very great deal of research and experimental work has been done in the last quarter of the twentieth century on the subject of Viking and earlier sails, rigs, and sailing techniques. There is archaeological evidence for the use of masts and perhaps sails in some of the Romano-Celtic boats, already described, of the second and third centuries AD. The evidence of a gold model from Broighter, County Derry, in Ireland dated by association to the first century BC which has a mast and yard together with Julius Caesar's description of the vessels of the Venati with their hide sails, already referred to, takes the history of the sail in northern Europe back to an earlier period.

A tiny carving, less than half an inch across, found at Karlby in Jutland in Denmark which shows a boat with a low, broad squaresail has not been dated but the earliest evidence for the widespread use of the sail comes from the picture stones in the island of Gotland in Sweden. I have already referred in Chapter 13 to the evidence for the existence of possibly flat-bottomed sailing vessels in trade in the Baltic as early as AD 700 but the Gotland stones, the earliest of which date from the fifth century AD, are a very rich source of illustration and show very many later vessels with complex rigging controlling big square sails of low aspect ratio (Figures 251 and 252). The first evidence of sails is on stones from circa AD 600.

It is evident from the numbers of the crew depicted on these stones that the vessels were relatively small – of 25 to 40ft (7 to 12m) in length. These were vessels for the Baltic trade and for trade eastwards, perhaps down the Russian rivers to the Black Sea, which involved portages where only relatively small vessels could be dragged over dry land.

These vessels have been the subject of a most valuable archaeological experiment. A clinker-built boat, named *Krampmarken*, 26ft (8m) long, was built on Gotland in 1980 (Figure 253), based on a Gotland find, the Bulverket boat of approximately AD 1200, which shows traces of Slavic influences in her structure, and subjected to three years of sailing trials in very differing conditions. These trials suggested that the low aspect ratio sails shown on the picture stones followed from the necessity of shipping both mast and yard when the vessel was rowed – as must very frequently have been necessary in the Baltic archipelagoes and especially on the Russian rivers. The sail was made from the water-resistant wool of the horned Gotland sheep and by using the narrow strips of cloth which contemporary looms would have produced, of different colours, and plaiting them together, a sail with a chequerboard pattern but not quite that of the picture stones was reconstructed. Sailing trials strongly suggested that the complex of lines depicted under the sails were multiple sheets which, with these small vessels, could be adjusted along the length of the foot thereby trimming the sail and controlling the airflow over it (Figure 254). This system would be ideal for the flukey winds of river sailing and would depend on a highly skilled crew. The sail was not suitable for windward work when the boat could easily be rowed. Under the leadership of the Swedish archaeologist Erik Nylén, who was largely responsible for this experimental reconstruction, a voyage was made in *Krampmarken* up the Vistula and Bug through Poland as far as the then Soviet

252
Sail on a Gotlands picture stone.
[Gotlands Historical Museum

253
Krampmarken *at Kovik, Gotland, before her great voyage to the former Soviet frontier. [Basil Greenhill*

border, covering the most difficult, upstream, part of the most southerly possible trade route to the Black Sea. Much was learned on this expedition, which proved the route and vessel as practical. Nylén concluded that the round voyage to Istanbul could have taken as much as four years. Recent research reported by Dan Carlsson in *Aspects of Maritime Scandinavia* has underlined the great importance of Gotland as a shipping and trading centre in Viking and pre-Viking times.

The Danish National Museum began practical experimental work in 1974 with a Nordlands *ottring* (Figure 255). The Nordlands boat was probably the last European seagoing boat type to work in any numbers under a single squaresail. Eric Andersen, working in association with the National Museum, has made a very detailed study of these boats (which were in use until the early twentieth century), their sails and rigging and the way they were handled. With a number of volunteers in 1974 he restored and re-rigged the National Museum's Nordlands boat and slowly began to learn to sail her. In the summer of 1975, working closely with Eric Andersen, the National Museum's reconstruction of the Gokstad *faering* was rigged and experience gained in sailing her.

The Nordlands boat requires five men to handle her (Figure 256) and she needs skilful sailing, but she is a beautiful boat to handle within these limitations, far more close-winded than might be expected, and very fast. Indeed the sailing of this boat has demonstrated that the flexibility of the squaresail is much greater than has been supposed in recent years, now that the tradition of single squaresail sailing has completely died away. The squaresail is highly flexible and adaptable, and should perhaps be thought of in the same way as the dipping lug of British fishing boats of the late nineteenth century. By definition the differences from the lug are, of course, that the luff of the squaresail changes from one edge of the sail to the other as she

255
The Danish National Museum's Nord-lands boat under sail in the Sound in 1974. [Basil Greenhill

256
Some of the crew of the Nordlands boat during sailing trials. Ole Crumlin-Pedersen is on the right in woollen hat. [Basil Greenhill

257
Viking vessel reconstructions assembling for sailing and rowing trials, Roskilde, 1992. [Basil Greenhill

goes about and the sail is always set outside the shrouds. But its aerodynamic characteristics are perhaps not so different from those of the dipping lug.

The Nordlands boat has, of course, a sail of high aspect ratio – and this has had its influence on many archaeological sailing experiments and on the rigging of reconstructions of Viking vessels. Much work of this kind has now been done (Figure 257) and reconstructions of, for instance, the cargo vessel Skuldelev 1 have sailed far and

258
Saga Siglar *and a reconstruction of Skuldelev 3 under sail. [Danish National Museum*

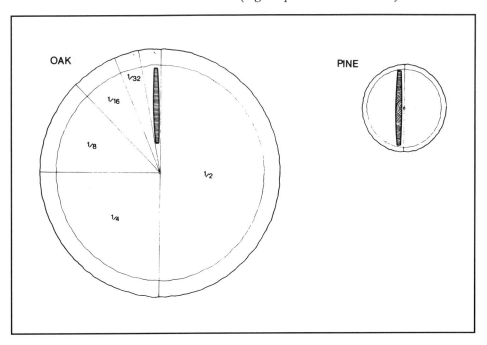

259
Wood splitting techniques. [Ole Crumlin-Pedersen

wide over the oceans with complete success. But in the late twentieth century broad low aspect ratio sails, being poor performers to windward, are not favoured by yacht designers. There has, perhaps, been an element of specialised sporting sailing, and also of playing to the public relations gallery, in some of the sailing of Viking ship reconstructions and, although the situation may be changing with some reconstructions of the 1990s, to give them a good windward performance and benefit from the experience with Nordlands boats they have been given high narrow sails though the great majority, if not all, of northern European illustrations up to 1300 or so show the shallow, broad, low aspect ratio, sails of the proportions of the sail of *Krampmarken*. Experience with sails of this shape has also been gained in the Åland Islands of Finland with the sailing of reconstructions of *Storbåten*, vessels of the size of Skuldelev wreck 3 and dating from the seventeenth century.

A reconstruction of Skuldelev 1 named *Saga Siglar* (Figure 258), equipped with a high aspect ratio single squaresail, a great deal of necessary modern equipment and sheltered accommodation for the crew, but navigating partly with the Viking sun compass identified by Vebaek and Thirslund, sailed round the world in 1984–86. With her sail she could lie within 60 degrees of the wind in good conditions, with leeway of 5 to 10 degrees her course made good was 65 to 70 degrees. The results of this round the world voyage, and even more of extended sailing trials along the coast of Norway and across the North Atlantic to Greenland, were summed up by Max Vinner, who participated extensively in the trials, in his contribution to *Viking Voyages to North America* edited by B L Clausen. He bore in mind that *Saga Siglar* was a very small Viking merchant vessel in comparison with, say, the Bergen ship which with her capacity of 200 tons of cargo, was probably a real Greenland trader. He wrote: 'We must therefore conclude that the ocean-going merchant vessel of the Viking period had no limits as far as seaworthiness is concerned . . .

The building of Viking vessels

Generally speaking, oak was the preferred timber for Viking shipbuilding whenever it was obtainable of the right dimensions. Where it was not available, as in Norway, frequently, pine was used and ash, particularly, apparently, for top strakes. As with

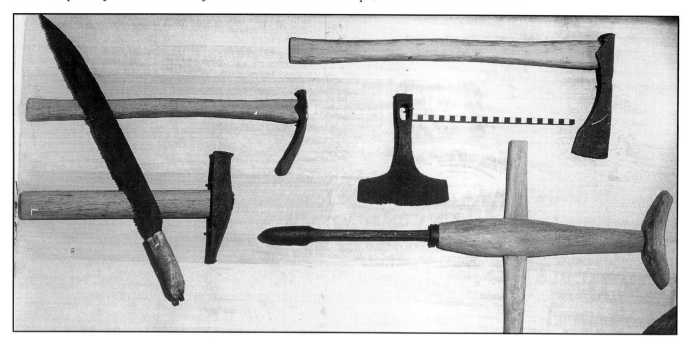

ship and boatbuilders throughout history, as far as possible the timber was matched to the job in hand. Curved grain material and natural crooks were preferred where they matched requirements and were available. Oak logs were converted into planks by splitting them into halves and then into halves again to produce radial planks (Figure 259). Pine was converted into planks from half logs. Keels, stems, frames and other pieces were shaped with axes by reduction from a log or half log to the required shape, using the natural run of the grain whenever possible. The Viking vessel built from radially cleft oak and treated with pine (Stockholm) tar was well placed to resist dry rot and Viking builders may not therefore have been so concerned to work with seasoned timber.

Boatbuilding tools have been recovered from Viking age graves and other sites in Scandinavia. Figure 260 shows a collection, once again from the island of Gotland

261
Building William the Conqueror's invasion fleet. [From Bayeux Tapestry *by F Stenton, Phaidon Press*

◀ 260
Tools from Mastermyr, Gotland, dated to about AD 1000: axe, adzes, hafted wedge, auger with spoon bit and a small saw. [Statens Historiska Museum, Stockholm

which is such a prolific source of information on early shipping. The adze was available and although there were saws of adequate size there is little or no evidence of their use to prepare planks at this period. Marking on the planks of the Skuldelev planks shows that planes were in use to finish the cleft timber. Figure 261 from the Bayeux Tapestry illustrates some aspects of Viking age shipbuilding.

Apart from the length of the cutting edge of the adze late twentieth-century hand tools still have many of the characteristics of the Viking age ancestors, though the hardened steel of which they are made probably retains an efficient cutting edge for a longer time. As Professor McGrail wrote in the earlier version of this book:

> the archaeological and technological evidence considered here points towards the formation of the following hypothesis. Without modern methods of analysis and of testing materials, boatbuilders of the Viking age evolved techniques of choosing the right tree, converting it at the right time and in the right manner to produce the best timber for building the types of boat which best suited their environment and economy . . . By trial and error methods, and by acute observation of the effects of varying certain factors, they could reject sub-optimal methods and materials and perfect those which gave their boats desirable characteristics.

Bibliography

ANDERSEN, B and E, *Råsejlet – Dragens Vinge*, 1989

ARBMAN, H, 'Der Årby-fund', 1940

ARBMAN, H, GREENHILL, B and ROBERTS, O, *The Årby Boat*, 1993

BINNS, A, *Viking Voyagers*, 1980

BRØGGER A W, *et al, Osebergfunnet*, 1917–28

BRØGGER, A W and SHETELIG, H, *Viking Ships, their Ancestry and Evolution*, 1951

BRØNDSTED, J, 'Oldtidsbaden fra Als', 1925

CHRISTENSEN, A E, *Boats of the North*, 1968

CLAUSEN, B L (ed), *Viking Voyages to North America*, 1993

CRUMLIN-PEDERSEN, O, 'Viking Ships of Roskilde', 1970
   'Five Viking Ships', 1974

CRUMLIN-PEDERSEN, O and VINNER, M (eds), *Sailing into the Past*, 1986

CRUMLIN-PEDERSEN, O (ed), *Aspects of Maritime Scandinavia*, 1991

ELLMERS, D, *Frümittelalterliche Handelsschiffahrt in Mittel-und Nordeuropa*, 1972

ESKERÖD, A, *Kyrkbåtar och Kyrkbåtsfarder*, 1973

FENWICK, V H (ed), *The Graveney Boat*, 1978

FOOTE, P G and WILSON, D M, *Viking Achievement*, 1970

GJELLESTAD, A J, 'Litt om Oselverbäter', 1969

GRAHAM-CAMPBELL, J, *The Viking World*, 1989

HAASUM, S, 'Vikingatidens segling och navigation', 1974

HÖGNÄS, P and ÖRJANS, J, *Storbåten*, 1985

JONES, G, *A History of the Vikings*, 1968

KRISTJANSSON, L, Graenlenzki Landnemaflotinn og Breidfirzki Báturinn', 1965

MCGRAIL, S, *Ancient Boats of North West Europe*, 1987
   Medieval Boat and Ship Timbers from Dublin, 1993

MCGRAIL, S and MCKEE, J E G, *Building and Trials of the Replica of an Ancient Boat: The Gokstad Faering*, 1974

MAGNUSSON, M, *Viking Expansion Westwards*, 1973

NICOLAYSEN, N, *Viking Ship discovered at Gokstad in Norway*, 1882

NYLÉN, E and LAMM, J P, *Stones, Ships and Symbols*, 1988

OLSEN, O and CRUMLIN-PEDERSEN, O, 'Skuldelev Ships', 1967

ROSENBERG, G, *Hjortspringfunnet*, 1937

SAWYER, P H, *Age of the Vikings*, 1971

SJØVOLD, T, *Oseberg Find*, 1969

STENTON, F M, *Bayeux Tapestry*, 1957

THORVILDSEN, K, *Ladby-Skibet*, 1957

VARENIUS, B, *Bulverket båten*, 1979

VEBAEK, C L and THIRSLUND, S, *The Viking Compass*, 1992

VIKINGESKIBSHALLEN, *Nordlandsbåden Rana*, Roskilde, 1981

WILSON, D and KLINDT-JENSEN, O, *Viking Art*, 1966

CHAPTER
17

The Clinker-Built Boat After the Viking Period

With the general development of Europe in the eleventh and twelfth centuries the Viking age passed away, but the Scandinavians during this period had given great impetus to the development of the clinker-built boat. There is a good deal of evidence about the development of ship- and boatbuilding in the twelfth, thirteenth and fourteenth centuries, not all of it yet adequately published. This is provided partly by carefully drawn seals of seaport towns on the shores of the Baltic, the North Sea, the English Channel and the Bay of Biscay which often show contemporary ships in considerable detail, and by medieval wrecks and boat- and shipbuilding materials which have been excavated in Sweden, Norway, Germany, Poland, Denmark, Holland, Britain and Ireland. The latter have been very fully published in Professor McGrail's *Medieval Boat and Ship Timbers from Dublin*. Murals in the thirteenth-century church at Sitjon, Telemark, Norway, and the fourteenth-century church at Skamstrup, Zealand, Denmark, also provide evidence.

This and other evidence suggests that northern European boats and ships followed three very broad main lines of development between the eleventh century and the fifteenth century when the technique was generally adopted of building large vessels without edge-joining. Meanwhile the older traditions persisted in small vessels and boats. Before this happened the three main lines of development AD 1100–1400 were:

1. the improvement and development of the round-hulled clinker-built vessel. The medieval English word for this sort of vessel appears to have been *ceol* or *keel*. The latter term is used by some archaeologists.
2. the development of the flat-bottomed boat into the medieval ships called cogs.
3. the development of that still mysterious vessel, the hulk.

As the Viking age drew to a close, clinker-built ships became bigger and more complicated. They grew broader and deeper and the planks of their shells and their timbers became bigger and heavier. The evidence of the seals shows that they could carry a ship's boat and that they had windlasses for hoisting anchors and the yard.

216

They acquired decks and 'castles' fore and aft, and beams protruding through their sides (Figure 262).

In 1962 excavations near Tyskerbryggen, Bergen's old harbour, revealed some remains of a very large vessel built in the Scandinavian round-hulled clinker tradition, which may have been partly destroyed in the great fire in Bergen in 1248 and its timbers re-used in buildings. The surviving material suggests a vessel some 36m long with a beam of 11m and a depth of 4.5m. The mast was over half a metre in diameter at its heel and the vessel is assumed to have carried a single squaresail of about 400 square metres in area. The vessel would have carried about 200 tons of cargo,

262
The second seal of Winchelsea of the late thirteenth century clearly shows developments in the clinker-building tradition, castles, a windlass, cross beams protruding through the sides. The crew appear to be standing on a deck providing covered space below.
[*National Maritime Museum*

equipment and people. Dated in the middle of the thirteenth century, a time when Norse contact with the Greenland settlements was at its height, it is thought that she represents some of the bigger vessels with which this business was conducted. The seagoing experience with the much smaller *Saga Siglar* reconstruction (see Chapter 16), considered with the Bergen find, leads to the conclusion that the big cargo vessels of the Viking period had no limits as far as ocean sailing is concerned. British seals of the same period illustrate similar large clinker-built vessels.

Two other archaeological finds of this period of great importance are Hedeby Wreck 3 not yet firmly dated (1995) but believed to be of the mid-eleventh century and the Lynaes ship of the mid-twelfth century. Hedeby is on an arm of the sea on the east side of Schleswig, Lynaes at the north of the Roskilde Fjord near

Copenhagen. Hedeby 3 could carry at least 40 tons of cargo and was probably built for long distance North Sea or Baltic trade. The Lynaes ship is estimated to have been capable of carrying 60 tons. Her framing apparently shows parallels with some of the ship timbers studied by McGrail in Dublin. Figure 263 shows very well the general development which appears to have taken place in cargo vessels of Scandinavian origin from the eleventh to the thirteenth centuries.

The long overhanging stem and stern of the Saxon/Scandinavian tradition gave way in many larger vessels to a relatively straight, much more upright stem and stern post. An important find made at Kalmar Castle in Sweden shows several small clinker-built merchant ships of the thirteenth century. Some of their beams projected through the sides of the vessel in the manner shown on contemporary seals. They had short fore and after decks and were equipped with windlasses, stern rudders hanging from a straight stern post and upright stems. Their general proportions suggest the traditions of Skuldelev Wreck 3 rather than the other Viking ship finds.

The importance of the straight sternpost of the Kalmar vessels rests not only in the use of the stern rudder but also in that its use meant that the problem of establishing the run of the strakes to a straight sternpost in a round-hulled vessel (as opposed to the chine construction of the cog) had to be solved.

The tradition is carried on even into the twentieth century in the Norwegian Nordfjord *jegt*. Figure 264 shows an example of this great single-masted clinker-built merchant vessel, now preserved in Norway, of a type which existed in great numbers in the nineteenth century, carrying on an extensive trade between north and south Norway and further afield. Some of these vessels even crossed the Atlantic in the late nineteenth century. Figure 265 shows one of them discharging firewood at one of the old quays at Bergen.

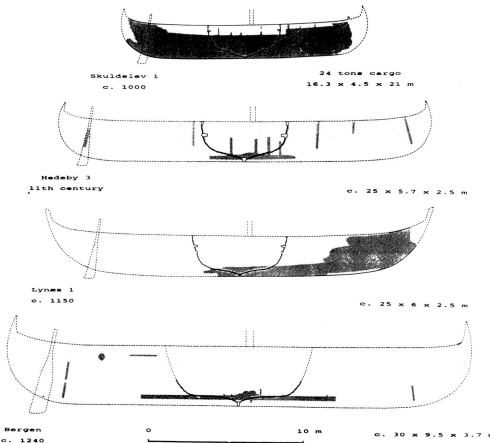

Skuldelev 1
c. 1000

24 tons cargo
16.3 x 4.5 x 21 m

Hedeby 3
11th century

c. 25 x 5.7 x 2.5 m

Lynæs 1
c. 1150

c. 25 x 6 x 2.5 m

Bergen
c. 1240

0   10 m

c. 30 x 9.5 x 3.7 m

263
Silhouettes of Scandinavian cargo vessels in the clinker-building tradition, eleventh to thirteenth centuries. [Ole *Crumlin-Pedersen*

264
Holvikjekten *preserved at Sandane in Nordfjord, Norway. [Arne Emile Christensen Jnr*

265
A late nineteenth-century photograph of a jekt *at Bergen. [Bergens Sjøfartsmuseum*

266
H371 in the foreground is a fine example of a coble. [*Basil Greenhill*

Warships also continued to be constructed as round-hulled, clinker-built vessels, but they suffered from a peculiar disadvantage in that a new type of ship, the cog, which was coming into use, was much higher-sided and this gave a great advantage to her fighting men, who could rain arrows and spears down on the decks of the old longships. To overcome this, longships were fitted with 'castles', fore and aft – this can be seen in some of the seals like that of Winchelsea (Figure 262). But the cogs also had castles built onto them and the use of the old type of clinker-built ships for war purposes really came to an end in the 1300s. Karl Leyser, the medieval historian, writing in *The Times Literary Supplement* in October 1978, drawing on Henry of Lettland's *Chronicon Livoniae*, ascribes the German success in the penetration of the eastern Baltic territories in the 1200s (the Baltic Crusades) largely to the cogs with their great cargo capacity and high freeboard.

Nevertheless the huge *Grace Dieu*, with which a very large ancient wreck lying in the river Hamble and now the property of Southampton University has been identified, was clinker-built in a very special way in the early 1400s. This very large vessel, a very early three-masted ship, which has not yet been fully investigated and represents an attempt to build in clinker a structure on the scale of the non edge-joined semi skeleton-built vessels soon to begin to appear on the coasts of Britain (see Chapter 20), presented grave difficulties in construction. To obtain the longitudinal strength necessary to maintain the integrity of the vessel's shape at sea it was necessary to use thicker planking for the strakes. Simple doubled or trebled planking would have put shearing strains on lengthened rivets which would have been very dangerous. The solution adopted appears to have been ingenious. We do not know if it worked because the *Grace Dieu*'s seagoing career was limited to one voyage to the Solent and to a passage to the laying up ground – where she still lies today.

Similar problems and an attempt to solve them appear to be demonstrated by the 'copper ore wreck' of the mid-1400s excavated in Gdánsk bay in Poland. This clinker-built vessel appears to demonstrate a transitional stage of development borrowing from the cog (see Chapter 18). She is round in the bilge but she has cog features in her construction. According to Crumlin-Pedersen, another Danish find, the Gedesby ship, dated around AD 1300, has planks assembled in the Viking way but also has cog features.

267
Setting the seine net from a locally built clinker salmon boat, Appledore, north Devon, 1946. [Basil Greenhill

But although clinker-building for large vessels went out of use, it persisted for boats and small ships down to the end of wooden boatbuilding and remained the principal tradition in Britain and Scandinavia and parts of North America. A number of examples of clinker-built boats built in different parts of Britain and North America for different purposes are illustrated here. All carry on the ancient tradition developed long before the Graveney boat was built, more than 1000 years ago, of shell-construction, edge-joined with inserted frames.

The coble (Figure 266) is a very distinctive boat type from the northeast coast of England. She was normally equipped with a tall narrow dipping lug sail and oars worked over a single thole pin. Her deep sharp forefoot and long rudder enabled her to work to windward despite her flat run. In some aspects her hull anticipates modern motorboat practices. Bob Strongman's lobster boat (see Chapter 2) is in some ways a big smooth-skinned coble. The long rather narrow North Devon salmon boat, (Figure 267) was used in the River Torridge for generations until pollution stopped the fishery. The clinker-built schooner *Peggy* (Figure 268) was built in 1791 in the Isle of Man as a working boat. She carried out the maritime equivalent of the combined role of a cart and a small carriage for the family who owned her. She is still in existence and is displayed in the Nautical Museum of the Manx Museum at Castletown, Isle of Man. The *Peggy* is remarkably similar in shape, size and sailplan to the Chebacco boats, the small schooners in which the fisheries of New England and Nova Scotia were carried on in the years immediately after the American Revolution. These had their descendants as late as the 1960s in the Gaspé schooners of Quebec, clinker-built vessels almost unaltered from the schooners of two centuries ago (Figure 269). In Prince Edward Island, Canada, miniatures of these little schooners, tiny shallops only 14ft (4.27m) or 16ft (4.88m) long and lapstrake-built, were used in the lobster fishery until the first motorboats came into common use after the First World War (Figure 270). Quite recently clinker or lapstrake boats are still being used in the fishery off the north shore of Cape Breton in Canada, and in the Magdalen Islands in the Gulf of St Lawrence (Figure 271). The famous Block Island boats of southern Massachusetts were also lapstrake built, as were also the fishing boats of Lake Michigan (Figure 272), and the beautiful Adirondack Guide boats (Figure 273).

268
The schooner-rigged clinker-built working boat Peggy, *built in 1791, displayed at the end of the twentieth century in her boat cellar at Castletown, Isle of Man.* [*Basil Greenhill*

269
Below left – a lapstrake-built Gaspé schooner near Bonaventure, Quebec, in 1962. [*Basil Greenhill*

272
Below – Schooner-rigged lapstrake-built fishing boats on Lake Michigan, 1890s. [*Rowley Murphy*

271
Above – a fine example of a lapstrake-built seine net boat at Havre Aubert, Magdalen Islands, 1976. [*Basil Greenhill*

273
Above right – an Adirondack Guide Boat type in the workshops at Mystic Seaport, Connecticut. [*Basil Greenhill*

270
A lapstrake-built Prince Edward Island two mast boat hauled out on her wooden slip or 'landing', early twentieth century. [*Public Archives of Prince Edward Island*

Eric McKee's brilliant study, *The Working Boats of Britain*, with its broad approach to its subject and its consideration of geographic, social and economic factors in the development of boats introduced new dimensions into the subject. Many of the later wooden working boat types of Britain are described and illustrated in detail in this masterly work. In these British boats, in all their multitudinous variations, the frames were steamed and bent and were more numerous than the stronger grown timbers of Scandinavian boats and the earlier British boats. This steamed frame technique was developed perhaps as late, in fact, as the mid nineteenth century.

In Scandinavia and northern Britain the oldest traditions of boat-building have been followed down to very recent years. Big clinker-built boats were used in the northern fisheries of Norway and the Shetland Isles until well into the twentieth century. A number of examples of these Norwegian clinker-built boats are preserved in the boat hall of the Maritime Museum in Oslo, including a superb *femboring*, a type of single squaresail boat in which deep sea fishing was carried out until the latter part of the nineteenth century, and even into the twentieth. A smaller example of the same general type, the Nordlands boat, in the possession of the Danish National Museum was referred to and illustrated in the last chapter (Figure 255). In

274
A clinker-built Danish fishing jagt, *the* Otto Mathiason, *H.K. 69, beautifully restored.* [*Basil Greenhill*

Shetland very similar boats were used until the present century. A long-range fishery, operating 90 miles offshore, was carried on in six-oared boats using squaresails, very similar to those of the Nordlands boat. In all three Scandinavian countries there has been a revival of interest in wooden working boats in the last twenty years. This has led to the restoration of old boats and the construction of new boats on the lines of local craft of the pre-plastic period (Figure 274).

The diffusion of clinker-building has been widespread. Quite apart from its separate appearance in the eastern part of the Indian sub-continent clinker-built wooden boats have recently been in commercial use in northwest Spain and on the Russian lakes.

Bibliography

ÅKERLUND, H, *Fartygsfynden i den forna hamnen i Kalmar*, 1951
ANDERSON, R C, 'The Bursledon Ship', 1934
BRINDLEY, H H, *Impressions and casts of seals, coins, tokens, medals and other objects of Art exhibited in the Seal Room of the National Maritime Museum*, 1938
BURWASH, D, *English Merchant Shipping 1460–1540*, 1947
CHRISTENSEN, A E, *Boats of the North*, 1968
CLAUSEN, B I (ed), *Viking Voyages to North America*, 1993
CRUMLIN-PEDERSEN, O (ed), *Aspects of Maritime Scandinavia*, 1991
DADE, E, *Sail and Oar*, 1933
    'The Cobles', 1934
EWE, H, *Schiffe auf Siegeln*, 1972
FRIEL, Ian, 'Henry V's *Grace Dieu*', 1993
GILLIS, R H C, 'Pilot gigs of Cornwall and the Isles of Scilly', 1969
HUTCHINSON, G, *Medieval Ships and Shipping*, 1993
LITWIN, J in VILLAIN-GADNOSSI, BOSUTTIL and ADAM (eds), *Medieval Ships and the Birth of Technological Societies*, Vol 1, 1989
MCGRAIL, S, *Medieval Boat and Ship Timbers from Dublin*, 1993
MCKEE, E, *Working Boats of Britain*, 1983
MARCH, E J, *Inshore Craft of Britain*, 1970
MOORE, A, *Last Days of Mast and Sail*, 1925
PYRNNE, M, 'Some general considerations applying to the examination of the remains of old ships', 1973
UNGER, R W (ed), *Cogs, Caravels and Galleons*, 1993
URBAN, W, *The Baltic Crusade*, 1975
WARINGTON-SMYTH, H, *Mast and Sail in Europe and Asia*, 1906
WESTERDAHL, C (ed), *Crossroads in Ancient Shipbuilding*, 1994
WHITE, E W, *British Fishing Boats and Coastal Craft*, 1950

The Cog
and the Flat-Bottomed Boat
After the Vikings

275
*The seal of Kiel, c1365, showing 're-
verse clinker' planking in a cog. The
stern rudder is clearly visible. [National
Maritime Museum*

The vessel that was to prove such a formidable rival to the northern round-hulled clinker-built vessel in the 1200s was the cog. She was particularly associated with the towns of the north German Hanse. She appears to have been developed from the flat-bottomed plank-built river boat traditions of northwest Germany and the Low Countries and was a flat-bottomed vessel with clinker-built sides. Sometimes the planks of the sides appear to have been laid with the upper edges of the lower planks outboard instead of inboard (Figure 275), as in the main North European clinker-building tradition.

She was a totally different shape from the northern round-hulled clinker-built boat, with high sides, little flare, a straight stem and stern post and a stern rudder. In twentieth-century terms she was something like a gigantic Banks dory. The cog was a high-sided, deep-draughted sailing vessel, probably able to carry more cargo than the round-hulled types in the same overall length and draught and more suited to shallow tidal waters, if less easy to handle at sea, and because of her high sides, she was able to defend herself against attack in an age of perpetual piracy. She was also, for reasons which will now be obvious to the reader of this book, easier and cheaper to build than boats and vessels in the northern round-hulled clinker tradition and she could be built by less skilled people. Not least, she was built of wide sawn planks instead of the narrow split planks of the Viking tradition and therefore required fewer fastenings.

The constructional differences between a cog and a vessel of the Scandinavian tradition are very clearly shown by Figures 276 and 277. Figure 276 shows a reconstruction in the National Maritime Museum in Stockholm of a section towards the stern of a moderately sized vessel of the late thirteenth century built in the Scandinavian traditions described in Chapter 16. Figure 277 shows the reconstruction of approximately the midships section of the complete cog of about 1380 excavated from the mud of the river Weser at Bremen and now under conservation at the German

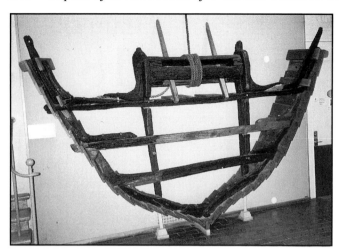

National Maritime Museum at Bremerhavn. It is very clear that these two vessels were the products of very different shipbuilding cultures.

Dr Detlev Ellmers of the German National Maritime Museum and others have researched the probable origins of the cog tradition of shipbuilding in great detail. A full and convenient summary by Dr Ellmers is to be found in Chapter 2 of the volume *Cogs, Caravels and Galleons* in the series of twelve volumes that comprise *Conway's History of the Ship*. To summarise further, archaeological and ethnographic evidence indicates the evolution of the cog in the general area of the southwestern Baltic and German and Netherlands North Sea coasts. In these areas small, primitive cog forms survived into the twentieth century.

The early seagoing cogs appear to have been three or four strakes high at the sides with straight stem and stern posts giving them at first a potential laden capacity less than that of the major Viking vessels. It is believed that the seagoing cog developed on the eastern coasts of the North Sea, trading from the Netherlands to Hollingstedt on the west coast of Schleswig Holstein, whence its cargoes were carried overland to the great shipping place of Hedeby on the east coast and there trans-shipped for destinations in the Baltic. Soon cogs began to be built in Hedeby and then in the southern Baltic ports generally. In Dr Ellmer's words:

> Instead of Hedeby forming one small bridgehead, there is a long series of harbour towns founded between about 1150 and 1250 from Kiel in the west to Elbing (Elblag) in the east, which, in their seals, presented themselves as home ports for cogs. With these towns the base for shipping using cogs has been remarkably enlarged.

The cog indeed played a very important role in the expansion of trade and commerce and the development of towns in the middle ages as she did in the Baltic Crusades which brought strong German interest into Sweden and German hegemony to the areas now known as Estonia, Latvia and Lithuania – and through them German influence in due course into Russia.

Her field of operation expanded rapidly. The cog was the ship of the Hanse. After the foundation of Lübeck in 1159 the new business methods which the Hanse represented led to the rapid expansion of its trade, and to a demand for more and bigger cogs. A century after it was founded Lübeck was the centre of a trading community which included London and Bruges, Bergen and Visby in the north and Reval (Tallin) and Novgorod in the east. Clear scratchings representing cogs have been found on the coast of Cornwall (Figure 278).

What is probably the earliest extant lading contract from northern Europe covers a passage in May 1323 from Bordeaux to Newcastle by the cog *Our Lady*, Master,

276
Above left – reconstructed section of a moderately sized vessel of the late thirteenth century built in the Scandinavian tradition displayed in the National Maritime Museum, Stockholm. [Basil Greenhill

277
Above – reconstructed midships section of the Bremen cog of the late fourteenth century displayed in the National Maritime Museum, Bremerhavn. [Basil Greenhill

278
Cogs moored in reeds. Graffiti on an undated corner stone discovered at the site of Crane Godrevy Manor, Gwithian, Cornwall. [Professor Charles Thomas

Walter Giffard, of Lyme. This document gives a good deal of information about the shipping business of the early fourteenth century. The passage was to be made and cargo delivered within fifteen days. This appears to have been achieved which suggests that Walter Giffard had considerable knowledge of the winds likely to be met on the passage at that season. The cargo was of 93 tuns and 18 pipes of wine and 44 tuns of flour. The freight was 9 shillings sterling per tun, discounted at the rate of 21.5 tuns for the cost of 20 tuns. Master Giffard received seven pounds two shillings in advance and forty-six pounds ten shillings on arrival in Newcastle. In October 1323, Giffard was granted a one-year safe conduct in which he is described as a 'king's merchant to go beyond the seas' in what appears to have been the *Our Lady*.

In the summer of 1304 the Florentine chronicler Giovanni Villani wrote:

> At this time people came from Bayonne in Gascony in their ships, which in Bayonne they call cogs, through the Straits of Gibraltar, on bucaneering expeditions in the Mediterranean, where they inflicted much damage. After that time people from Genoa, Venice and Catalonia began to employ cogs for their seafaring and abandon the use of their own large ships owing to the seaworthiness and lower cost of cogs. Thus great changes were wrought in the ship form of our fleet.

The reign of the cog seems to have lasted until the first half of the 1400s. It was perhaps less the result of the cog's superior cargo capacity over contemporary vessels of the Scandinavian tradition (the facts of this capacity have recently been challenged by Crumlin-Pedersen) or even the fact that she was cheaper and simpler to build and maintain than vessels of the Scandinavian tradition – though this must have been a big factor – that ensured the very widespread adoption of the cog. The Hanse in the thirteenth and fourteenth centuries took control of many Baltic shipping places and became the dominant factor in Baltic trade, pushing Scandinavians and Slavs out of business. And the cog was the traditional tool of the ascendant German culture.

She is shown most clearly in contemporary illustration in the two seals of Kiel and Elbing. The Kiel seal dated from about AD 1365 and the Elbing seal some fifteen years earlier (Figures 275 and 279). But conclusive evidence as to the shape and structure of the cog was obtained by the excavation of a very large part of the hull of one in the harbour of Bremen, Germany, in 1962. Like the Graveney boat, she has been subjected to a long process of recording which has revealed her to be 77ft (23.5m) long and 23ft (7m) in breadth. She has been dated at about the year 1380. The Bremen cog has high clinker-built sides, a straight sloping stem and a stern post. She is in fact pretty well what was expected from contemporary illustrations. As might be expected from her late date, she demonstrates a tendency towards a refinement of

279
The seal of Elbing, c1350. [National Maritime Museum

form which is a constantly recurring factor in the history of different kinds of flat-bottomed boats. The flat smooth plank bottom has been reduced to a relatively small area, the ends sharpened, a small keel added. She had an after castle which is not part of the permanent structure of the vessel herself. Altogether she looks remarkably like the cogs of medieval seals, and Figure 280, a photograph of a model taken from the port bow, shows the type very well as far as the evidence provided by the Bremen cog herself is concerned. What it does not show is that the planks of her flat bottom were not edge-joined, but fastened only to the floor timbers with trenails (see Figures 277 and 281) and that her clinker strakes were joined not with clenched rivets but with iron nails, the points of which are bent back on themselves twice. It could therefore be that she and her numerous sisters represent a development of a different strand in boatbuilding traditions from some of the other flat-bottomed vessels that have been examined here (see Chapter 3). In the 1990s the vessel is undergoing conservation totally immersed in a tank in the Maritime Museum at Bremerhavn, a situation that has led to her being spoken of as 'the cog in aspic'.

280
A reconstruction model of the Bremen cog in the German National Maritime Museum at Bremerhavn. [Basil Greenhill

281
The stern of the Bremen cog before she went into her conservation tank at Bremerhavn. The clinker laid, edge-joined, planks of the sides clearly contrast with the planks of the flat bottom, brought up to the sternpost, which are not overlapping and not edge-joined. [Basil Greenhill

282

The reconstruction built at Bremerhavn of the Bremen cog under sail. [*Deutsches Schiffahrtsmuseum*

Since the discovery of the Bremen Cog other, usually fragmentary, cog remains have been found in the Netherlands, at Lübeck and Rostock and in Danish and Swedish waters. These show variations in local detail as the cog developed in the 1200s and the 1300s. There is now beginning to be sufficient archaeological, iconographic, literary and ethnographic evidence for a comprehensive history of the cog and the immensely important role she played in the development of modern Europe.

The very detailed information obtained from all these sources, and especially from the Bremen cog, has made possible the building of two reconstructions of her, one at Bremerhavn (Figure 282) and one at Kiel. From the sailing trials of these vessels a great deal has been learned about the handling of cogs at sea. As the photograph in Figure 280 shows, the hull shape of a cog was well suited to the environment in which she evolved, of relatively shallow draught for her cargo-carrying capacity, with a flat bottom to enable her to take the ground fully laden in the tidal waters of the North Sea coast, quite a good entrance and a fine run. The single squaresail with which she was rigged however on this hull did not make for windward ability. The reconstructions have shown that she makes enormous leeway in anything of a sea and will not point up more than roughly 80 degrees to the wind, although further experience in sailing reconstructions may lead to much improved performance.

Sailing the Bremerhavn cog along the Hanseatic trade routes in the Baltic has underlined the necessity of familiarity with all the cracks in the rocks and sheltered roadsteads which could be used for sheltering from adverse winds, and usually overnight, for these places are often a day's sail apart. Cogs are pictured on stones and in churches on the island of Gotland, beautifully in Finström Church in the Åland Islands, (Figure 283) and in many other places in Scandinavia and Finland. Along the north coast of the Baltic, through the Åland Islands, and along the south coast of Finland, names on the modern map, like Kugshamn, Kugsholm, and Kuggsund, show the sheltering places of the cogs on their way to the Gulf of Finland and Tallinn.

283

Mural of a cog in Finström Church, Åland Islands, Finland. [*Tourist Office of Åland*

284
Gaddtärnen, the Pike's Belly, a sheltering place of cogs off Hanko in southwest Finland. On the smooth rocks are inscriptions left by medieval seafarers. [*Basil Greenhill*

The last stage of the journey, from what is now Hanko, meant crossing the open sea. The cogs waited in a little harbour between islands called the Gaddtärnen (the Pike's Belly) for favourable conditions for the open sea passage to Estonia (Figure 284). While they waited, the crew escaped the smelly confines of the cog to stretch their legs ashore in this wild, remote, place and to immortalise themselves, their vessels, and their employers by leaving their names and crests carved in the hard granite of the islands. Over 400 of these carvings survive today, most from the 1500s, but the earliest from the last days of the cogs a century earlier. It is as if the contemporaries of Columbus and Cabot, and their predecessors, had left their names and crests on the rocks of one of the Scilly Isles or an island off the Maine Coast.

The draining of the polders in the Netherlands has revealed the remains of many vessels which had sunk to the floor of the shallow sea. Wrecks have been found, of very varying sizes, that have been dated from the eleventh to the end of the seventeenth centuries and which show the general characteristics of construction of the cog. Figure 285 shows an eleventh-century shipwreck being excavated from section Q75 of the Northeast Polder. The bottom of this ship is flat and the sides are clinker – she is a very early example of the family of the cog.

285
An eleventh-century early cog type wreck under excavation in the northeast Polder in the Netherlands. [*G D van der Heide*

But it is not only in Holland that there have been survivals of the great north European flat-bottomed clinker-sided boatbuilding tradition. Eric McKee has shown that until recent years a series of boat types existed in Somerset which suggest the possible evolution in some local circumstances of sophisticated boats even as large as small cogs from a simple flat-bottomed boat of the type of the turf boat (Chapter 2).

For fishing off the adjacent coast and in the estuary of the river Parret near the home of the turf boat on the Somerset levels, a larger more seaworthy boat of very similar construction, locally known as the flatner, was used. She had both fore and aft and athwartships rockers to make her easy to handle ashore on the extremely muddy banks of the Bridgwater river (Figure 286). For lightering and barge work in the Parret estuary and on the river, big double-ended barges with straight stem and stern post, flat bottoms and clinker sides were built (Figure 287). These boats were in the shape of small cogs and were locally known as 'Bridgwater boats'. Perhaps they were the last of the medieval cogs' near relations to survive in commercial use in Britain, although boats of similar construction operated until the early twentieth century on the river Teign in Devon, and were sailed under single square sails. It is a

286

Structural and lines drawing of a Bridgwater flatner. [Eric McKee

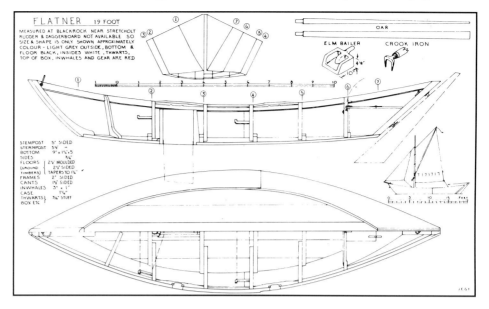

287

Structural and lines drawing of a Bridgwater 'boat' or barge. [Eric McKee

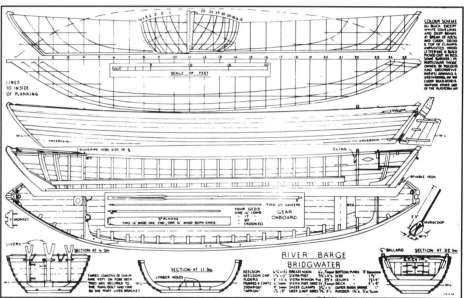

reasonable hypothesis that the cog type served on in local places where it was particularly suitable long after its general abandonment as a seagoing type. One of the most pleasing flat-bottomed clinker-sided survivals in Britain is the Fleet trow (Figure 288). These boats are still used on the shallow arm of the sea between the mainland and Chesil Beach in Dorset and are still being built of wood at the end of the twentieth century. Very similar boats are in use on the North Sea coast of Denmark and on the coast of Lithuania, whence they have migrated to Poland. On the eastern shore of south Sweden and on the island of Gotland, a type of double-ended flat-bottomed boat is still built for leisure use which is locally called a *Kåg*, (Figure 289).

Indeed the simple flat-bottomed boat is a worldwide phenomenon in different forms adapted to working requirements and local conditions. Jerzy Litwin of the Polish National Maritime Museum at Gdańsk has made an exhaustive study of the boats of the Vistula river system where there is a complex series of flat-bottomed boats from the head waters to the Vistula lagoon (Figures 290, 291 and 292). It is to be noted in Figure 290 that the block ends of the middle river boats provide a

291
The birth of a flat-bottomed Polish river boat, the beginning of the assembly of the bottom planks. Jerzy Litwin and Ann Giffard interview the boatbuilders' family at Laskowiec. [Basil Greenhill

solution to the problem of the strake ends reminiscent of the *goloi* of a boat from Bangladesh.

Dr Wolfgang Rudolph and others in 1958 established an ethnological inventory of boats and associated material on the north German coast between the Bay of Wismar and the delta lagoon at the mouth of the Oder. Over the next ten years the group visited numerous maritime communities, boatyards, smiths, ropemakers, sailmakers and other maritime tradesmen and examined every boat they could find. Much of what they saw has now gone, but was in varying degrees recorded in time. The majority of the boats recorded were flat-bottomed, some of them of very simple construction with the ends closed with carved solid blocks, the *blockkahn* (Figure 293).

Amongst the most aristocratic of European flat-bottomed boats is the Venetian gondola (Figure 294) and all her numerous humbler relatives in the Lagoon (Figure 295). Here we have the flat-bottomed boat in its most elegant varieties from the gondolas themselves to their fishing and load-carrying contemporaries.

A most striking example of the separate development of a closely similar solution to the problem of building cheaply a shallow draught boat capable of carrying a large cargo and of sailing under a single squaresail, occurred in the state of India now known as Uttar Pradesh. She was the *patalia*. I never saw one myself, but I heard of them from boatmen of the Ganges and it is clear that this obsolescent, if not now completely obsolete, boat type was in some ways structurally parallel with the European cog. She had a flat bottom built of two layers of heavy planking, one running fore and aft and the other athwartships, and fastened with heavy iron spikes. This bottom was forced up at bow and stern to give it a pronounced fore and aft rocker and on to it were built sides of very heavy planks laid in ordinary clinker fashion. In the bigger boats, I was told, the overlap of the planks was so deep that the sides were

◄◄ 288

A Fleet trow photographed in 1994. The bottom has a small fore and aft rocker but is not dished. Note the balanced oars and single thole pins. A similar arrangement was still used in the older Finnish Lake Boats in the late twentieth century. [*Basil Greenhill*

◄ 289

A kåg *sailing among the skerries of a Swedish archipelago in a fresh wind.* [*Postcard*

◄◄ 290

Boats of the middle river Vistula at Kaliszany Stare. [*Basil Greenhill*

292

A Leba Lake boat in the Fisheries Museum at Hel at the mouth of Gdánsk Bay. The bow structure is unusual. The late Dr Smolarek, Director of the Polish National Maritime Museum, described this flat-bottomed boat as derived from an extended, but not expanded, logboat. [*Basil Greenhill*

293

The structure of a mid-twentieth-century blockkahn *from Gotmmund near Lübeck.* [*Detlev Ellmers*

actually three planks thick. The *patalia* had no floor timbers, but she had knees where the sides joined the floor and she had side timbers. She must have been prodigiously expensive in timber.

Many smooth-skinned, edge-joined, river sailing vessels of Uttar Pradesh in the 1950s were still equipped with boats about 18ft (5.49m) long, flat-bottomed with clinker-built sides in the manner of the *patalia* (Figure 296). Once again the small boats of today represent big vessels now vanished.

The tradition of the simple flat-bottomed boat in many variations (straight sides and curved sides; with bottom rocker fore and aft; and athwartships; with refined bows and sterns; smooth-skinned and clinker-built; double-ended and with transom sterns; with straight stems and curved stems; or upright and sloping; shell-built and skeleton-built) can be traced through illustration, description and surviving boat types in Europe, from the southern Baltic to the Mediterranean, from medieval times and, of course, earlier in some of the Romano-Celtic boats already described in Chapter 3, to the present day. Despite the almost universal use of plastic for new construction numerous examples exist at the end of the twentieth century in Denmark, southern Sweden, Germany, Holland, France and especially in North America.

These are the main streams of European and Asian boat development, and the long, narrow, flat-bottomed boat is one of the most widely distributed of all boat forms. It occurs wherever simple, cheap boats, which do not need great skill to build, are needed for use in shallow, rough water. There is always a tendency to refine the bows and broaden the stern to make the boat more seaworthy, easier and safer under sail. In the twentieth century with the introduction of motors, this tendency has been demonstrated again and again. In that some of them show in miniature the constructional characteristics of the cog, so again do the last wooden small boats illustrate the designs and practices which gave rise to the big ship, long obsolete.

The most numerous and best known in the English-speaking world of these small flat-bottomed boats is the Banks dory. Like the cog her bottom planks run fore and aft, which distinguishes her from the skiff with her athwartships planking (Chapter 2). Unlike the skiff which is built sides first and therefore represents shell construction, if you like, the dory is built bottom-first and then planked up to pre-erected side frames, skeleton construction. The difference suggests widely different ultimate origins. The typical northeast coast North American Banks dory shown here (Figure 297) was photographed under construction in the Lawrence Allen Dory Shop at Lunenburg, Nova Scotia, in 1981. She represents a very well-known late nineteenth-century manifestation of the flat-bottomed tradition. The dory in this form is the product of an industrial age. Because only one plank in her structure need essentially be of curved shape in the flat (often the other strakes were shaped a little as well, though less so in the mass-produced dories, the hull form of which was conditioned by the method of production) she is simple to build and can be put together with

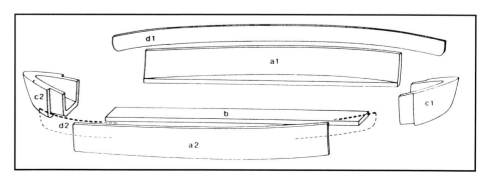

294
Gondolas at the building yard at Squero di S Trovaso, Venice. [*Basil Greenhill*

295
A fishing versison in the same tradition at Guidecca, Venice. [*Basil Greenhill*

296
Flat-bottomed, clinker-sided boat from Uttar Pradesh. [*Basil Greenhill*

297
Banks dory under construction in the Lawrence Allen Dory Shop, Lunenburg, Nova Scotia. [*Basil Greenhill*

minimum wastage in quantity by unskilled labour from pre-cut parts made from stock sawn planks.

In the second half of the nineteenth century, the increasing demand following on the increase of the population in North America led to the expansion of the North American Banks fishery from Massachusetts, from Maine, and from almost every port in Nova Scotia. In order to extend the fishing capacity of individual vessels the custom was adopted (probably from a French practice in vessels from St Pierre) of carrying a number of small boats which were dropped over the sides of the fishing schooners and from which one or two men fished with one kind of gear or another (Figure 298). These boats had to be cheap, partly because the initial capital available was not large, and secondly because they were highly expendable. They were not only lost by the sheer perils of the trade but also by being washed overboard in large numbers from the decks of hard-driven vessels on their way back from the fishing grounds with the fish for market. Because they did not need the strength of permanent thwarts they could be carried nested inside one another on a vessel's deck (Figure 299). The dory, produced in great numbers in boatbuilding workshops, some using almost mass production methods, was the answer, and, because they became readily available cheaply from this source, dories became almost the standard small fishing boat for beach work all the way down the east coast of North America from Massachusetts to Newfoundland. They were also the chosen boat type for many other functions, some very remote from the dory's origins. The early exploration of

298
Trawl fishing on Grand Bank, a contemporary primitive oil painting. [*Maritime Museum of Maine*

299
Nested dories on board the banking schooner Theresa E Connor *preserved at the Maritime Museum of the Atlantic at Lunenburg, Nova Scotia. Aled Eames, the Welsh merchant shipping historian, without hat, with the vessel's curator.* [*Basil Greenhill*

300
Dory boat type used on an early expedition through the Grand Canyon, Arizona. [Basil Greenhill

the Grand Canyon was done in dory type boats (Figure 300), and today you can spend a very adventurous week transiting part of the Colorado river through the canyon in a dory.

The dory has become part of the North American scene and almost the typical flat-bottomed rowing boat of the modern world. She was also used by the French and Portuguese North Atlantic fishermen. Her possible history is therefore worth looking at in a little more detail, especially as in recent years it has been the subject of minor international controversy between Nova Scotia and New England, and Europe and North America. She is a simple case of a boat developing when required for a very special purpose, suited to that purpose, but adaptable to a very limited range of other purposes, and not to be judged on other grounds than her fitness for the job for which she was designed (see Chapter 1).

Given the age and widespread extent of the flat-bottomed tradition, the particular form assumed by the dory could have developed at any time when the need arose. Dories were, and are, of all sizes from 11ft (3.35m) to 28 ft (8.53m) in overall length. Most had a tall, narrow transom, introduced to enable the boat to be sculled with a single oar, but some were double-ended. The general type existed in numerous forms in North America from the seventeenth century onwards and played its part in United States history (Figure 301), but the most spectacular form was perhaps the big lumberman's *bâteau*, of which an example from Maine is in Figure 302.

But the local development of the Banks dory seems to have come from another source. Charles de la Morandière gives an interesting account.

When St Pierre and Miquelon were returned to France in 1763 their inhabitants lacked capital to build sophisticated boats. They therefore copied the flat-bottomed,

301
The Continental gunboat Philadelphia, *built and sunk on Lake Champlain in 1776 displayed in Washington DC.* [*Museum of History and Technology*

302
Lumberman's bâteau *in the Maine Maritime Museum, Bath, Maine.* [*Basil Greenhill*

double-ended boats currently in use by the equally poor English fishermen of the south coasts of Newfoundland, who presumably had inherited the flat-bottomed tradition from Britain – and perhaps even from the flat-bottomed boats in use on the coast of Dorset, like the Fleet trows, an area with strong Newfoundland connections at the time. One of the factors in the development of these flat-bottomed boats had been the necessity of beaching after each use, easier in general with rockered flat-bottomed boats than with keel boats (see the references to the Jersey skiff types later in this chapter). In St Pierre these boats, locally dubbed wherries, were built in great numbers. Morandière suggests that it was the wherry that inspired the American and Canadian development of the dory handline fishing which Innes records as taking place at Southport, Maine, in 1858. By the early 1870s dories, bought from American

303

Dories were often equipped with sails of one kind or another. Here Sam and Susan Manning of Camden, Maine, prepare for a winter sail in the dory they built. [*Basil Greenhill*

schooners, were in use at St Pierre. In 1885 more than 1000 dories were bought from the United States. French fishing vessels visiting St Pierre were quick to adopt the new, cheap boats and dory factories were established, notably at St Malo, where exact copies of New England dories were made in great numbers. The type was also adopted by the Portuguese schooner owners and at Lunenburg, Nova Scotia, where dory fishing was adopted in 1872 and rapidly grew in scale until in the twentieth century it rivalled the fishery of New England. It did not end until 1963.

Because she is relatively easy and cheap to construct, and yet is of an ancient boatbuilding tradition (and, since this is a boat which at its best requires skilful handling, she must be very carefully designed), a well-designed small dory is perhaps the best boat from which to learn something of the problems and skills of an ancient boatbuilding tradition. Both working and pleasure dories have been equipped with sails (Figure 303) and in 1939 on the north coast of Brittany I came across a dory employed in a local beach fishery which had been equipped with a centre board. But dories under sail require very careful handling.

The development of the transom-sterned, flat-bottomed boat in the nineteenth century was particularly associated with the east coast of North America and in general, in contrast with European practice, flat-bottomed craft were the most widely used of North American boat types in the days before the introduction of small gasoline and diesel marine engines and outboards. In Chapter 2 of this book we saw George Adams at work on building skiffs, vessels built the other way round from the dory, which begins with its bottom, planked fore and aft, and has the sides added;

while George Adams started with the sides and fastened the bottom planks athwartships, cutting off the ends to shape. Variations of George Adams' skiffs are still to be found all the way from Georgia to Newfoundland. Some reached a high degree of development and size, like the Newhaven sharpie, developed for oyster fishing in Long Island Sound in the middle of the nineteenth century. She was, of course, very economical to build for her size, easy to handle, and, in the words of Howard I Chapelle in *The Migrations of an American Boat Type*, she was 'manoeuvrable, fast and seaworthy, the type was soon adopted for fishing along the eastern and south eastern coasts of the United States and in other areas. Later, because of its speed, the sharpie became popular for racing and yachting . . . The Newhaven sharpie proved that a long, narrow hull is most efficient in a flat-bottomed boat.'

Figure 304 shows the hull of a Newhaven sharpie preserved at the Mariner's Museum at Newport News. Some of the biggest of the sharpies, notably those in the oyster fishery of the North Carolina Sounds, were schooner-rigged.

By way of contrast with the sharpie, another type is illustrated. Figure 305 shows a rowing and sailing skiff from Maine, equipped with a wheel and handles for easier launching and pulling out. The type is fairly common in the eastern states and obviates the necessity for a launching trolley. This particular variation was developed at Seal Cove, south of Portland, Maine, in the second half of the nineteenth century as a tender for large sailing lobster boats. A replica built by Alan Hinks at Appledore from drawings by Howard I Chapelle has been subjected to extensive trials by the author, and has proved a good rowing boat for use in a swift flowing tidal river and its estuary. She is pulled up a slipway after use.

There are two further variations on the flat-bottomed boat, both particularly associated with North America, which should be described here. These are the skiff with curved plank-built sides above a narrow flat rockered bottom and the V-bottomed boat.

The first form occurs among other places in Denmark and in Britain, where it was built at Weston-super-Mare and at Clevedon in Somerset. Eric McKee's drawing in Figure 306 shows the Weston version. But it was in the United States and Canada, in the Sea Bright skiffs of the New Jersey shore, the Staten Island skiffs and the oyster skiffs of the Virginia shore of the Chesapeake (Figure 307), and the skiffs of the Magdalen Islands (Figures 308 and 309) and the south shore of the Gaspé Peninsula, that the type was developed most highly.

These boats, as Figure 308 shows, could be beached easily on sand, shingle or pebbles, or on a wood or concrete landing slip and once beached could be moved around without difficulty. The Magdalen Islands skiffs were still built and in use in great numbers in the 1970s and were particularly associated with small scale sealing. Their shape made them very suitable for use in pack ice, over which they could easily be pulled. Some were fitted with rockered skids specifically for the purpose (Figure 309). There is a parellel here with the ice *öka* used in the Finnish archipelagoes (see Chapter 2). They were at the same time safe and handy in the water, particularly in surf, and they were cheaper and easier to build than keel boats. It is just possible (bearing in mind the geographical proximity) that the skiffs of the Magdalen Islands and the south shore of the Gaspé, like those illustrated here, are the descendants of the wherries of southern Newfoundland and St Pierre which in turn, according to Morandière's theory, gave rise to the dory. There were dozens of variations of the type in use in eastern North America and Europe a century ago and less.

But the most spectacular of these round-hulled, flat-bottomed vessels in use in

304
A Newhaven sharpie in the Mariner's Museum at Newport News. [Basil Greenhill

305
A reconstruction of a skiff from Seal Cove, Cape Elizabeth, Maine. Eric McKee is the passenger. [Basil Greenhill

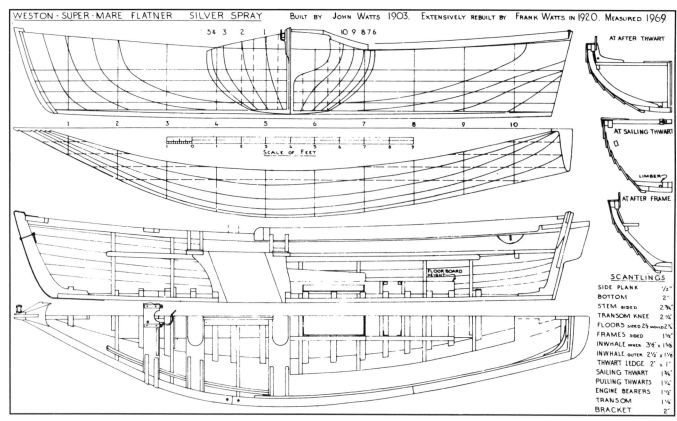

WESTON-SUPER-MARE FLATNER SILVER SPRAY. BUILT BY JOHN WATTS 1903. EXTENSIVELY REBUILT BY FRANK WATTS IN 1920. MEASURED 1969.

AT AFTER THWART

AT SAILING THWART

AT AFTER FRAME

SCANTLINGS

SIDE PLANK	1/2"
BOTTOM	2"
STEM SIDED	2 3/4"
TRANSOM KNEE	2 1/2"
FLOORS SIDED 2 1/2 MOULD	2 1/4"
FRAMES SIDED	1 1/2"
INWHALE INNER	3 1/2" x 1 5/8"
INWHALE OUTER	2 1/2" x 1 7/8"
THWART LEDGE	2" x 1"
SAILING THWART	1 3/4"
PULLING THWARTS	1 1/2"
ENGINE BEARERS	1 1/2"
TRANSOM	1 1/4"
BRACKET	2"

SCALE OF FEET

308

Dignity and impudence, a Magdalen Islands skiff rests upright on her rockered flat bottom on the landing at Leslie while a Northumberland Strait type lobster boat is propped up by a box under her starboard bilge keel. [Basil Greenhill

309

Right – a Magdalen Islands skiff fitted with heavy steel skids for hauling over ice floes when sealing. [Basil Greenhill

306

Opposite, top – Weston-super-Mare flatner. [Eric McKee

307

Opposite, bottom – Chesapeake oyster skiff in the Mariner's Museum at Newport News, Virginia. Note that she is lapstrake built. [Basil Greenhill

310
The St Lawrence goelette GH Marie, *ex* Emerillon, *ex* Francoise G: *built at Riviere-du-Loup, Quebec, in 1947, 150 tons gross. She ceased to trade in 1974. Here, laid up in her old age in 1978 she sits bolt upright on her flat bottom on the foreshore at Riviere-du-Loup.* [Basil Greenhill

recent years, and the largest modern descendant of the family of the cog (though built very differently from the medieval cog) was the St Lawrence '*goelette à fond plat*'. These big wooden vessels, latterly motor-driven, carrying perhaps 100 tons of cargo, worked around the small ports of the great estuary of the St Lawrence and in the western part of the Gulf. Seen afloat they appeared to be ordinary small wooden motorships. Lying dried out on the shore they were seen for what they were, completely flat-bottomed and in effect gigantic forms of the Magdalen Islands skiff (Figure 310). The model (Figure 311) in the excellent Musée Maritime Bernier at L'Islet sur Mare in Quebec Province shows the shape of the bottom perfectly. The last to be built was launched in the late 1950s. Very fortunately, the National Film Board of Canada recorded her construction in a most valuable documentary film *The Jean Richard*, and two of the *goelettes* have been restored and preserved in the harbours of Quebec townships, *Marie Clarice* at Jonquières and *St André* at La Malbaie.

The V-bottomed boat (the name is self descriptive) was the last of the classic boatbuilding traditions to develop on a large scale, probably in North America in the eighteenth century although, as we have seen in Chapter 9, V-bottomed sewn plank boats existed among the Saamish people of northern Finland. It was not until a hundred years later that it began to come into general use when a boat with better seakeeping abilities than those of the flat-bottomed boat was required, but building costs called for simpler construction than that of the normal round-hulled, non edge-joined fully skeleton-built vessel. Great developments of the V-bottom took place on Chesapeake Bay where it was used in a number of forms and sizes of boat and vessel, the largest of which was the oyster-dredging skipjack (Figure 312), which took over from the bugeyes described in Chapter 8 when the construction costs of the latter became prohibitive, as the principal vessel of the great oyster fisheries of Maryland. Figure 313 shows the type developed as a small yacht.

The V-bottom has, of course, been greatly developed in high speed motor pleasure craft, but it also has its modern commercial applications, of which a very handsome example is the V-bottomed lobster boat (a variation of Bob Strongman's boat) of which an example appears in Figure 314.

Of course, the flat-bottomed boat has evolved in many other forms, some of which are interrelated. There still exist in the world today examples of all the stages in the evolution of the logboat, punt or scow shown in Figure 315, which illustrate a possible sequence of development from the prehistoric logboat canoe into the punt or scow. The first stage is a simple logboat, then planks are added to increase stability; two logboats are then joined together and as a further refinement two half logboats to give a broad-beamed hull. Finally the punt or scow with a plank keel between two half logboats anticipates the fully-planked boat of the same general shape. Dr Detlev Ellmers has suggested that there may be two distinct roots of the scow, the split logboat, which will always have chine girders, the L-shaped timber at the turn of the bilge, as in the last drawing in Figure 315, and scow-shaped boats without chine girders which may have evolved from rafts. But we have already seen (Chapter 9) that the chine girder also exists in Saamish-built V-bottomed boats.

From these roots come the punt with transoms at both ends and many kinds of scow and broad-beamed flat-bottomed boat. Large cargo vessels derived ultimately from this form are still in use in many parts of the world. Punts and scows of all kinds are in use as pleasure boats and working boats (Figure 316). Many made in fibre-glass are capable of very high speeds with powerful outboards and are highly

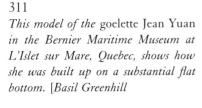

311
This model of the goelette Jean Yuan in the Bernier Maritime Museum at L'Islet sur Mare, Quebec, shows how she was built up on a substantial flat bottom. [Basil Greenhill

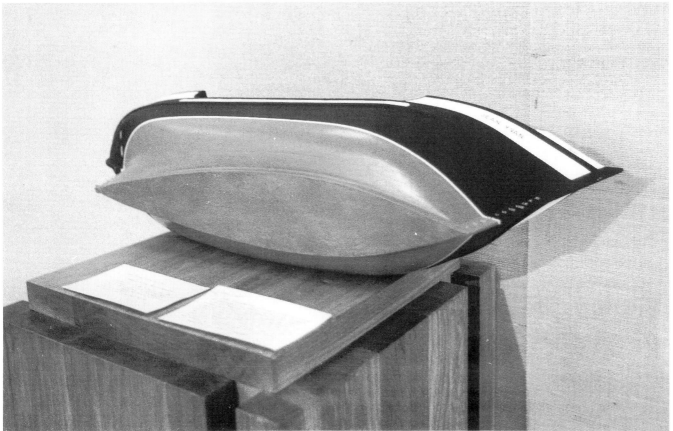

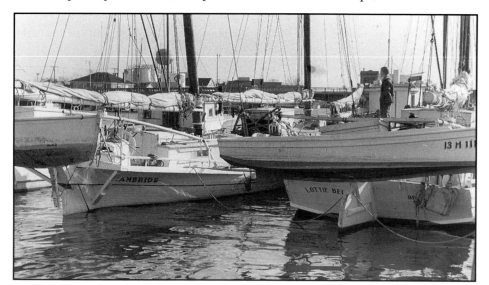

312
A V-bottomed skipjack and a frame bugeye in harbour at Cambridge, Maryland, 1954. [*Basil Greenhill*

313
A small V-bottomed skipjack built on Chesapeake Bay as a yacht discovered in Harley Cox and Co's yard at Shelburne, Nova Scotia in 1982. Note the planking of the bottom. [*Basil Greenhill*

314
The long lean hull of the V-bottomed lobster boat Bayfield Cape. [*Basil Greenhill*

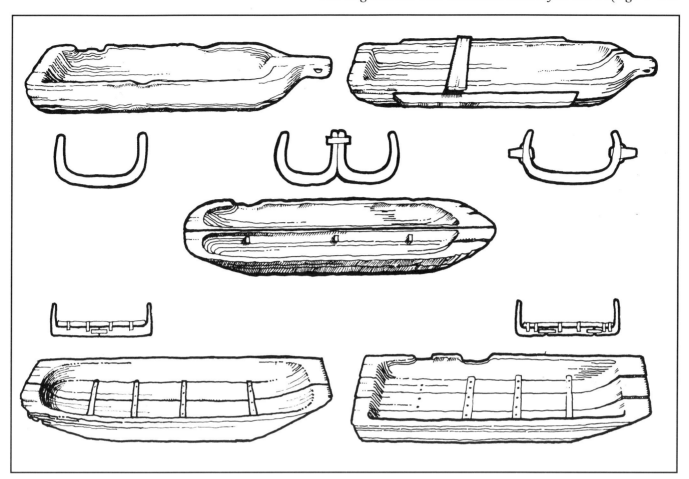

315

Logboat to scow. [Landström, The Ship

316

A lobsterman's punt, used as a tender to a lobster boat moored afloat, photographed at South Bristol, Maine. [Basil Greenhill

317
New Zealand schooner rigged scows, one, the Lake St Clair, *built in 1876 and one of the first scows, derelict and the other with sails bent, still in working condition.* [Clifford W Hawkins

318
Scow schooner Alma *at San Francisco.* [Dr John H Harland

practical vessels for many purposes; very sophisticated ones are marketed in Britain with the totally inaccurate brand name of 'dory', in the United States, even worse, as 'whalers'.

Figure 317 shows a very developed form of sailing scow which was built in New Zealand in the late nineteenth century for service in the extremely rough waters around North Island. It is thought that the type was almost certainly taken to New Zealand by settlers from the east coast of the United States and Canada. Many of these scows, equipped with big drop keels and rigged as ketches or schooners, survived years of sailing. They carried their cargo on deck and can be regarded, if you like, as gigantic hollow sailing rafts. A few have been restored in recent years.

Scows also developed on both coasts of the North American continent. Scow sloops were used in the coastal trade of New England, scow schooners in the Carolina Sounds and on the west coast around San Francisco. One of the latter is now preserved at the San Francisco Maritime State Park, and her photograph (Figure 318) illustrates well the ultimate development of this type.

Bibliography

ABEL, H (ed), *Die Bremer Hanse-Kogge*, 1969

BAYKOWSKI, V, *Die Kieler Hanse Kogge*, 1991

BRINDLEY, H H, *Impressions and casts of seals, coins, tokens, medals and other objects of Art exhibited in the Seal Room of the National Maritime Museum*, 1938

BURWASH, D, *English Merchant Shipping 1460–1540*, 1947

CHAPELLE, H I, *Boatbuilding*, 1947
   American Small Sailing Craft, 1951
   'The Migrations of an American Boat-type', 1961

CRUMLIN-PEDERSEN, O, 'Cog-Kogge-Kaage', 1965
   (ed), *Aspects of Maritime Scandinavia*, 1991

DADE, E, *Sail and Oar*, 1933

EADDY, P A, *'Neath Swaying Spars*, 1939

ERICSSON, C, *The Routes of the Sea*, 1988

EWE, H, *Schiffe auf Siegeln*, 1972

FLIEDNER, S, 'Kogge und Hulk', 1969

GARDNER, J, with illustrations by MANNING, S, *The Dory Book*, 1978

GREENHILL, B and MANNING, S, *The Evolution of the Wooden Ship*, 1988

HAWKINS, C, *Out of Auckland*, 1960
   Maritime Heritage, 1978

HEIDE, G D van der, 'Ship Archaeological Investigations in the Netherlands', 1970

HUTCHINSON, G, *Medieval Ships and Shipping*, 1944

INNES, H A, *Cod Fisheries, the History of an International Economy*, 1954

MCGRAIL, *Ancient Boats in North West Europe*, 1987
   (ed), *The Archaeology of Medieval Ships and Harbours of Northern Europe*, 1979
   (ed), *Aspects of Maritime Ethnology and Ethnography*, 1984

MCKEE, J E G, *Working Boats of Britain*, 1983
   'Weston-Super-Mare Flatners', 1971

MACPHERSON RICE, W, 'Account of an Ancient vessel recently found under the old bed of the River Rother, Kent', 1824

MARCH, E J, *Inshore Craft of Britain*, 1970

MESSENGER, A H, 'Notes on the New Zealand Scow', 1969

MOORE, A, *Last Days of Mast and Sail*, 1925

MORANDIÈRE, C de la, *History of the French Cod Fishing Industry in North America*, 1966

PERGOLIS, R, *The Boats of Venice*, 1981

RUDOLPH, W, *Handbuch der volkstumlichen Boote im ostlichen Nieder Deutchland*, 1966
   Inshore Fishing Craft of the Southern Baltic from Holstein to Curonia, 1974

SHAW, A, 'Bridgwater Flatner', 1969

UNGER, R W (ed), *Cogs, Caravels and Galleons*, 1994

WARD, R H, 'A Surviving Charter Party of 1323', forthcoming for publication in *The Mariner's Mirror*.

WARINGTON-SMYTH, H, *Mast and Sail in Europe and Asia*, 1906

WESTERDAHL, C (ed), *Crossroads in Ancient Shipbuilding*, 1994

WHITE, E W, *British Fishing Boats and Coastal Craft*, 1950

ZIMER, F, *Bluenose, Queen of the Grand Banks*, 1970

CHAPTER

19

The Mysterious Hulk

While in the years before AD 800 the northern clinker-built ship was developing in Scandinavia and northern Germany and the cog was developing in the Low Countries, another type of vessel must have been evolving at the same time in Europe. This was the hulk, *hulc* or *holc*, an Anglo-Saxon word meaning a hollow and applied to a husk of corn or a peapod, whose shape the hulk closely resembled. I have already referred to her several times and she is illustrated in Chapter 3. Her basic characteristic, the solution adopted by her builders to the problem of the plank ends (to have them all out of the water) is one that, as we have seen, occurs elsewhere in the world, notably in modern Bangladesh. The evidence is much less complete for the development of the hulk than for the clinker-built boat and there is also less evidence than there is for the story of the cog. No recognised and identified remains of a hulk had been identified by the mid-90s of the twentieth century. Somewhere in the mud of an estuary or buried in saltings, this most important discovery in the archaeology of boats and ships is still waiting to be made. In the meantime, we are dependent for our knowledge of her entirely on pictures, seals and representations on coins and so forth. Documentary evidence indicates that in the 1300s the cog began widely to be supplanted by the hulk. Her image appears on town seals in Britain, the Low Countries and France, but, apparently, not east of the Isselmeer. She is illustrated in numerous forms more widely, for example, in graffiti in Tofta in Gotland and on a brass of the late fifteenth century of possibly Flemish origin in Nousiainez Church near Turku in Finland. Hulk types can also be seen in numerous illustrations collected from many sources in the first volumes of the *Mariner's Mirror* (1911–1920).

The available iconographic material suggests that the hulk was quite different in construction from either the cog or the Scandinavian clinker-built boat. She appears to have been curved both longitudinally and transversely, probably with a long, narrow, flat keel, curved up at the ends, and always without a stem or sternpost. Most of the illustrations suggest clinker-laid planking, running in a uniform curve parallel to the sheer line and bottom, ending on a horizontal line at the ends well above the waterline. Such a vessel is completely different from the traditional clinker with stem and sternposts, and has a characteristic dishlike shape – in profile, something like a banana.

Having described the apparent characteristics of the vessel identified (by Ole Crumlin-Pedersen, Detlev Ellmers and others) with the type-name 'hulk' as it appears in medieval documents, we must examine very briefly some of the evidence we have for the existence of a distinct shipbuilding tradition, quite different from the traditions which produced the Scandinavian, Slav, or middle northern European clinker-built boats, and quite different from the traditions that produced the cog.

Ellmers believes the hulk to have been predominant in the North Sea as early as the second half of the eighth century, in the form illustrated on contemporary coins of the town of Dorestad, near Utrecht. These in turn, Crumlin-Pedersen has pointed out, are copies of coins of Quentovic, the French shipping place south of Boulogne, which perhaps pushes the origins of the hulk a little further back in time. It has been noted that medieval Shoreham was called 'Hulkesmouth' and that the vessel roughly depicted on its seal of *c*1295 (Figure 319) appears to have some of the characteristics described above. It is largely on this evidence that the name 'hulk' has been identified with this type of vessel.

319

The Common Seal of the Corporation of New Shoreham, Sussex, dated about AD *1495 shows a vessel with the characteristics attributed to the hulk. Shoreham was known at this period as Hulkesmouth.* [*National Maritime Museum*

What is quite certain is that medieval craftsmen seeking to illustrate vessels in illuminated manuscripts, in stonecarving, and in fine metalwork, were by the early twelfth century deliberately and carefully depicting a vessel quite different from the clinker-type with stem and sternpost, equally carefully depicted in other contemporary works of art. Let us take a few examples. The Lewes capital of *c*1120 from Lewes Priory, now in the British Museum, depicts scenes from the life of St Peter and in one of them a vessel of the hulk type is very carefully shown. The Worcester Chronicle of *c*1130–40, in the possession of Corpus Christi College, Oxford, shows an equally carefully depicted vessel of the same type. English enamel plaques dated

320

A misericord in the choir stalls of St David's Cathedral in Pembrokeshire depicts a hulk type vessel under (somewhat leisurely) construction. [University of St Andrews

321

Far left – the Seal of the Admiralty Court of Bristol, established in 1446, depicts a hulk in some detail. Note the reverse clinker planking and the rope girdling at the bows. [Basil Greenhill

322

Hulk on a British coin of 1473/4. [National Maritime Museum

by art historians to *c*1170–80, now in the Germanisches National Museum in Nuremburg, show a less carefully depicted vessel which is evidently of the same type. All these vessels have side rudders and one of them a clearly drawn single squaresail. The well-known depiction of *c*1180 of the same type of vessel, on the font of Winchester Cathedral Figure 323, shows a stern-rudder as does a similar carving at Zedelgem near Bruges; these may well be the first depictions of a stern-rudder so far noticed. A misericord in the choir stalls of St David's Cathedral in Pembrokeshire shows a vessel of hulk type, under construction (Figure 320).

The seal of the Admiralty Court of Bristol, established in 1446 (Figure 321) clearly depicts a hulk in some detail. The fifteenth-century gold coin illustrated here (Figure 322) is from a hoard showing representations of hulks which was found in 1971 on the site of the palace of Placentia in the grounds of the Royal Naval College, Greenwich. The coin is an angel of Edward IV, 1473–4. Although it is so late, it shows an unmistakable hulk. The hulk by the late 1400s was obsolescent if not obsolete and as so often with designs of coins, etc, the designer seems deliberately to

323
Hulk on the font of Winchester Cathedral, CAD 1180. Note the clearly depicted stern rudder. [Albert W Kerr

NOTE *In August 1995, when this book was being printed, I found in the church on Fårö, north of Gotland, an oil painting apparently of the early 1600s clearly showing a three masted hulk with a single high aspect ratio square-sail set from each mast.*

have chosen an anachronistic form to illustrate. All these examples of illustrations of the hulk except one are English or Welsh, some from the west coast.

A distinct type of vessel therefore undoubtedly existed and was widespread in its use in Britain. We can deduce some of her characteristics, and also the reasons for them, but can go no further until archaeological evidence becomes available. Of the hulk's origins we really know little. Crumlin-Pedersen and others, following him, have seen a possible ancestor in the Utrecht boat, an extended logboat of about AD 900, but there are few structural characteristics to connect this vessel with the hulk. Equally, there seems little evidence to support the theory which has been put forward that the hulk is represented today by the two-transom boat miscalled a pram by yachtsmen in the English-speaking world. This has none of the hulk's apparent structural characteristics and is at least equally likely to have been developed in comparatively recent years from the willow tree logboat of the middle Baltic region.

Recent research by Mrs Jones-Baker, presented at the Society of Antiquaries in London but unfortunately not published, into the vessels illustrated by graffiti in churches in East Anglia has revealed the images of many vessels which appear to be of the hulk type, associated with river and coastal trade. This may suggest that the hulk developed in Britain from the inland and sheltered-water vessels of the area north of the Thames in the way that the cog developed from similar boats in the Friesian area. Certainly the development of the hulk would seem to be a prime subject for British research and its study should be given priority in anticipation of the inevitable archaeological discovery, which may occur at any time. It would be possible, for instance, to determine with model structures the degree to which simplicity of construction using the natural run of straight-plank shaped only on the bottom edge may have encouraged the development of the hulk, just as relative economy of structure may have been important in the development of the cog.

The hulk seems to have become predominant in northern sea commerce in the fourteenth century because she was capable of greater cargo capacity in relation to building cost than even the cog (with its definite size limits) at a time when vessels of greater capacity were becoming profitable to operate. The reign of the hulk seems to have been rather short, for by the middle of the next century she began to be overtaken by a new type of ship, capable of development to a degree which was to make her superior in seaworthiness, sailing ability, size, economy and range of operation to any vessel which had existed before (see next chapter).

An ethnographic parallel

The construction of many boat types in different districts of Bangladesh in the third quarter of the twentieth century appeared to have striking similarities with the building tradition of the hulk. The illustrations Figures 324, 325, 326 and 327 show the planking techniques employed very well. In both smooth-skinned and reverse clinker construction the strake ends were brought up and cut off on a level plane not on transoms, and capped with horizontal strakes (Figure 324). Figure 326, a photograph taken fairly early in the building of a large cargo boat, shows the technique particularly well with the unfinished ends of the lower strakes coming up at the bows of the vessel.

In some Bangladesh boats the fore ends of the strakes were laid in this way, the after end faired to the garboard strake as to a stern post. Figure 327 shows this type of construction. The iconographic evidence for the hulk shows similar hybrids in western Europe in the 1300s. Here the after planking is brought up to a sternpost

324

A big river cargo boat from Sylhet, Bangladesh. Her planking appears closely to resemble that of a European hulk. [Basil Greenhill

325

This drawing made from a photograph shows the planking pattern of a big smooth planked cargo boat of Bangladesh. [Cicely Hill

326
The hulk-like planking pattern of a Bangladesh cargo boat under development at an early stage in building. [Alan Villiers

327
Boat with hybrid hulk type planking under construction, Sylhet, Bangladesh. [Basil Greenhill

which can accommodate the stern rudder, then just coming into use. This cannot be the reason for adopting this form of construction in Bangladesh, where all boats of the local building traditions except the *sampan*, already described, steer with a steering oar or a side rudder.

Bibliography

BRINDLEY, H H, *Impressions and casts of seals, coins, tokens, medals and other objects of Art exhibited in the Seal Room of the National Maritime Museum*, 1938

BURWASH, D, *English Merchant Shipping 1460–1540*, 1947

CRUMLIN-PEDERSEN, O, 'Das Haithabuschiff', 1969

ELLMERS, D, *Frümitteralterliche Handelsschiffahrt in Mittel und Nordeuropa*, 1972

EWE, H, *Schiffe auf Siegeln*, 1972

FLIEDNER, S, 'Kogge und Hulk', 1969

HUTCHINSON, G, *Medieval Ships and Shipping*, 1944

MCGRAIL, S, *Ancient Boats in North West Europe*, 1987

UNGER, R W (ed.) *Cogs, Caravels and Galleons*, 1994

VLEK, R, *The Medieval Utrecht Boat*, 1987

VON BUSCH, P, HAASUM, S and LAGERLÖF, E, *Skeppsristningar på Gotland*, Stockholm, 1993

WASKÖNIG, D, 'Bidliche Darstellungen des Hulk', 1969

CHAPTER
20

Skeletons Everywhere

The cog, the hulk and the clinker-built ship of the north influenced one another. Cogs were evidently built in which the flat bottom became almost vestigial and they were fitted with keels. The terms cog and hulk became confused and interchangeable and ship types appear to have become even less clearly defined in contemporary usage (at least in the usage of the officials who kept the records) than before. In the early fifteenth century the same ship may have been called a cog in one port and a hulk in the next one she visited. It depended, perhaps, on which elements in her construction were locally thought to predominate. Many other names were used with reference to ships: thus we read of the barge, balinger, crayer, navis, neif or nef, scoute, dogger, farcost, spinece, hoy, hayne, topship, foucet, galley and batella (which term is still used in Pakistan). Sometimes these terms seem to have been used almost indiscriminately, and differently from port to port. Only rarely do we have any information about the structure of the vessels concerned.

But a great change which was to sweep away much that was traditional was already under way, and the roots of some of it lay in the stresses to which every boat and vessel is subjected. There was of course a limit to the size to which a vessel dependent for the greater part of its strength on edge-joining could be built, if it were to be strong enough for sea service with heavy loads. However massive the planks of which she was constructed and however many of them were used (in clinker construction overlapping and overlapping again), still the shell of a big edge-joined vessel without very heavy frames was weak in relation to its size and the great stresses to which it was subjected, deep laden with guns, stores and cargo in a rough sea. As has already been said the remains of the probable hull of the *Grace Dieu*, Henry V's great clinker-built warship launched in 1418 and of a size comparable with that of HMS *Victory*, as they lie in the Hamble river today show her to have been massively constructed.

The alternative method of construction involved a great and complex technical revolution with roots and implications reaching deep into the structure of the societies in which it took place. For reasons already explained, the technique of full non edge-joined construction on a pre-erected skeleton was completely different from the old and very widespread traditions of edge-joined boat- and shipbuilding. The builder could no longer shape the vessel according to tradition, use and available material as she grew on the slipway; she had to be conceived as a whole before she could be built. The parts that determined her shape ceased to be the strakes, shaped to fit as she grew, but became her frames, which had to be shaped according to a pre-determined design.

As I said in Chapter 3, it is possible to become philosophical on this theme. Given that there were periods of varying length in different societies in which transitional building methods may have been used, at what point does shell-building become skeleton-building? Is it, as suggested in Chapter 3, when the builder, whatever transitional method he may use to obtain his frame shapes, visualised his vessel in terms of the framing rather than the planking? Or is it at the point at which the shape of the entire vessel is determined by a pre-erected framework – full skeleton construction as defined by McGrail?

We have seen in Chapter 3 that some intermediate forms, including the use of some non edge-joined planks, and even something moving close to full skeleton construction as in the Serçe Limani vessel of AD *c*1000, developed in different parts of the world, as in the Mediterranean in the first millennium AD, and that evidence, including the earliest finds found in the City of London, indicate that a rather similar Romano-Celtic tradition may have existed in Britain and in Europe from very early in the present era. Some of these vessels, as the Guernsey wreck, were probably seagoing.

One development, which may possibly have come out of these traditions, the cog, was very successful as a vessel for limited seagoing. The archaeological evidence shows that some cogs had the planks of the flat, or near flat, bottom not joined edge to edge. But other than in some of these flat-bottomed boats what developments may have taken place towards full skeleton construction in the centuries after Serçe Limani are not yet known. There is little or no evidence in Scandinavia, where good fortune has left us more information than anywhere else, so that we really do know something about the development of boat and shipbuilding over a limited period and area. All this evidence indicates highly developed edge-joined techniques.

The development of non edge-joined fully skeleton shipbuilding (that is, the building of vessels the shape of which is determined entirely by a pre-erected frame-work) with all its possibilities for extended seafaring, trading and the establishment of authority, is one of the great technical achievements in the history of European (and, at one remove, of North American) man. The ultimate result of the great change was the building of ships which were strong and big enough to carry adequate supplies, cargo, men and women at a time when the wastage of human life at sea of more than 50 per cent was normal, and, perhaps most important of all initially, sufficient heavy guns to make long ocean voyages with profitable results to the sponsors. The vessels were strong enough to survive the stresses imposed on them for months, sometimes years, on end without needing repairs greater than could be done on some remote beach by their own skilled people. In other words, the result was ships in which it was possible for European man, given many other factors in his favour, to make his travels, and eventually his domination, worldwide.

This does not imply that the right ship was necessarily developed to meet the demands of profitable world travel with the authority established by shipborne guns. The cause may have been largely other, and the world travel may have followed upon the possession of the right vehicle, initially brought into existence, or partly brought into existence, for other purposes, and the travel may have encouraged its further development. Indeed, given the extreme difficulty and slowness of the innovation, clearly demonstrated by the history of its very slow spread over the next five hundred or so years, this is likely to have been the order of events. We must look therefore before the development of ocean voyaging for traces of the early development of the non edge-joined skeleton-built vessels and, as with so many other things

The last wooden three-masted square-rigged merchant sailing vessel in the world is the Sigyn *of Wårdö, Åland Islands, built in Göteborg in 1887 which today lies restored in her specially built floating dock in the harbour of Turku, Finland. This view from the forecastle head shows the rocker arm of the pump handle windlass, the deck house forecastle and galley and the rigging of the fore lower mast.* Sigyn *is a maritime monument of the greatest international importance. [Basil Greenhill*

328

This panel, before conservation, from an altar piece in the church in Satopy near Olsztyn in Poland, painted CAD 1500, is a late depiction of a two-masted vessel. [Musuem Warmii i Mazur, Olsztyn

in the history of shipbuilding and navigation, the innovation probably began earlier than has been thought. It may have happened more than once, in different places in different ways.

Ocean voyaging, in the sense in which we are considering it now, perhaps began in the shadows of the early fifteenth century from the west coast of Europe, that is the Iberian Peninsula, Biscay France and Britain. It is in these areas that we might look for evidence of the beginnings of the great but prolonged revolution, say between 1200 and about 1400, stretching back well into, and even before, the era of the cog, hulk and the great clinker-built ship. The evidence may take a number of forms. Insofar as the material exists it could be useful, for instance, to examine in this context the development of the trades of the areas concerned in the thirteenth and fourteenth centuries from the point of view of the demands that changes may have made for larger and stronger vessels.

There is one factor which has perhaps been rather overlooked. It is very widely known that the scant evidence shows that between the late fourteenth century and the late fifteenth century the European sailing ship, north and south, underwent dramatic development in matters of sails and rigging. In those years the sailing ship appears to have grown suddenly in matters of rig from a single master with a single squaresail through two masts to a three-masted vessel with squaresails on each mast, topsails and even topgallants (Figures 328, 329 and 330). A great deal of work still needs to be done to determine what further unrecognised evidence exists for this great development in the sailing ship, which produced a vessel capable of sailing to windward and of efficiently going through the wind when on a passage to windward.

But further evidence has come to light in recent years. A chart of the mid-1300s shows a Mediterranean vessel with a single squaresail amidships and a lateen mizzen. Anna-Lisa Stigell has drawn attention to a picture for the month of June in the manuscript of *De Sphaera Estense* from *c*1350, now in Modena, which appears to show a three-masted vessel. L V Mott has found and published a sketch clearly

s manuscript illustration from c1450 shows a y developed, wooden three-masted square-ed sailing vessel, a basic type which was to tinue to be constructed in Europe until 20. [The Hastings Manuscript

depicting a three-masted vessel in a Catalan manuscript dated 1406. From the middle 1400s onwards illustrations of ships with three masts begin to appear widely on manuscripts, church walls and bench ends, on coins, on pottery and on seals and eventually in paintings. In the Victoria and Albert Museum is a Hispano-Moresque bowl, a very beautiful object, dated by the specialists in this kind of material at about 1425, which clearly shows a three-masted vessel. In these early illustrations the first two masts aft from the bows are equipped with squaresails, the third mast with a lateen sail.

The spread of three-masters into northern Europe was rapid. Because depictions show the masts of ships clearly, but tell us nothing of their construction, we know far more about the progress of this second revolution than the first, the development of skeleton construction. By the end of the fifteenth century the three-masted vessel was fully established. Even the cogs were equipped with three masts, as is shown in a carving on a 'calendar stick' in the Norwegian Museum of Art in Oslo, dated from its inscription to as early as 1457. The frames of early three-masters may not have been continuous and they may have been built partly using shell techniques to develop their shape. The birth of this type of vessel has rightly been called 'the invention of the sailing ship', an expression which may be taken to mean a vessel capable of ocean voyages.

So the tool of the European expansion, the three-masted non-edged joined skeleton-built sailing ship was born. She was the vehicle of achievement at an almost explosive rate. Just as she herself seems to have developed at a pace which can almost be compared with that of the aeroplane in the twentieth century, so the discovery of the oceans and of the true extent of the world which she made possible took place in less than a century. Most histories of the ship draw attention to this period of development. There may have been many and complex causes, but a contributing factor may well have been developments occurring, again rather earlier than has been thought, towards fully skeleton construction, the results being stronger, more burdensome vessels, able to carry the three-masted rig really essential for prolonged ocean voyaging in all conditions.

An important contribution as far as northern Europe is concerned has been made by the Swedish maritime historian, Dr Olof Hasslöf, formerly Professor of Maritime

331
Caulking the new wooden three-masted schooner Linden *in Mariehamn, Åland, Finland in July 1992.* [*Basil Greenhill*

Ethnology at the University of Copenhagen. There is, of course, always the danger in this kind of research that the discussion will in the end be about a word rather than about the realities behind it. Bearing this in mind, and bearing in mind also that we do not know what the word meant at the time, it is nevertheless interesting that the earliest appearance of the term carvel, in one form or another, which Hasslöf quotes is a Portuguese one of 1255, in which *caravela* refers to small fishing boats along the Portuguese coast. The term is used later of larger vessels and the history of both the term and of shipbuilding in the next two centuries is very obscure. In Mediterranean countries it has been difficult to associate the term carvel with a method of shipbuilding because all vessels, whether edge-joined or not, were smooth-skinned. In northern and western Europe, however, the distinction was clearer because edge-joined vessels were usually clinker-built. It is in this area, therefore, that the word carvel can first be associated with a method of building distinct from the old traditions. At the end of the fifteenth century hard evidence perhaps begins to appear in English written records. Hasslöf points out that in English shipyard ledgers of the thirteenth, fourteenth and fifteenth centuries the terms 'spiknayl', 'clinch-nayl' and 'rivetts' are frequently used and would appear to refer to fastenings used in clinker-building. But in the 1490s items begin to appear which refer to 'carvell nayles'. Early in the 1500s the Great Galley, clinker-built in 1515, was ordered to be broken up and rebuilt carvel. A State Paper of 1545 records that clinker-built vessels were 'both feeble, olde and out of fashion'.

Walther Vogel, in *Geschichte der Deutschen Seeschiffahrt* (Berlin, 1915) quotes evidence suggesting much the same development at a slightly earlier period and under western European influence. *The Chronicle of Zeeland* by Jan Reygersbergen, which dates from the mid-sixteenth century, contains the following passage:

about 1459, at first in Zierikzee, following the example of a Breton named Julian, carvel built ships began to be built instead of the hulks and craiers up to then solely in use. Velius, the Chronicler, who however wrote about three-quarters of a century later, supplements this information to the effect that the older ship type has been . . . the old clinker built type with the planks overlapping. Which kind of work was changed about this time and hence carvel-built types began to be made . . .

Clearly, even more research and more evidence are needed before statements can be made with any confidence on the questions of when, where and why skeleton

construction, moving slowly towards fully skeleton building, began to be developed seriously. But there are some obvious difficulties which faced the early builders. Beyond a certain general size the edge-joined shell-constructed vessel did not really work for a number of reasons, not the least of which must have been the sheer difficulty of building large structures by this method with the resources available. But up to a certain point in size she was almost ideally suited to face the alternating tension and compression stresses imposed at sea. The numerous fastenings of the plank edges resisted both the forces pulling them apart and those pushing them apart. In some southern traditions heavy wales gave great strength. To replace this tough strength, massive internal support was needed in the form of very strong and large continuous frames. But something else was needed as well to replace the loss of the strength provided by the edge-joining, or else the working of the vessel would result in heavy leaking, if not weakening of the whole structure.

The answer, of course, was to provide an inner lining of planks, the ceiling, and to jam the outside planks as closely together as possible and then to ram caulking between them, not only to produce a watertight vessel, but also to seek to make the whole structure as near as possible a unity, so that it could withstand best the continually varying stresses to which it was subjected. This caulking had to be properly done or else it was spewed out between the planks by the compression, or it dropped out when the planks were forced apart. It had often to be re-done, and at its best was always a compromise. In old vessels it became more and more difficult to caulk them satisfactorily and so an old non edge-joined wooden ship rapidly deteriorated once a certain stage in her wearing out was passed. Not for nothing were some of them spoken of in several languages as 'baskets'. The caulking was a skilled business, even a full-time occupation for some men. The plank edges were slightly bevelled for the outer half and oakum driven in with shaped irons and caulking mallets, which were specially made for the job. The seam was then sealed off with pitch (Figure 331).

The builders who developed the new non edge-joined construction, wherever and whenever it was that they did so, had many problems to face. As I have already said in Chapter 3, it is not certain whether the various intermediate forms of construction, such as starting with the shell-construction of the lower part of the vessel and then fitting shaped frames, ending with non edge-joined strakes in the upper structure and so forth (Figure 332) may be taken to give evidence of how non edge-joined

333
Non edge-joined planking temporarily joined with cleats and set up to moulds which will in due course be replaced by frames, Karachi, 1954. [Basil Green-hill

construction evolved from edge-joined, or whether they represent borrowings from already developed non edge-joined traditions. Certainly in some cases the latter is undoubtedly true. In Japan, as was explained in Chapter 8, Government pressure was brought to bear to bring about the adoption of non edge-joined construction. In the late 1950s many small vessels were still being constructed partly by the traditional methods with borrowings from the new. In Pakistan different combinations of edge-joining with borrowings from non edge-joined constructions have been used for many years (Figure 333).

Indeed the whole question of the role of the frames in the development of wood shipbuilding is becoming almost philosophical, as some of the papers in the published collections listed in the bibliography at the end of this chapter show. It would not be appropriate in this elementary introduction to the archaeology of boats and ships to go into questions of whether the individual builders of transitional types saw their shape as strake or frame determined, important as these matters may be in the detailed study of individual archaeological discoveries. But, among all the finds of the remains of vessels of different intermediate types from the 1500s and 1600s which have been made in recent years and published in varying degrees of completeness, it will be useful to look very briefly at four important finds, two of them very well known, to see something of what has been learned about the systems of building used in each case.

1. *The* Mary Rose, *built 1510 in Britain, found in British waters, the Solent off the Hampshire coast.*

    As with all reasonably intact wrecks, there is a problem. As Dr Margaret Rule, who has been so intimately associated with the *Mary Rose* for so many years, has said in a personal communication, it was decided in the mid-eighties not to dissect parts of the hull in order to answer questions about the framing, the sequence of construction and subsequent modifications, but to concentrate on recording and preserving what could be seen and to leave the hull as a unit until after the completion of the active and continuing conservation programme.

334

The diving barge above the wreck in Red Bay, Labrador, 1983. [Basil Greenhill

335

Robert Grenier, Chief Archaeologist of the expedition, showing the stem of one of the whale boats recovered in Red Bay. [Basil Greenhill

Margaret Rule continues to say that:

The use of fore and aft trenails to secure frames elements on the Mary Rose was confined to the bow (2 cases) where they were used to secure the Y frames to the first futtock and at the stern (1 case) . . . Elsewhere massive rebated stringers (clamps) ride over and between each frame and the ends of the futtocks are secured to these clamps. A simple notch in the lower element is used to locate the end of the upper element. My assumption from this is that the ship was skeleton built and construction began with the keel, stem and sternpost. Scarfs in the frames are rare and in the upper parts of the hull a simple 'notch' technique is used to locate the frame elements which are then secured by the clamps. In the hold the same method seems to have been used with notches to locate the futtock with the floor and stringers or 'thick stuff' used to secure the joint. The lack of scarfs and fore and aft fastenings would suggest that planking (internal and external) followed as soon as each frame element was in place. The presence of shavings and other debris between the lower ends of the frames may also suggest that the skeleton was not open for long and any debris falling between the frames became inaccessible very quickly.

2. *The Red Bay wreck, built c1550 in northern Spain, found in Canadian waters, the coast of southern Labrador.*

This find was made in the natural harbour at Red Bay on the south coast of Labrador (Figure 334). The vessel was there to load the products of the whale fishery established by the Basques from the area of northern Spain in the Straits of Belle Isle (Figure 335). She has been identified with a vessel called the *San Juan* from Pasajes which sank in Red Bay in the mid 1560s. The identification is not certain but the period is. Certainly she is a large vessel for her period which, of course, is that of Drake and the Elizabethan seafarers.

Much of the timber of the Red Bay wreck was preserved with little or no deterioration because the low temperature of the harbour had ensured a biologically inert environment. Intensive study of the frames and strakes, together with study of contemporary Portuguese literary sources, has shown that the vessel was built not as a planked skeleton but in a manner that could perhaps be described as a development of the midships frame and battens principle described in Chapter 3. Construction began with keel, stem and sternpost. A dozen or so scarfed frames were fabricated and erected amidships together with single scarfed frames about a quarter of the vessel's length forward of the transom and the same distance aft of the stem. These frames were assembled from units scarfed together, unlike those of the *Mary Rose* which were secured only by the fore and aft stringers (Figure 336).

336
Floor timbers from the Red Bay wreck, the scarfs for the first futtocks clearly visible. [Basil Greenhill

A series of battens were then secured from stem to sternpost around these frames and the remainder of the frames fabricated to the natural run of the battens, not all the futtocks being scarfed to the lower members of the frames since planking appears to have begun before framing was complete and the planks supported these timbers. The whole process can be understood very easily from the drawings in Figure 337. The research has led to the conclusion that shipbuilding in the Basque country in the mid-1500s was already a highly organised business in which frame timbers were fabricated in the woods (as with the building of the big schooners in the United States in the late nineteenth century) and the timber merchants played a leading part. There are other whalers under the icy waters of Red Bay. One day it may be possible to examine and record them and to add yet further to our knowledge of this period of transition. As Mark Redknap has shown in *Post-medieval Boat and Ship Archaeology*, the Cattewater wreck, a vessel of *c*1520, wrecked at Plymouth, England, has some structural features in common with the *San Juan*.

3. *The Western Ledge Reef Wreck, built c1575 in Spain, found off the coast of Bermuda.* The vessel is thought to be a Spanish despatch vessel lost in the last quarter of the 1500s. The lower hull section and the lower part of the stern structure are extremely well preserved – probably because the vessel carried a large quantity of ballast which protected the remains underwater. It is thought that the vessel's construction sequence was very similar to that adopted in the Red Bay wreck. After erecting the keel, stem, and sternpost several frames were set up on the keel. Battens were then attached to the end posts and run down the length of the vessel outside the few erected frames. She was then framed up, partly to the battens and partly to planking begun before the framing was complete.

4. *Wasa, launched 1628 in Sweden, found at the bottom of Stockholm Harbour, raised, conserved and now magnificently displayed in Stockholm (Figure 338) where she is one of the great sights of Europe.*
The Swedish warship *Wasa*, like the *Mary Rose* but more so, is too much intact for the dismantling necessary to study her construction on any scale to be thought of. Björn Landström, the Finnish-born artist and writer on the archaeology and history of the ship has hypothesised on the available evidence that she was built up to the turn of the bilge on the keel, stem, and sternpost with shell construction without moulds, the strakes being temporarily edge-joined with wooden cleats. He suggests that three frames were then erected, one amidships, together with the lower stern transom and a stern frame. Battens were then run around these frames and the vessel framed up to them. Landström based his reconstruction of the building

338
The starboard quarter gallery of the Swedish warship Wasa *as she is today in Stockholm. The whole stern area of the vessel is covered with magnificent wood carvings closely paralleling those on contemporary buildings in the old city ashore.* [Basil Greenhill

337

These four drawings illustrate the probable building sequence of the wreck of the supposed San Juan *of the mid-1500s in Red Bay, Labrador. [Parks Canada via Robert Grenier*

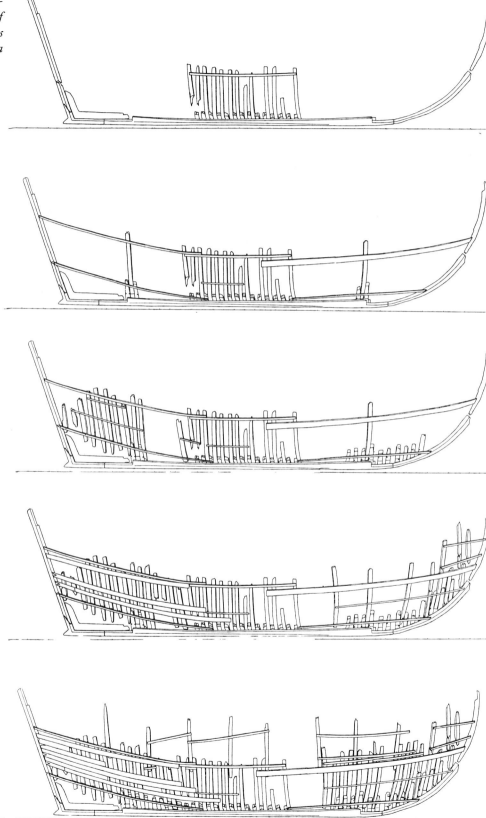

339
Master Shipwright Tom Perkins presenting a shaped frame piece to the shell of the Shamrock *during her reconstruction. The* Shamrock *is currently (1995) on display at the National Trust's Cotehele Quay on the river Tamar in Cornwall. [Basil Greenhill*

method principally on seventeenth-century publications on shipbuilding, Rålamb, Witson, Furttenbach and Anderson, listed in the bibliographies in this book, rather than on the detailed examination of the material evidence as did Grenier at Red Bay, which is currently impossible with *Wasa*, though technology may one day make it possible.

However, since Landström's work was originally published in Swedish in 1980, Carl Olof Cederlund has published an account of a wreck of a merchant vessel of *c* 1650 found on Jutholm in the Stockholm archipelago. The vessel was probably of Swedish origin and was a typical merchant vessel of the period of the type contemporarily referred to as a *flute* built for the Baltic trade. Here it is possible to examine the structure in some detail. Cederlund reports her as 'definitely Dutch fashion. The vessel belongs to the same construction traditions as the *Wasa* and there are a number of similarities between the two ships.' She appears, however, to have been even more transitional in that her upper frames are notched to receive clinker planking.

Because of the low level of biological activity in the Baltic, the sea is a veritable potential treasurehouse for the maritime archaeologist. Carl Olof Cederlund lists in his publication *Old Wrecks of the Baltic Sea* eighty-six wrecks under the waters of east central Sweden alone of which twelve are 'well preserved' and forty-one more or less intact.

It is becoming increasingly clear, I suggest, that there are, in very general terms, in fact in history three general classes of round-hulled wooden vessel construction. The first is shell-building, which persisted widely with smaller craft as long as wood was the building material. The second is intermediate building involving in one way or another, in varying degrees, elements of both shell and skeleton techniques in determining the vessel's shape and the order of her construction. Although intermediate forms and virtually full skeleton construction had existed in the Mediterranean centuries before, they appear again and begin to develop in western Europe perhaps in the early 1400s. They lasted as long as wood was the main material used in vessel construction. The third form was fully evolved skeleton construction (that is, with the shape of the entire vessel determined by a pre-erected framework) which was, perhaps, a product of the 1600s and lasted to become most people's idea of how a wooden ship was built.

It can be strongly argued that the term intermediate is not appropriate and that the real distinction is between vessels the shape of which is determined by the planking and those whose shape is determined by framing elements. If this is accepted then the Red Bay wreck is 'frame-based' and not 'intermediate' and the only true intermediate archaeological discovery so far is the Yassi Ada wreck of the seventh century AD, already described, which has a frame-based upper structure on top of a plank-based lower hull.

My case for seeing a period of intermediate techniques rests in the fact that with all of them, as with my friends of long ago who worked on the building of ketches in Cornwall in the 1870s, the vessel was partly designed on the building slip as she grew and some, perhaps many frame shapes were derived from the planking, or at least from the 'run of the batten'. This usually applied to the ends of the vessel which became increasingly difficult to form, fore and aft of amidships. In full skeleton construction, the vessel was conceived as a whole, her shape (once again) determined by a pre-erected framework, the shape of which was derived from a half model or later in big shipyards from drawings, or both; both were used, for instance, at Appledore during the building of wooden minesweepers in World War Two.

This was the really great leap forward. To achieve it, to commit oneself to a pre-designed structure which could not be changed in building (or 90 per cent could not be changed – it is to be remembered that very few half models exactly check with the vessels built from them, which is one of the difficulties in identifying half models) involved crossing a great psychological barrier into a new kind of thinking and taking risks, economic, physical, social, of a new kind. Now that we know so much more of how, where and when 'intermediate' forms of construction developed, perhaps the detailed investigation of the history of the development of full skeleton construction should be the next step.

But whatever was the sequence of events, it was a long time before non edge-joined fully skeleton-built became the universal way of building a large wooden vessel in Britain and in northern Europe and North America. The method is described and illustrated in detail in Greenhill and Manning *The Evolution of the Wooden Ship*. In most cases it comprised, in outline, first the making of a scale model of one side of the complete vessel, the half model. This could take several forms, but from it the general shape of the finished vessel was ultimately derived. The half model was therefore very important in the development of the design of the vessel.

Measurements taken from the half model were scaled up to full size on the scrieve board or mould loft floor. This was the process known as lofting. The shapes of the frames were taken from these full-sized drawings and these, of course, determined almost entirely the shape of the finished vessel. The frames, once sawn out and made up from their constituent parts, floors, first and second futtocks, etc, were erected on the keel (Figure 340). Either initially, or as the framing developed, the stem and sternposts were erected and fastened. The beam shelves and clamps bound the skeleton together and provided lodging for the ends of the deck beams (Figure 341). Fastening was by thick bolts of galvanised iron, or, in high quality construction of copper alloy. Trenails were also usually used. The whole structure was bound together with reinforcing knees of wood or iron, by iron straps, and by other means.

The strength of some of these latter day smaller wooden vessels was as great as the limitations of the materials would allow. For example, according to her master and owner for many years, Captain W J Slade, the schooner *Millom Castle* (Figure 343) had a beam shelf of 9in (23cm) timber and three sternposts, one inside the other. The framing in the first 25ft (7.6m) of her and in the last 25ft–50ft (7.6m–15m) of her

340

The sternpost and midships frames of a wooden dragger (trawler) rise above the keel at Mahone Bay, Nova Scotia, in 1963. The scrieve board on which the frames are made up is visible in the foreground. The piled timber and general mess around is typical of any wood shipbuilding yard anywhere at any period. [*Basil Greenhill*

341

The framed up structure of the four-masted schooner Rachel W Stevens, *1,032 tons net, built at Bath, Maine by the New England Company in 1898. She foundered off Cape Matteras, December, 1924. Note in particular the huge keelson, made up of a series of 16in (39cm) squared baulks, scarfed and bolted together.* [*W J Lewis Parker*

342
Above – planking up a wooden dragger at Smith and Rhuland's Yard, Lunenburg, Nova Scotia, in 1962. [Basil Greenhill

343
Above right – the hull of the schooner Millom Castle, *78 tons net, still intact and retaining her shape, abandoned in a Cornish creek, 120 very hard worked years after she was launched at Ulverston in 1870.* [Basil Greenhill

approximate 80ft (24m) length was almost solid, the frames nearly touching. Her upper frames were 5½in (14cm) square and her floors and futtocks 9in (23cm) square, and all of oak. The 10in (25.5cm) deck beams were of hackmatack. As a result, she is still in existence as an abandoned hulk in 1995, a century and a quarter of rough use since she was built.

The complex structure, a skeleton of timber, which now stood on the building slip was ready for planking. The long planks, softened when necessary by soaking with steam, were wrapped around the skeleton structure, shoved, shouldered, wedged, shored and clamped into place (Figure 342). The deck planks presented fewer problems, but the ceiling, the inner lining of the vessel, required nearly as much skilled shaping of the planks as did the outer skin. The vessel was caulked with oakum driven into the wedge-shaped seams between the planks with irons and mallets and the hull was then virtually complete.

Despite the strength and vigour with which European technological development was projected around the world, except to a degree in Japan, the style of construction outlined in the last few paragraphs never became the normal method of construction of local vessels over most of the rest of the world. Indeed even in Britain and northern Europe it spread much more slowly than is generally realised. C H Ward Jackson has noted in his studies of the ship registration records of the port of Fowey in Cornwall that it is not until the end of the eighteenth century and the beginning of the nineteenth that there was a sudden transition from 'clinker' to 'carvel' in the registered descriptions of the majority of new vessels. Only at this late date was non edge-joined construction generally adopted at this Cornish seafaring centre for smaller vessels, and I think it likely that similar detailed study of shipping registration records will in due course show similar late transitions at some other ports of registration, particularly those remote from centres of population. What cannot be determined from shipping registration documents, however, is the process of the introduction of full skeleton construction.

Olof Hasslöf has many examples of the use of the intermediate methods in

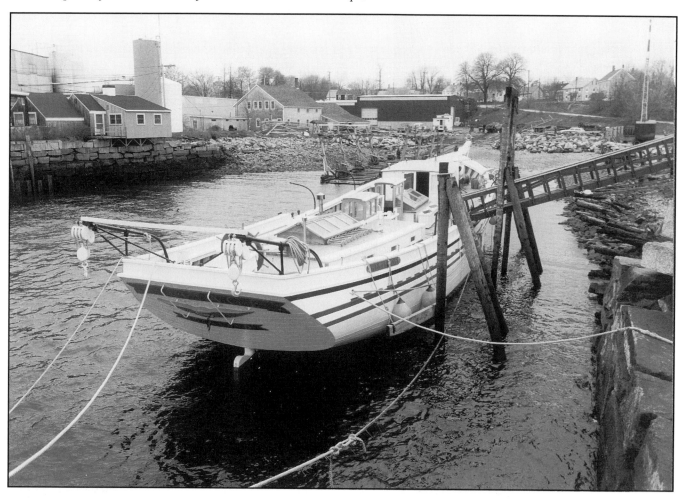

344
The beautiful hull of the newly launched schooner Heritage *built by Doug and Linda Lee at Rockland, Maine, for the Penobscot Bay cruise business in 1980.* [*Basil Greenhill*

346
A great builder of wooden vessels in the late twentieth century, Alexander Noble of Girvan, Ayrshire, Scotland, in his yard with some of his products, 1987. [*Basil Greenhill*

345

The Bonaventure, *a modern wooden trawler (dragger) with full lightweight metal shelterdeck and all electronic equipment at Buckie, Banffshire, Scotland, 1987 shortly after her launch by Herd and Mackensie. [Basil Greenhill*

347

The three-masted schooner Linden *built for the cruise business and for social purposes at Mariehamn, Åland Islands, Finland, in 1993. [Justus Harberg*

Scandinavia and indeed Arne Emil Christensen has recorded that after the middle of the sixteenth century the central governments of all the Scandinavian countries tried to convince shipbuilders and shipowners that non edge-joined vessels were best. Despite continuous government efforts the general introduction of this kind of construction was very slow indeed, and only in the twentieth century did the use of full skeleton construction penetrate to the small vessels used in coastal fisheries. As late as 1900 in Norway a special 'state travelling teacher of carvel work' was appointed, but it was only the adoption of motor power with the peculiar stresses it imposes that finally led to the general acceptance of full skeleton construction. Even then, edge-joined construction and intermediate methods have lingered on to the present day, and we know that in Norway, as in Japan, the use of moulds in edge-joined construction was a recent innovation from non edge-joined skeleton building, and not a transitional stage in the development of the latter. As late as the year 1975 the restoration of the coasting ketch *Shamrock* at Cotehele Quay in Cornwall involved the adoption of intermediate methods. The planking of the vessel being in good repair it was retained and new frames shaped to it and inserted into the shell (Figure 339). Such methods, which eliminated the necessity for lofting, were used frequently in the nineteenth century in rebuilding old vessels.

348

The end of one story, and of very many wooden vessels. This was the brigantine Cameo, *built at Bath, Maine, in 1878, 244 tons. She sailed for years in the West Indian trade from New York, then became a whaler from New Bedford from 1908 to 1921 and then freighted box-boards and other cargo on the New England coast. In the 1930s she was laid up on the Frankfort Marsh at the mouth of the Penobscot river, Maine where this photograph was taken in May 1983.* [*Basil Greenhill*

Fully skeleton construction blossomed in an age of big ships and big capital, extensive deep sea seafaring, relatively widespread literacy and the use of half models. The use of drawings came slowly and later with the gradual adoption of this technique of communication. Right down to the very end of large scale wooden shipbuilding in the early twentieth-century drawings were hardly ever used in small shipyards building small merchant vessels in Britain or North America. At its most sophisticated the design stage still took place in the half model, on the mould loft floor and on the slips as the vessel developed.

But in due course and very slowly fully skeleton construction became 'normal' in Britain, northern Europe and North America and until even the 1980s it was still possible to see in Spain, Greece, Finland, Denmark, Sweden and Norway, in Scotland, Maine and Nova Scotia, the skeletons of wooden vessels rising above the keel blocks in small shipyards. The development of the market for cruising in vessels with sails, for the building of reconstructions of historic vessels, for restoration work, and the continuing demand for wooden fishing vessels has ensured the survival of wooden ships at the end of the twentieth century (Figure 3). These vessels are part of a very long and very complex story, about which, despite the length of this book and the great amount of work which has been done on the subject in the last twenty years, we really still know remarkably little.

Bibliography

ANDERSON, R C, 'The Bursledon Ship', 1934

ARNELL, J C (ed), *Bermuda Journal of Archaeology and Maritime History*, Vol 5

BARKHAM, S H, *The Basque Coast of Newfoundland*, 1989

BURWASH, D, *English Merchant Shipping 1460–1540*, 1947

CEDERLUND, C O, *Vraket vid Jutholmen*, 1982
   Old Wrecks in the Baltic Sea, 1983
   (ed) *Post Medieval Boat and Ship Archaeology*, 1985

CHRISTENSEN, A E, 'Lucien Basch: Ancient Wrecks and the Archaeology of Ships, A Comment', 1973

CURTISS, W H, *The Elements of Wood Ship Construction*, 1919

ESTEP, H C, *How Wooden Ships are Built*, 1918

FURTTENBACH, J, *Architectura Navalis*, 1629

GREENHILL, B, *Merchant Schooners*, 4th edn, 1988

GREENHILL, B and MANNING, S, *The Evolution of the Wooden Ship*, 1988
   The Schooner Bertha L. Downs, 1995

HASSLÖF, O, 'Wrecks, Archives and Living Tradition', 1963
   'Sources of Maritime History and Methods of Research', 1966
   'Main Principles in the Technology of Shipbuilding', 1972

HIDALGO, M, *Columbus' Ships*, 1966

HUTCHINSON, G, *Medieval Ships and Shipping*, 1994

LANDSTRÖM, B, *The Royal Warship Vasa*, 1988

MCGRAIL, S, *Rafts, Boats and Ships*, 1981

MORTON NANCE, R, 'The Ship of the Renaissance', 1955

MOTT, L V, *Development of the rudder: a technological tale*, 1994

NOBLE, A, *Scottish Fishing Vessel Design, Construction and Repair*, 1978

PARKER, W J L, *Great Coal Schooners of New England, 1870–1909*, 1948

PARRY, J H, *The Discovery of the Sea*, 1975

PROULX, J P, *Basque Whaling in Labrador in the 16th century*, 1993

PYRNNE, M, 'Some general considerations applying to the examination of the remains of old ships', 1973

RÅLAMB, A C, *Skeps Byggerij eller Adelig Öfnings Tionde Tom*, 1691

REINDERS, R and PAUL, K (eds), *Carvel Construction Technique*, 1991

SALISBURY, W and ANDERSON, R C, *A Treatise on Shipbuilding and a Treatise on Rigging*, Written about 1620–1625, 1958

STIGELL, Anna-Lisa, *Kyrkans Tecken och Årets Gång*, 1974

STORY, D, *Frame Up!*, 1964
   The Building of a Wooden Ship, 1971

TUCK, J A and GRENIER, R, *Red Bay, Labrador, World Whaling Capital, 1550–1600*, 1989

UNGER, R (ed), *Cogs, Caravels and Galleons*, 1994

WESTERDAHL, C (ed), *Crossroads in Ancient Shipbuilding*, 1994

WILSON, G, *Scottish Fishing Boats*, 1995

WITSON, N, *Architectura Navalis et Regimen Nauticum*, 1690

Selected Bibliography

BOOKS

NOTE

Carvel = REINDERS, R and PAUL, K (eds), *Carvel Construction Technique*, Oxford, 1991

Celts = MCGRAIL, S (ed.), *Maritime Celts, Frisians and Saxons*, London, 1990

Crossroads = WESTERDAHL, C (ed.), *Crossroads in Ancient Shipbuilding*, Oxford, 1994

NMM MM+R = National Maritime Museum Monographs and Reports

Marine Archaeology = BLACKMAN, D J (ed.), *Marine Archaeology*, London, 1973

Ships and Shipwrecks = BASS, G F (ed.), *Ships and Shipwrecks of the Americas*, London, 1988

Ships and Shipyards = HASSLÖF, O (ed.), *Ships and Shipyards, Sailors and Fishermen*, Copenhagen, 1972

Shipshape = OLSEN, O (ed.), *Shipshape*, Roskilde, 1995

ABEL, H (ed.), *Die Bremer Hanse-Kogge*, Bremen, 1969

ABELL, W, *Shipwright's trade*, Cambridge, 1948

ADDYMAN, P *et al.* (eds), *The Vikings in England*, London, 1981

ADNEY, E T and CHAPELLE, H I, *Bark Canoes and Skin Boats of North America*, Washington, 1964

ALONSO, F, 'Prehistoric Boats in Rock-paintings of Cadiz and in the Rock-carvings of N–W Spain' in *Crossroads*

ALONSO, F, 'Traditional clinker and carvel techniques in the NW of Spain' in *Carvel*

ALOPAEUS, H, 'Aspects of the Lapuri find' in *Shipshape*

ANDERSEN, E, 'Woollen material for sails' in *Shipshape*

ANDERSEN, B and E, *Råsejlet-Dragens Vinge*, Roskilde, 1989

ANDERSEN, S H, New Finds of Mesolithic Logboats in Denmark' in *Crossroads*

ANDRINGA, A J, *Chinese Jonken*, Droningen, 1970

ANON, *Oman, A Seafaring Nation*, Oman, 1979

ARBMAN, H, GREENHILL, B and ROBERTS, O, *The Årby Boat*, Stockholm, 1993

ARBMAN, H, *The Vikings*, London, 1961

ARIMA, E Y, *A Contextual Study of the Caribou Eskimo Kayak*, Ottawa, 1975

ARNELL, J C (ed.), *Bermuda Journal of Archaeology and Maritime History*, vol. 5, Hamilton, Bermuda, 1993

ARNOLD, B, 'Batellerie gallo-romaine sur le lac de Neuchâtel', *Archéologie Neuchâteloise*, vols. 12 and 13, 1992

ARNOLD, B, 'The Gallo-Roman boat of Bevaix and the bottom based construction' in *Carvel*

ARNOLD, B, 'The heritage of logboats and Gallo-Roman boats of Lake Neuchâtel: technology and typology' in *Celts*

AUDEMARD, L, *Les Jonques Chinoises*, Rotterdam, 1957–69

BALCOM, R A, *History of the Lunenburg Fishing Industry*, Lunenburg, 1977

BANG-ANDERSEN, A, GREENHILL, B, and GRUDE, E H (eds), *The North Sea*, Stavanger, 1985

BARKHAM, S H, *The Basque Coast of Newfoundland*, St John's, 1989

BARNES, G W, *Building your first wooden boat*, New York, 1979

BARSS, P, *Images of Lunenburg County*, Toronto, 1970

BASS, G F, *Archaeology Under Water*, London, 1970

BASS, G F (ed.), *A History of Seafaring based on Underwater Archaeology*, London, 1974

BASS, G F (ed.), *Ships and Shipwrecks of the Americas*, London, 1988

BASCH, L, *Le musée imaginaire de la marine antique*, Athens, 1987

BAYKOWSKI, U and HOHEISEL, W–D, 'A full-scale Replica of the Hanse Cog of 1380' in *Crossroads*

BAYKOWSKI, V (ed.), *Die Kieler Hanse Kogge*, Kiel, 1991

BEAGLEHOLE, J C (ed.), *The Endeavour Journal of Joseph Banks, 1760–1771*, Sydney, 1962

BEST, E, *The Maori Canoe*, Dominium Museum Bulletin 7, Wellington, N.Z., 1925

BETLYON, J W, *The coinage and mints of Phoenica in the pre-Alexandrian period*, 1982

BETTS, J H, *Ships on Minoan Seals*, in *Marine Archaeology*

BILL, Jan, 'Getting into business – Reflections of a market economy in medieval Scandinavian shipbuilding' in *Shipshape*

BILL, J, 'Iron Nails in Iron Age and Medieval Shipbuilding' in *Crossroads*

BINNS, A, *Viking Voyagers*, London, 1980

BLACKMAN, D J (ed.), *Marine Archaeology*, London, 1973

BLOESCH, P, 'Inventing the *Barque du Leman*, Lake Geneva' in *Crossroads*

BONDE, Niels and JENSEN, J S, 'Dating the coin beneath the mast' in *Shipshape*

BOUNEGRU, O and ZAHARIADE, M, 'Roman Ships on the Lower Danube (1st–6th Cent. AD) Types and Functions' in *Crossroads*

BREWINGTON, M V, *Chesapeake Bay Bugeyes*, Newport News, 1941

BREWINGTON, M V, *Chesapeake Log Canoes*, Newport News, 1937

BREWINGTON, M V, *Chesapeake Bay Log Canoes and Bugeyes*, Cornell, 1963

BRINDLEY, H H, *Impressions and casts of seals, coins, tokens, medals and other objects of Art exhibited in the Seal Room of the National Maritime Museum*, London, 1938

BRUCE-MITFORD, R L S, *Sutton Hoo Ship Burial*, British Museum, London, 1968

BRUCE-MITFORD, R L S, *The Sutton Hoo Ship Burial*, vol. 1, London, 1975

BRØGGER, A W and SHETELIG, H, *Viking Ships, their Ancestry and Evolution*, Oslo, 1951

BRØGGER, A W *et al.*, *Osebergfunnet*, Oslo, 1917–28

BRØNSTED, J, 'Oldtidsbaden fra Als', *Nationalmuseets Bog*, Copenhagen, 1925

BRØNSTED, J, *The Vikings*, London, 1967

BURWASH, D, *English Merchant Shipping 1460–1540*, Toronto, 1947

BUTLER, V, *The Little Nord Easter: Reminiscences of a Placentia Bayman*, St John's, Nfld., 1975

CARPENTER, A C *et al.*, *The Cattewater Wreck*, NMM MM+R, No 13, 1974

CARVER, M O H, 'On – and off – the Edda' in *Shipshape*

CARVER, M O H, 'Pre-Viking traffic in the North Sea' in *Celts*

CASSON, L, *Ships and Seamen in the Ancient World*, Princeton, 1972 (reprinted 1985) = SSAW

CEDERLUND, C O, *Ett Fartyg Byggt med Syteknik*, Stockholm, 1978

CEDERLUND, C O, *Old Wrecks in the Baltic Sea*, Stockholm, 1983

CEDERLUND, C O (ed.), *Post Medieval Boat and Ship Archaeology*, Oxford, 1985

CEDERLUND, C O (ed.), *The Årby Boat*, Stockholm, 1994

CEDERLUND, C O, 'The European Origin of Small Water Craft in North America' in *Crossroads*

CEDERLUND, C O, *Vraket vid Jutholmen*, Stockholm, 1982

CHAPELLE, H I, *American Sailing Craft*, New York 1936

CHAPELLE, H I, *American Small Sailing Craft*, New York, 1951

CHAPELLE, H I, *Boatbuilding*, New York, 1947

CHRISTENSEN, A E, 'Boat fragments from Mangersnes' in *Shipshape*

CHRISTENSEN, A E, *Boats of the North*, Oslo, 1968

CHRISTENSEN, A E, 'Boatbuilding Tools and the Process of Learning' in *Ships and Shipyards*

CHRISTIANSEN, A E, *The Northern Crusades*, London, 1980

CLAUSEN, B L (ed.), *Viking Voyages to North America*, Roskilde, 1993

CLOWES, L, *History of the Royal Navy VII*, London, 1923

COATES, J, 'Power and Speed of Oared Ships' in *Crossroads*

COLES, J, FENWICK, V and HUTCHINSON, G (eds), *A Spirit of Enquiry*, Exeter, 1993

CROVATO, G, CROVATO, M and DIVARI, L, *Barche della Laguna Veneta*, Venice, 1975

CRUMLIN-PEDERSEN, O. See separate full list of publications

CUNLIFFE, B, 'Hengistbury Head: a late prehistoric haven' in *Celts*

CURTISS, W H, *The Elements of Wood Ship Construction*, New York, 1919

DADE, E, *Sail and Oar*, London, 1933

DAMINIADIS, K, 'Planking up a carvel boat in the Aegean' in *Carvel*

DEAN, M *et al.* (eds), *Archaeology under Water*, London, 1992

de la MORANDIERE, C, *History of the French Cod Fishing Industry in North America*, Paris, 1966

de JONG, N J, and MOORE, M F, *Shipbuilding on Prince Edward's Island*, Hull, Quebec, 1994

de WEERD, M D, 'Barges of the Zwammerdam type and their building procedures' in *Celts*

de WEERD, M D, 'Gallo-Roman plank boats: Shell-first building procedures between "sewn" and "cog" ' in *Carvel*

de WEERD, M D, 'Rib Insertion in Phases: The Type Zwammerdam Shell First Building Procedure, 500BC(?)–1500AD' in *Crossroads*

DONNOLLY, I A, *Chinese Junks and other Native Craft*, Shanghai, 1924

DUFFY, M., FISHER, S, GREENHILL, B, and STARKEY, D (eds), *The New Maritime History of Devon*, vol. 2, London, 1994

EADDY, P A, *'Neath Swaying Spars*, Wellington, 1939

EDGREN, T, 'De Aspo usque Orsund. vi. Inde usque Hangethe.iij . . .' – An archaeological research project concerning one of the harbours in Finland's s.w archipelago referred to in the 'Danish itinerary' in *Shipshape*

EDWARDS, C R, 'Aboriginal watercraft on the Pacific coast of South America', *Ibero Ámericáná*, 47, University of California, 1965

EGLINTON, E, *The last of the Sailing Coasters*, London, 1982

EGLINTON, E, (ed. GREENHILL, B), *The Mary Fletcher*, Exeter, 1990

ELLMERS, D, 'Crew structure on board Scandinavian vessels' in *Shipshape*

ELLMERS, D, *Frühmittelalterliche Handelsschiffahrt in Mittel-und Nordeuropa*, Neumünster, 1972

ELLMERS, D, 'The Frisian monopoly of coastal transport in the 6th–8th Cent. AD' in *Celts*

ESKERÖD, A, *Båtar*, Stockholm, 1970

ESKERÖD, A, *Kyrkbåtar och Kyrkbåtsfärder*, Stockholm, 1973

ERICSSON, C and MONTIN, K, *Maritima Medeltidsstudier*, Åbo, 1989

ERICSSON, C *et al.*, *The Routes of the Sea*, Helsinki, 1988

ESTEP, H C, *How Wooden Ships are Built*, New York, 1918

EVANS, A C, 'The Sutton Hoo Ship' in *Three Major Ancient Boat Finds in Britain*, NMM MM+R No. 6, pp. 26–43, 1972

EVANS, A C, *The Sutton Hoo Ship Burial*, London, 1986

EWE, H, *Schiffe auf Siegeln*, Rostock, 1972

FAERØYVIK, B and O, *Inshore Craft of Norway*, London, 1979

FENWICK, V H (ed.), *The Graveney Boat*, London, 1978

FILGUEIRAS, O L, 'Gelmirez and the reconversion of the W Peninsular shipbuilding tradition (XIth–XIIth cent.) in *Carvel*

FILIPOWIAK, W, 'Shipbuilding at the Mouth of the River Odra' (Oder) in *Crossroads*

FILMER-SANKEY, W, 'A new boat burial from the Snape Anglo-Saxon cemetery, Suffolk' in *Celts*

FILMER-SANKEY, W and PESTELL, T, 'The Snape Logboats: Excavation, construction and performance' in *Shipshape*

FLIEDNER, S, 'Kogge und Hulk' in ABEL, H (ed.), *Die Bremer Hanse Kogge*, pp. 39–121, Bremen, 1969

FOOTE, P G and WILSON, D M, *Viking Achievement*, London, 1970

FROST, H, 'Where did the Carthaginians see clinkers?' in *Shipshape*

FULLER, B A G, 'The Origins of American Boatbuilding' in *Crossroads*

FURTTENBACH, J, *Architectura Navalis*, Ulm, 1629

GADNOSSI, VILLAIN-, BOSUTTIL and ADAM (eds), *Medieval Ships and the Birth of Technological Societies*, vol. 1, Malta, 1989

GARDNER, J and MANNING, S F, *The Dory Book*, Camden, Me., 1978

GAWRONSKI, J H, 'The archaeological and historical research of the Dutch East Indiaman *Amsterdam* (1749)' in *Carvel*

GEIPEL, J, *The Viking Legacy*, Newton Abbot, 1971

GILLMER, T C, 'The Importance of skeleton-first ship construction to the development of the science of naval architecture' in *Carvel*

GILLMER, T C, *Working Watercraft*, Camden, Me., 1972

GJELLESTAD, A J, 'Litt om Oselverbäter' in *Norsk Sjøfartsmuseum Arbok*, pp. 18–29, Oslo, 1969

GJESSING, G, 'Båtfunnene fra Bårset og Øksnes', *Tromsø Museum Arshefter*, 58, Tromsø, 1935

GODAL, J B, 'The use of wood in boatbuilding' in *Shipshape*

GOODBURN, D M, 'Anglo Saxon Boat Finds from London, Are They English?' in *Crossroads*

GOODMAN, W L, *History of Woodworking Tools*, London, 1964

GOTHCHE, M, 'Three Danish 17th-19th cent. wrecks as examples of clinker building vs. carvel building techniques in local shipwrightry' in *Carvel*

GOTHCHE, M, 'The Stinesminde Wreck of AD 1600, Denmark' in *Crossroads*

GRAHAM-CAMPBELL, J, *The Viking World*, London, 1980

GRAY, D, *Seewesen*, Archaeologia Homerica I.G. Göttingen, 1974

GREEN, J N, 'Arabia to China – the Oriental Traditions' in *The Earliest Ships*, CHRISTENSEN, A E (ed.), Forthcoming

GREEN, J N, 'The Planking-first construction of the VOC ship *Batavia*' in *Carvel*

GREENHILL, B, *Boats and Boatmen of Pakistan*, Newton Abbot, 1971

GREENHILL, B, *Merchant Schooners*, 4th edn, London, 1988

GREENHILL, B, *Sailing for a Living*, London, 1962

GREENHILL, B, 'The Graveney Boat – an exercise in Anglo-Danish collaboration' in *Shipshape*

GREENHILL, B and MANNING, S F, *The Evolution of the Wooden Ship*, London, 1988

GREENHILL, B. and MANNING, S F, *The Schooner Bertha L. Downs*, London, 1995

GRENIER, R, LOEWEN, B and PROULX, J–P, 'Basque Shipbuilding Technology c.1560–80: The Red Bay Project' in *Crossroads*

GRENIER, R, 'Basque whalers in the New World: the Red Bay wrecks' in *Ships and Shipwrecks*

GUTHORN, *The Sea Bright Skiff*, New Brunswick, N.J., 1971

GUY, C, *The Weymontaching Birchbark Canoe*, Ottawa, 1974

HADDON, A C and HORNELL, J, *Canoes of Oceania*, 3 vols, Honolulu, 1936–8

Handbook of Hardwoods, Forest Products Research Laboratory, HMSO, 1969

Handbook of Softwoods, Forest Products Research Laboratory, HMSO, 1968

HANSEN, K. *Umiaq*, Svendborg, 1980

HARDING, A F (ed.), *Climatic Change in Later Pre-History*, Edinburgh, 1982

HARRIS, L D, 'The development of the coble: Evidence from Maritime Anthropology' in *Carvel*

HASSLÖF, O (ed.), *Ships and Shipyards, Sailors and Fishermen*, Copenhagen, 1972

HASSLÖF, O, 'Main Principles in the Technology of Shipbuilding' in *Ships and Shipyards*

HASSUM, S, 'Ship grafitti in the medieval churches of Gotland' in *Shipshape*

HASSUM, S, LAGERLÖF, E and von BUSCH, P, *Skeppsristningar på Gotland*, Stockholm, 1993

HASSUM, S, 'Vikingatidens segling och navigation', *Theses and Papers in North European Archaeology*, 4, The Institute of Archaeology at the University of Stockholm, 1974

HAWKINS, C W, *Maritime Heritage*, Wellington, NZ, 1978

HAWKINS, C W, *Out of Auckland*, Wellington, NZ, 1960

HAWKINS, C W, *The Dhow*, Lymington, 1977

HAYWOOD, J, *Dark Age Naval Power*, London, 1991

HIDALGO, MARTINEZ-, J M (ed.), CHAPELLE, H I, *Columbus' Ships*, Barre, Mass., 1966

HIDALGO, MARTINEZ-, J M, *Las naves de Colóm*, Barcelona, 1969

HOCKMANN, O, 'Post-Roman Timbers and a Floating Mill from the Upper Rhine' in *Crossroads*

HOCKMANN, O, 'Roman Danube vessels from Oberstimm (Gernaby) as examples of shell-first construction' in *Carvel*

HOHEISEL, W–D and BAYKOWSKI, U, 'A full-scale replica of the Hanse cog of 1380' in *Crossroads*

HOLMQUIST, W, *The Swedish Vikings*, Stockholm, 1979

HORBERG, P U, 'Nuts, Bricks and Pewter – preliminary notes on three new ship-finds in Scania, Sweden' in *Shipshape*

HORNELL, J, *Water Transport*, Newton Abbot, 1970

HORNELL, J, *Fishing in Many Waters*, Cambridge, 1950

HORSTMANN, H, *Die Rechtszeichen der europaischen schiffe im Mittelalter*, Bremen, 1971

HOURANI, G R, *Arab Seafaring in the Indian Ocean in Ancient and Early Medieval Times*, Princeton, 1951

HOVING, A J, 'A 17th cent. 42-feet long Dutch pleasure vessel: A research into original building techniques' in *Carvel*

HOWARTH, D, *Dhows*, London, 1977

HUMBLA, P, 'Om Björkebaten fran Hille socken', *Fran Gastrikland 1949*, Gavle, 1949

HUTCHINSON, G, 'Early 16th century wreck at Studland Bay, Dorset in *Carvel*

HUTCHINSON, G, *Medieval Ships and Shipping*, Leicester, 1994

HUTCHINSON, Gillian, 'Two English side rudders' in *Shipshape*

HÖGNÄS, P and ÖRJANS, J, *Storbåten*, Mariehamn, Åland, 1985

INGSTAD, A S, *The Discovery of a Norse Settlement in North America*, Oslo, Bergen, Tromsø, 1977

INGSTAD, H, *The Norse Discovery of America*, Oslo, Bergen, Stavanger, Tromsø, 1985

INNES, H A, *Cod Fisheries, the History of an International Economy*, Toronto, 1954

ITKONEN, Suomen Kansanomaiset Veneet, in *Suomen Museo*, XXXIII, Helsinki, 1926

JANSEN, E G and BOSTAD, *Sailing Against the Wind*, Dhaka, 1992

JANSEN, E G *et al.*, *The Country Boats of Bangla Desh*, Dhaka, 1989

JASINSKI, M E, 'Tracing Crossroads of Shipbuilding Traditions in the European Arctic' in *Crossroads*

JENKINS, J G, *Nets and Coracles*, Newton Abbot, 1974

JENSEN, J S, 'Dating the coin beneath the mast' in *Shipshape*

JEWELL, J H A, *Dhows at Mombasa*, Nairobi, 1976

JOHNSTONE, P (ed. S. MCGRAIL), *The Sea-Craft of Prehistory*, London, 1980

JONES, G, *A History of the Vikings*, Oxford, 1968

KEITH, D H, 'Shipwrecks of the explorers' in *Ships and Shipwrecks*

KENTLEY, E, 'Some aspects of the Masula surfboat' in *Sewn Plank Boats*, MCGRAIL, S (ed.) and KENTLEY, E, BAR S276, Oxford, 1985

KLAUSEN, D (ed.) *et al.*, *Nordlandsbaden*, Copenhagen, 1980

KIRK, G S, 'Ships on Geometric Vases', *Annual of the British School at Athens*, 44: 93–153k

KRISTJANSSON, L, 'Graenlenzki Landnemaflotinn og Breidfirzki Báturinn', *Arbok Hins Islenzka Fornleifafelags*, pp. 20–68, Reykjavik, 1965

LAGERLÖF, E, HAASUM, S and von BUSCH, P *Skeppristningar på Gotland*, Stockholm, 1993

LAMM, J P and NORDSTRÖM, H–A, *Vendel Period Studies*, Stockholm, 1983

LANDSTRÖM, B, *Columbus*, Stockholm, 1966, London, 1967

LANDSTRÖM, B, *Ships of the Pharaohs*, Stockholm, 1970

LANDSTRÖM, B, *Regalskeppet Vasan*, Stockholm, 1980

LANDSTRÖM, B, *The Royal Warship Vasa*, Stockholm, 1988

LANDSTRÖM, B, *The Ship*, London, 1961

LAVERS, G M, *Strength Properties of Timbers*, Forest Products Research Laboratory Bulletin No. 50, 1969

LEHMANN, L Th, 'The Romano-Celtic boats from Druten and Kapel Avezaath' in *Celts*

LEHMANN, L Th, 'Variations in boatbuilding under the Roman Empire' in *Carvel*

LESLIE, R C, *The Sea Boat. How to build, rig and sail her*, London, 1892

L'HOUR, M and VEYRAT, E, 'The French Medieval Clinker Wreck from the Aber Wrac'h' in *Crossroads*

LIEBGOTT, N–K, 'A ship and its cargo' in *Shipshape*

LINDER, E, 'Naval warfare in the El Amarna Age' in *Marine Archaeology*

LIPKE, P, *Royal Ship of Cheops*, BAR, S225, Oxford, 1984

LITWIN, J, 'Clinker and carvel working boats on Polish waters: Their origin, development and transformations' in *Carvel*

LITWIN, J, 'Shipbuilding Traditions in the Southern part of the Vistula Lagoon' in *Crossroads*

LITWIN, J, 'The first Polish galleon and its construction register from 1570–72' in *Carvel*

LITWIN, J, 'The Puck Bay wrecks – an opportunity for a Polish "Skuldelev" ' in *Shipshape*

LOYN, H R, *The Vikings in Britain*, London, 1977

LOWELL, R, *Boatbuilding Down East*, Camden, Me., 1977

LUNT, R K, *Lobsterboat Building on the Eastern Coast of Maine: A Comprehensive Study*, Ann Arbor, Mich., 1975

MCCAUGHAN, M, 'The enigma of carvel building traditions in Ireland' in *Carvel*

MCGRAIL, Seán, See separate full list of publications

MACKEAN, R and PERCIVAL, R, *The Little Boats. Inshore Fishing Craft of Atlantic Canada*, Fredicton, NB., 1979

MCKEE, J E G, *Clenched Lap or Clinker*, London, 1972

MCKEE, J E G, *Working Boats of Britain*, London, 1983

MAARLEVELD, T J, 'Double Dutch Solutions in Flush-planked Shipbuilding' in *Crossroads*

MAARLEVELD, T J, 'Environment factors in underwater heritage management. A reflection on the Dutch situation' in *Shipshape*

MADSEN, J S, OLSEN, O and RIECK, *Shipshape*, Roskilde, 1995

MAGNUSSON, M, *Viking Expansion Westwards*, London, Sydney, Toronto, 1973

MAITLAND, D and WHEELER, N, *Setting Sails*, Hong Kong, 1981

MARCH, E J, *Inshore Craft of Britain*, 2 vols, Newton Abbot, 1970

MARSDEN, P R V, 'A re-assessment of Blackfriars 1' in *Celts*

MARSDEN, P R V, 'Early Ships, Boats and Ports in Britain' in *Shipshape*

MARSDEN, P R V, *A Ship of the Roman Period from Blackfriars in the City of London*, Guildhall Museum, undated.

MARSDEN, P R V, *Ships of the Port of London*, London, 1994

MARSTRANDER, S, *Østfolds jordbruksristninger, Skjeberg*, 2 vols, Oslo, 1963

MARTIN, C J M, 'The Spanish Armada Expedition, 1968–70' in *Marine Archaeology*

MARTINEZ-HIDALGO, J M, *Columbus' ships*, Barre, Mass., 1966

MARTINEZ-HIDALGO, J M, *Las naves de Colóm*, Barcelona, 1969

MASS, V, 'A Unique 16th cent. Estonian Ship Find' in *Crossroads*

MILNE, G, 'Maritime traffic between the Rhine and Roman Britain: a preliminary note' in *Celts*

MOORE, A, *Last Days of Mast and Sail*, Oxford, 1925

MORLING, S, 'Clinker Built Keel Boats in the Iberian Peninsula' in *Crossroads*

MORRISON, J S and COATES, J F, *Greek and Roman Oared Ships*, Oxford, 1995 = GROW

MORRISON, J S and WILLIAMS, R T, *Greek Oared Ships 900–322 BC*, Cambridge, 1968 = GOS

MORRISON, J S, *Long Ships and Round Ships*, London, 1980 = LSRS

MORRISON, J S (ed.), *The Age of the Galley*, London, 1995

MORRISON, J S and COATES, J F, *The Athenian Trireme*, Cambridge, 1986 = AI

MORSE, E W, *Canoe Routes of the Voyageurs*. Reprinted from the *Canadian Geographical Journal*, May, July & August, 1961, for the Quetico Foundation of Ontario and the Minnesota Historical Society, St. Paul, Minnesota and Toronto, Ontario, 1962

MORSE, E W, *Fur Trade Canoe Routes of Canada, Then and Now*, Ottawa, 1968

MULLER-WILLE, M, 'Two early medieval sites near Wismar and Rostock at the southern Baltic Coast' in *Shipshape*

NEEDHAM, J, *Science and Civilisation in China*, 4, Part 3, Cambridge, 1971

NICHOLAYSEN, N, *Viking Ship discovered at Gokstad in Norway*, Kristiania, 1882. Republished Farnborough, 1971

NICOLAISEN, I, 'Salui'. A Dugout from Borneo, Roskilde, 1986

NEILSON, C, *Danske badtyper*, Copenhagen, 1973

NIELSEN, C, *Wooden Ship Designs*, London, 1980

NISHIMURA, S, *Ancient Rafts of Japan*, Tokyo, 1925

NOBLE, A, *Socttish Fishing Vessel Design, Construction and Repair*, London, 1978

NORDLINDER, G, *Singbåtar*, Borås, 1982

NYLÉN, E and PEDERHAMM, J, *Bildstenar*, Visby, 1978, Stockholm, 1987 and Tokyo, 1986

NYLÉN, E and LAMM, J P, *Bildsteine auf Gotland*, Neumünster, 1981

NYLÉN, E, *Bygden, Skeppen och Havet*, Lund, 1973

NYLÉN, E and LAMM, J P, *Stones, Ships and Symbols*, Stockholm, 1988

OHLMARKS, Å, *Graveskeppet*, Stockholm, 1946

OLSEN, O and CRUMLIN-PEDERSEN, O, *Five Viking Ships*, Copenhagen, 1978

OLSEN, O, 'Malmo – a medieval sea port without a harbour' in *Shipshape*

OLSEN, O (ed.), *Shipshape*, Roskilde, 1995

OOSTING, R, 'Preliminary Results of the research on the 17th cent. merchantman found at lot E 81 in the Noordoostpolder (Netherlands)' in *Carvel*

OOSTING, R and van HOLK, A, 'The Excavation of a Peat Barge found at Lot LZ 1 in Zuidelijk Flevoland' in *Crossroads*

PARIS, F E, *Essai sur la Construction Navale des Peuples Extra-Européen*, Paris, 1841

PARKER, W J L, *Great Coal Schooners of New England, 1870–1909*, Mystic Seaport, Conn., 1948

PARRY, J H, *The Discovery of the Sea*, London, 1975

PARRY, S and MCGRAIL, S, 'A Bronze Age Sewn Boat Fragment from Caldicot, Gwent, Wales' in *Crossroads*

PAYSON, H D, *How to Build the Gloucester Light Dory*, Brooklin, Me., 1982

PERGOLIS, R, *The Boats of Venice*, Venice, 1981

PESTELL, T, 'The Snape log-boats: Excavation, construction and performance' in *Shipshape*

PETERSEN, H C, *Skinboats of Greenland*, Roskilde, 1986

PETTERSSON, S S, *Roslagsjakter*, Stockholm, 1969

POMEY, P, 'La construction à franc-bord dans l'Antiquité Méditerranéenne: Principes et méthodes in Sardinia, Italy' in *Carvel*

POMEY, P, 'Shell Conception and Skeleton Process in Ancient Mediterranean Shipbuilding' in *Crossroads*

PRINS, A H J, *A Handbook of Sewn Boats*, NMM MM + R 59, 1986

PRINS, A H J, *Sailing from Lamu*, Assen, Netherlands, 1965

PROBST, N M, 'The Introduction of Flush-planked Skin in Northern Europe and the Elsinore Wreck' in *Crossroads*

PROULX, J P, *Basque Whaling in Labrador in the 16 th Century*, Ottawa, Ont., 1993

PROULX, J P, *Les Basques et la pêche de la baleine au Labrador aux XVIe siecle*, Ottawa, Ont., 1993

REDNAP, M, *Cattewater Wreck*, BAR, 131, Oxford, 1984

REINDERS, R and PAUL, K, *Carvel Construction Technique*, Oxford, 1991

RICCARDI, E, 'Note on the construction of the Lazzaaretto wreck, 4th cent. AD, Sardinia, Italy' in *Carvel*

RICCARDI, E, 'The Wrecks off the Camping Site "La Mariposa", Alghero, Sassari, Sardinia, Italy' in *Crossroads*

RIECK, F, 'The Iron Age Boats from Hjortspring and Nydam' in *Crossroads*

RIETH, E, 'L'epave du debut de XVIeme siecle de Villefranche-sur-Mer (France): un premier bilan de l'etude architecturale' in *Carvel*

REITH, E, 'The Flat-bottomed Medieval (11th cent.) Boat from Orlac, Charente (France): Regional Boatbuilding Tradition' in *Crossroads*

ROBERTS, K G and SHACKLETON, P, *The Canoe*, Toronto, 1983

ROBERTSON, F L, *Evolution of Naval Armament*, London, 1968

ROLFSEN, P, *Båtnaust på Jaerkysten*, Stavanger, 1974

ROSE, S (ed.), *Navy of the Lancastrian Kings*, Navy Records Society, 123, 1982

ROSENBERG, G, *Hjortspringfundet*, Copenhagen, 1937

RUDOLPH, W, *Handbuch der volkstumlichen Boote im ostlichen Nieder-deutchland*, Berlin, 1966

RUDOLPH, W, *Inshore Fishing Craft of the Southern Baltic from Holstein to Curonia*, NMM MM+R No. 14, 1974

RUDOLPH, W, *Segelboote der Deutschen ostseekuste*, Berlin, 1969

RULE, M, *The Mary Rose*, London, 1982

RULE, M and MONAGHAN, J, *Gallo-Roman Trading Vessel from Guernsey*, Guernsey Museum Monograph No. 5, 1993

RULE, M, 'The Romano-Celtic Ship excavated at St. Peter Port, Guernsey' in *Celts*

RÅLAMB, A C, *Skeps Byggerij eller Adelig Ofnings Tionde Tom*, 1691, reprinted Stockholm, 1943

SALISBURY, W (ed.), *Treatise on Shipbuilding*, issued as Occasional Publication No. 6 by Society for Nautical Research, 1958

SANDISON, C, *Sixareen and her racing descendants*, Lerwick, 1954

SARSFIELD, J P, 'Master frame and ribbands: A Brazilian case study with an overview of this widespread traditional carvel design and building system' in *Carvel*

SAVORY, J G, *Prevention of decay of wood in boats*, Forest Products Research Laboratory Bulletin No. 31, 1966

SAWYER, P H, *Age of the Vikings*, 2nd edn, 1971

SHACKLETON, P and ROBERTS, K G, *The Canoe*, Toronto, 1983

SHAW, T (ed.), *Trireme Project*, Oxbow Monograph No. 31, Oxford, 1993

SJØVOLD, T, *Oseberg Find*, Oslo, 1969

SLADE, W J, *Out of Appledore*, Newton Abbot, 1970

SMITH, R C, 'Voyages of Columbus: search for his ships' in *Ships and Shipwrecks*

SMOLAREK, P, 'Aspects of Early Boatbuilding in the Southern Baltic Region' in *Crossroads*

STEFFY, J R, 'The Mediterranean shell to skeleton transition: A N–W European parallel??' in *Carvel*

STEFFY, J R, *Wooden Shipbuilding and the Interpretation of Shipwrecks*, Texas A & M University Press, 1994

STENTON, F M, *Bayeux Tapestry*, London, 1957

STIGELL, Anna-Lisa, *Kyrkans Techen och Arets Gång*, Helsinki, 1974

STORY, D, *Frame Up!*, Barre, Mass., 1964

STORY, D, *The Building of a Wooden Ship*, Barre, Mass., 1971

SWINEY, H W and KATZEV, M L, 'The Kyrenia Shipwreck' in *Marine Archaeology*

TAYLOR, J du PLAT, *Marine Archaeology*, London, 1965

TAYLOR, D A, *Boatbuilding in Winterton, Trinity Bay, Newfoundland*, Ottawa, 1982

TEISEN, M, 'A Medieval Clinker-built Wreck from Hundevika, Norway' in *Crossroads*

THESIGER, W, *Marsh Arabs*, London, 1978

THIRSLUND, S and VEBAEK, C L, *The Viking Compass*, Helsingør, 1992

THIRSLUND, S and VEBAEK, C L, *Vikingernes Kompas*, Helsingør, 1990

THOMAS, A V, *Timbers used in the Boatbuilding Industry*, Forest Products Research Laboratory Industrial Survey No. 6, 1964

THORVILDSEN, K, *Ladby-Skibet*, Copenhagen, 1957

TRAUNG, J O (ed.), *Fishing Boats of the World*, 3 vols, London, 1955–67

TUCK, J A and GRENIER, R, *Red Bay, Labrador, World Whaling Capital, 1550–1600*, St. John's, Nfld., 1989

TÖRNROOS, B, *Båtar och-båtbyggeri i Ålands östra skärgård 1850–1930*, Åbo, 1968

TÖRNROOS, B, *Öståländska Fiskebåtar*, Jakobstad, 1978

URBAN, W, *The Baltic Crusade*, DeKalb, Ill., 1975

UNGER, R W (ed.), *Cogs, Caravels and Galleons*, London, 1994

van der HEIDE, G D, 'Ship Archaeological Investigations in the Netherlands' in *Aspects of the History of Wooden Shipbuilding*, NMM MM+R No. 1:24–31, 1970

van HOLK, A and OOSTING, R, 'The Excavation of a Peat-Barge found at Lot LZ 1 in Zuidelijk Flevoland' in *Crossroads*

van de MOORTEL, A, 'Functional Analysis of a Small Zuyderzee Cog' in *Crossroads*

van de MOORTEL, A, 'The construction of a cog-like vessel in the Late Middle Ages' in *Carvel*

VARENIUS, B, *Bulverket båten*, Stockholm, 1979

VARENIUS, B, 'The Baltic itinerary of Codex Holmiensis A 14, a contextual approach' in *Shipshape*

VEBAEK, C L and THIRSLUND, S, *Vikingernes kompas*, Helsingør, 1990

VEBAEK, C L and THIRSLUND, S, *The Viking Compass*, Helsingør, 1992

VEYRAT, E and L'HOUR, M, 'The French Medieval Clinker Wreck from Aber Wrac'h' in *Crossroads*

VIKINGESKIBSHALLEN, *Nordlandsbåden Rana*, Roskilde, 1981

VILLAIN-GADNOSSI, BOSUTTIL, and ADAM (eds), *Medieval Ships and the Birth of Technological Societies*, vol. 1, Malta, 1989

VILLIERS, A J, *Sons of Sinbad*, New York, 1940

VINNER, M, 'A Viking ship off Cape Farewell' in *Shipshape*

VINNER, M and CRUMLIN-PEDERSEN, O (eds), *Sailing into the Past*, Roskilde, 1986

VLEK, R, *The Medieval Utrecht Boat*, BAR S382, Oxford, 1987

von BUSCH, P, HAASUM, S and LAGERLÖF, E, *Skeppristningar på Gotland*, Stockholm, 1993

WACHSMAN, Shelley, 'Paddled and Oared Ships before the Iron Age', *The Age of the Galley*, pp. 10–35, London, 1995

WALLINGA, H T, *Ships and Sea-Power before the Great Persian War*, Leiden, 1993

WALLINGA, H T, 'The Ancestry of the Trireme: 1200–525 BC', *The Age of the Galley*, London, 1995

WARINGTON-SMYTH, H, *Mast and Sail in Europe and Asia*, Edinburgh, 1929

WASKONIG, D, 'Bidliche Darstellungen des Hulk', *Altonaer Museum in Hamburg*, pp. 139–66, 1969

WEIBUST, K, 'Holmsbuprammen', *Norsk Sjøfartsmuseum 1914–1964*, pp. 87–96, Oslo, 1964

WELLS, K, *The Fishery of Prince Edward's Island*, Charlottetown, PEI, 1986

WESTERDAHL, C (ed.), *Crossroads in Ancient Shipbuilding*, Oxford, 1994

WESTERDAHL, C, *et sätt som liknar them uti theras öfriga lefnadsart*, Umeå, 1987

WESTERDAHL, C, 'Traditional zones of transport geography in relation to ship-types' in *Shipshape*

WHITE, E W, *British Fishing Boats and Coastal Craft*, London, 1950

WILSON, D M, 'Anglo Saxon Carpenters' Tools' in CLAUS, M (ed.), *Studien zur Europaischen vor-und Fruhgeschichte*, pp. 143–50, Neumünster, 1968

WILSON, D M, *The Vikings and their Origins*, London, 1970

WILSON, D M and KLINDT-JENSEN, O, *Viking Art*, London, 1966

WILSON, G, 'Computer Documentation and Analysis of Historic Ship Design' in *Crossroads*

WILSON, G, *Scottish Fishing Boats*, Beverley, 1995

WITSON, N, *Architectura Navalis et Regimen Nauticum*, Stockholm, 1690

WITTY, A, 'North America's Small Craft Network: Research and Exchange' in *Crossroads*

WORCESTER, G R G, *Junks and Sampans of the Yangtze*, Shanghai, vol. 1, 1947, vol. 2, 1948

WORCESTER, G R G, *Sweep and Sail in China*, London, 1966

WORCESTER, G R G, *The Floating Population in China*, Hong Kong, 1970

WORCESTER, G R G, *The Junkman Smiles*, London, 1959

WRIGHT, E V, *The Ferriby Boats*, London, 1990

WRIGHT, E V, 'The Boats of North Ferriby' in *Three Major Boat Finds in Britain*, NMM MM+R No. 6: 3–7, 1972

WRIGHT, E V, 'The North Ferriby Boats – a Final Report' in *Crossroads*

ZACKE, A and HAGG, M, *Allmogebåtar*, Stockholm, 1973

ZAHARIADE, M and BOUNEGRU, O, 'Roman Ships on the Lower Danube' in *Crossroads*

ZIMMERLY, D W, *An Annotated Bibliography of Kayaks*, Ottawa, 1978

ZIMMERLY, D W, *Hooper Bay Kayak Construction*, Ottawa, 1979

ZINER, F, *Bluenose, Queen of the Grand Banks*, Philadelphia, Pa., 1970

ÅKERLUND, H, *Fartygsfynden i den forna hamnen i Kalmar*, Stockholm, 1951

ÅKERLUND, H, *Nydamskeppen*, Göteberg, 1963

ARTICLES

NOTE

IJNA = International Journal of Nautical Archaeology
MM = Mariner's Mirror

ALBION, R G, 'Timber Problems of the Royal Navy 1652–1862, *MM*, 38: 5–10, 1952

ANDERSON, R C, 'The Bursledon Ship', *MM*, 20: 158–70, 1934

ARBMAN, H, 'Der Årby-fund', *Acta Archaeologica*, 11:43–102, 1940

ARNOLD, B, 'Gallo-Roman boat from the Bay of Bevaix, Lake Neuchâtel, Switzerland', *IJNA*, 4: 123–6, 1975

BARNWELL, E L, 'Caergwrle Cup', *Archaeologica Cambrensis*, 4th series, 6:268–74, 1875

BASCH, L, 'Ancient Wrecks and the Archaeology of Ships', *IJNA*, 1:1–58, 1972

BASCH, L, 'Another Punic wreck in Sicily: its ram. 1. A typological sketch', *IJNA*, 2:201–19, 1975

BASS, G F, 'Cape Gelydonia, a Bronze Age Shipwreck', *Transactions of the American Philosophical Society*, 57, part 8, 1967

BASS, G F, 'Byzantine Trading Venture', *Scientific American*, 224:23–33, 1971

BLACKMAN, D J, 'Further Early Evidence of Hull Sheathing', *IJNA*, 1:117–9, 1972

BOCZAR, M L, 'The Craft in Use at the Rivergate of the Dunajec', *MM*, 52:3, 1966

BOWEN, R Le Baron, 'Primitive watercraft of Arabia', *American Neptune*, 12, 186–221, 1956

BRUCE, R S, 'More about sixerns', *MM*, 20:312–22, 1934

CARR-LAUGHTON, L G, 'Clove-board', *MM*, 43: 247–9, 1957

CASSON, L, 'New Light on Ancient Rigging and Boatbuilding', *American Neptune*, 24:86–9, 1964

CASSON, L, 'Bronze Age Ships. The evidence of the Thera Wall Paintings', *IJNA*, 4:3–10, 1975

CHAPELLE, H I, 'The Migrations of an American boat-type', *US National Museum Bulletin 228*, Washington, 1961

CHITTICK, N, 'Sewn Boats in the western Indian Ocean', *IJNA* 9, 297–309, 1980

CHRISTENSEN, A E, 'Boat finds from Bryggen', *Bryggen Papers*, 1, 47–280, Bergen University Press, 1985

CHRISTENSEN, A E, 'Lucien Basch: Ancient Wrecks and the Archaeology of Ships. A comment', *IJNA*, 2:137–45, 1973

COATES, J, 'Hogging or breaking of frame-built wooden ships', *MM* 71, 437–442, 1985

CORBETT, N H, 'Micro-morphological studies on the degradation of lignified cell walls by ascomycetes and fungi imperfecti', *Journal of Wood Science*, 14:18–29, 1965

CRUMLIN-PEDERSEN, O. See separate full list of publications

DADE, E, 'The Cobles', *MM*, 20:199–207, 1934

de CERVIN, G B R, 'The Evolution of the Venetian Gondola', *MM*, 42:3, 1956

de WEERD, M D and HAALEBOS, J K, 'Schepen voor het Opscheppen', *Spiegel Historiael*, 8: 386–97, 1973

DORAN, E, Jnr, 'The Origin of Leeboards', *MM*, 53: 1, 1967

DUVAL, P–M, 'La forme des navires romains d'après la mosaïque d'Althiburtus', *Mélanges d'archéologie et d'Histoire de l'Ecole Française de Rome*, 61–62 anée, pp. 119–49, 1949

ELLMERS, D and PIRLING, R, 'Ein mittelalterliches Schiff aus dem Rhein', *Die Heimat*, 43:45–8, 1972

ELLMERS, D, 'Keltischer Schiffbau', *Jahrbuch des Romische-Germanischen Zentralmuseums Mainz*, 16:73–122, 1969

EVANS, A J, 'Votive Deposit of Gold Objects', *Archaeologia*, 55:391–408, 1897

FARRELL, A W and PENNEY, S, 'Broighter boat: a re-assessment', *Irish Archaeological Research Forum*, 2.2:15–26, 1975

FRIEL, Ian, 'Henry V's *Grace Dieu*', *IJNA* 22:1 3–19, 1993

FROST, H, 'First season of excavation on the Punic Wreck in Sicily', *IJNA*, 2:33–49, 1973

FROST, H, 'The Punic Wreck in Sicily, second season of excavation, *IJNA*, 3:35–42, 1974A

FROST, H, 'The Third Campaign of Excavation of the Punic Ship, Marsala, Sicily, *MM*, 60:265–6, 1974B

FROST, H, 'Another Punic wreck in Sicily: its ram. 2 The ram from Marsala', *IJNA*, 4:219–28, 1975

GILLIS, R H C, 'Pilot gigs of Cornwall and the Isles of Scilly', *MM*, 55:117–38, 1969

GREENHILL, B, 'The Karachi Fishing Boats', *MM*, 42:1, 1956

GREENHILL, B, 'Japanese Inshore Fishing Boats', *MM*, 45:1, 1959

GREENHILL, B, 'More Evidence of the Separate Evolution of the Clinker Built Boat in Asia', *MM*, 47:4, 1961

GREENHILL, B, 'A Boat of the Indus', *MM*, 49:4, 1963

GUTHRIE, J, 'Bizarre Craft of Portugal', *MM*, 35:3, 1949

HASSLÖF, O, 'Wrecks, Archives and Living Tradition', *MM*, 49:3, 1963

HASSLÖF, O, 'Sources of Maritime History and Methods of Research', *MM*, 52:127–44, 1966

HAWKINS, C W, 'The Tuticorn Thoni', *MM*, 51:2, 1965

HOEKSTRA, T J, 'A note on the Utrecht boats', *IJNA*, 4:390–2, 1975

HORNELL, J, 'Fishing luggers of Hastings', *MM*, 24: 39–54, 1938

JOHNSTONE, P, 'A Medieval Skin Boat', *Antiquity* 36:32–7, 1962

JOHNSTONE, P, 'Bronze Age Sea Trial', *Antiquity* 46:269–74, 1972

JOHNSTONE, P, 'Stern first in the Stone Age?', *IJNA* 2:3–11, 1973

JOHNSTONE, P, 'The Bantry Boat', *Antiquity* 38: 277–84, 1964

KENTLEY, E, 'Some Aspects of the *Masula* surfboat, in MCGRAIL, S (ed.) *Sewn Plank Boats*, BAR S276, 1985

LLOYD, A B, 'Triremes in the Saite Navy', *Journal of Egyptian Archaeology*, 63:268–79, 1972

MCGRAIL, S. See separate full list of publications

MCKEE, J E G. Unpublished Study of East Sussex and Chesil Bank beach boats, undated

MCKEE, J E G, 'Flatners', *MM*, 56:232–4, 1970

MCKEE, J E G, 'Weston-super-Mare Flatners', *MM*, 57:25–39, 1971

MACMURRAY, C. Unpublished transcripts of interviews with former merchant and naval seamen, archives of the Royal Naval Museum, Portsmouth

MACPHERSON, N, 'Notes on Antiquities from the Isle of Eigg', *Proceedings of the Society of Antiquaries of Scotland*, 12:594–6, 1877–8

MACPHERSON RICE, W, 'Account of an Ancient Vessel recently found under the old bed of the River Rother, Kent', *Archaeologia*, 20:553–65, 1824

MARSDEN, P R V, 'Boat of the Roman period found at Bruges, Belgium in 1899, and related types', *IJNA*, 5:23–56, 1976

MESSENGER, A H, 'Notes on the New Zealand Scow', *MM*, 55:461–5, 1969

MOLL, F, 'History of Wood Preserving in Shipbuilding', *MM*, 12:357–74, 1926

MORRISON, J S, 'Review of Casson (1971)', *IJNA*, 1: 230–3, 1972

MORTON NANCE, R, 'The Ship of the Renaissance', *MM*, 41:180–92 and 281–98, 1955

NICHOLLS, R V, *Archaeological Reports*, No. 17 for 1970 – 1:85, no. 28, fig 14, Hellenic Society, 1970–1

OLSEN, O and CRUMLIN-PEDERSEN, O, 'Skuldelev Ships', *Acta Archaeologica*, 38:73–174, 1967

OWEN, D I, 'Excavation Report', *IJNA*, 1:197–8, 1972

PETERSEN, J, 'Vikingetidens Redskaper', *Skrifter utgitt av Det Norske Videnskaps-Academi i Oslo*, Oslo, 1951

PHILIPSEN, J P W, 'Utrecht Ship', *MM*, 51:35–46, 1965

PRYNNE, M, 'Henry V's *Grace Dieu*, *MM*, 54:115–28, 1968

PRYNNE, M, 'Some general considerations applying to the examination of the remains of old ships', *IJNA*, 2:227–38, 1973

RENFREW, C, 'Cycladic Metallurgy and the Aegean Early Bronze Age', *American Journal of Archaeology*, 71:1–20, 1967

SHAW, A, 'Bridgwater Flatner', *MM*, 55:411–5, 1969

STEFFY, J R, 'Reconstruction of the 11th century Serçe Liman vessel', *IJNA*, 11:13–34, 1982

van der HEIDE, G D, 'Archaeological Investigations on New Lands', *Antiquity and Survival*, 1:221–52, 1955

WACHSMANN, Shelley, 'The Ships of the Sea Peoples', *IJNA*, 10.3, 187–220, 1981, Additional Notes, *IJNA*, 11., 4, 297–304, 1982

WARD, R M, 'A Surviving Charter Party of 1323', forthcoming for publication in *MM*

WATERS, D W, 'Chinese Junks – The Antung Trader', *MM*, 24:1, 1938

WATERS, D W, 'Chinese Junks – The Pechile Trader', *MM*, 25:1, 1939

WATERS, D W, 'Chinese Junks – An exception, the Tongkung', *MM*, 26:1, 1940

WATERS, D M, 'Chinese Junks – The Twaqo', *MM*, 32:3, 1946

WATERS, D M, 'Chinese Junks – The Hangchow Bay Trader and Fisher', *MM*, 32:1, 1946

WILLIAMS, R T, 'Early Greek Ships at Two Levels', *Journal of Hellenic Studies*, 78, 121–130, 1958. Addenda: *JHS* 79, 159–160, 1959

WORCESTER, G R G, 'Four Small Craft of Taiwan', *MM*, 42:4, 1956

WORCESTER, G R G, 'Six Craft of Kwantung', *MM*, 45:2, 1959

WORCESTER, G R G, 'Four Junks of Kiangsi', *MM*, 47:3, 1961

ZIMMERLY, D W, 'An illustrated glossary of Kayak terminology', *Canadian Museums Associated Gazette*, 9(2): 27–37, 1976

PUBLICATIONS BY OLE CRUMLIN-PEDERSEN

(List reprinted from OLSEN, O (ed.), *Shipshape*, Roskilde, 1995)

1958 The Skuldelev Ships (I). A preliminary report on an underwater excavation in Roskilde fjord, Zealand *Acta Archaeologica* 29, pp. 161–175 (with Olaf Olsen)

1959 Skuldelev-skibene. *Skalk* 4/59, pp. 7–8

1959 Arkæologi under vandet. *Nationalmuseet's Arbejdsmark* 1959, pp. 5–20 (w/Olaf Olsen)

1959 Vikingeskibe i Roskilde. *Søens Verden* 1959–60/2, pp. 53–63

1960 Berømte vrag langs Danmarks kyster. *Hvem-Hvad-Hvor*. Politikens årbog 1961, pp. 268–273

1960 Sideroret fra Vorså. *Kuml* 1960, pp. 106–116

1961 The Skuldelev Ships. *Actes du Ile Congrés International d'Archaéologie Sous-marine*. Albenga 1958, pp. 266–269

1962 Skibene. *Skalk* 2/62, p. 6

1962 Stævnen. *Skalk* 4/62, pp. 16–17

1962 *Vikingeskibene i Roskilde fjord*. Årets fund, Nationalmuseet, 28p. ill. (with Olaf Olsen)

1962 Reclamation of Viking Ships in the Roskilde Fjord. *CN-Post*, Nov. 1962, pp. 13–17 (with H. Bank Petersen)

1962 Trækutterens fremtid? *Ingeniørens Ugeblad* nr. 29, 1962

1963 Skibe i havn. *Skalk* 1/63, pp. 3–7

1963 The Viking Ships in Roskilde Fjord (with Olaf Olsen). *The Mariner's Mirror*, vol. 49, 1963, pp. 300–302

1963 Viking Ships. The Undersea Challenge. *Proceedings of the Second World Congress of Underwater Activities*, London, 1962, pp. 88–98

1963 Vikingeskibene i Roskilde fjord. *Jul i Roskilde* 1963, pp. 5–9

1964 Træskibsbyggeriet i støbeskeen. *Ingeniørens Ugeblad* nr. 9, februar 1964

1964 Navires et Navigation des Vikings. *Courrie des Messageries Maritimes* No. 62, 1964

1965 Til søs med vikingeskibet 'Imme Gram'. *CN-Post*, Februar 1965, pp. 20–23 (with T. Hartvig Nielsen)

1965 Cog-kogge-kaag. Træk af en frisisk skibstypes historie. *Handels-& Søfartsmuseet på Kronborg, Årbog* 1965, pp. 81–144

1966 En kogge i Roskilde. *Handels-& Søfartsmuseet på Kronborg, Årbog* 1966, pp. 39–58

1966 Sjællands-vraget. *Skalk* 6/66, pp. 5–9

1966 Vikingeskibshallen og Roskilde. Kronik, *Roskilde Tidende*, d.27/9 1966

1966 Two Danish Side Rudders. *The Mariner's Mirror*, vol. 52, 3, pp. 251–261

1967 Parallel to Dunajec Craft? *The Mariner's Mirror*, vol. 53, 1, p. 31

1967 Czy odpowiednik jednostki Dunajeckiej? *Kwartalnik Historii Nauki i Techniki*, Rok XII nr. 3, pp. 595–597

1967 Grestedbro-skibet. *Fra Mark og Montre* 1967, pp. 11–15

1968 The Skuldelev Ships II. A Report of the Final Underwater Excavation in 1959 and the Salvaging Operation in 1962 *Acta Archaeologica* 38, pp. 95–170 (with Olaf Olsen)

1968 TRÆskibET. Fra langskib til fregat. Udgivet af Træbranchens Oplysningsråd, København, 48p., ill.

1968 Die Nordische maritim-historische Arbeitsgruppe. Bericht. *Kolloquium Balticum Ethnographicum 1966*. R. Peesch & W. Rudolph (eds), Berlin, pp. 39–42

1969 The Grestedbro Ship. The remains of a Late Iron Age Vessel. Found in 1945 in South Jutland. *Acta Archaeologica* 39, pp. 262–267

1969 *Fem vikingeskibe fra Roskilde fjord*. Roskilde 1969, 136p., ill. (with Olaf Olsen)

1969 Skibe i hus. *Skalk* 2/69, pp. 18–27

1969 Das Haithabuschiff. Vorläufiger Bericht über das im Jahre 1953 in Haddebyer Noor entdeckte Schiffswrack. *Berichte über die Ausgrabungen in Haithabu*, 3. Neumünster, 38p., ill.

1970 *Skonnerten Fulton af Marstal*. Roskilde, 52p. ill.

1970 *Fulton. En rapport undervejs*, (editor). Roskilde, 55p. ill.

1970 Skind eller træ? En studie i den nordiske plankebåds kontruktive oprindelse. *Sømand, fisker, skib og værft. Introduktion til maritim etnologi*. København, pp. 213–239. (Also separate edition Vikingeskibs-hallen 1970)

1970 The Viking Ships of Roskilde. *Aspects of the History of Wooden Shipbuilding*. Maritime Monographs and Reports. No. 1, London, pp. 7–23

1971 Viking Ships and a three-masted Schooner. *J L News*, No 73, July 1971, pp. 16–18

1971 Introduction. *Danske Småskibe* by Andreas Laursen. Blade fra sejlskibenes tid. København, pp. 7–16

1971 Bådebygger and Skibstømrer. *Gamle danske Håndvoerk*. København, pp. 95–102 and pp. 242–248

1971 *Et dyk i fortiden*. Preface and contributions. Dansk Sportsdykker-Forbund.

1972 Gokstadskibet, Hjortspringbåden, Ladbyskibet, Nydambåden, Osebergskibet, Skibe, Skuldelevskibene, Tuneskibet and Undervandsarkæologi. *Arkæologisk ABC*, København.

1972 Wrecks in the North Sea and the Baltic. Underwater Archaeology, a nascent discipline. *Museums and Monuments* XIII, Unesco, pp. 65–75 (also French edition)

1972 Kællingen og kløften. Nogle jyske fund af kølsvin og mastefisk fra 800–1200 e. Kr. *Handels-& Søfartsmuseet på Kronborg, Årbog 1972*, pp. 63–80

1972 *Skin or Wood? A Study of the Origin of the Scandinavian Plankboat. Ships and Shipyards. Sailors and Fishermen*. Copenhagen, pp. 208–234

1972 The Vikings and the Hanseatic Merchants: 900–1450. *A History of Seafaring, based on Underwater Archaeology*. G. Bass (ed.), London 1972, pp. 181–204

1973 Ein Kielschwein aus der Schleswiger Altstadt, *Beiträge zur Schleswiger Stadtgeschichte*, Heft 18, pp. 18–19

1974 Helnæs-spærringen. *Fynske Minder* 1973, Odense, pp. 29–48

1974 Five Viking Ships. The Saga of a new Danish Museum. *CN-Post*, No. 104, Februar, pp. 3–6

1975 The Viking Ship Museum of Roskilde. The Saga of a new Danish Museum. *Museum* XXVII, no. 1, 1975. Unesco, pp. 17–21 (also French edition)

1975 The Viking Ship Museum of Roskilde. A Museum of Nautical Archaeology in Denmark. *Transport Museums Yearbook* 1975, vol. 2, Gdansk, pp. 84–104

1975 'Æ Lei' and 'Margrethes Bro'. *Nordslesvigske Museer* 2, pp. 9–25

1975 Viking Seamanship Questioned. *The Mariner's Mirror* 61, pp. 127–131

280 • Selected Bibliography

1975 Notes and News, Vigsø. *The International Journal of Nautical Archaeology and Underwater Exploration*, vol. 4,2 September, pp. 389–390

1975 La tradition nordique de la construction navale a travers les decouvertes archáeologiques, 200–1200 ap. J.C. *Le Petit Peroquet*, nr. 17, Grenoble 1975, pp. 42–54

1976 Boot. Das Bootkammergrab von Haithabu. M. Müller-Wille (ed.). *Bericht über die Ausgrabungen in Haithabu*, 8, Neumünster 1976, pp. 20–28

1976 Skatten fra havet. *Nationalmuseets Arbejdsmark*, pp. 183–185

1976 Koggen med guldskatten. *Skalk* 6/76, pp. 9–15 (with J. Steen Jensen et al.)

1977 *From Viking Ship to 'Victory'*. London, 48 p. ill. (with Roger Finch)

1977 Some Principles for the Recording and Presentation of Ancient Boat Structures. Sources and Techniques in Boat Archaeology. Sean McGrail (ed.), National Maritime Museum, Greenwich, Archaeological Series No. 1, *BAR Supplementary Series* 29, pp. 163–177

1977 'Guldskibet' ved Vejby Strand. *Vejby-Tibirke Årbog* 1977–78, pp. 35–43

1977 TRÆskibTO. Sømand og Købmand. Træbranchens Oplysningsråd, København, 48p., ill.

1977 Pælespærringer and Skibstyper. *Kulturhistorisk Leksikon for nordisk Middelalder*. København.

1978 The Ships of the Vikings. *The Vikings. Proceedings of the Symposium of the Faculty of Arts of Uppsala University*, Uppsala, pp. 32–41

1978 Søvejen til Roskilde, *Historisk årbog fra Roskilde amt*, 1978, pp. 3–79

1978 Fünf Wikingerschiffe aux Roskilde Fjord. København, 145 p., ill. (with Olaf Olsen)

1978 Five Viking Ships from Roskilde Fjord. København, 136 p., ill. (with Olaf Olsen)

1978 Arkæologisk dokumentation og tolkning af fartøjsfund. *NAM-förtryck*, Stockholm

1979 Danish cog-finds. The Archaeology of Medieval Ships and harbours in North. Europe. *BAR International Series* 66, pp. 17–34

1979 Dronning Margrethes Stiger, en pælespærring ved Vordingborg Nordhavn. §49 -udgravninger 1969–79. København, pp. 44–45

1979 Lynæsskibet og Roskilde søvej. 13 bidrag til Roskilde by og omegn's historie, Roskilde, pp. 63–77

1980 Havnen i Hedeby, *Skalk* 1980/3, pp. 4–10 (with Kurt Schietzel)

1980 Kyholm 1978. A joint archaeological-geological investigation around a 13th century wreck at Kyholm, Samsø, Denmark (with Lis Nymark, Chr. Christiansen et al.) *International Journal of Nautical Archaeology*, vol. 9,3, pp. 193–216

1980 The Ships of the Vikings. *Danish Journal*, special issue, pp. 21–25

1981 Mit skib skal hedde Fulton! Mennesker omkring et Marstalskib i tiden omkring 1. verdenskrig. *Det skabende menneske 2, festskrift til P. V. Glob*, København, pp. 97–122

1981 Træskibsejernes Sammenslutning 1971–81, forhistorien. Under sejl påny, *Maritim Kontakt* 4, København, pp. 9–14

1981 Indledning til Aksel Sandemose: Marstalskonnerterne under Labrador. Under sejl påny, *Maritim Kontakt* 4, København, pp. 181–184

1981 Søforsvaret and Skibe og havn. *Vikingernes spor i det danske landskab*, København, pp. 18–19 and 26–37

1981 Viking shipbuilding and seamanship. *Proceedings of the Eighth Viking Congress*, Odense, pp. 271–286

1981 Skibe på havbunden. Vragfund i danske farvande fra perioden 600–1400 *Handels-og Søfartsmuseet på Kronborg, Årbog* 1981, pp. 28–65

1983 Schiffe und Seehandelsrouten im Ostseeraum 1050–1350. *Lübecker Schriften* 7, pp. 229–237

1983 *From Viking ships to Hanseatic cogs*. National Maritime Museum, London. Occasional lecture 4

1983 Med Nordisk maritimhistorisk arbejdsgruppe hos Christian Madsen i Lynæs. *Handels-og Søfartsmuseet på Kronborg, Årbog*, Helsingør, pp. 52–68

1983 Fotevik-projektets mål og midler. *Meta* 1983/3–4, Lund, pp. 27–31

1983 Skibe, sejlads og ruter hos Ottar og Wulfstan. *Ottar og Wulfstan, to rejseberetninger fra vikingetiden*. N. Lund (ed.). Roskilde, pp. 32–44

1984 Ships, Navigation and Routes. *The Reports of Ohthere and Wulfstan. Two Voyagers at the Court of King Alfred*. N. Lund (ed.). York, pp. 30–42

1984 Vikingeværk. *Skalk* 1984/2, pp. 16–17

1984 Experimental boat archaeology in Denmark. *Aspects of Maritime Archaeology and Ethnography*, London, pp. 97–122

1984 Die Schiffe von Haithabu. *Archäologische und naturvissenschaftliche Untersuchungen an Siedlungen im deutschen Küstengebiet*, Bd. 2, Weinheim, pp. 241–250

1984 Fotevik. De marinarkæologiske undersøgelser 1981 og 1982. *Pugna Forensis - ? Arkeologiska undersökningar kring Foteviken, Skåne 1981–83*, Lund, pp. 7–68

1984 Ekkolod. *Arkæoeologi og geofysiske sporingsmetoder*, København, pp. 178–182 and 187–196

1985 Ship Archaeology in Denmark 1979–82. Postmedieval boat and ship archaeology. *BAR International Series* 256, pp. 373–379

1985 Cargo Ships of Northern Europe AD 800–1300. *Proceedings of the Second Waterfront Archaeology Conference*, Bergen 1983, pp. 83–93

1985 Ship Finds and Ship Blockages AD 800–1200. *Archaeological Formation Processes*. København, pp. 215–228

1985 Skibsfund etc. *Arkæologi Leksikon*, København

1985 Havne og søfart i romersk og germansk jernalder. *Gudmeproblemer*, Odense, pp. 68–91

1985 Wrecks as a Source for Ships and Sea Routes. *5th International Congress of Maritime Museums. Proceedings*. J. Bracker (ed.), Hamburg, pp. 67–73

1986 *Sailing into the Past*. Editor and Introduction, Roskilde, p. 7

1986 The Roar-Projekt. *Sailing into the Past*, Roskilde, pp. 94–103

1986 Aspects of Wood Technology in Medieval Shipbuilding. *Sailing into the Past*, Roskilde, pp. 138–148

1986 Introduction. *Skinboats of Greenland* by H C Petersen. Ships and Boats of the North, vol. 1, Roskilde, 1986

1987 Aspects of Viking Age Shipbuilding *Journal of Danish Archaeology*, vol. 5, 1986, pp. 209–228

1987 Le projet Roar Ege. Reconstitution et expérimentation d'un caboteur viking. *Le Chasse-Marée* no. 30, Tours, pp. 16–45

1987 Häfen und Schiffahrt in der Römischen Kaiserzeit sowie in der Völkerwanderungs-und Merowingerzeit Dänemarks. *Frühmittelalterliche Studien* 21, Berlin, pp. 101–123

1988 A note on the speed of Viking ships. *The International Journal of Nautical Archaeology*, vol. 17,3:270–271

1988 *Både fra Danmarks oldtid*. Roskilde, 180 p., ill. (with Flemming Rieck)

1988 Gensyn med Skuldelev 5-et ledingskib? *Festskrift til Olaf Olsen*, København, pp. 137–156

1988 'Imme Gram' og forskningen. *Råsejl og rorskarle*, Tønder, pp. 37–43

1989 Schiffe und Schiffahrtswege im Ostseeraum während des 9.–12. Jahrhunderts. Oldenburg-Wolin-Staraja Ladoga-Novgorod - Kiev. M. Müller-Wille (ed.) *Bericht der Römisch-Germanischen Kommission* 69, 1988, Mainz, pp. 530–563

1989 Vikingernes 'søvej' til Byzans - om betingelserne for sejlads ad flodvejene fra Østersø til Sortehav. *Beretning fra Ottende tværfaglige Vikingesymposium*. T. Kisbye & E. Roesdahl (eds). Århus, pp. 33–51

1989 Wood Technology and the Forest Resources in the Light of Medieval Shipfinds. *Medieval Ships and the Birth of Technological Societies*, vol. 1. C Villain-Gandossi et al. (eds). Malta, pp. 25–42

1989 Skibet i Bøtøminde - en falstersk middelalderskude. *Lolland-Falsters historiske Samfund*, Årbog 1989, Maribo, pp. 33–44 (also printed in To skibsfund fra Falster. Roskilde 1989)

1990 The boats and ships of the Angles and Jutes. *Maritime Celts, Frisians and Saxons*. S. McGrail (ed.). CBA Research Report No. 71, London, pp. 98–116

1990 The dating of Wreck 2, the Longship, from Skuldelev, Denmark. *Newswarp* No. 7, Exeter, pp. 3–6 (with Niels Bonde)

1990 Marinarkæologien i Danmark. *Arkæologiske Udgravninger i Danmark*. København, pp. 9–15. English summary pp. 16–21

1990 Sejle op ad åen. Skibsfund og sejlspærringer i danske indvande. *Vandløb og kulturhistorie*. Skrifter fra Historisk Institut, Odense Universitet, nr. 39, Odense pp. 93–104

1990 Introduction. *Råsejlet-Dragens Vinge* by Bent & Erik Andersen. Roskilde

1990 Arkæologiens våde ende og Der må være en grænse. *Danske Museer* 1990, pp. 2 og 12–14

1990 Mit skib skal hedde Fulton . . . *Fulton-Posten*, 1990, pp. 8–16

1991 Bådgrave og gravbåde på Slusegård. *Slusegård-gravpladsen* III, pp. 93–266. Jysk Arkæologisk Selskabs Skrifter XIV, 3. Århus.

1991 *Aspects of Maritime Scandinavia* AD 200–1200. Editor and Introduction. Roskilde.

1991 Maritime Aspects of the Archaeology of Roman and Migration-Period Denmark. *Aspects of Maritime Scandinavia* AD 200–1200, pp. 41–54

1991 Ship Types and Sizes AD 800–1400. *Aspects of Maritime Scandinavia* AD 200–1200, pp. 69–82

1991 Søfart og samfund i Danmarks vikingetid. *Fra Stamme til Stat i Danmark* 2. Høvdingesamfund og Kongemagt. Jysk Arkæologisk Selskabs Skrifter XXII: 2. Peder Mortensen & Birgit M. Rasmussen (eds). Århus, pp. 181–204

1992 Søfart og skibe. *Viking og Hvidekrist.* Else Roesdahl (ed.). København, pp. 42–46. (Also English, French and German edition)

1992 Ellingåskibet - fundet og genfundet. *Bangsbo Museum, Årbog* 1991. Frederikshavn, pp. 31–47

1992 Maritime Aspects of the Archaeology of Roman and Migration-Period Denmark. *Der historische Horizont der Götterbild-Amulette aus der Übergangsepoke von der Spätantike zum Frühmittelalter.* K. Hauck (ed.). Göttingen. pp. 385–402

1992 Skibsfund spejler fortidens samfund. *Humaniora* nr. 2. København

1993 Handelsskibets kulturhistorie and Reisebeskrivelse fra vikingetiden. *'Saga Siglar's forlis. Vikingenes seilaser.* O. Nilsen (ed.). Ålesund 1992/93, pp. 78–87 & 88–89

1993 The Rise and Decline of Hedeby/Schleswig as a Major Port of the Baltic Trade. *Ellevte tvoerfaglige Vikingesymposium,* Københavns Universitet 1992. Århus. pp. 27–37

1993 Les lignes elegantes du navire de guerre de Marsala. *Les Dossiers d'Archaeologie.* No. 183, Juin, pp. 58–65

1993 The Nydam Ships. Old and new investigations at a classical site. *A Spirit of Enquiry. Essays for Ted Wright.* John Coles et al. (eds), Exeter, pp. 39–45 (with Flemming Rieck)

1993 Roar og Helge af Roskilde - om at bygge og sejle med vikingeskibe. *Nationalmuseets Arbejdsmark* 1993, pp. 11–29 (with Max Vinner)

1993 Stato attuale della nave pinica. *Fenici e vichingi: le navi.* Marsala, pp. 9–21

1993 Skibe og spærringer. *Da klinger i muld . . . 25 års arkæoeologi i Danmark.* Steen Hvas & Birgit Storegaard (eds). Århus, pp. 254–259

1993 Ships and Blockages. *Digging into the past, 25 years of archaeology in Denmark.* Steen Hvass & Birgit Storegaard (eds). Århus, pp. 254–259

1993 Danish Marine Archaeology Research Center. *Newswarp.* Wetland archaeology research project no. 14. November, pp. 12–14

1993 Editor of and contributor to *Maritime Archaeology Newsletter* from Roskilde No. 1. Roskilde. (Danish and English version)

1993 Razmery i tipy korablej 800–1400 gg. n.e. *Izutenie Pamjatnikov Morskoj Archeologij.* Rossijskaja Akademija NAUK. Institut Istorii Materialnoj Kultury. Sankt-Petersborg, pp. 46–58

1994 Atlas over Fyns kyst i jernalder, vikingetid og middelalder. *Nordisk Bygd* nr. 8, 1994 - Havets landskaber. Esbjerg, pp. 16–19

1994 Introduction & Medieval Ships in Danish Waters. *Crossroads in Ancient Shipbuilding.* Proceedings of the Sixth International Symposium on Boat and Ship Archaeology. Roskilde 1991. Christer Westerdahl (ed.). Oxbow Monograph 40, Oxford pp. v & 65–72

1994 Marinarkæologisk Forskningcenter i Roskilde - en aktuel orientering. *Fortid og Nutid,* pp. 24–52

1994 Editor of and contributor to *Maritime Archaeology Newsletter* from Roskilde No. 2 & 3. Roskilde. (Danish and English version)

1994 Fotevikens fem skeppsvrak har nära slägtingar i Danmark. *Populär Arkeologi.* Stockholm

1994 Marinarkæologi. *Den Store Danske Encyklopædi* bd. 1. København

1994 Foteviken - en tidligmiddelalderlig naturhavn, slagmark og markedsplads i Skåne. *Sjöhistorisk årsbok* 1994. Stockholm.

PUBLICATIONS BY SEÁN McGRAIL

1974A 'A 17th century gunner's tallystick', *International Journal of Nautical Archaeology* 3, 157–160

1974B *Building and trials of the replica of an ancient boat: the Gokstad faering Part I,* NMM Monograph 11

1975A 'Models, replicas and experiments in Nautical Archaeology', *Mariner's Mirror* 61, 3–8

1975B 'Brigg "Raft" re-excavated' *Lincs. Hist & Arch.* 10, 5–13

1975C 'Early British boats and their chronology', *International Journal of Nautical Archaeology,* 4, 191–200 (with R. Switsur)

1975D 'Archaeology of wooden boats', *J. Inst. Wood Science* 7 (37th issue) 16–19 (with C. Gregson)

1975E 'Progress towards a centre for the conservation of waterlogged wood' in Oddy, A. (ed.) *Problems in the Conservation of Waterlogged Wood,* 107–108. NMM Monograph 16

1975F 'Viking raft, pontoon bridge or boat', *Mariner's Mirror* 61, 180

1975G 'Brigg, Lincolnshire', *International Journal of Nautical Archaeology* 4, 387

1976A 'Further aspects of Viking Age boatbuilding' in Greenhill, B., *Archaeology of the Boat,* 234–249. A & C Black

1976B 'Wreck in the Dark', *Spectrum* 143, 5–6 (with P. v.d. Merwe)

1976C 'Wood Quay, Dublin', *International Journal of Nautical Archaeology* 5, 180 (with P. Wallace)

1976D 'Problems in Irish Nautical Archaeology', *Irish Arch. Research Forum* 3 (1), 21–31

1976E 'Nautical Archaeology' section in *International Book of Wood,* Mitchell Beazley.

1977A *Sources and Techniques in Boat Archaeology* (ed). NMM Archaeological Series 1/BAR (Oxford) S.29

1977B 'Aspects of Experimental Boat Archaeology' in McGrail, 1977A, 245–258

1977C 'Searching for a pattern among the logboats of England and Wales' in McGrail, 1977A, 115–135

1977D 'Axe, adze, hoe or slice?', *International Journal of Nautical Archaeology* 6, 62–4

1977E 'McKee's "Timbers from old ships" – a comment', *International Journal of Nautical Archaeology* 6, 248–251

1977F 'High speed capability of ancient boats', *International Journal of Nautical Archaeology* 6, 352–3 (with E. Corlett)

1978A *Logboats of England and Wales,* NMM Archaeological Series 2/BAR (Oxford) 51

1978B 'Dating ancient wooden boats' in Fletcher, J. (ed) *Dendro-chronology in Europe,* 239–258. NMM Archaeological Series 4/BAR (Oxford) S.51.

1978C 'Medieval logboat from Giggleswick Tarn, Yorkshire' in Annis, P. (ed.) *Ingrid and other studies,* 25–46. NMM Monograph 36

1979A 'Boat finds on land', *Current Archaeology,* 65, 171–5 (with others)

1979B 'Rowing: Aspects of the ethnographic and iconographic evidence', *International Journal of Nautical Archaeology* 8, 155–166 (with A. Farrell)

1979C *Medieval Ships and Harbours in Northern Europe* (ed.) NMM Archaeological Series 5 /BAR (Oxford) S.66

1979D 'Medieval logboats of the R. Mersey – a classification study' in McGrail, 1979C, 93 –115 (with R. Switsur)

1979E 'Giggleswick Tarn logboat', *Yorks. Arch. Journal* 51, 41–9 (with S O'Connor)

1979F 'Prehistoric boats, timber and woodworking technology', *Proceedings of the Prehistoric Society* 45, 159–163

1979G 'Medieval logboats', *Medieval Archaeology* 23, 229–231 (with R Switsur)

1980A 'Ships, Shipwrights and Seamen' chapter in Graham-Campbell, J, *The Viking World,* Weidenfeld & Nicholson

1980B *Seacraft of Prehistory* (P Johnstone) Edited. Routledge & Kegan Paul

1981A *The Brigg 'raft' and her prehistoric environment,* NMM Archaeological Series 6/BAR (Oxford) 89

1981B *Rafts, Boats and Ships* – water transport from prehistoric times to AD 1500. HMSO/NMM

1981C 'A Medieval logboat from Stanley Ferry, Yorkshire' *Medieval Archaeology* 25, 160–4

1981D 'Medieval boats, ships and landing places' in Milne, G and Hobley, B, *Waterfront Archaeology in Britain and Northern Europe,* 17–23. CBA Research Report 41

1981E 'Water Transport before 1400' in *The Commanding Sea,* 39–41. BBC Publications

1981F 'Reconciling tree-ring sampling with conservation' *Antiquity* 55, 90–5. (With R A Morgan, J Hillam & J M Coles)

1982A *Woodworking techniques before 1500* (ed.) NMM Archaeological Series 7/BAR (Oxford) S.129

1982B 'Woodworking techniques, technological change and attribute analysis' in McGrail, 1982A, 25–72. (With G Denford)

1983A *Ancient Boats,* Shire Archaeology

1983B 'The interpretation of archaeological evidence for maritime structures' in Annis, P. (ed.) *Sea Studies*, 33–46, NMM Greenwich

1983C 'Cross-Channel Seamanship and Navigation in the 1st Millennium BC', *Oxford Journal of Archaeology* 2, 299–337

1984B Boat Ethnography and Maritime Archaeology, *International Journal of Nautical Archaeology* 13, 149–150

1984B *The Greek Trireme of 5th century BC*, (ed.) with J Coates. NMM Greenwich

1984C *Aspects of Maritime Archaeology and Ethnography*, NMM Greenwich

1984D 'Maritime Archaeology – present and future' in McGrail, S (ed.) 1984C, 11–40

1985A 'Towards a classification of water transport', *World Archaeology* 16.3, 289–303

1985B 'Hasholme logboat', *Antiquity* 59, 117–120, with M Millett

1985C *Sewn Plank Boats* (ed.) with E Kentley. BAR (Oxford) S276, NMM Archaeological Series 10

1985D 'Brigg "raft" – problems in reconstruction and the assessment of performance' in McGrail & Kentley, 1985C, 165–194

1985E 'Early Landing Places' in Herteig, A E (ed.) *Conference on Waterfront Archaeology* No. 2. Bergen 1983, 12–18

1986A Recovering the Hasholme logboat *Current Archaeology* 99, 112–3 (with M Millett)

1986B Experimental boat archaeology – some methodological considerations in O Crumlin-Pedersen (ed.) *Sailing into the Past* Roskilde. 8–17

1986C 13th century oak timbers from Cornmarket St Cork in Hurley, M F Excavations in Medieval Cork: St Peter's Market *J Cork Historical & Archaeological Soc.* 91, 24

1987A *Ancient boats in NW Europe* Longman

1987B Need we wreck our past? *Country Life* (16. 4.87) 192–3

1987C A medieval wreck in the R Hamble in M Hughes (ed.) *Archaeology & Historic buildings in Hampshire* 38–9

1987D Early boatbuilding techniques in Britain & Ireland – dating technological change *Int. J. of Nautical Archaeology* 16, 343–6

1987E Archaeology of the Hasholme logboat (with M Millett) *Archaeological J.* 144, 96–155

1988A Assessing the performance of an ancient boat – the Hasholme logboat *Oxford J. of Archaeology* 7, 35–46

1988B *Seacraft of Prehistory* (P Johnstone) Edited. 2nd Edition. Routledge

1989A Tredunnoc boat (with S Parry) *Int. J. of Nautical Archaeology* 18, 43–9

1989B Pilotage and navigation in the time of St Brendan, in *Atlantic Vision* (ed.) de Courcy Ireland, J & Sheehy, D C, 25–35. Boole, Dun Laoghaire

1989C The Clapton logboat – boatbuilding characteristics *Int. J. of Nautical Archaeology* 18, 103

1989D Ships, Shipwrights & Seamen, Chapter in Graham-Campbell, J. *The Viking World* 2nd Edition. Frances Lincoln

1989E Prehistoric water transport in NW Europe *MM* 75, 297–312

1989F The shipment of traded goods and of ballast in Antiquity *OJA* 8, 353–8

1989G Maritime Archaeology in Britain *Antiq. J.* 69, 10–22

1990A Early boats of the Humber basin in Ellis, S, and Crowther, D R (ed.) *Humber perspectives*, 109–130. Hull University Press

1990B The UK Advisory Committee on historic wreck sites (with A Flinder) *Int. J. of Nautical Archaeology* 19, 93–99

1990C Theoretical performance of a hypothetical reconstruction of the Clapton logboat *Int. J. of Nautical Archaeology* 19, 93–99

1990D *Maritime Celts, Frisians & Saxons* (ed.) London: CBA Research Report 71

1990E Boats & boatmanship in the southern N. Sea and Channel region in McGrail, 1990 D, 32–48

1991A Early Sea Voyages *Int. J. of Nautical Archaeology* 20, 85–93

1991B A flat-bottomed boat from the R. Usk at Tredunnoc, Gwent, Wales (with S Parry) in Reinders, R, & Paul, K, (ed.) *Carvel Construction Techniques* 161–170. Oxford: Oxbow Monograph 12

1991C Bronze Age Seafaring in the Mediterranean – a view from NW Europe, in Gale, N H (ed.) *Bronze Age trade in the Mediterranean*, 83–91. Studies in Mediterranean Archaeology vol. XC Jonsered, Sweden: Paul Astroms Forlag

1991D Finds from Maritime Sites in Britain in Southworth, E (ed.) *Whats Mine is Yours* Museum Archaeologist 16. Society of Museum Archaeologists, 23–29

1991E A prehistoric plank boat fragment and a hard from Caldicot Castle Lake, Gwent, Wales (with S Parry). *IJNA* 20, 321–4

1992A Boat & Ship Archaeology at Roskilde. *IJNA* 21, 61–64

1992B Boat and ship timbers from 10th to 13th century Dublin – recording and interpretation in Carver, M (ed.) *Maritime Studies, Ports & Ships* 119–124. Medieval Europe 1992, vol. 2 University of York

1992C Replicas, reconstructions and floating hypotheses *IJNA* 21, 353–5

1992D Columbus' trans-Atlantic voyages in 1492/3 *Medieval History* 23. 76–91

1993A Recent work on the R Hamble wreck near Bursledon, Hampshire (with others) *IJNA* 22, 21–44

1993B The future of the Designated Wreck site in the R Hamble *IJNA* 22, 45–51

1993C Experimental Archaeology and the Trireme in Shaw, T (ed.) *The Trireme Project*, 4–10. Oxbow Books

1993C *Medieval boat and ship timbers from Dublin* Dublin: Royal Irish Academy

1993E From the Ice Age to Early Medieval times in Duffy, M, Fisher, S, Greenhill, B, Starkey, D J, and Youings, J (ed.) *New Maritime History of Devon* 1, 35–44. London: Conway Maritime Press

1993F Prehistoric Seafaring in the Channel Scarre, C and Healy, F (ed.) *Trade and Exchange in Prehistoric Europe*, 199–210. Oxbow Monograph 33.

1994A Ship Timbers for Wood Quay, Dublin and other medieval sites in Ireland. *Bullán* 1.1, 49–61

1994B Bronze Age sewn boat fragment from Caldicot, Gwent, Wales in Westerdahl, C, (ed.) *Crossroads in Ancient Shipbuilding*, 21–8, Oxbow Monograph 40 (with S Parry)

1994C Barland's Farm, Magor, Gwent: a Romano-Celtic boat. *Antiquity*, 68, 596–603 (with N Nayling & D Maynard)

1995A Training maritime archaeologists in Olsen, O, Madsen, J S and Rieck, F (ed.) *Shipshape*, 329–334

1995B Maritime Research in India. *S. Asian Studies*, 11:177–8

1995C Brigg "raft": a flat-bottomed boat. *IJNA*, 24:

1995D Celtic Seafaring & Transport in Green, M (ed.) *Celtic World*, 254–281

1995E Romano-Celtic boats and ships: characteristic features. *IJNA*, 24:

1995F Study of boats with stitched planking in Ray, H P and Salles J–F (ed.) *Techno-Archaeological Perspectives of Seafaring in the Indian Ocean*. New Delhi.

Glossary

Boatbuilding terms are not standardised in Britain: Essex will interpret a word differently from Wessex. In addition, the same parts of a boat or the same boatbuilding technique may be known by different names in different counties. This glossary, therefore, defines the terms as they are used in this text, and is based on the glossaries in Seán McGrail's *Building and Trials of the Replica of an Ancient Boat* and Eric McKee's *Clenched Lap or Clinker*.

BAULK   a tree trunk which has been roughly squared.

BEVEL   a surface which has been angled to make a fit with another.

BLIND FASTENING   one in which the point of the nail does not protrude through the timber.

BOTTOM BOARDS   lengths of timber fastened together and laid over the bottom of a boat as flooring.

BRAIL   rope used to bundle a fore-and-aft sail rapidly. It may be rigged singly or with others, generally on boomless sails that have their peaks extended by a sprit or a standing gaff, which are not readily lowered.

BREASTHOOK   stemlock, fore hook. In wooden ships a stout knee fitted internally across the bows, holding the sides together. In boats this knee is at gunwale level.

CARVEL BUILD   there are several definitions in use; in particular, this term is sometimes taken to be synonymous with skeleton build with flush-laid strakes. The term is confusing and ill defined and is not used here.

CAULK   to insert material between two members *after* they have been assembled, and thus make the junction watertight. (see **luting**)

CHINE BEAM   longitudinal strength member fitted at the turn of the bilge and into which the planking is rabbeted and fastened above and below. If an angle is formed, this is known as a hard chine, and is usual in 'V'-bottom designs.

CLENCH   rivet. To deform the end of a fastening so that it will not draw out – usually done over a rove.

CLINKER BUILD   a form of boatbuilding in which the strakes are placed so that they partly overlap one another – usually upper strake outboard of lower strake, but occasionally the reverse arrangement is found.

CONSTRUCTION PLAN   a scale drawing of a boat with a longitudinal section, horizontal plan, and several transverse sections. The position and nature of the scarfs, and other important constructional details and scantlings, may also be given.

COVE   scotia. A hollow shaped moulding. May be used to hold the luting between two strakes.

CRAMP   clamp, gripe. A device for holding elements of a boat together temporarily.

CROOK   a curved piece of wood which has grown into a shape useful for boatbuilding.

DAGGER PLATE   a metal retractable device on the centre-line for combating leeway.

DOLLY   a metal billet held against the head of a boat nail whilst it is being clenched.

DOUBLE-ENDED   a boat which is (nearly) symmetrical about the transverse axis – pointed at both ends. It would not be normal usage to describe a pram as double-ended.

DROP-KEEL   centre board or centre plate. A wood or metal retractable device on the centre-line for combating leeway.

FAIR (n)   a line is fair when it passes through its guide marks without any abrupt changes in direction. The lines of a boat are fair when the level lines, half breadths, buttock lines and diagonals, being themselves fair, all correspond.

FAIR (v)   to render a set of lines eyesweet and mutually true on a ship's draught.

FEATHER-EDGE   tapering to nothing.

FLOOR   a transverse member – often a crook – extending from turn of bilge to turn of bilge, and set against the planking.

FRAME   a transverse member made up of more than one piece of timber, usually extending from sheer to sheer and set against the planking. (see **rib** and **timber**).

FUTTOCK   any of the timbers used to make up a frame in a wooden ship. More exactly, not the floor or top timbers.

GARBOARD   the strake next to the keel or keel plank.

GROMMET   strand(s) of rope layed up in the form of a ring.

GUNWALE   a longitudinal member fitted round the inside top edge of the sheer strake of an open boat. In open boats, mainly positional – the timber or arrangement of timbers that make up the sheer line.

HOG   a longitudinal strength member of a boat fastened to the top of the keel to provide a landing for the inner edge of the garboard between the forward and aft deadwoods. Also a form of distortion which causes the ends of a boat to drop.

HORN   to check the squareness of a mould, relative to the boat's centre-line.

JOGGLE   to cut out a notch in a piece of timber so that it will fit close against another member.

KEEL   the main longitudinal strength member, scarfed to the stempost forward and the sternpost aft.

KNEE   a naturally grown crook used as a bracket between two members set at about right angles to each other or more.

LAND   that part of a strake which is overlapped by the strake immediately above it.

LAY-OFF   to draw out the lines of a boat full size.

LINES   the interrelation of sections in different planes which show the shape of a boat's hull. They usually consist of (a) sheer plan with longitudinal sections, (b) half breadth plan with waterlines or horizontal sections, (c) body plan with transverse sections. Diagonal lines, longitudinal section lines on the half breadth plan, and water-lines on the sheer plan, enable the three plans to be related to each other and checked for fairness. Lines converted to numbers are known as a Table of Offsets.

LOOM that part of an oar inboard of the point of pivot; it includes the grip. The section of an oar between the loom and the blade is called the shaft.

LUTING traditionally, luting is a plastic substance such as paint used between two adjacent members. In this text the term is used to de-scribe any material inserted between two members *before* they are assembled. (see **caulk**)

MAST STEP fitting used to locate the heel of a mast.

MOISTURE CONTENT the weight of water in a specimen of wood expressed as a percentage of the weight of oven dry-wood. Thus the figure can be greater than 100%.

MOULDS transverse wooden patterns taking their shape from the body plan. (see **lines**)

MOULD LOFT loft with a levelled floor on which the lines of a vessel are drawn out full size and faired.

MOULDING a pattern of linear decoration cut into a length of timber.

PAY cover caulking in seams with a layer of hot pitch. Loosely but commonly used – to coat a ship's bottom with tar.

PLANK a component of a strake that is not all in one piece.

RABBETT rabet, rebate. A groove or channel worked in a member to accept another, without a lip being formed.

RAYS layers of parenchyma cells in horizontal strands running out from the centre of a tree towards the circumference.

RIB a simple form of frame. This term may be more appropriate than frame, when applied to small open boats.

ROVE roove. A washer-like piece of metal, which is forced over the point of a nail before it is clenched.

SCARF scarph, scarve. A tapered or wedge shaped joint between pieces of similar section at the join.

SCRIVE OR SCRIEVE BOARD the floor of the mould loft or (more frequently) a board erected in the open air for the same purpose.

SHAKE a crack or split forming in wood, usually during drying or seasoning. Examples are: cup shakes – curved clefts between the growth rings; heart shakes – splits radiating from the centre of a tree.

SHEER sheer line. The curve of the upper edge of the hull.

SHEER STRAKE the top strake of planking.

SHELL CONSTRUCTION a method of boatbuilding in which the shell (ie the watertight envelope of stems, keel and planking) is built or partly built *before* the ribs and other internal strengthening members are fitted. (see **skeleton construction**)

SHROUDS ropes leading from the masthead to the sides of the boat to support the mast athwartships.

SKELETON CONSTRUCTION a method of boatbuilding in which a framework of stems, keel *and ribs* is first erected, or partly erected. This skeleton is then clothed in a 'skin' of planking. Skeleton and shell construction merge into one another with the use of 'intermedi-ate methods' of uncertain age.

SPALL a light batten used during building to brace parts of the boat from floor, rafters or other strong point.

SPANISH WINDLASS a simple rope and rod device for forcing two elements closer together, and holding them there.

SPILE to transfer a curved line on to a pattern which, when laid flat, will give the shape to cut the lower edge of a plank.

STATION the horizontal position of the transverse sections on the lines. They are used as datum lines when building from drawings, and moulds are generally made of transverse sections at some or all of these stations.

STEALER a tapered plank or plate worked into the entry or run of a vessel to preserve the general lie of the strakes without making the ends too thick or thin.

STOCKHOLM TAR a blackish semi-liquid prepared by the destructive distillation of various trees of the *Pinaceae* family.

STOCKS set-up. The temporary wooden support on which a boat is built.

STRAKE a single plank or combination of planks which stretches from one end of a boat to the other.

STRETCHER an athwartships length of timber against which a rower braces his feet.

TEMPLATE a shaped pattern of an element or section of a boat, made of plywood or hardboard, etc.

THOLE a pin projecting upwards at sheer level to provide a pivot for an oar. Strictly thole-pin, but frequently used as above.

THWART a transverse member used as a seat.

TIMBER an element of a frame or rib. May also be used generally referring to any piece of wood used in boatbuilding. One piece ribs or frames, especially those steamed or bent into place, are frequently called timbers.

TRENAIL treenail, trunnel. Wooden peg or through fastening used to join two members. It may be secured at each or either end by the insertion of a wedge.

Index

Actium, battle of 164
Adams, George 26–8, 30–1, 187–8,
  239–40
ad balams 123
Adirondack guide boats 221, *222*
Aelian 158
Africa 21, 80, *81*, 97, 100–1, 112, 132,
  159
Agrigentum 164
Agrippa 165
Åland Islands 126, 213, *229*, 229
Alba Fucentia graffito *164*
Alexander the Great 153, 156–7, 159,
  161, 163
  successors 160–3, *161–3*
Als boat *see* Hjortspring boat
Amandus fresco 167
Amathus gem *155*, 156–7
Ameinocles 151, *155*
America *see* Canada, North America,
  South America, Eskimos,
  Cajuns
Amorgos, battle of 160
anchors 216
ancient world 131–72
  see also under edge-joined planks,
  frames, keels, oars, round-
  hulled boats, sails, shell
  construction, and
  individual states and ship
  types
Andersen, B 19
Andersen, E 19, 210
Andersen, N 35–7, 45
Anderson, RC 266
Anglo-Saxons 22, 173, 175, 177–8,
  180–1, 192–3
Annotated Bibliography of Kayaks
  (Zimmerly) 91
Antigonus I 163, 165
'Antimenes painter' *148*, 148–9
Antipater 160
Appian 161, 165
Appledore *1*, 15–16, 51, *221*, 240, 267
Arabs 112, 151, 159
Arados coins 153, *153*, *155*, 155–6
Årby boat 64, *64–5*, 207
Archaeological Research Centre 12,
  17, 121, 204, 208
architects' drawings 45–6, 58–9, *62–3*,
  63, 273
Argo
  as two-level ship 149–50, *150*
  as three-level ship 152, *154*
Aristoboulos 159
Aristonothonos vase *143*, 144
Arnold, B 186
Arrian 159
ash wood 97, 99, 213
Asia 101, 118–19
askomata 153–4, *154*, 155, 168, 171
Athenaeus 161
Athens 151–2, 155, 159–61, 165

Australia 11, 97, 100, 181
auxiliaries *see kerkouroi*
Avenches find 186

baggalas 112, *112*
Baker, S *29*
balams *105*, 122–4, *124–5*
balingers 256
Ballinderry find 92
Baltic 37, 113, 174, 186, 188–90, 209,
  216, 218, 220, 226–7, 229, 233,
  266
bamboo 121, 123
Bangladesh 19, 38–48, *39–43*, *45*, 58,
  62, 80, *81*, 109–11, *111*, 123–4
  clinker-building 20, 39–43, 52, 58,
  174, *185*, 250, 254–5, *254–5*
  logboats 76, 81, 102, 104, *105*, 106,
  107, 109–11, *110–12*, 174,
  183, *185*
  sewn plank boats 119–20, 121–6,
  122, *124–5*
  see also balams, ad balams
Banks, Sir Joseph 22–3
Banks dories *see under* dories
Bantry boat *95*, 96
bardes 189, 203
barges 30, 183, 185, 256
bark boats 20, 74, *75*, 77, 97–101
Barlands Farm find 56
Barnes, RH 118
barquentines 52–3
barques 33
Bårset boat 126, *175*, 176, 182
basket boats 75, 77
Basques 263–4
bâteaux (Maine) 111, 237, *238*
batellas 256
Bayeux Tapestry 199, *200*, *214*,
  215
Bayonne 227
Beer boat 173, *174*
beitiass 124, 198
Bergen 61, *219*, 226
  runes 194–5, *195*
  ship 203, 213, 217, *218*
Bermuda 264
Betlyon, J W 159
bhums 112, *113*
Billiot, A 108, *109*
biremes *see* twos
Birka coins 189, *189*
Biscay, Bay of 216, 258
Björke boat 67, *68*, *175*, 176–7, 178
Blackfriars find 56
Black Sea 151, 192, 194, 209–10
block ends 113, 124, 186, 232, *233*
  see also golois
Block Island boats 221
Blockkahn 232, *233*
Bonaventure 271
Bonino, M 118
Brazil 21, 102, *103*

Bremen cog 17–18, 225, *226*, 227–8,
  228
  reconstructions 229, *229*
Brewington, M 116
Bridgewater flatners 20, 66, 188, 230,
  231
brigantines 33, *272–3*
Brigg boat 12, 17, 24, *120*, 120–1
Bristol seal 252, *252*
Britain 12, 17, 19–22, 43, 46, 48, 56,
  91, 96, 101, 106, 108, 119–21,
  177, 180, 183, 196, *196*, 204,
  208
  clinker-building 37, 59, 106, 173,
  175, 180–1, 192–3, 203–4,
  216, 220–1, 223, 250–3, 260
  flat-bottomed boats 119–21, 186,
  188, 226–7, 238, 240, 249
  frame-joining and skeleton
  construction 58, 77, 258,
  260, 262–3, 269, 273
  Vikings 62, 63, 191–2, 194, 197, 199,
  201–6, 208, *208*, 210, 212
  see also Appledore, Cornwall,
  Devon, London, Somerset,
  and individual finds
Brohier model 208–9
Brønsted, J 194
Bronze Age 12, 50, 56, 91
Bruges 186, 226
bugeyes 114–16, *116*, 245
  sails 116
  see also oyster skiffs
Bug river 209
Bulverket boat 209
bundle boats and rafts 75, 76, 80,
  85–6, 93
Burness Corlett and Partners 204
Byblos coins *155*, 156–7
Bygdøy 197, 207

Caergwle bowl *95*, 96
Cajuns 108, *109*
Caldicot find 119–20
'calendar stick' carving 259
Calenian dishes 167, *167*
Canada 27, *27*, 33–5, 52–3, 91, 181,
  192, 201–2
  canoes 97–100, *98–100*
  flat-bottomed boats 188, 233, 235,
  236, 237–40, 244, 249
  logboats 109
  see also Gaspé schooners, kayaks,
  Lunenburg,
  Newfoundland, Nova
  Scotia, Prince Edward
  Island, Red Bay wreck
canoes 17, 20, 33, *23*, 65, 97–100, *98–9*,
  104, 109, *115*, 115, 123, 207
  'Montreal canoe' 100, *100*
  see also kayaks
Cape Islander boats 33–5

caravela 260
Caria 152, 160
Carlsson, D 210
Carolina skiffs 26–8, 47
Carthage 150–2, 158–61, 163, 165
  Carthaginian/Roman oar system
  144, 159, 165–7, *166–7*
  fives 159, 164–5, 167
  grave stele 167, *167*
carvels 59–60, 260, 269, 272
  frames 60
Casa del Atrio Corinzio fresco 168
Caspian Sea 159
castles 168, 217, 220, 228
catapults 158
Cattewater wreck 264
cedar 26, 97, 99
Cederlund, C O 118–19, 266
ceilings 52, 87, 261
Chapelle, H I 21, 240
Charles A Dean 51
charring 40–1, *41*
Chebacco boats 221
Cheops ship 86, 118, *131*, 131–2,
  139
China 19, 44, 46, 79–81, *82*, 82–5,
  106, 111
  'palmiped' shape 85
chine logs 128, *128*, 190, 245, *247*
Chios, battle of 161
Chittagong Gazetteer 123
Christensen, A E 16, 48, 197, 272
The Chronicle of Zeeland
  (Reygersbergen) 260
Chronicon Livoniae (Henry of
  Lettland) 220
Cilicia 160
Clausen, B L 213
Clement of Alexandria 146
clinker-building techniques 28, 31,
  31, 36–7, 58–61, *def* 59, *60*,
  173, *174*, 176–82, 191,
  197–200, 202–4, 213–17, 256,
  260, 266
  Northern European tradition 18,
  20–1, 46, 50–1, 53, 56, 58–
  9, 61, 63, 78, 92–3, 106, 173,
  183, *187*, 187–94, 203–4,
  206, 216–26, 217–24, 273
  outside Europe 20, 58–60, *106*, 106,
  109–11, 119, 183, *185*, 224,
  232–3, *234*
  reversed clinker *71*, 71–2, 109–10,
  173, 225, *225*, 252, 254
  Romano-Celtic tradition 56, 91–6,
  92–5, 116, 186, 208, 233,
  257
  Scandinavian tradition 93–4, 96,
  126, 173–82, *175–7*, *179*,
  181, 189–90, 191–3, 207,
  213–18, *214*, *218–19*, 221,
  223–5, *226*, 227, 229, 250–1
  see also under Vikings

Slavonic tradition 35, 189–90, 201, 209, 227, 251
see also edge-joined planks, *and under Bangladesh, Britain, North America, shell construction, Vikings*
Coates, J 161–2, 165–70
cobles 220, *220*
cogs 17–18, 30, 225–30, *225–30*, 250, 253, 256–8
    construction 56, 72, 111, 188–9, 218, 220, 225–6, *226*, 256–7, 259
    see also Bremen cog
compasses 213
Cook, Capt James 23
copper 267
'copper ore wreck' 220
coracles 74, 91, *92*, 96
Corcyra 151–2
Corinth 144, 151, 158
    oar system 144, 146, 155–7, *157*, 167
Cornwall 30, 36, 51–2, 124, 226, 267, 269
crayers 256
Crete 131, *140*, 140–1
Crumlin-Pedersen, O 17, 66, 104, *105*, 177, 189, *196*, 197–8, *198*, 201, 203, 220, 227, 250–1, 253
curraghs 74, 91, *92*
Curtius 159
Cypriot Salamis, battle of 160–2, 165
Cyprus 137, 145, 156, 160, 163
    see also Amathus gem

Dahshur boats 87, *89*, 90
deal 31
Deir-el-Bahari relief *133*
Demetrius Poliorketes 160–1, 163, 165–6
    coin 165, *165*
Denmark 16–17, 19–21, 24, 96, 177–80, 190, 216
    flat-bottomed boats 35, 183, *184*, 185, 188, 229, 231, 233, 240
    sewn plank boats 126–7
    skeleton construction 259–60, 273
    Viking boats 191–4, 199, 201, 203–4, 210
    see also Gredstedbro boat, Hedeby boat, Nydam boat, Shuldelev finds
Denyen *see* Sea Peoples
De Sphaera Estense 258
Devon 22, 63, 173, *174*, 230
    see also Appledore
Diodorus 158, 163
Diogenes of Sigeion 144
Dipylon kraters *141*, 141
Dipylon vases 144
doggers 256
dories 21–2, 34, 59, *66*, 66, 188, *188*, *236*, 237, *238–9*, 239, 249
    Banks dories 225, 233, *235*, 237–8
Dover find 120
draggers *268–9*
dragon boats 135
drashels 29, 186
Drew, Sawyer 51–2
dunnage 143

East Anglia graffiti 253
Ecnomus 158
edge-joined planks 20, 27, *31*, 31, 39, 46–54, 58–61, *60–1*, 63, 93, *174*, 187, 190, 256
    ancient world 50, 131, *132*, 143
    as critical distinction 47–56, 59
    decline 256–7, 261–2, 272
    outside Europe 39–42, *40*, 59, 83–4, 86–7, *87*, *106*, 106–7, *108*, 109–12

techniques 53, 58, *60–1*, 66, 256–7, 260–1
    see also clinker-building techniques, overlapping planks, *and under skeleton construction, shell construction*
Egypt 58, 80, 85–90, *89*, 131–3, *131–3*, *136–8*, 137–40, 143, 151–2, 160–1, 163–5, 168, 188
    hull shapes 86, 90, *138*, 139
    see also Sea Peoples
Eigg island 193
eights 165
eikosoroi *140*, 141, *143*, 144
Elbing 226
    seal 227, *227*
Elea 164
elevens 161, 163
Ellesmere Island 192
Ellmers, Dr D 56, 91–2, 226, 245, 250–1
elm 20, 30
enamel plaques 251–2
Epirus 164
Ericsson, Prof C *126*
Erment model *156*, 156–7
Erythrae 144, 149
Eskimos 91, 192
Estonia 118, 190, 220, 226, 229
Etruscans 150, *150*, 151
Exekias dinos *148*, 149
'eyes' 141, *141*, 153, *153*

femboring 223
Ferriby boats 17, *119*, 119–21
    Ferriby I boat *67*, 67
fifteens 163
Filipowiak, W 190
Finland 21, 37, 59, 70, *71*, 118–19, 126–30, *127–9*, 186, 189, 199–200, 213, 229, 244, 273
    see also Saamish people
Finström church murals 229, *229*
fives *155–7*, 156–61, 163–8, *167*
    Carthaginian/Roman oar system 159, 166–7, *167*
    Greek oar system 159, 165
flat-bottomed boats 26–8, 30, 35–7, *39*, 81–2, *84*, 85–7, 111, 119–20, 183–90, *184*, 187, 209, 216, 225–49, 256–7
    advantages 26–8, 37, 225, 227, 233, 235
    bottoms 119, 228, *229*, 257
        joining with strakes 26–8, *27*, 66, 82, *83*
    outside Europe 54, *54–55*
    rockers 26–7, 40, 54–5, 82, 136–7, 190, 232–3, 238, 240
    see also cogs, dories, prams, skiffs
flatners 20, 66, 230, *231*
Fleet trows 231, *232*, 238
flutes 266
Foochow pole junk *85*, 85
forefeet *140*, 141, *141*, 142–3, *143*, 144, 145, 146, *147–148*, 149, *149*, 156, *156–157*, 157, 221
Formosa 80
Forssell, H 118, 126, *126*
foucets 256
fours *153*, 158–61, 163–4, *164*, 165
frames *see* steam-softening *and under intermediate types, shell construction, skeleton construction, Vikings*
France 21, 108, 188, 191, 194, 197, 202, 226, 233, 237, 239, 250–1, 258
Fribodre find 190
Frisia 180–1, 189, 253

Gaddestärnen carvings 230, *230*
gadus 123

galars 12, 120, *120*
galeases *261*
galleys 256
Gallo-Roman tradition *see* Romano-Celtic tradition *under* clinker-building
Gardner, J 21
Gaspé peninsula 221, *222*, 240
Gdánsk 114, 220, 231
Germany 17–18, 121, 177–8, 180, 186, 188–90, 201, 203–4, 216, 220, 226–7, 233, 252
    see also Hanseatic League
Geschichte des Deutschen Seeschiffart (Vogel) 260
Gibraltar 227
Giffard, Walter 226–7
Gifford, Dr E 204
Godel, I 22
Godesby ship 220
goelettes 244, *244–5*
Gokstad ship 61, 68, *69*, *175*, 176, *197*, 197–203, *200*, *203*
    faering 62–3, *63*, 187–8, 207–8, 210
    meginhufr 198, 200
Goldcliff find 120
golois 40, 42, 110, *111*, 232
gondolas 232, *234*
Goths 190
Gotland 209–10, 231, 250
    picture stones 19, *189*, 189, *208*, 209, *209*, 229
    tools *214*, 214–15
Grace Dieu 220, 256
Graveney boat 17, 20–1, 66, 68, *69*, 70, *175*, 176, 180–1, 189, 193, 203–6, *204–6*, 208, 220, 227
Great Galley 260
Gredstedbro boat *175*, 176, 178–80
Greece 50, 58, 121, 131, *133–5*, 133–7, *141*, 141–55, *143*, *147–50*, 161–6, 169–72, 273
    Greek rowing model 149–50, *150*, 159–60, 164–8, 165
    see also Macedon and individual city-states and islands
Green, J N 80, 83
Greenland 24, 192, 194, 201–2, 213, 217
Greenwich coins *252*, 252–3
Guernsey find 56, 257
guns 57, 256–7
Guy, C 99
Gwithian graffito 227

Hackman, J *126*
Hallström, G 127–8, *128*
Hanseatic League 226–7, 229
Hardanger boat 208
Hasslöf, Dr O 48, 53, 58, 259–60, 269, 272
Hedeby 226
    coins 189, *189*
    ships 203, 217–18, *218*
Helen Barnet Gring 51
hemioliai 161, 161–2
Herakleides 159
Heritage 270
Herodotus 151–2
Hinks, A 240
Hittites 137
Hjortspring boat 67, *68*, *93*, 93–4, 96, 126, 176, 199, *200*
Hobah 51–2
hogging 48–9, 132–3, 135
hogs *see* keel planks *under* keels
Holvijekten 219
Homer 24, 140, 142–4
Hong Kong 83, *83*, 85
horas 60, *61*
Hornell, J 16, 53, 80, 102
hoys 256
hrungs 29, 186
hulks 18, 216, 250–5, 256, 258

planking 57, *57*, 70–2, *71*, 110–11, 250, 253–5, *254–5*
hybrids *see under* intermediate construction
Hyrkania 159

Iceland 24, 175, 192, 194, 201–2
Ijeket *see* Sea Peoples
ikria 142–3
Images of Lunenburg County (Barss) 22
Inari boat 128–9, *129*
India 58, 78, 112, *112–13*, 224
    see also Bangladesh, Pakistan
Indonesia 97
'intermediate' construction 49–57, *57*, 59, 61, 257, 259, *261*, 261–4, 266–7, 269, 272
    frames 50, 257–9, *262–6*, 262–6
    hybrids 49–50, 53, *57*, 57, 220
    see also shell construction, skeleton construction
International Journal of Nautical Archaeology 56
Iolkos sherds 133, *135*, 136–7
Ionia 151
Ipsos, battle of 165–6
Iraq 75
Ireland 74, 92, *95*, 96, 101, 193–4, 197, 199, 201, 207, 216, 218
Isola Tiberina monument 165–6, *166*, 168
Istanbul 210
Italy 118, 151, 158
Itkonen, T 129–30, 186

jalyanaos 123
Japan 46, 81, 173, 262, 269, 272
    logboats 106–7, *107*
    see also Yamato-gata building
jekts 218, *219*
Jenkins, G 96
Johnstone, P 94
Jones-Baker, Mrs 253
Julius Caesar 24, 56, 209
junks *84–5*, 85
Jutes 180
Jutholm wreck 266

kågs 231, *232*
Kalmar Castle find 218
Karlby carving 209
karves 202
    see also Gokstad ship, Oseberg ship
Kasion 163, 165
Kaupang 36
kayaks 91, *92*
keels 23, 43, 49, 52, 126, *189*, 189–90, 214, 238, 250, 256, 263–4, 267, 273
    ancient world 135–7, 139, *140*, 141, 143, 157, *157*
    drop keels 32, 78, *79*, 80, *80*, 85, 249
    keel planks 40, 106, *107*, 107, *108*, 110, 178, 180, 183, 191, 203, 245
    T-shaped 178, 182, 191, 197
keelsons 268
keels see round-hulled boats
Keltischer Studien 56
Kentley, E 118
kerkouroi 145, 145–6, 150
ketches 51–2, 249, 267
Keying 85
Kida River rafts 80, *82*
Kiel 226, 229
    seal *225*, 227
Kition 160
Klåstad ship *197*, 197–8
Kleitias *krater* *147*, 147–8
knarrs 202, *202*
Kola peninsula boat 127–30, *128*
korsha 111

Krampmarken 209–10, *209–10*, 213
Kuhn, K 106, *107*, 186, *187*
Kuwait 112
Kvalsund boat *175*, 176, *181*, 181–2

Ladby ship *175*, 176, *198*, 199–202, *200*
Lake Inati boat 128–30. *129*
Lake Neuchâtel finds 186
Lal Mian 38–46
Lamu Archipelago 112
Landström, B 86, 132, 264
L'Anse aux Meadows 192
Lapps 119, 130
    see also Saamish people
lapstrake *see* clinker-building techniques
larch 31
Larisa 160
Latvia 220, 226
Lebanon 159
Lenormant relief 154–5, *155*
    reconstructions 155
    see also Olympias
Leptines 158
Leslie, R C 49
Levant 132, 137, 151
Lewes Priory carving 251
Leyser, K 220
lifts *140*, 140–1
Limavady find 96
Linden 260, 271
Lindos prow *161*, 161–2
    relief 162, *162*
Lithuania 220, 226, 231
Litwin, J 118, 231
lobster boats *33–4*, 33–5, 47–8, *48*, 99, 221, 240, 245, *246*
Locri 158, 164
logboats 20, 24–5, 92–3, 101–16, *102–3*, 177
    construction 67, *68*, 101–2, 104, 124, 183
    developments from 20, 28, 37, 46, 55, 75, 77–8, 81, 93, 101–15, 119, 176, 178, 180, 183, 186, 190, 245, *247*, 249, 253
    expansion and extension 59, 80–1, 92, 102, 104, *104–105*, 106–7, 121, *122*, 123, *125*, 126, 174, 176–7, 178, 253
    outside Europe 17, 21, 76, 81, *81*, 102, *102–12*, 104, 106–12, *115–16*, 174
London 85, 226
    finds 56, 257
Long Island Sound 114
Lübeck 226, 229
luggers 124, 173, *174*
lug sails 124, 210, 212, 221
Lunenburg, NS 15–16, *17*, 22, 66, 188, 233, 239
Lyme 227
Lynaes ship 203, 217–18, *218*
Lysimachus 163

Maarleveld, T J 52, 190
Macedon 159–61, 164
    see also Alexander the Great
MacMurray, C 14
Magdalen Islands 221, *222*, 240, *243*, 244
Maine 22, 111, 235, 237, *238*, 238, 240, *272–3*, 273
Maine Coast Fisherman, The 21
Man, Isle of 194, 221
maple wood 99
Marguin, P Y 118
Mariner's Mirror 250
Mark Antony 164
Marstrander, Prof 94
Mary Rose 262–3, 264
Massachusetts 235

Massalia 152
masts
    two-masters *258*
    three-masters 220, *258*, 258–9, *260*
    four-masters *268*
Matsuki, Prof S 107
May, Bob 31
McGrail, Prof S 16, 51, 56, 101, 118, 120, *126*, 193, 215–16, 218, 257
McKee, E 59, 61, 66–7, 93, 204, 206, 230, 233, 240
Medinet Habu frieze *136–7*, 137–8, 140, 144
Mediterranean 50, 93, 118, 131–72, 192, 194, 202, 233, 266
meginhufr 197–8, 200
Melos 131, *133*
Merchant Shipping Acts 32
Michigan, Lake 221, *222*
Miletus 151
Millom Castle 267, 269, *269*
Minoan seals *134*, 136–7, 137
Miquelon 237–8
Miramichi river 109, 192
mistris 58, 121
models 24, *84*, 85–6, 96, 109, *110*, 112, *114*, 139, *181*, 182, 196, *196*, 228, *228*, 244, *245*, 253
    half models *48*, 51, 58, 61, 267, 273
    see also Naxos models
Morandière, C de 237–8, 240
mortise-and-tenon joining 50, 58, 131, 142
Motya, siege of 158
moulds 31, 34, 40, 48–51, 57, *57*, 59, 272
mtepes 112, *114*
murinas 124, *125*, 126
Mycenae 140
Mylai, battle of 165

Naples 164
National Fisherman, The 21
navis 256
Naxos models 133, *134*, 135, 137
Nearchos 159
Necho, Pharoah 151
Needham, J 80, 82–3
neif 256
Netherlands 30, 52, 121, 183, 188–9, 191, 203, 216, 225–6, 229–30, *230*, 233, 250
Neusiainez Church 250
Newfoundland 16, 52, 192, 235, 238, 240
Newhaven sharpies 239–40, *241*
New Zealand 181, *248*, 249
nines 160–1, 168
Nineveh relief *145*, 145–6, 148, 152, *153*
Nishimura, Prof S 80
Noble, A *270*
Noordlands *ottring* 210, *211*, 212–13, 223–4
Nordfjord *ject* 218, *219*
Normans 199, *214*, 215
    see also Bayeux Tapestry
Norrköping carvings *94*, 94, 96
North America 15–24, 43, 46, 50, 101, 104, *105*, 121, 181, 267
    canoes 97–100, *98–100*, 115
    clinker-building 173, 221
    flat-bottomed boats 21, 26–8, *27*, 47, 59, 186–8, 233, 235, *237*, 237–40, *242–3*, 249
    logboats 100, 102, 108, *109*, 114–16
    native Americans 97, 108, *109*, 115
    skeleton construction *33–4*, 33–5, 47, 52, 77, 257, 273
    V-bottomed boats 244–5, *246*, 248, 249
    and Vikings 192, 194

    see also Cajuns, Canada, Eskimos, Maine, South America
Northern European tradition *see* *under* clinker-building techniques, oars
Norway 16, 24, 43, 178, 181–2, 216, 218, 223, 259, 272–3
    prams 35–7, *36*, 70, *71*
    sewn plank boats 127
    skin boats 91, 93–4
    Vikings 17, 19–1, 63, 182, 194, 196–7, 197–8, 202, 213
    see also Oselver boat
'nosers' 186
Nova Scotia 35, 188, 235, 237, 273
nuggars 90, *90*
Nugget 30–2, *30–2*, 72
Nydam boats 176, 198–9, *200*
    oak *175–6*, 177–80
    pine *175*, 176, 178, 182, 197
Nylén, E 19, 126, 209–10

oak 30, 119, 182, 198, *213*, 213
oars 25, 30, 32, *55*, 95, 96, *125*
    ancient world 69, *132*, 132–41, *137–8*, *140*, *143*, 144–50, *145*, *147–50*, 152–7, *154–7*, 159, 161–2, *162*, *164*, 164–8, *166–7*, 171–2
    see also Carthaginian/Roman oar system *under* Carthage
    double-manning 143, 157–8, 161, 165
    Northern European tradition 177, 181–2, 189, 221, 224
    steering oars 191, 255
    Viking 61, 191, 202, 207
Oceania 118
Octavian 164–5
Oder 114, 190, 232
ökas 37, *37*, 240
Olsen, O 17
Olympias 18, *169*, 169–72
Orchomenos fragments *133*, 133, 135–7
Oseberg ship *175*, 176, *196*, 196–9, *200*, 202–3, *203*
    meginhufr 197–8, 200, 203, *203*
oselver boats 61, *208*, 208
ottrings see Noordlands *ottring*
Our Lady 226–7
outriggers 144, 146, *149–50*, 150, 153–5, *153–5*, 157, *157*, 165, 167

paddles 25, 87, 123, 132, 135–7, 207
pahee 23
Pakistan 54–6, 60, *61*, 86, 159, 161, 256, 262
Palakaistro model *134*, 135–6
Palazzo Barberini mosaic 162, *163*
Palazzo Spada relief 162, *163*
Papias 165
patalias 232–3, *234*
peat boats 29
Pechili junk *84*, 85
Peggy 221, *222*
Peleshet *see* Sea Peoples
pentecontors 140, *140*, 143–4, *147*, 148–50, *150*, 150, 152, 158, 164
    two-level *153*, 153
Persia 150–2, 159
    seals *145*, 157, *157*
Persian Gulf 112, *112*, 159
Peshawar Valley 54–6
Petäjävesi boat 199–200, *200*
Phaistos disc 136
Philadelphia 238
Philostephanos of Cyrene 146
Phocaea 150, 152
Phoenicians 58, 160, 167
    twos 149

threes 144, *145*, 146, 151–3, *155*, 155–7
fives 159, 164, 167
Phrygia 160
Phylakopi fragment *133*, 133, 135–6
pine 31, *213*, 213
    tar 214
piracy 151, 161, 165, 192, 225, 227
pirogras 108, *109*
plank-built boats, evolution of 25, 80–96, *81–5*, *87–90*, 92–5, 101–16, *103*, *106–16*, 190
    see also sewn-plank boats
planks
    floor 28, 35, 40, 43, 56, 83–4, 86, 113–14, *122*, 228
    overlapping
        outside Europe 20, 59, 106, *106*
        techniques 31, 39, 53, 59–60, *60–1*, 67, *67–8*, 71–2, 173–4, *174*, 232–3, 256, 260
    see also clinker-building techniques
    plank ends 36, 59, 67–71, *67–72*, 201, 250, 254–5
    shaping 23, 31, 34, 36, 40–3, *41*, 61–8, *68–69*, 86, 102, 104, 187–8, *213*, 214–15, 233, 253
    width 191, *196*, 197, 220, 225, 226, 226
    see also edge-joined planks, strakes *and under* keels
Pliny 158–9
Plutarch 163
Poland 78, 101–2, *103*, 114, 120–1, 189–90, 209, 216, 220, 231
poling 25, 29, 85, 87, 186
    see also punts
Polybius 164
Polycrates 152
Polynesians 22–3
Pomerania 114
Pomey, P 118
Pompeii fresco *167*, 167–8
Poole seal 71
A Poor Man's House (Reynolds) 22
Poplicola frieze 167, *168*
Portugal 21, 188, 237, 258, 260
Pozzuoli reliefs 153
Praeneste relief 165, *165*, 168
prams 35–7, *36*, *38*, 47, 70, *71*, 82, 190, 253
Prince Edward Island 27, 33–5, *50*, 52–3, 221, *222*
Prins, A H J 118
Prussia 190
Punic Wars 161, 163–5
punts 35, 86, *88–89*, 190, 245, *247*
    Indus punts 86–7, *87*
Punt (Somalia) 132
Pylos-Tragana ship *140*, 140–2

Quentovic coins 251

Rachel W Stevens 268
rafts 11–12, 20, 46, 74, *75*, 77–90, *79*, 101, 106
    boat-shaped 21, 78, *79*, 80, *81*
    evolution from 55, 86, 245, 249
    sailing 78, *79–80*, 80
    skin rafts 78, *79*
Raiatea 23
Rålamb, A C 266
rams 136, 141, *141*, 144, *145*, 146, 148, 149–51, *153*, 153, 156–7, *156–7*, 165, 168
    upper rams *164*, 165
Raphia 165
reconstructions and replicas 11, 18–19, 23–4, *50*, 62, *64–5*, 94, *95*, *131*, 155, *161*, 162, *198*, 198–9, 204, *205*, 206, 208, *208*, *212*, 212–13, 224, *224*, 240, 273

see also Olympias
Red Bay wreck 52, *263–5, 263–7*
Reynolds, S 22
Rhegium 158
Rhodes 160–3
Rio de Janeiro 19, 21
Ristilä boat *129,* 129–30
Roberts, O 19, 207
rockers *see under* flat-bottomed boats
Romano-Celtic tradition *see under* clinker-building
Rome 50, 58, 158–61, 163–8
and Carthaginian oar-system 159, 164, 166–7, *167*
Roskilde find *see* Lynaes, Skuldelev finds
Rostock 114, 229
round-hulled boats 56, 73, 92, 96, 183–93, 197, 216–18, 220, 225
ancient world 142–3, *145,* 149
outside Europe 38, 109–11
see also Romano-Celtic tradition
'rower' tablets 140
Rudolph, Dr W 106, *107,* 113, 232
Rule, Dr M 56, 262–3
Russia 118–19, 127, *128,* 192, 194, 209–10, 224, 226
Ruvo vase 153–4, *154,* 155

Saamish people 119, 126–7, 129, 244–5
Saga Siglar 212, 213, 217
sagging *48–9*
Sahure ship 132, *132*
Sailing Into The Past 22
sails 25, 30, 32, 85, 109, 273
ancient world 87, *132,* 132–3, 134, *137,* 138, *140,* 140–1, *147,* 147, 149, *157,* 157, 165, 171–2
flat-bottomed boats 37, 189, *189,* 225, 229–30, 232, 239, *239,* *248,* 249
'invention of the sailing ship' *258–9, 258–9*
Northern European tradition 182, 189, 223–4, *227,* 229
schooner-rigging 221, *222*
Viking 19, *195–9,* 201–2, *208–12,* 208–13
see also cobles *and under* Bangladesh, bugeyes, China, rafts
Salamis, battle of 155
salmon-boats 30–2, *30–2,* 36, 47, *221,* 221
Samos 151–2, 155
sampans 80, *81,* 81, *125,* 255
chicken 82, *83,* 85
duck 80, 82, *83,* 85
San Juan see Red Bay wreck
Sarazin 97
Sardinia 150
Scandinavia *see* individual countries *and under* clinker-building techniques
Schleswig-Holstein 92, 177, 181, 203, 226
see also Hedeby
schooners 30, 33, 51–2, 221, *222,* 264
Scotland 101, 193–4, 197, 273
scoutes 256
scows 245, *247–8,* 249
seals 24, *134,* 136, *140,* 140–1, 216–17, *217,* 218, 250
see also individual seals

Sea Peoples *136–7,* 137–40, *139*
Serçe Limani wreck 50, 257
sevens 159–61, 163–5
sewn plank boats 23, 40, 50, 56, 67, *67–8,* 86, 90, 96, 109, *110,* 112, *114,* 118–30, 123, 127, *128*
see also under Bangladesh, Norway, Sweden, Vikings
Sextus Pompeius 165
shallops 221
Shamrock 266, 272
shell construction 26–32, *31,* 35–48, 52–4, *57,* 57–9, 97, 110–11, *142,* 142–3, 186–7
ancestry 113–14
in ancient world 50
frames 26–8, 30–1, 35–7, 39, *42,* 43, 47–50, 52–3, 97, *98,* 106, 110, 112, 125, 131–2, 176, 181–2, 186, 190, 259, 261
not edge-joined 52, 257
and skeleton construction 49–54, 257–9, 264, 266
techniques 48–50, 66, 110, 261
see also intermediate construction, skeleton construction
Shetlands 182, 208, *208,* 223
Shoreham seal 251, *251*
Siberia 97
Sicily 151–2, 158, 163–5
see also Syracuse, Dionysius
Sidon 145–6, 156–7, *8*
Sitjon murals 216
sixes 158–9, 160–1, 163–5, *166,* 166
sixteens 163
Skamestrup murals 216
Skaw 17, 174, *175,* 192
skegs 35–6
Skeklesh see Sea Peoples
skeleton construction 33–5, 46–59, *51,* 61, 97, 112, 173, 187, 253, 256–73
development of *48–9,* 48–52, 56–9, 257–67
edge-joined 52–3
frames 34, 46–9, *48–50,* 51–60, *57,* 93, 97, 99–100, 112, 115, *196,* 197–8, 203, 207–8, *208,* 257, 259, 261–2, *262,* 263–4, 267, *268,* 269
technique 34–5, 46, 256–7, 267–73, *268–73*
see also intermediate construction, shell construction
skiffs 26–8, *27,* 30, 47, 118, 186–8, 239–40, *241–2,* 244
see also bugeyes
skin boats 20, 25, 56, 74, *75,* 77–8, 80, 91–7, *93,* 101–2, 192
skipjacks 245, *246*
Skuldelev finds 16–17, *175,* 176, 190, 199–203, 215
Skuldelev 1 *70,* 70, *202,* 202–3, *212,* 212–13, *218*
Skuldelev 2 193, 199, 201
Skuldelev 3 201, *201,* 203, *203, 212,* 218
Skuldelev 5 *198,* 199
Slade, W J 267
Slavonic tradition *see under* clinker-building techniques
smacks 30, 51
smooth-skin vessels 21, 28, 34, 39, 50, 58–60, *61,* 110, *110,* 174, 233, *254,* 260
Society Islands 23

Somerset 28–9, 31, 186–8, 230, 240
see also turf boats
South America 19, 78, 97, 100–1
Spain 224, 258, 263–4, 273
Sparta plaque 146–7, *147*
spruce 52, 97, *99*
Sri Lanka 109, *110*
St David's Cathedral 252, *252*
steam-softening *34,* 34, 40, 48, 99, 130, 223
Stigell, A-L 258
St Lawrence river 244
St Malo 239
St Pierre 237–8, 238–40
strakes
construction 31, 61, 63, 191, 213–14, 218
garboard strakes 40, *40,* 183, 254, *255*
overlapping *see* clinker-building *and under* planks
strake diagrams 62–6, *62–6,* 107, *108,* 206, *206*
Strongman, Bob 33–5, 45, 221, 245
Sukkur 54
Suojoki boat 126, *126*
Sutton Hoo ship *76, 175, 179,* 180, *181,* 193, 199
Sweden 21, 58–9, 72, *175,* 176–7, 188–90, 216, 218, 225, *226,* 226, 229, 231, 233, 264, 266, 273
prams 37, 70, *71*
sewn boats 118–19, 126–30
skin boats 93–4, *94*
Vikings 194, 197–8, 207–8
see also individual finds
Switzerland 186
Syracuse 158–9, 161, 163–4, 167
Syria 152–3, 160
Syros fans *134,* 135–7

Talus painter 153–4, *154*
Tarentum 164
Tenojoki river 130, *130*
tens 159–60, 164
Thapsacus 159
Theophrastus 163
Thera 138, *138*
Thirslund, S 213
thirteens 161, 163
thirties 161
threes 144, *145,* 146, 149, 151–65, *152–4, 156–7,* 167, 192
oar system 144, 152–6, 165, 170, 172
replicas 18, *169,* 169–72
see also Olympias
see also fives
Thucydides 151–2, 155
tillers 87, 135, *138,* 138, 140, *140*
Times Literary Supplement 220
Ti relief *133*
Tofta Church 250
triacontors 140, *147,* 148, *148,* 148–9, *149,* 149, 159, 161
trieres see threes
trihemioliai 161, 161–3
triremes *see* threes
Trireme Trust 169–70
Tune boat 126, *175,* 176, 207
turf boats 28–31, *29,* 186–8, 230
Turkey 50
twelves 161
twenties 161
twos 143–6, *144–5,* 148, 149–52, *150,* 159

see also fours, nines, pentecontors
Tyre 151–2, 159–60, 167
evacuation of *144–5,* 145–6, 156

Ulelia 52
umiaks 91
USA *see* America
Utica 161
Utrecht boat *175,* 176, 183, *184,* 185, 253
Uttar Pradesh 174, 232–3

Valsgärde find 207
vargords 124
V-bottomed boats 128, *129,* 208, 240, 244–5, *246*
see also under North America
Velius 260
Vendel find 207
Veneti 24, 56, 209
Victory of Samothrace monument 162, 162–3
Vienna fragment 153, *154,* 155
Vikings 16–17, 19–22, 24, 30, 35–6, 59, 106, 124, 137, 173, 175, 178, 182, 191–216, *195–8,* *199–214,* 226
clinker-building 93, 126, *175,* 191–3, 207, 213–15, *214,* 221
frame-joining 93, 191, 197–8, 200–1, 203
sewn planks 126
see also individual finds, *and under* Britain, North America, sails
Vilkuna, J 126, *126*
Villani, G 227
Vinland 192
Vinner, M 213
Visby 226, 250
Vistula 114, 190, 209, 231–2, *232*

Wachsmann, S 137–8
Waldron, Sawyer 51
Wales 19, 30, 56, 74, 91, *95,* 96, 101, 119, 253
Ward Jackson, CH 269
Wasa 57, 264, *264,* 266
Waters, D 83–5
Wens 201
Westerdahl, C 118–19, *126*
Western Ledge Reef wreck 264
West House wall paintings *138,* 140
'whalers' 249
Williams, R T 144
willow 37
Winchelsea seal *217,* 220
Winchester Cathedral font 71, 252, *253*
windlasses 85, 133, 216, 218
Wismar, Bay of 232
Wooden Boat 21–2
Worcester Chronicle 251
Wright, E V 67, 119

Xenagoras 158
Xerxes 152

Yamato-gata building 107–8, *108–9*
Yassi Adda wrecks 50, 267
yew 119

Zea shipsheds 155
Zedelgem carving 252
Zuyder Zee wrecks 56